The Therapist's Answer Book

Therapists inevitably feel more gratified in their work when their cases have better treatment outcomes. This book is designed to help them achieve that by providing practical solutions to problems that arise in psychotherapy, such as the following:

Do depressed people need an antidepressant, or psychotherapy alone? How do you handle people who want to be your "friend," who touch you, who won't leave your office, or who break boundaries? How do you prevent people from quitting treatment prematurely? Suppose you don't like the person who consults you? What if people you treat with cognitive behavioral therapy (CBT) don't do their homework? When do you explain defense mechanisms, and when do you use supportive approaches?

Award-winning professor Jerome S. Blackman answers these and many other tricky problems for psychotherapists. Dr. Blackman punctuates his lively text with tips and snippets of various theories that apply to psychotherapy. He shares his advice and illustrates his successes and failures in diagnosis, treatment, and supervision. He highlights fundamental, fascinating, and perplexing problems he has encountered over decades of practicing and supervising therapy.

Jerome S. Blackman, MD, is Professor of Clinical Psychiatry at Eastern Virginia Medical School. He has taught at Beijing University, Tulane School of Social Work, Virginia Wesleyan College, Old Dominion University, MIT Educational Studies Program, and Naval Medical Center–Portsmouth, and presented at programs in Germany, Italy, China, and the United States. His first book, *101 Defenses*, has been translated into Chinese and Romanian.

The Therapist's Answer Book

Solutions to 101 Tricky Problems in Psychotherapy

Jerome S. Blackman

First published 2013
by Routledge
711 Third Avenue, New York, NY 10017

Simultaneously published in the UK
by Routledge
27 Church Road, Hove, East Sussex BN3 2FA

Routledge is an imprint of the Taylor & Francis Group, an informa business

© 2013 Taylor & Francis

The right of Jerome S. Blackman to be identified as author of this work has been asserted by him in accordance with sections 77 and 78 of the Copyright, Designs and Patents Act 1988.

All rights reserved. No part of this book may be reprinted or reproduced or utilized in any form or by any electronic, mechanical, or other means, now known or hereafter invented, including photocopying and recording, or in any information storage or retrieval system, without permission in writing from the publishers.

Trademark notice: Product or corporate names may be trademarks or registered trademarks, and are used only for identification and explanation without intent to infringe.

Library of Congress Cataloging in Publication Data

Blackman, Jerome S.
  The therapist's answer book : solutions to 101 tricky problems in psychotherapy / Jerome S Blackman.
      p. cm.
   Includes bibliographical references and index.
 1. Psychotherapy—Popular works. 2. Psychotherapist and patient—Popular works. 3. Self-help techniques. I. Title.
   RC480.515B53 2012
   616.89′14—dc23
   2012012479

ISBN: 978-0-415-88891-2 (hbk)
ISBN: 978-0-415-88892-9 (pbk)
ISBN: 978-0-203-09474-7 (ebk)

Typeset in Stone Serif
by Apex CoVantage, LLC

Printed and bound in the United States of America by Sheridan Books, Inc. (a Sheridan Group company)

Contents

Some Answers…		xi
Acknowledgments		xv

SECTION A	**A VERY QUICK TAKE ON ASSESSMENT AND TECHNIQUE**		**1**
	General Comments		**1**
PROBLEM 1	*What Do I Say? (Technique)*		3
PROBLEM 2	*When Do I Say It? (Diagnosis)*		6
SECTION B	**GENERAL PRINCIPLES ABOUT TREATMENT**		**9**
	General Comments		**9**
PROBLEM 3	*The Alliance and the Frame of Therapy*		11
PROBLEM 4	*People Without a Clear Problem (or "Chief Complaint")*		13
PROBLEM 5	*Can You Diagnose From the Presenting Problem (the "Chief Complaint")?*		17
PROBLEM 6	*When to Use Medicine and When Not To*		21
PROBLEM 7	*Should I Medicate Depressions or Try to Figure Out the Causes Instead?*		23
PROBLEM 8	*Planes of Psychotherapy: Where to Intervene?*		28
PROBLEM 9	*Alternating Supportive and Interpretive Techniques*		33
PROBLEM 10	*How to Stop People From Quitting Therapy*		37
PROBLEM 11	*What to Do With People's Early Resistances*		39
PROBLEM 12	*What to Do Before Each Therapy Session*		42

SECTION C	**TECHNIQUES WITH DIFFERENT TYPES OF DISTURBANCES**	**45**
	General Comments on Varying Technique	45
PROBLEM 13	Is Being a "Container" or Providing a "Holding Environment" Enough? With Whom?	47
PROBLEM 14	Are Obsessional People Neurotic, Borderline, or Schizophrenic?	51
PROBLEM 15	People With Physical Illnesses and Conversion Symptoms	55
PROBLEM 16	Financially Successful People	58
PROBLEM 17	Highly Intelligent People	61
PROBLEM 18	People Who Are Chronically Late to Sessions	65
PROBLEM 19	Do All Alcoholics Need AA?	68
PROBLEM 20	What Do You Do With Different Types of Alcoholics?	71
PROBLEM 21	Bullies	75
PROBLEM 22	Procrastinators	80
PROBLEM 23	Passive, Wimpy People	84
PROBLEM 24	The Male "Yes, Dear"	87
PROBLEM 25	Self-Centered People Who "Need a Spanking"	89
PROBLEM 26	Can You Understand the Meanings of an Obsession?	93
PROBLEM 27	People With Visible and Nonvisible Disabilities	96
PROBLEM 28	Counterphobic People Who Risk Their Lives	100
PROBLEM 29	Seniors Who Feel Entitled	102
PROBLEM 30	Promiscuous People	105
SECTION D	**TECHNIQUES WITH ACTING IN AND ACTING OUT**	**109**
	General Comments About Boundaries	109
PROBLEM 31	What About Boundaries?	111

PROBLEM 32	*"Let's Make a Deal" and Gifts—Boundary Crossings*	112
PROBLEM 33	*Boundary Violations, Erotic and Erotized Transferences*	116
PROBLEM 34	*People Who Berate or Verbally Attack You*	119
PROBLEM 35	*"Acter-Outers," or Impulsive People*	122
PROBLEM 36	*Those Who Get to Understandings of Themselves Before You Do*	126
PROBLEM 37	*People Who Ask You to Hug Them or Want to Hug You*	129
PROBLEM 38	*People Who Try to Undress in Front of You or Attempt to Seduce You During a Session; Also, People Who Touch You*	133
PROBLEM 39	*People Who Talk to Your Secretary*	137
PROBLEM 40	*People Who Date Your Secretary*	140
PROBLEM 41	*Enactors: "Actor-in-ers"*	142
PROBLEM 42	*People Who Bring Their Spouse to a Session*	146
PROBLEM 43	*People Who Bring Their Parents to a Session*	151
PROBLEM 44	*People Who Do Not Want to Leave Your Office on Time*	155
PROBLEM 45	*People Who Accuse You of Not Paying Attention*	159
PROBLEM 46	*People Who Don't Let You Get a Word in Edgewise*	162
PROBLEM 47	*Women Who Bring an Infant to the Session*	165
PROBLEM 48	*Silent People*	170
PROBLEM 49	*People Who Stand Up and Walk Around*	174
PROBLEM 50	*People Who Check Their Watches*	177
PROBLEM 51	*Parting Shots*	181
PROBLEM 52	*People Who Ask How You Are Feeling*	184
PROBLEM 53	*Adolescents Who Sit in Your Chair*	188
PROBLEM 54	*People Who Bring Their Own Drinks to the Office*	190
PROBLEM 55	*People Who Don't Hang Up Their Coats*	195

PROBLEM 56	*People Who Ask to Borrow a Magazine*	198
PROBLEM 57	*People Who Don't Pay the Bill*	200
PROBLEM 58	*People Who Miss Many Appointments*	204
PROBLEM 59	*People Who Demand Medicine*	208
PROBLEM 60	*People Who Move Your Furniture*	211
PROBLEM 61	*People Who Fall Asleep in Your Waiting Room*	215
PROBLEM 62	*Suicidal People*	217
PROBLEM 63	*When CBT Alone Is Not Working*	227
PROBLEM 64	*Those Who Have Had a Bad Experience With a Prior Therapist*	231
PROBLEM 65	*People Who Ask You Questions*	235
SECTION E	**YOUR REACTIONS TO PEOPLE IN TREATMENT**	**239**
	General Comments	**239**
PROBLEM 66	*What Is Countertransference and How Is It Different From Empathy?*	241
PROBLEM 67	*Countertransference to Unfaithful People*	242
PROBLEM 68	*Compliant Talkers*	245
PROBLEM 69	*Those Who Have Figured You Out*	248
PROBLEM 70	*Countertransference to Marital Arguments*	250
PROBLEM 71	*People You Don't Like and People Who Don't Like You*	254
PROBLEM 72	*People Who Do Not Respond to Your Explanations About Their Problems*	258
PROBLEM 73	*People Who Want Your Advice*	262
PROBLEM 74	*Questions About Your Theoretical Orientation*	268
PROBLEM 75	*People Who Read Your Professional Articles and Books*	272
PROBLEM 76	*People Who React to Any Intervention as an Invasion*	274
PROBLEM 77	*When You Find Yourself Asking Too Many Questions*	276

| PROBLEM 78 | *People Who Threaten You* | 279 |

SECTION F	**MODIFICATIONS TO THE "FRAME" OF TREATMENT**	**283**
	General Comments About Exceptions	**283**
PROBLEM 79	*Bumping Into People Outside of the Office*	285
PROBLEM 80	*When You Lower Your Fee*	288
PROBLEM 81	*What About E-mail and Skype?*	290
PROBLEM 82	*Bosses Who Have Their Assistants Contact You*	293
PROBLEM 83	*People Who Want to Be Your Friend—Use Your First Name*	297
PROBLEM 84	*Elevator Phobics Who Must Take an Elevator to Your Office*	301
PROBLEM 85	*Lawyers Wanting Evaluations for Their Clients Versus People Who Call at the Suggestion of Their Attorneys*	303
PROBLEM 86	*People Who Want You to Give a Second Opinion While They're in Treatment With Someone Else*	305
PROBLEM 87	*People Who Consult You Because of Third-Party Pressure*	308
PROBLEM 88	*Child-Centered Counseling*	310
PROBLEM 89	*People Who Travel a Long Distance to Sessions*	315
PROBLEM 90	*What If You Opt Out of Medicare or Are an "Out of Network" Provider?*	319

SECTION G	**SPECIAL ISSUES**	**321**
	General Comments About Unusual Situations and Behaviors During Treatment	**321**
PROBLEM 91	*People Who Say "You Know" Repetitively*	323
PROBLEM 92	*Loud Throat Clearing and Globus Hystericus*	325
PROBLEM 93	*Women Who Wear Ultra-Short Skirts and/or See-Through Blouses*	329

PROBLEM 94	*Wiseguys*	333
PROBLEM 95	*People Who Are Friends With Other People You Are Treating*	338
PROBLEM 96	*People Who Are Involved With Someone Who Is Driving Them Crazy*	341
PROBLEM 97	*People Who Are Dating Someone Who Sounds Severely Mentally Ill*	344
PROBLEM 98	*People Who Write Down Long Dreams*	348
PROBLEM 99	*Consulting With and Treating Family Members of People You Are Already Treating*	353
PROBLEM 100	*When People "Don't Get It": Are They Using Denial or Are They Psychotic?*	357
PROBLEM 101	*How to Improve Diagnosis and Choice of Techniques*	361
	A. More on Supportive and Interpretive Techniques	362
	B. More Information on Diagnosis	366

References   371
Index   381

Some Answers...

for my friends, colleagues, trainees, relatives, and interested social acquaintances who have asked me hard questions about psychotherapy. This book is intended for all mental health practitioners who engage in psychotherapy and for others who have an interest in learning about psychotherapy.

You will read about some of my successes and failures in diagnosis, treatment, and supervision; the highlights of the most perplexing, fundamental, and fascinating questions I have encountered over decades of practicing and supervising psychotherapy; and my ideas about practical solutions for handling those questions.

Over the years I have taught, supervised, or consulted with many mental health practitioners about psychotherapy technique. They have included social workers, psychologists, pastoral counselors, educational counselors, licensed professional counselors, psychiatrists, and psychoanalysts.[1] Despite their wide variety of backgrounds, I have found that many of these practitioners have grappled with common practical problems and difficult technical questions like the ones I attempt to answer in this book.

I was initially somewhat surprised to learn that, even though many therapists felt their training prepared them for one particular type of approach to treating mental conditions, most practitioners were not "purists" in adhering only to one therapeutic approach. They often combined useful features from other technical approaches that were not covered in their training. Sometimes they did this deliberately; at other times, they did it without realizing that the technique they used in a particular case actually had its origins in a different body of theory.

---

1   Their theoretical backgrounds have included supportive therapy, cognitive psychology, interpersonal therapy, neurosciences, cognitive behavioral therapy, electroconvulsive therapy, psychopharmacology, developmental psychology, addictionology, social work, eating disorder specialties, neuropsychology, child psychiatry, child abuse, ethology, geriatrics, music therapy, art therapy, college counseling, hospital-based practice, and psychoanalytic theories of Klein, Lacan, Jung, Freud, Bion/Tavistock, Kohut, Mahler, Kernberg, Bowlby/Ainsworth, Arlow and Brenner, and existentialists.

What I have observed is that most therapists develop their own "style" and technique through common sense, professional judgment, experience, empathic attunement to people in treatment, trial and error, and reading. Many of the most valuable skills they have cultivated were learned on the job and/or through research, postlicensing supervision, and consultations with other colleagues.

I consider a multidisciplinary approach to have many benefits both to practitioners and to the people receiving treatment. As the saying goes, "If the only tool you have is a hammer, everything starts to look like a nail." Most seasoned practitioners learn that their professional training provided a starting viewpoint as to how to approach people in therapy. And we all find that we learn something new from every person we treat. That is one of the great sources of intellectual stimulation the field of mental health has to offer: No matter how long we practice, we can always learn something new just by treating people.

I personally like to study a wide array of theories concerning the treatment of mental conditions and take something from the best ideas that each theory has to offer. In my conversations with colleagues, I inevitably find that practitioners who are flexible in their theoretical approach and are skilled in tailoring technique to particular people they treat enjoy three benefits:

1. they have better treatment outcomes overall;
2. they find more gratification in their work; and
3. they are ultimately financially successful in building a practice (largely because of #1 and #2).

To become proficient in tailoring the treatment to the individual requires you to develop your diagnostic toolset. More information about diagnosis can be found in certain problems addressed in this book, particularly Problem 2 (When Do I Say It?) and Problem 101 (B) (More Information on Diagnosis). My earlier book, *Get the Diagnosis Right: Assessment and Treatment Selection for Mental Disorders* (Routledge, 2010), provides a more in-depth exploration of the topic.

All psychotherapies are designed to influence people's disturbances through the interaction with the therapist. Sometimes the therapist tries to help others understand conflicts they have not previously seen. At other times, the therapist attempts to provide comfort, solutions to practical problems, and/or advice about work and relationships. In this book, I have included some of my thoughts on gray areas and mixtures of therapeutic approaches.

You'll recognize many of the dilemmas. Some are almost universal. Some are unusual and only occur on rare occasions. Most are in the middle, common enough but not ubiquitous. A few of the problems are mundane; some are ironic and manageable through a bit of humor in the session. Others are extraordinarily sad, irritating, or even dangerous.

I hope that you learn from my answers as much as I have learned from having had such difficult questions put to me by supervisees and by people I have treated. Such questions have kept me interested and broadened my thinking about treating people.

You will, no doubt, think of questions that I have omitted or not considered. If you do, please e-mail me your thoughts on the matter. Since I started writing this book, colleagues have been extremely forthcoming with new and ever more challenging problems they have encountered. I have also, as expected, heard answers I had not thought of, and look forward to hearing more of those, as well.

The essential thrill in asking and answering questions is for me, the pleasure of intellectual expansion and continuing progress toward mastery.

Enjoy!

Jerome S. Blackman, MD
jeromesblackmanmd@gmail.com

N.B. This book is filled with clinical examples. Many are amalgams of different people, and all are extremely disguised as to their actual identity, but I have preserved the pertinent dynamic elements.

Acknowledgments

First, thanks to the many therapists who have consulted me for supervision, who forced me to think of how to explain complicated situations in therapy. Second, I owe much to people I have treated, who allowed me access to the recesses of their minds; they taught me about human nature and mental functioning.

Special appreciation goes to my wife, Susan, who, in the midst of her busy legal practice, took pains to help me edit this book; and to my son, Ted, who took time from his hectic business activities to criticize my writing style.

My colleagues who read and offered very useful opinions about various sections of the book include, but are not limited to, Dr. Steven Waranch, in Virginia Beach, VA; Janet Schiff, LCSW, in Norfolk, VA; and Dr. Andrea Bandfield, in Greenville, SC. Dr. Ji Xuesong, in Beijing, and Dr. Cao Lingyun, in Shanghai, read earlier versions of the manuscript, and Drs. Emad Daniel (U.S. Navy) and Aileen Kim (Washington, DC) read and contributed to the text. To all of you, my warmest thanks.

Last but not least, I owe much to my stalwart office manager, Mrs. Jean Broughton, who, as usual, was invaluable in organizing and editing this project.

SECTION A

A Very Quick Take on Assessment and Technique

GENERAL COMMENTS

Not every therapy is for everyone. Not every theory explains all people's behaviors and problems.

In this section, I briefly go over some ideas about what types of interventions psychotherapists can make. I also discuss what types of problems seem to respond best, in general, to which types of interventions—and which theories are most suited to those different problems.

For a full discussion of these issues, please see *Get the Diagnosis Right: Assessment and Treatment Selection for Mental Disorders* (Blackman, 2010).

What follows here is, I hope, a pithy summary of the actually complex undertaking of determining the most likely diagnosis and then figuring out what types of things to say to people in treatment, depending on that determination. For a bit more detail, see Problem 101.

Problem 1
What Do I Say? (Technique)

Doing any type of psychotherapy involves you telling people things that affect them. What you say to them falls, essentially, into two groups:

- things that calm them down and
- things that stir them up.[1]

Calming interactions are often called "supportive," whereas stirring comments are often referred to as "clarifying," "understanding," or "interpretive." In Problem 2, you will find my thoughts about when to use each type of intervention, and throughout this book, I give illustrations of each.

Supportive techniques involve things you say to people to make them feel better—sort of like giving an analgesic for physical pain. Explanatory techniques are more like surgery: The things you tell people may hurt a bit at first and require some time to take effect, but they aim to remove or correct the problem in the long run.

Cognitive-behavioral techniques are a bit of an amalgam of supportive and explanatory approaches, but they are mainly supportive. You are basically attempting to help people feel better and think more rationally.

So what is it that you should say? (I address the question of *when* in Problem 2.)

SHORT ANSWER

Support

Support requires careful attunement to people's emotions and the realities of their lives. You are interested in where people are making errors in judgment and communication so that you can discuss solutions with them. You also try to find their overwhelming emotions and express openly (as you are able) your attunement to these.

If you decide supportive therapy is required, you

- ask people questions about their current situation in order to obtain details,
- explore areas of difficulty in their work situations and their current personal relationships, and

---

1 Schlesinger (1995).

try to intervene to help people make better decisions and to feel better about themselves.

Some therapists add cognitive-behavioral techniques to

- clarify areas of people's unrealistic expectations about themselves or others,
- have them write about significant events and their thoughts and reactions to them ("homework"),
- consider alternative ways of viewing issues causing dysfunctional emotions,
- validate their correct perceptions and help them learn to modify incorrect perceptions, and
- teach relaxation exercises/guided imagery.

Understanding ("Interpretation")

Interpretation involves explaining to people what you think is causing their problems, whether they are aware of it or not (conscious and unconscious). You are looking for elements of conflict[2] among their

- loving, sexual, and violent wishes;
- guilt and shame;
- reality;
- emotions ("affects"); and
- defense mechanisms.

You will find these elements as you listen closely to people's descriptions of their symptoms, their troubled relationships, and sometimes their reactions to you.

If you decide on an explanatory approach, you

- **Instruct**

    people to tell you about their thoughts, dreams, and feelings about their problems in relationships, in life, and in treatment;

- **Point out**

    conflicts, present and past, among wishes, their conscience, people, and the environment;

---

2 Brenner (2006).

- **Clarify**

    the bases for their anxiety and depressive affect; and

- **Confront**

    the defensive operations that are interfering with adequate solutions to the conflicts.

When you have figured all this out with people, they may feel a bit unhappy at first, but the knowledge they gain can help them understand their own actions, make better decisions, and obtain relief of symptoms.[3]

---

3 For the Long Answer, see Problem 101 (A).

Problem 2
When Do I Say It? (Diagnosis)

After hearing people's problems, you are faced with a choice: Should you intervene supportively or interpretively?

SHORT ANSWER[4]

Use *explanatory* (interpretive) *techniques* (Problem 1) more or less exclusively when the following are intact:

> **THEORY**
> To try to explain people's conflicts, they need
>
> - **AIRS:** Abstraction, Integration, Reality testing, Self-preservation
> - **ARTS:** Affect tolerance, Regulation of impulses, Trust, Superego (conscience)

- understanding symbolism (abstraction ability),
- organization of thought (integration),
- relation to reality,
- self-preservation (not harming themselves),
- emotional controls ("affect regulation"),
- capacity for trust ("object relations"), and
- conscience ("superego").

Use *medication* and/or *supportive/relational* techniques more or less exclusively when there are serious lapses in

- abstraction,
- organization of thought,
- reality functions,
- capacity for trust, and/or
- capacities for
    - impulse control (like alcohol abuse or sexual addiction) and
    - emotional control.

---

[4] For the Long Answer on diagnosis, see Problem 101 (B).

Use *cognitive-behavioral* techniques for people's problems with perspectives

- about reality,
- about themselves,
- about the future,
- about people with whom they are involved, and
- factors that overwhelmed them with anxiety.

> **TIP**
> - Medicate deficits
> - Explain conflicts

SECTION B

General Principles About Treatment

GENERAL COMMENTS

The "frame" or "working alliance" consists of people

- arriving and leaving on time,
- identifying their problems,
- agreeing to talk to you (and nothing else),
- agreeing to tell you what they think of what you tell them,
- paying the fee, and
- paying for missed sessions according to your policy.

When one of these parameters is breached by people you treat, you need to discuss it with them. If you breach any of the parameters, you have to think about "countertransference" (see Section E).

Problem 3
The Alliance and the Frame of Therapy

Psychotherapy, when it goes well, is similar to a normal conversation with a good friend, in that:

- You encourage people to speak openly with you.
- You try to be honest, though tactful, with them.
- People form an attachment to you and care about you.
- You care what happens to them and feel attachment to and responsibility for them.
- You develop some empathic understanding of how they feel.
- They develop some empathic understanding of you and your efforts to help them.
- You both value each other's time.
- You develop mutual respect.
- As people get more objective with themselves, they may joke a bit with you.
- You discuss honestly their reactions to what they tell you and what you tell them.
- You resonate emotionally with them when they are very upset.

Psychotherapy is different from a normal conversation with a good friend in that:

- You do not see people outside of your office.
- You do not usually tell people much detail about your personal life.
- People identify certain emotional problems that are *really* bothering them, which are so embarrassing they would not even tell their best friend.
- You try to help people make decisions, cope better, or understand themselves better.
- You sometimes tell people things about themselves that get them upset (like telling them about a defense mechanism they hadn't seen).
- People tell you their reactions to what you say.
- You only see people for a limited amount of time (often 30 or 45 minutes).

- People agree to be on time, leave on time, and be as honest as possible.
- People pay you for your input.
- If people cannot meet with you at the appointed time, they will have to abide by rules you have made about missed appointments.
- You encourage people to tell you about their thoughts about their relationships, fantasies, and secrets (like masturbation fantasies or extramarital affairs).
- You encourage people to reveal positive and negative thoughts about their relationship with you, including fantasies that would be inappropriate in any other situation, to see if you can figure out the childhood and adolescent problems that still haunt them.
- You do not touch the people who are talking with you (except a handshake at the beginning of the first and at the end of the last meeting in the United States; and a quick handshake at the beginning and end of each session in many other parts of the world).
- You accept certain responsibilities and liabilities regarding their mental health.
- You do not expect them to help you in return.
- You cannot repeat what people tell you to anyone (confidentiality)—except to get professional supervision without revealing people's names to the supervisor, or in rare legal situations such as involuntary commitment proceedings.

The above elements are often referred to as the "working alliance."[1]

---

1 Greenson (2008).

Problem 4
People Without a Clear Problem
(or "Chief Complaint")

This may seem strange to contemplate. If you are practicing, you already know that most people will not call you for an appointment until they have first tried umpteen things to solve their own problems.[2] Usually, people have tried, in no particular order, talking with friends, yoga, meditation, consultations with mentors, various medications, acupuncture, exercise, working harder, travel, masturbation, or extramarital affairs.

Every once in a while, however, people will come to see you who seem a bit obscure about what is troubling them. They speak vaguely, or normalize the problems they do mention (in passing). What do you do with this?

> **REMINDER**
> The working alliance means that people in treatment with you
>
> - attend their sessions,
> - arrive and leave on time,
> - pay the fee the way you wish,
> - pay for any missed sessions according to the policy you have set,
> - *agree they have specific problems for which they want help,*
> - only talk (and nothing else) with you, and
> - give you feedback about your comments to them.
>
> You, reciprocally,
>
> - focus entirely on their problems (and not your own or someone else's),
> - try to figure out what is wrong,
> - make comments designed to help them cope or understand the problems you and they have identified,

---

2 By the way, this is where insurance carriers and third-party payers (including the U.S. government) make incorrect assumptions about the availability of psychotherapy causing people to overuse it: The vast majority of people resist seeing therapists because
   a) it is embarrassing to talk about their problems, especially sexual matters and masturbation;
   b) it feels too much like a teenager giving up autonomy to consult an "authority" figure about anything; and
   c) they would rather spend their time on something else that is pleasurable.

- also are on time, and
- take them seriously.

SHORT ANSWER

The usual wisdom is that if people do not clarify their problems, the working alliance has not been established. It's then usually necessary to attend to the problem in the alliance before trying to tackle other matters (unless the person is in an emergency situation). When they are vague about their main problems, I bring this to their attention.

For example, I might say, "I understand that you have communication problems in your marriage, but I've noticed you've left out what those problems concern." That would be a confrontation of vagueness. When I do that, I hope to hear people tell me more details about their problems, such as, "Well, it's embarrassing to tell you. We haven't had sex in 2 years…"

Sometimes, however, the person may respond, "I don't know what it's about. We just wind up arguing; I can't remember what we argue about." In other words, their vagueness may be complicated by them forgetting ("repression"). You will then have to try to find out what the details may be. You can do that by getting more history or by confronting the repression with a comment like, "I see; the devil's in the details, but it sounds like the details are so upsetting that your mind kind of shuts them off."[3]

Watch out for asking too many questions, such as, "Do you argue about money?" There are reasons people forget (repression is a defense mechanism). If you dig into the content of what's upsetting them, people may repay you by quitting treatment or not showing up for the next session ("avoidance" as a defense—see Problem 10).

> **TIP**
> If you have to dig deep to find a chief complaint, you may be missing a person's use of suppression of fantasies and conflicts.

LONG ANSWER

Aside from vagueness, people who consult you may just start talking about their childhood or adolescence. If people are focusing on Family Of Origin

---

3 **Theory:** This uses Paul Gray's (1994) concept of focusing on the (unconscious) resistance as it occurs.

Issues too much, at any time, this may be a way of avoiding their current problems. For this reason, I have sometimes lightly referred to this focus as FOOI.[4]

> **TIP**
> FOOI focus may cloak current problems.

EXAMPLE 1

Joe, age 41, was depressed. When he came to my office, he began, "Well, my father was bipolar, I think. He saw a psychiatrist for a while. Later he drank too much, but went to AA, which was helpful until he got emphysema from smoking. I had my first drink when I was 13, and thought it was a big deal. All my friends did it. My parents never knew. I met Sandy when I was 14, and we started dating. I remember she had blue eyes and long, brown hair. But she broke up with me...."

At this point, I had a number of choices. I could wait a few more minutes to see if Joe got around to linking what he was telling me about his past history with his current depression. I could explore his relationship to Sandy or his relationship with his father in order to see, myself, if any of that shed light on his depression, or I could gently point out that although the material he was telling me seemed important, I was still in the dark about what caused him to call me.

Or I could add that it seemed somehow easier for him to start with his life story than to "get into" the difficult situation in which he found himself lately. I decided on the last of these approaches. Joe responded, "That's the way I always handle hard things: I wander around Robin Hood's barn and never get to the point. My wife says the same thing." I eventually learned that Joe's current depression centered on conflicts regarding emotional closeness and sexual relations with his wife.

EXAMPLE 2

Karen, age 22, who was working in a rural, underserved area for AmeriCorps, was referred by Arlene, a social worker who had once been a student of mine and now had a position with AmeriCorps. Karen had had panic attacks while at the rural worksite, the last of which necessitated a medevac to bring Karen home.

---

4 The technical name for this defense is temporal regression. See Blackman (2003a).

I began Karen's evaluation session by saying, "Why don't you tell me something about your problem?" Karen looked nonplussed; she responded, "What problem?" I related to her that Arlene had told me about the anxiety attacks. Karen nodded her head and said, "Oh, that. But that was a long time ago." It had been 2 weeks (!).

Karen added, "I don't like to think about it!" I explained that it must have been particularly painful or embarrassing for her to have shut it out of her mind like that. She looked at me tentatively, and said she just "blew it off." Her use of an expression that had a possible double entendre[5] tipped me off that she might be suppressing conflicts of a sexual nature.

Unfortunately, when I pointed out her avoidance of her chief complaint, Karen got more defensive. I therefore asked her if she would be willing to tell me about her experiences in AmeriCorps. She agreed. Over the next 20 minutes or so, she explained that, at the job site, she had become "close friends" with Ken, one of the other volunteers. Her panic attacks had started when she and Ken had been working together late at night. Karen said, "But he wasn't like my boyfriend. My boyfriend, John, is in Canada."

In fact, John had not seen Karen for months, and their e-mails had become less frequent. I was able to clarify with Karen that she would have felt very guilty about getting involved with Ken under those circumstances. She agreed, and became more interested in her conflicts about John, who, it turned out, had cheated on her once, but she had forgiven him. By the end of the evaluation session, we agreed that she had been having some mixed feelings about her relationship with John, and would like to get more clarity about what she was doing; we now had a chief complaint.

Karen and I worked in psychotherapy, once a week, for about 3 months. During that time, we were able to understand that she had been suppressing anger at John for ignoring her but let him off the hook (rationalized) by thinking he was busy with "friends." Her guilt had caused her to avoid facing her wish to retaliate by getting involved with Ken.

Ironically, her panic attacks had gotten her away from Ken at the same time they made her unavailable to John (still in Canada); she was punished by the loss of both men. Her conflicts were exacerbated because of an adolescent tendency to inhibit judgment: avoiding judgment about John regarding his infidelity, for example.

Regarding family origins, Karen's father had cheated on her mother when Karen was 15, but her mother had forgiven him. Karen had identified with her forgiving mother. Karen thereby avoided criticizing her mother's "doormat" mentality in accepting her father back and hung onto John.

---

5 S. Freud (1901).

Problem 5
Can You Diagnose From the Presenting Problem (the "Chief Complaint")?

Sometimes. If you can, you save yourself a lot of time. At least, the presenting problem can guide you as to what type of material you need in order to confirm or negate your initial hunches about diagnosis.

SHORT ANSWER

If the presenting problem is bizarre, chances are people may be psychotic. Example 1: A man had shot himself in the neck. Example 2: A woman had sliced off her own breast. Such people will need medicine and, no doubt, periodic hospitalization.

If the presenting complaint is not too bizarre (e.g., "I can't seem to get over my mother's death," or "I'm hitting the bottle too much and too often"), I often ask what the person has already figured out about the issue. Favorable responses might be, "I think I feel guilty about something with my mother" or "I've had some financial reversals lately, and maybe I'm drowning out my feeling of failure." Such answers indicate reasonable self-observation and abstraction abilities—required for therapy to understand conflicts.

> **DIFFERENTIAL DIAGNOSIS**
> The process and results of considering the various complaints, signs, symptoms, and findings in a person that lead to a variety of possible diagnoses.
> After the various possible diagnoses and causes (etiologies) are considered, each must be "ruled out" or "ruled in" by further study in any specific case.

LONG ANSWER

EXAMPLE 1

Amir, a psychiatry resident, presented in class the case of Joan, a 33-year-old woman hospitalized on the internal medicine ward for "depression." Actually, Joan was hearing voices telling her to kill people; she was also seeing dead relatives and a dog that appeared and then disappeared from her bed; she could not stop these upsetting experiences, which made her depressed.

I asked the residents in the class to attempt to diagnose from the actual chief complaint: auditory hallucinations. The residents' opinions included "paranoid schizophrenia," "major depression with psychotic symptoms," and "borderline personality with psychotic episodes." They all agreed on one thing: Joan was currently psychotic.

The *differential diagnosis* (other possibilities) also included drug abuse and a variety of physical illnesses. Therefore, we were not looking to understand conflict but needed to find the cause of the psychotic symptoms.

Amir then said Joan missed her boyfriend, who had just jilted her. She had five children, ages 6 through 17, all by different men; none was paying child support. She had never been married and was now alone. MRI of the head was normal. Blood work was normal, as was physical exam (i.e., "organic" etiologies were ruled out). Amir then reported that for a 2-year period, Joan had been homeless. Following Bleuler (1911/1950), homelessness likely indicated schizophrenia.

Amir then recalled that Joan had said to him, "Your spirit was like mine. Now you have changed; I don't want to hurt your feelings, but now I don't like you."

> **TIP**
> Not all people who say they are "depressed" have a diagnosis of depression.

I explained that these statements indicated that Joan had some conscience functioning;[6] also, Joan was "splitting": a deficit in her ability to entertain both positive and negative thoughts about a person simultaneously, common in borderline and psychotic people. Joan's break in her reality testing about Amir (a shift in perception without external evidence) made psychosis a bit more likely.

Amir then added that Joan had shown him a nude picture of herself. In the photo, Joan was standing next to naked male transvestites, as "a model." Amir verified that Joan had never been a model, although her pictures were posted on the Internet. Amir wondered about Joan's grandiosity—a delusion, characteristic of schizophrenia? He reported a discussion among faculty members about her "Axis II-ishness" (probable antisocial traits), based on Joan's lying, exhibitionism, and grandiosity.

I agreed that Joan manifested "histrionic traits"—her exhibitionism could be listed on Axis II; also, her lying would fit with "factitious" or "antisocial" traits. These features did not rule out psychosis, where pathological

---

6 She felt guilty about hurting Amir's feelings—possibly poorly integrated guilt (Ticho, 1972).

character traits[7] are commonly present—the reasoning behind establishing the *Diagnostic and Statistical Manual of Mental Disorders (DSM)* multiaxial diagnostic system.

In sum, the internist's diagnosis of "depression" was not reliable for determining Joan's true diagnosis, although it had been her chief complaint.

EXAMPLE 2

Fred, a 28-year-old married attorney, could not get a young woman who worked for him "out of [his] head." The woman, Ann, "sexted" him, but when they saw each other, she was stand-offish. He felt guilty about being attracted to her, although he and his wife had been considering a divorce. He was "obsessed" with Ann—his chief complaint. Fred felt competitive with one of his married male law partners, who took Ann with him on trips. She would never acknowledge this, which made Fred even more frustrated.

Fred seemed to have adequate reality testing, he could observe himself, and he was interested in understanding himself (he could "mentalize"). He presented his problems in an organized way (intact integrative function), realized something was inhibiting him (intact abstraction ability) and that his attraction to Ann was "nuts." My initial diagnosis included obsessional symptoms with neurotic inhibitions of judgment and executive function (making decisions about love and aggression).

I treated Fred for about 2 years. We figured out that his attraction to Ann reflected

- a salve to his injured feelings of loss about his wife, who was rejecting him;
- a secret way of expressing anger at his wife;
- a way of getting himself punished (she tortured him); and
- a repeat of severe frustrations he had felt because his mother idealized him.

Fred and his wife eventually got divorced. It turned out his wife already had another lover. Fred was jealous but relieved of guilt.

Ann confessed to Fred that she had been having an affair with Fred's partner but was afraid that the partner would not leave his wife to marry her. After a long talk, they decided to just "stay friends." When Fred finished up therapy with me, he was dating again.

---

7   Hoch and Polatin (1949).

The point is that, in his chief complaint, there was evidence that Fred possessed observing ego, abstraction ability, and reality-testing.

He also experienced longing and guilt, other good prognostic signs for therapy designed to help him understand himself better.

> **TIP**
> Before choosing to help people understand their problems, look for
>
> - good abstraction ability,
> - good organization of thought,
> - ability to observe themselves, and
> - conflicts involving guilt.

Problem 6
When to Use Medicine and When Not To

I prescribe medicine when someone I am treating experiences a dangerous upsurge of emotions (depression, panic, rage) that causes more than a brief breakdown in functions. Damaged functions may include

- sleep–wake cycle
- memory
- work
- concentration
- judgment about danger
- speech and language
- intellect

Neuroleptic medicine, in particular, may be necessary; even if people are not schizophrenic, they can experience a breakdown in containment of primary process thinking—where bizarre (condensed, symbolic) thoughts flood their conscious thinking.

Of course, it's best not even to try to do explanatory work with people who show too much *deficit*

- in integration (loose associations, flight of ideas);
- in abstraction (concrete thinking);
- in relationship to reality; or
- in self-preservation (severe suicide attempts). (See Problem 101 [B])

Sometimes, as you are trying to help people understand themselves, they become so overwhelmed by emotion that understanding their conflicts is relatively ineffective. At the times when their basic functions are overwhelmed, they may benefit from short courses of medication.[8]

SHORT ANSWER

Medicate deficits; understand conflicts. Not vice versa.

---

[8] Blackman (2003a), Introduction.

LONG ANSWER

EXAMPLE

Brad, a 30-year-old graduate student, revealed during treatment that Trey, the brother who had protected him during childhood, had died in a motorcycle accident. After the funeral, Trey's widow seduced Brad. He had sex with her but afterward felt confused. I explained to Brad that sex with his sister-in-law seemed to have guarded him from grief (sex as a defense); he then began to cry. His crying became overwhelming and at one point was so severe that Brad fell off the couch.

A few hours later, Brad was having trouble studying. He telephoned me and sounded disorganized. I therefore called in a prescription for a low dose of neuroleptic medicine. When I saw him 2 days later, he felt much better. He continued to grieve, but without the breakdown in integration and orientation. He needed medicine for several weeks but eventually recovered his functions of abstraction, integration, reality testing, and orientation and was able to resume his analytic treatment.

Problem 7
Should I Medicate Depressions or Try to Figure Out the Causes Instead?

Regardless of the precipitating factors for depression, if AIRS (*A*bstraction, *I*ntegration, *R*eality testing and *S*elf-preservation—see Problem 101 [B]) are intact, and impulse control and affect regulation are adequate, medication is generally not advisable (*contraindicated*). Nevertheless, many depressed people request antidepressants. What should you do?

> **TIP**
> Just because people ask for an antidepressant does not mean they should receive one.

SHORT ANSWER

For depression associated with deficits in functions (i.e., psychosis, recognizing the limits of treatment of psychosis, or shame over embarrassing debility due to psychosis), *antipsychotic medicine* is usually needed. If this is not enough, antidepressants may be needed as well. You may also try supportive interventions, including

- expressing empathic understanding,
- substituting your reality for the psychotic person's,
- explaining other people's motives,
- suggesting defenses (like rationalization), and
- offering opportunities for sublimation (occupational therapy, music therapy, art therapy).

Antidepressants may be indicated when depression overwhelms psychomotor functioning (when people can't get out of bed). In addition, consider an antidepressant for people with weakness in controlling their temper. They get depressed because they feel guilty (critical of themselves) about their weakness in affect tolerance. When antidepressants take the edge off the anger, they make the defense of *turning criticism onto the self* less necessary; the depression may then lessen.

> **TIP**
> Medicate with neuroleptics when there is a breakdown in AIRS (Abstraction, Integration, Reality testing, Self-preservation) or a breakdown in containing bizarre thoughts. Consider antidepressants and anxiolytics for damaged affect tolerance.
>
> When these mental operations are functional, do not medicate, even if people are depressed. Instead, try to figure out the causes for the depression and explain them.

When people (who have adequate functioning) request medication, I

- explain the contraindications, or
- try to figure out the meanings of their request.

For depression caused by excess (conscious or unconscious) guilt, explain the conflicts and defenses caused by the guilt (provocation of punishment, turning of anger on the self, being too nice). *Do not medicate.*

For depressive affect due to unresolved mourning, find and discuss impediments to (defenses preventing) grieving; abreact (suggest affective flexibility); "contain" the grieving process. *Do not medicate.*

> **TIP**
> People with no major deficits (in AIRS) may still benefit from antidepressants if they suffer with (an ego weakness in) affect tolerance or impulse control.

For depressive affect generated by people's mistakes (caused by personality conflicts or neurotic inhibition of functions), confront the errors

- in judgment (about danger),
- in executive function (poor decisions),
- in work (wrong job choice or counterproductive efforts), and
- in social skills (awkward interactions).

Then explain the conflicts causing the mistakes and character problems. *Do not medicate.*

EXAMPLE 1

Glenda, age 37, depressed because of marital disappointments, asked me about taking an antidepressant. I responded with irony: "I wish I had one that would make your husband come home earlier and pay attention to you and the children." Glenda responded, "Yeah, it would be nice if there were some magic pill; then I wouldn't have to tell him what's wrong with him. I really dread that. And I wouldn't have to talk to you about all this disgusting stuff."

Glenda's wish for medication was a defense (to relieve the pain of her reality). She was responsive when I explained her magical thinking to her: she realized no magic pill would fix her marriage. Her only chance of improving the marriage required difficult conversations which she was afraid to begin. After these clarifications, she spoke to her husband.

LONG ANSWER

One common cause of depressions is turning on the self of anger and/or criticism, which relieves guilt (superego pressure) over a homicidal wish toward someone else.[9] Since the guilt is based largely on *identifications* from the latency (elementary school) and adolescent phases of child development, they are called "introjective" depressions.[10] When the cause of the depression is introjective, explanation of turning of anger on the self to avoid guilt (blaming oneself unfairly) is usually the intervention of choice.

Depressions caused by loss are called "anaclitic" depressions.[11] To get over such depressions, grieving is required. If people are not grieving, but instead become attached to keepsakes in a kind of permanent mausoleum in their home, you can show them that these souvenirs are guarding against grief—termed "established pathological mourning."[12] If you are successful in explaining this, the person in treatment will become unhappy and grieve for a while.

This is the reason *antidepressant medicines are relatively contraindicated in nonsuicidal, nonpsychotic people with anaclitic depressions*—these depressed people need to feel the grief, discuss it, and eventually gain perspective on the loss. The same principle governs people who are depressed because of going through a divorce. Medication usually interferes with the grieving process over the lost marriage.

What I call "secondary depressions" occur in situations where people's *pathological character traits* (such as pseudoindependence, obnoxiousness, passivity, or impulsivity) have caused havoc in their lives.[13] Then they become

---

9 S. Freud (1917) and Menninger (1933).
10 Blatt (1998).
11 Blatt (1992), following Spitz and Wolf (1946).
12 Volkan (1982).
13 T. Wolfe (1987).

unhappy because of the unsolvable melodrama that has developed. These cases, when possible, require understanding the origins and purposes of the character pathology. If you are successful in explaining the conflicts producing the pathological character traits, the depression should lift some; but if people have caused too much damage to their lives, they will still have lots of regrets.

EXAMPLE 2

Jessica, a 31-year-old obstetrician, consulted me for depression. She was unhappy, easily irritated, and complained of loss of interest in her relationship with her husband. They had not had sexual relations for several months.

Since she had frequently prescribed antidepressant medicine for women who consulted her, she asked me about antidepressants. I encouraged her to tell me more about her marriage and her work, so we might see what was indicated.

Jessica explained that she had been married for about a year. They had met eight months prior to the wedding while she was traveling on a church mission to Indonesia. He was an agronomist in the Peace Corps, also working in Indonesia. They had a torrid sexual affair for about 2 months.

When they returned to the United States, he went back to his hometown in Idaho. They got together about one weekend a month and eventually decided to get married. Since he did not have stable employment, he moved to be with her.

He had been "looking" for a job since they got married, but could not find one. He stayed out till 4:00 a.m. drinking with "friends" and smoking pot. When Jessica complained, he became irascible and drank more. During the day, he slept and smoked pot. She lamented that if he did not become more responsible, they could not start a family; he responded that he was not sure he wanted children.

Jessica had suggested marital therapy, but he adamantly refused. She feared her "depression" was somehow driving him away.

Instead of prescribing medicine, I pointed out to Jessica that she seemed to be looking right at the problem that was getting her depressed, but somehow not seeing it (denial of reality) and then she blamed herself for being depressed. She also hoped[14] her husband would get better; she did not want to feel disappointed with him. She responded, "You're right. I've known for months what I have to do, but I haven't wanted to face it."

---

14 Akhtar (1996). The "someday" fantasy used as a defense.

A week later, Jessica returned for a follow-up session. She had moved out of the apartment and filed for divorce. She now confided that what had stopped her previously included

- not wanting to grieve over the marriage, and
- not wanting to admit she had made such a terrible mistake.

She had always prided herself on getting things right; she had been a "counselor" to friends and patients. She had been an excellent student. Her mistake in choosing the man she married was "embarrassing."

For Jessica, staying married and taking an antidepressant may have alleviated (defended against) depression but not relieved the problem. At the end of that second (and final) session, she commented, "Next time I'll be a lot more careful. No more romantic fantasies until I get to know the guy."

I have also treated a number of women in their late 40s who had not married because they thought that job success meant not getting involved with a man emotionally. To paraphrase Irina Dunn (Yoest, 2007), they felt "a woman needs a man like a fish needs a bicycle." The women who consulted me, however, had also wanted to bear children. They presented with significant depression over that loss, and even after understanding the various defenses (including identification with feminist mentors) that caused them to avoid getting married, they still needed to grieve about the painful loss of childbearing.

Still another type of depression occurs when there is a failure to live up to certain ideals. At times the ideals are set too high for the person to achieve because the person does not possess the skills needed. In some instances, however, the ideals are reasonable for people, but inhibitions of functioning impair their ability to reach the ideals.

Problem 8
Planes of Psychotherapy: Where to Intervene?

You can think of the material you hear from people who consult you as falling into "planes" (geometric, not the flying ones or the tools). The problems people present have a history that can be broken down into conflicts at each phase (or plane) of their development (infancy—attachment; preschool—separation; school-age—conscience; adolescence—identity; adulthood—generativity).

SHORT ANSWER

Make connections within the same plane (see Figure 1).

LONG ANSWER

Figure 1, modeled after Waelder's (1936/2007) formulations of conflict, has been modified to summarize the brief, (mostly) explanatory treatment of Henry.[15] (See pages 28–29.)

EXAMPLE

Henry, a 32-year-old married man, complained of depression. When I asked about his marriage, he described his "lovely" wife and "delightful" 1½-year-old daughter. The marriage was "fine." When I attempted to confirm this by saying, "And the sex is good, too?" Henry laughed. He admitted there had been no sex since his daughter was born because she slept in the bed with him and his wife.

    Henry had acceded to his wife's (unrealistic) fear of being separated from the child at night, although he would have preferred the child sleep in her own room. I pointed out that Henry shied away from his own judgment (passivity and inhibition of executive functioning). He responded that he did not want to upset his wife.

    This entire discussion took place *at his current level of development* (adulthood), where he became passive to guard against guilt over the "aggressiveness" he needed to argue with his wife about the sleeping arrangements and

---

15   Blackman (2003a), Defense #48, and S. Freud (1926).

to encourage her back into a regular sex life. That is, Henry unconsciously equated activity (verbal expression of his preferences) with insensitivity and destructive-aggression. He then felt guilty about speaking. He remembered how he had been shy about speaking with girls, starting in grade school.

In the follow-up session, Henry reported that he had told his wife what he wanted. She expressed understanding, but was unsure about when to have the child sleep alone. He did not know, either. They wanted my opinion.[16]

I decided to "answer his question" (see Problem 65), to give him information. I explained that child development studies suggest it is best for the child never to sleep in the parents' bed, since this tends to prolong symbiotic attachment and therefore interferes with the child's internal sense of security.[17]

Since his daughter was, at this point, bound to be a bit behind in feeling comfortable when alone (some persistence of symbiosis and increased separation anxiety at night),[18] I recommended that he or his wife sit in his daughter's room until she fell asleep. Taking action now could probably help the child over any disturbance during her rapprochement.[19] I also recommended Gil Kliman's book, *Responsible Parenthood*.[20]

In his third and final meeting with me, Henry said he was "well-armed" and had persuaded his wife to put the child to bed in her crib in her own room. Either he or his wife sat with her for a few minutes until she fell asleep. Freed from the presence of a "third" (as it has been described lately),[21] Henry and his wife then had gratifying sexual intercourse, and his depression lifted.

Henry then compared me to his father. His father had been passive with Henry's mother, so Henry said he had "come by" his passivity "honestly." I inquired about the stage of his life when he recalled his father's passivity. He at first said, "Always," but then thought of incidents from grade school and adolescence where his father "took the easy way out." Henry remembered always hating the way his father caved in and found it strange that he

---

16 I am perpetually dismayed by the unfortunate failure to disseminate, to the general public, the work on early childhood development by Bowlby (1944); Bretherton (1992); Mahler (1968); McDevitt (1983, 1997); S. Kramer (1978, 1983); Kramer and Akhtar (1988); Blum and Galenson (1978); Galenson and Roiphe (1980); Stoller, Buxbaum, and Galenson (1976); Kleeman (1966); Marcus and Francis (1975); Parens (1991); and Sandler (1960).

   I believe the findings of these child development experts support the conclusion that sleeping in the same bed with your child has more downsides than upsides (contrary to the viewpoint of those who currently promote "the family bed" or "co-sleeping").

17 Mahler (1968).
18 Mahler, Pine, and Bergman (1975).
19 Mahler, Pine, and Bergman (1975).
20 Kliman and Rosenfeld (1983).
21 *Psychoanalytic Quarterly* (2004).

30 GENERAL PRINCIPLES ABOUT TREATMENT

Conflict at Current-day Plane: Adult level
Henry wishes for sex and to move his daughter out of the marital bed (aggression); these wishes conflict with guilt (over hurting wife), and the reality of his wife's attitude. When he uses the defenses of passivity, rationalization, and inhibition of speech, he winds up in a pickle, with the compromise formation of being depressed.

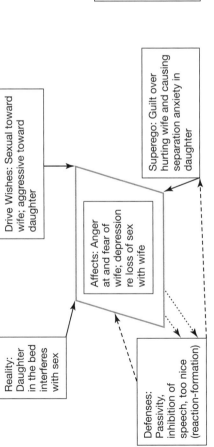

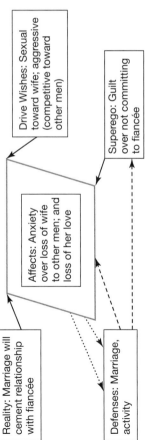

Conflict at Plane of Early Adulthood (specifics unknown): Henry's wish for sex and children, superego factors, and the reality of his love (attachment) for the woman he will marry are resolved by Henry getting married (compromise formation)—this defensively relieves guilt, resolves whatever anxieties about loss (of the object) exist, allows him sexual pleasure and gratification of (aggressive) wishes to possess his wife's fidelity.

PROBLEM 8   PLANES OF PSYCHOTHERAPY: WHERE TO INTERVENE?   31

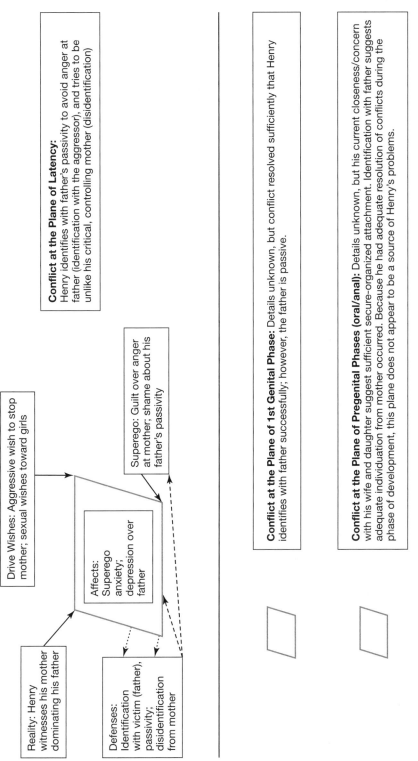

Figure 1. Henry's Phases of Conflict.

- Warning: Theory Ahead

was doing the same thing. He also felt critical of his mother's dominance. I offered the possibility that Henry had not wanted to be mad at his father and his mother at the same time. He confirmed that he was close to his father and never wanted to be mad at him.

In other words, we had now completed explaining his

- identification with his father, so he would not lose his father's love, and
- shifting into the current-day the conflicts he had had about his father at the *developmental levels of latency and adolescence.*

Henry did not get to other phases with me, as it was not necessary. With other people, where resolution is not as straightforward, further understanding might be needed from other planes of conflict. You can find connections *between planes as well*—as Henry had started doing. A good rule of thumb is not to jump between distant planes often. The reasons for this are as follows:

- It is easier for people to understand conflicts within the same plane.
- It is more accurate to stay within the same plane; when jumping back to a previous plane, you can miss conflicts that had occurred in between.

Problem 9
Alternating Supportive and Interpretive Techniques

Some people have only the minimum requirements needed for therapy aimed at helping them understand themselves. Their ability to organize their thoughts (integrative function) and/or understand symbols (abstraction ability) may be somewhat weak, although not exactly defective. Others have weaknesses in maintaining close, trusting relationships (object relations problems) and a related weakness in affect tolerance. How can you approach their problems in a flexible manner?

SHORT ANSWER

Oscillate in your technique. Use supportive techniques (see Problem 1) when people show weaknesses in sustaining themselves in the face of powerful emotions, in organizing their thoughts, in speech, in making decisions, in social skill, and in judgment. Supportive techniques include

- supplying a(n ego) function—telling people your version of reality, explaining abstract concepts, organizing what they report for them;
- "containing" their affects (see Problem 13)—listening and "absorbing" their overwhelming feelings; and
- advising and persuading them regarding their decision making.

At other times, when people avoid childhood-based anxiety, you point out the avoidance. When they repeat something from childhood with you (transference), you discuss this. If they are impeding their own functioning because of symbolism, you demonstrate how the symbolism causes the impairment in functioning (see example in Problem 8 and "Example of Neurotic Symbolism" in Problem 44).

Further, if people have conflicts regarding your advice, you may have to shift to understanding their conflicts; if they become overwhelmed by your explanations, then you shift to offering support: containing, understanding, clarifying, or persuading.

LONG ANSWER

When people demonstrate weaknesses in functioning, but are also suffering from conflicts, this poses a serious problem. Explaining their conflicts may be necessary but may not be enough to help them. Sometimes, the explanations are too upsetting.

On the other hand, too much support can be insulting, may be experienced as invasive or presumptuous, and sometimes is so controlling that someone in treatment may get worse or quit. The difficulty in watching for uneven functioning in people you are treating was managed very nicely by Dr. Emad Daniel, who was in supervision with me at the time.

EXAMPLE

Dr. Daniel[22] asked me about Irma, age 45, who was depressed and confused about her life. She was living separately from her husband of 18 years; she left her 15-year-old daughter and 13-year-old son in his care voluntarily because she "couldn't take it." Irma had her own apartment, worked a 50-hour week, and saw her children on weekends. She was taking an antidepressant prescribed by her family doctor.

During supervision, Emad formulated that Irma was depressed because she could not speak to her teenage daughter without getting mad; this had caused distance between her and her daughter. He felt Irma had a weakness in affect tolerance (she had "given up" on talking with her daughter); therefore, Emad had expressed understanding of her weakness and of how difficult her daughter was to reach (supportive technique of *expression of empathic understanding and clarifying the reality of other people*).

He *advised* Irma to try to speak to her daughter rationally without expressing too much anger (Irma knew her angry criticisms made her daughter rebellious).

Irma expressed appreciation for his concern, but said she "just couldn't" speak calmly with her daughter; she felt critical of her daughter for being messy with dirty clothes, for spending too much time texting friends, for ignoring her studies, and for talking back.

At this juncture, I advised Emad to switch technique. Irma was shutting off her speech and executive function (interfering with her choosing when to express criticism or aggression). I thought he should discuss how she *inhibited her ego functions*.[23]

---

22 Dr. Daniel, at the time chief psychiatry resident, agreed to using material from our supervisory meetings regarding this case and requested I use his real name. The name Irma, however, is fictitious, and other identifying information about her is heavily disguised.
23 S. Freud (1926), H. Hartmann (1939), Blackman (2003a).

He reported, in his next supervisory session with me, that he had brought Irma's inhibitions of decision-making and speech to her attention (*confrontation*). She agreed, but had no idea what was causing the inhibition. I reminded Emad that defenses usually guard against some part of an affect, and of Brenner's (1982) clarification that all affects have two parts, sensation and thought. He then recalled he had asked Irma what she thought she was avoiding by not talking to her daughter; she had replied, "The first thing I think of is fear." She did not know what she was afraid of, but it was intense.

I explained that Irma had now become aware of part of her affect (the sensation) after Emad's confrontation of her defensive inhibition. We still didn't know the thought content, which was *repressed* (shut off from consciousness). Emad recognized that to complete an explanation of the conflicts causing her inhibition (the compromise formation), he would need to help her find the repressed thought content. He voiced pessimism about Irma's ability ever to get to the thought content through free association. He had noticed some weakness in integration during sessions.

I suggested he consider the 18 types of thought content that affects routinely may contain,[24] and explore the thought content by letting her endorse whichever thought content sounded right to her (e.g., loss of daughter, loss of daughter's love, loss of self-image, physical injury, punishment of some other sort, or loss of identity). He would be using a supportive technique (*supplying possible thoughts,* an ego function), while looking toward eventually completing the understanding (interpretive technique).

Emad then raised an important question: Even if Irma realized that she was anxious about caving in to her daughter (loss of identity), what could she do about it?

---

24 Blackman (2010), Chapter 11. The thought contact of anxiety, depressive affect, and anger can contain material concerning
   1. ego (function) fragmentation,
   2. annihilation (of the self),
   3. loss of the object,
   4. loss of the object's love,
   5. self-object fusion,
   6. separation (and basic trust),
   7. power of the drives,
   8. objectivity,
   9. reality,
   10. castration,
   11. feminine genital injury,
   12. penetration,
   13. lack of ego function development (inadequacy),
   14. superego (guilt and shame),
   15. loss of body integrity,
   16. social awkwardness,
   17. identity diffusion, and
   18. performance/nongenerativity.

I suggested the first approach would be to see if they both agreed on that explanation; that is, that she was guarding against some loss of identity, herself, by avoiding talking to her daughter.

Next time, Emad reported that Irma's fears about her own intactness led her to *disidentify* from her own mother. Irma vividly described her mother's invasiveness, which had led Irma to hate saying anything the slightest bit invasive or critical. One reason she left her children with her husband was that she felt she was, unnervingly, becoming more like her own mother.

Emad showed Irma how she was displacing anger onto her daughter from her mother. Irma could then see how she was reacting to her daughter as though her daughter were Irma's demanding mother (*transference interpretation*).

These interventions were not totally effective, however. Irma was still afraid to talk to her daughter. I advised Emad to use *exhortation to behavior* (supportively encourage Irma to *practice* getting closer with her daughter by speaking calmly to her) and add that Irma was avoiding unrealistic anxieties based on experiences with her own mother.

He did this. She responded that her fears were childish. Emad and I then discussed adolescent development. We went over how teenagers need to develop affect tolerance through experiencing adversity and its painful affects. In a parallel fashion, parents who are emotionally sensitive to their children need to develop "parental-level ego strength" (in affect tolerance).[25] I suggested that Emad discuss this with Irma.

He explained to Irma that her daughter "had" to be "difficult" in order to feel separate from her mother. Irma needed to put herself "through it" in order to "get stronger."[26] That is, Emad used the *supportive techniques of teaching and exhortation to behavior.*

Interestingly, Irma responded to Emad's exhortation (to practice closeness with her daughter) as coercive. After first being able to handle her daughter, she failed and yelled at the daughter. Emad then skillfully shifted technique, again, by showing Irma how she was now rebelling against him as though he were her invasive, controlling mother (*transference confrontation*).

Because of Emad's sensitivity and ability to oscillate in his technique between supportive and explanatory modes of interaction with her, Irma not only got to know herself better but was able to withstand the struggles of interacting with her difficult teenage daughter.

---

25 Blackman (2002). What I mean is that, throughout a child's development, normal parents slowly become stronger in withstanding the emotional storms and provocations of their children.
26 Much as Marcus (2004) encourages men who have been avoiding emotional closeness with their wives (by being unfaithful) to make a conscious decision to try to get closer to their wives.

Problem 10
How to Stop People From Quitting Therapy

This question is an oxymoron, and yet it has been asked of me hundreds of times. I remind supervisees that one goal of psychotherapy is to have people quit. Of course, you want them to quit once they have resolved their problems. The goal of therapy is not to keep people in treatment; it is to help them resolve their problems so that they are able to stop treatment.

Nevertheless, the frequency with which people quit treatment prematurely is so high that therapists are often curious about how to prevent this. I have some thoughts about this, but no technique is entirely successful in preventing some people from quitting treatment prematurely.

SHORT ANSWER

1. Find the resistance at the end of the initial evaluation (or before).

I try to remember to leave 10 to 15 minutes at the end of the first evaluation to discuss with people any negative thoughts they have about treatment. Often, they are embarrassed about admitting this to you, but if they will, it helps. Sometimes the people who are the most agreeable to a follow-up appointment are no-shows (compliance being a way of avoiding guilt over defiance—see Problem 68).

When I forget to discuss this, invariably people start deliberating about making a follow-up appointment, and I wind up running overtime without being able to discuss their resistance.

In appointments following the initial evaluation, keep your eye on where the resistance is. Are people late, silent, have they forgotten to bring a check? Are they hesitant? Are you asking too many questions? When you see signs of their reluctance to cooperate with treatment, discuss this with them. If you can pick it up before they act on it, they will stay in treatment and learn about themselves.

LONG ANSWER

2. Don't depend on people for your income. If necessary, get a part-time job with salaried income.

If you rely on your private practice too much for sustenance, people in treatment sense that you see them as "food." They can then imagine you are greedy, using them for money. They may test you by threatening to quit. If you don't mind, financially, you will handle their threats with more equanimity, neutralizing their projections of their own greediness.

3. Do not indicate to people that their treatment is important or mandatory. It is elective.

A common technical mistake is to try to persuade people to stay in treatment. Some therapists explain that treatment is necessary. This can easily seem as though the therapist is "selling" therapy, and makes a lot of people quit.

I have heard some therapists explain that they tell some people that, in stopping therapy, they are doing themselves harm. People who have seen such therapists sometimes later told me, "I think (s)he was the one getting harmed—if you know what I mean [gesture indicating greediness]."

When people tell me they want to stop treatment, I do not argue with them. Unless they are overtly suicidal or overtly psychotic, and need intervention to protect them from themselves, their treatment is entirely elective. I also try not to make the mistake of saying, "Well, of course, whether you stay in treatment is 100% up to you..." This is obvious, and people who are not psychotic know it.

Whatever the reasons, when people want to stop treatment, they can. Those who have the courtesy to come to tell you so require the same courtesy in response, in my opinion.

When people want to stop treatment because they feel better and no longer want to pay for treatment, this is quite understandable. I understand their reasoning as a sort of cost-benefit assessment, where they have made progress and have decided they no longer want to spend the time and money on the hope of further progress. Very often, I have met with a response of relief; many people worried that I was going to be insulted, that I might disapprove, that I would try to talk them out of it, or that I would try to "hold onto them."

Problem 11
What to Do With People's Early Resistances

People who consult us have problems, but are uneasy about learning about them. How do we handle this?

SHORT ANSWER

The Reality of Dependency

It is best if you do not actually depend on people you treat for your income. They can easily test this and find out how you feel about it.

Many therapists unconsciously see the people they treat as "food" (i.e., income security that puts food on the table). Of course, the reality is that without people to treat, you will not have much of a practice. But if you feel too much this way and do not have some other way of subsidizing your income without people to treat, people will sense it, and then project onto you their own feelings of dependency. What this means is that

1. they fail to examine how frightened they are of starving to death, alone, with no one to take care of them. Instead,
2. they imagine that you "need" them to feed yourself because you are afraid of starving to death, alone (projection).

LONG ANSWER

Control

If people sense that you need them to be in therapy, they will, at least unconsciously, feel controlled by you, and rebel by stopping treatment (object-relations-based control). Some people may take pleasure in exercising their "leverage" over you by frequently changing appointment times.

If, on the other hand, someone tells you they are thinking about stopping treatment, and you simply respond that you are interested in their thoughts about this, they will then sense that you are not coercing them. They may say something like, "Gee, that's odd, I suddenly feel free. I thought you were going to try to talk me out of it." In other words, issues of autonomy often creep in, unconsciously, in people who are thinking about stopping treatment.

Avoidance of Pain

Pleasure–unpleasure Principle

This is a big problem. People want to stop treatment when they are beginning to touch on something painful or when they are feeling too close to you (in borderline personality). When something is painful, it is almost built into the human organism to try to avoid that something.[27]

The so-called pleasure principle or "pleasure–unpleasure principle"[28] operates in the vast majority of human beings most of the time. Is it any surprise that people would want to stop treatment if it is becoming uncomfortable or painful? In practice, approaching their most profound, deeply hidden truths about their problems may cause an intense urge to run away.

When this resistance occurs, you can express understanding of how people would like to run away from painful things—without putting pressure on them to stay in treatment.

> **REMINDER**
> One of the ironies about all types of explanatory (insight-directed) psychotherapy is that some of what you talk to people about is painful. This is sort of the opposite of giving them medicine to relieve anxiety and depressive affect.

Managing Emotional Overload During Treatment

How much should the therapist modulate how much emotional pain or overload people experience in treatment?

It is easy to make a mistake one way or the other. You can engage in interactions with people you are treating that relieve emotional stress but do not resolve their problems; or you may engage in discussions that create such overwhelming emotions that people no longer want to talk to you. Some balance, from a practical standpoint, is necessary.

In years past, this process has been called, somewhat mystically, "managing the regression" of people in treatment, or perhaps, "measuring the dosage of deprivation" that people incur. Pragmatically, this refers to how much you allow people to discuss painful things with you versus how much you sidetrack them from this by interacting with them about other issues or talking to them about more pleasurable topics.

---

27 S. Freud (1900) and Schur (1966).
28 Brenner (2006).

Sometimes, after people have gotten a peek at their more painful conflicts (much of which they had not known about previously), they are able to joke with you about those, too, and things aren't so maudlin.

EXAMPLE

Peter, a 62-year-old dentist, had a number of problems:

- sexual inhibition,
- spending too much money,
- getting his wife angry at him, and
- generalized lugubriousness.

After about 4 months of once-a-week therapy, we understood Peter was compensating for feeling small when he was a school-age child. His father had ridiculed him, and his mother did not protect him. Although part of his response to his father's ridicule was to incorporate some of his father's values (which made him a meticulous dentist), in other ways, these identifications had been problematic: He expected himself and his wife to be perfect. When he or his wife was not perfect, he became critical, and, often, then felt inhibited and depressed.

One day, Peter told me that he had decided to stop treatment. He didn't want to do it, and it was costing too much money. I found this surprising, but acknowledged to him that he had made some progress.

I thought Peter was fighting for autonomy. Although he had worked comfortably with me, I knew that his father had not given him freedom of choice. I gently pointed out to Peter that I could see that he wanted to have freedom of choice in this situation without me badgering him about it like his father had done. He quickly acknowledged that he thought that was true and important.

We parted on amicable terms, and Peter said he might call me in the future if he decided he wanted to do more work on himself. I told him that would be fine. About a year later, I received a thank you note from Peter, expressing gratitude for our final session.

Problem 12
What to Do Before Each Therapy Session

Most advice about psychotherapy technique suggests that you let people talk about their problems, listen carefully, and notice when they are fighting against themselves (resistance). When they are resisting, you discuss this with them.[29]

This is, of course, good advice, but the question is, if you are seeing somebody once a week, should you be doing more to help with continuity?

SHORT ANSWER

Yes. In doing once-a-week psychotherapy, you usually do not have the luxury of allowing people just to say what's on their mind, notice when they are resisting, and wait for them to have memories connected to previous material.

There are three major areas I consider before seeing someone for follow-up treatment sessions.

1. I either muse about or review notes from the prior session. I try to remember what the person had been talking about, and, more particularly, what I had said to them (explanations or advice).
2. I think about or review the person's past history that I consider important.
3. I get ready for resistance.

In baseball, you don't walk up to the plate and hold the bat with one hand. You must be ready for the pitch; different batters have different ways of doing this. All of them, however, get into a "stance." This means that they are relaxed, in the best position to hit the ball when it comes, and are intently watching the ball as it is pitched.

Similarly, when you are getting ready for a new psychotherapy session with people, you must be ready to handle resistance.

LONG ANSWER

The list of reasons people fight against themselves and do not help you with their own therapy is quite long.[30] Each person may fight you in his or her own

---
29 P. Gray (1994).
30 Volkan (2011).

particular way. Salman Akhtar has quipped that all people in treatment have a way of finding what annoys their therapist. (This is due to lifelong resistance to being controlled, which has its origins during the separation–individuation phases, between 7 and 36 months of age.[31])

Once-a-week psychotherapy is difficult because there is some lack of continuity. People can forget what they had said the last time, or distort it somehow. If they distort what you said to them, it may be hard for you to remember what you said exactly.

Interestingly, keeping voluminous notes probably is somewhat counterproductive, since long notes are rarely read.[32]

In the current litigious climate in the United States, it is wise to have some notes on people, particularly if they are suicidal or psychotic. You need a record of the work you have been doing with people in case there is an untoward event and you get sued for malpractice. Many third-party payers, institutions, and government-run clinics require notes be kept in a specific format.

For therapeutic purposes, it is useful to note what people discussed during a session, along with your interventions, and how people responded to your interventions.

Being in a "stance" to handle resistance is particularly useful because a lot of people exhibit some resistance at the beginning of the session and then drop it within seconds.

EXAMPLE

Nigel, 64 years old and still active in business, began his session by telling me that he was sorry he did not have a check to me by the 15th of the month but made an excuse about some various monies not being in the right accounts. He said he was sorry but would have me a check by the next week. Being in my "stance," and having thought about what was going on with him, I told him that I understood what he was saying, but this was the same pattern that I had been noticing over a period of months, where, with other people, he failed to do what he said he was going to do, inevitably found himself feeling guilty, and then tried to excuse himself and slide out of being punished.

> **TIP**
> Prepare for each session by reviewing, in your own thinking, what the issues and history have been; also, get in your "stance," ready to handle resistance.

---

31 Mahler et al. (1975).
32 Glover (1968).

This pattern was also maladaptive with his wife. He would promise her he was going to do something and then forget to do it. Inevitably, he had a good reason: he was overwhelmed, there was too much to do at work, et cetera, but the pattern was self-destructive: He had been behaving like this for years, and his wife's reaction included rejecting him sexually.

Instead of just recounting to me the issues that had gone on that week, I was able to engage Nigel in understanding how he provoked punishment, what the origins of his misbehavior (forgetting) were in adolescence, and how he was still angry about having to be "the good boy" who did everything for his mother.

SECTION C

Techniques With Different Types of Disturbances

GENERAL COMMENTS ON VARYING TECHNIQUE

People with different kinds of problems call for varying approaches. In this section, I discuss the techniques that can be used with such people, and some things to watch out for.

Problem 13
Is Being a "Container" or Providing a "Holding Environment" Enough? With Whom?

FIRST, AN EXPLANATION OF THE TERMINOLOGY

In 1963, Bion summarized his ideas about the therapist as "a container" who would "contain" people's emotions. Winnicott, also regarded as part of the British Object Relations School, discussed how some children grow up where there is chaos in the home; they are unsure of themselves and expect bad things to happen. They become quintessential pessimists. Winnicott described the "holding environment" as a house (of course, usually the people in the house) that promulgated the development of structure in the child's mind and diminished anxiety about what is sometimes called the "background of safety" or "sense of well-being."[1] Bion's approach was designed for "more disturbed" people and is loosely compatible with modern object relations theory.[2]

My own take on containing is that it offers a theory for "support," where one person listens to another person's feelings and somehow "absorbs" those feelings. This concept was popularized in the later book, *Men Are From Mars, Women Are From Venus*,[3] which puts forth the idea that women want to have their "needs understood" whereas men want to be appreciated for their accomplishments.[4]

Concepts about containing and holding environment fit with supportive elements in any therapy: "creating a safe environment" for people you treat as adults.

SHORT ANSWER

Listening attentively is a useful approach for therapists doing any type of treatment, but it is usually not sufficient. For some people who have psychotic or near-psychotic illnesses, an understanding, "absorbing" type of

---

1 Joffe and Sandler (1979).
2 Based on the work of Margaret Mahler et al. (1975). Although Bowlby had already published his *44 Thieves* paper (1944), which demonstrated that without stable human attachments, school-age children became criminals.
3 J. Gray (1993).
4 Also suggested by Beck (1983).

attitude is useful on the part of the therapist, but the therapist may have to take action to protect people with these illnesses.

> **TIP**
> Attentive listening, "containing," or "providing a safe environment" for people, although necessary, is usually not sufficient.

"Analytic listening"[5] starts with containing but adds processing your responses to people using theories of defense and developmental stages before intervening.[6]

Attentive listening is useful in the treatment of everyone but becomes a key ingredient in treating psychosis and borderline personality. Even then, corrections of breaks in reality testing and integration, arguments against irrational ideas, and confrontation of disturbances in judgment can also play a key role.

LONG ANSWER

Although attentive listening is usually a reasonable approach to people, being "understanding" can be a problem if people in treatment are bullying the therapist or have superego defects (disturbances in guilt, shame, integrity, or ethics). In these latter instances, activity on the part of the therapist is necessary to confront, correct, and try to figure out the causes of such damage and disturbance.

In treating people who can observe themselves and have the capacity to organize their thoughts, you want to listen attentively and then point out disturbed elements of mentation. These elements include pathological defenses, such as projection and denial.

There is a frequent conflation of "empathy" with passivity, and destructiveness with activity. When this occurs, therapists experience their interventions as harmful and "unempathic"—resulting in guilt over any intervention. If the therapist equates empathy with passivity, and insensitivity with activity, then the therapist will feel too inhibited to make necessary interventions.

In particular, managing resistances requires activity on the part of the therapist. People's unconscious rebellious hostility, transferred from a parent, which leads them to come late, miss sessions, and unconsciously provoke the therapist to be critical (repeating patterns from adolescence) need to be

---

5 Schwaber (1998).
6 Arlow (1979, 1995).

discussed by the therapist. Passive "containing" in these situations is not likely to help people with such problems.

On the other hand, if people are crying, it is best not to interrupt them. People who are crying will inevitably stop crying; it is best not to try to explain things to people when they are overwhelmed by affect.[7] It is also usually best to let people present dreams without interruption. You might have people repeat the report of the dream, and then note differences in the people's second report.[8]

It is good to be vigilant, "a container," and thoughtful. "Containing" for a while, when people are regressed, is usually indicated. The therapist may later "strike while the iron is cold."[9]

EXAMPLE

Nancy, 41 years old, was frustrated. Her husband was leaving at night, right after dinner, to visit his buddy "to watch sports." When her husband came home, he routinely smelled of marijuana. He would shower and brush his teeth before getting in bed, and pretend nothing had happened. He had not had sexual relations with Nancy for months.

When she presented these problems to me and expressed helplessness, I had several therapeutic options. I could have listened attentively to "contain" her frustration and depression. I could have advised her (supportive technique) to talk to her husband about his marijuana abuse and to investigate further with him what was going on.

Alternatively, I could have emphasized how her husband was being destructive toward her and the children, setting a bad model, and that this was worse than she thought (confrontation of denial). This posed two dangers:

- a *concordant identification* with Nancy's superego: exposing my criticism of her husband, ignoring her conflict; and
- inflaming her criticism of her husband that could lead her to use more passivity and inhibition.

Since her integrative function was working, her abstraction ability was good, and she could see that she was being passive. I opted to point out that she could see what her husband was doing, but there was some block she experienced in talking to him or attempting to rectify the problem.

---

7   Bird (1955).
8   S. Freud (1900).
9   Pine (1985).

> **COUNTERTRANSFERENCE**
> *Concordant identification:* You pick up the same attitude as the person you are treating.
> *Complementary identification:* You pick up the same attitude as important people in the life of the person you are treating.

She admitted she didn't like what he was doing, but she didn't want to act like her mother, who always nagged her father. After recognizing her disidentification from her mother, Nancy began crying. When she stopped, she remembered a dream where her husband was dressed like a dead woman.

We discussed how shame and guilt were causing her to feel inhibited. I added that I felt in the dream she turned her husband into a dead woman partly because she wanted to kill him, partly because she wished he understood her better, and partly because she was afraid that if she complained, he would feel emasculated and then abandon her. This last fear she tied to her boyfriend in college, who had, during their senior year, broken off their engagement. She did not want to go through that again. In other words, her inhibition was also guarding against anxiety over loss of the object, partly transferred from her prior fiancé.

The next time I saw Nancy, a few days later, she reported that she had spoken to her husband rationally and had not "castrated him." She had told him that his secrecy was a sham; she knew he was smoking pot with his friend. She also noted that he had been avoiding her sexually.

He then confessed that he had been having an affair with the wife of one of his employees. In the end, Nancy and he wound up divorced.

The point of this example is that if I had only "contained" Nancy's feelings of helplessness and depression, and/or sympathized with her, she could have stayed in the marriage for quite a while and continued to suffer.

Had I advised her to confront her husband, she may have done it in such a way that he lied and counter-attacked her. She might have turned anger against herself to avoid guilt and shame, culminating in a suicide attempt. An explanatory approach, looking at the different aspects of her conflict, namely the anger, the guilt, the shame, and the inhibition, allowed her to deal with the reality more actively and think her way through it in a way that was less destructive to her or to her husband.

The divorce was relatively untraumatic; they were able to work things out so that their children maintained a relatively positive view of both of them.[10]

---

10 About 10 years later, I heard in the community that Nancy's husband had gotten divorced from his second wife as well, and philandering was involved. He seemed to have the character problems, described by Marcus (2004), as the "Adulteen" and "Playmate."

Problem 14
Are Obsessional People Neurotic, Borderline, or Schizophrenic?

This is one of the biggest diagnostic problems in the mental health field. Literally hundreds of studies have been done on obsessional people. A variety of causes have been proposed to explain the peculiar symptoms.

Obsessional symptoms include rituals (such as double-checking and triple-checking things); self-doubt; thinking about the same thing over and over again ("rumination"); cleaning and recleaning the same spots; and, of course, ritualistic hand-washing.

A common obsession today involves the use of hand sanitizers. We no longer fear the plague or syphilis; those old objects of our "objective" anxiety[11] have been replaced by viruses.

Obsessional character traits include hyperpunctuality, hyperneatness, and perfectionism, all of which are the result of the mind turning something into its opposite ("reaction-formation"). In other words, people who are hyperpunctual really want to be late, people who are hyperneat really want to be sloppy, and people who are perfectionistic really would like not to care at all. Their rebellious feelings, however, conflict with guilt and shame; the mind then flips things into the opposite.

Other obsessional traits include being overly nice (although this is not a standard trait; some obsessional people are overtly sadistic)—reaction-formations; intellectualizing about things; making excuses (rationalization); and getting preoccupied with details ("circumstantiality").

SHORT ANSWER

People with obsessive-compulsive symptoms and character traits may be neurotic, be suffering with borderline personality disorder, or be schizophrenic. You want to attempt to distinguish these different disturbances since the treatment for them is entirely different. Neurosis calls for understanding symbolism; borderline necessitates attention to distancing in relationships; and psychosis requires antipsychotic medication.

> **TIP**
> People who have obsessive-compulsive symptoms do not necessarily have a diagnosis of simply OCD.

---

11 A. Freud (1936).

The typical obsessive-compulsive person is too nice, too intellectual, a bit passive, a bit too critical, too preoccupied with details ("circumstantial"), and often described as "fussy." Notwithstanding the presence of these defensive operations, deficits in various functions—like reality testing—may be present or not.

If abstraction, reality testing, or self-preservation functions are damaged, or if there is too much bizarre (condensed, symbolic) material in consciousness, then the so-called "obsessions" become delusions that require antipsychotic medication. What looks like "rumination" (thinking things over and over to punish yourself) can turn out to be a breakdown in the integrative function and may be a defect in containing "bizarre" fantasies—both more characteristic of schizophrenia.

In people suffering from borderline personality disorder who are also obsessive-compulsive,[12] reality testing and abstraction ability may be intact. But you will find impulsivity as well as perverse fantasies and/or functioning, extensive masturbatory rituals, sleep disturbance, and difficulties with judgment in interpersonal situations.

LONG ANSWER

When people present obsessional character traits or symptoms, you want to try to determine the quality of their reality testing and organization of thought. This is often not clear.

For example, some people who are preoccupied with germs (called a "germ phobia" but actually referring to an obsession) may carry around a hand sanitizer and disposable cloths to use after they touch any doorknob. If you bring to their attention that cleaning their hands may have meanings above and beyond the actual degree of danger from germs, some of them will admit this, although they may hold to some intellectual arguments about germs and doorknobs.

If obsessional people can understand symbolism, they will eventually see they are trying to "clean" something in themselves, maybe something that is not so pleasant. They project onto doorknobs their fear of retribution for their own hostile feelings. If people are concrete, tell you that not only are there viruses on doorknobs, but parasites and bugs also thrive on doorknobs, one must begin to consider a more serious illness necessitating antipsychotic medicine.

When people get lost in details, you can point out to them that they do this because they are afraid they will leave something out; if they leave out something, they may not get something perfect; and then they are afraid they will be punished. If they can see this, you have a more neurotic person, whom you can treat by figuring out symbolic conflicts. If they just observe

---

12 Kernberg (1975) and Blackman (2010), Chapters 13 and 14.

that they get lost in details, they may be observing their deficit in organization of thought, putting them in the classification of borderline personality disorder or some type of psychosis.

My usual procedure when I am confused about the diagnosis in obsessional people is to make a "trial interpretation." In other words, I will tell them what I think the meaning of their obsessional symptom may be. I then watch to see whether they have enough abstraction and integrative ability to understand any symbolism.

> **TIP**
> Attempting a "trial interpretation" of a possible symbolic meaning of an obsessional symptom may yield useful data as to whether a person is neurotic, concrete, delusional, or disorganized and psychotic.

EXAMPLE 1

LeShawn, a 10-year-old boy, double-checked the spigot in the bathroom sink to make sure it was not leaking. He was afraid that if it kept dripping, it could cause a flood, which might flood their whole house, and maybe his mother would drown because she did not know how to swim.

I told LeShawn that I thought his worries meant that he was trying hard not to be angry at his mother, and that checking the faucet indicated his very strong wish to keep his mother alive because he would feel so bad if she died. He responded by crying briefly, and then told me that he had had a lot of dreams in which his mother had died. He said he did not want to be without his mother, but, "She makes me so mad sometimes I could strangle her."

In his case, the obsessional checking was based on a neurotic conflict between anger and guilt that had led to the defenses of symbolic rituals, isolation of affect, and some repression of the conflict. After understanding his anger and his conflicts over it, his obsessional symptom went away.

In other cases that are more severe, obsessional thinking can obscure the diagnosis of psychosis.

EXAMPLE 2

After Matt shot his wife, Lena, to death and then killed himself, I was asked to review his records in a civil lawsuit brought by his descendants. I saw that when he had been initially admitted to a mental hospital, Matt had been diagnosed with obsessive-compulsive personality disorder and adjustment disorder.

In reviewing the hospital records and depositions of his relatives some time after the double murder, I learned that Matt had strangled Lena while they were having sexual intercourse to the point where she had lost consciousness. A few minutes later she awakened, jumped out of bed in her nightgown, and ran across the street to her neighbor's house where she called the police.

The police had taken Matt to the hospital, but the admitting professionals accepted his description of being "just angry" at Lena. They had not become aware of his (delusional) belief that Lena was having sexual relations with his brother.

Matt had a history that he had gone on several "fastidious" diets in the past (including a diet of only water for 11 months), he had been critical of his wife, and he tried not to have any feelings toward anybody (isolation of affect). In other words, he showed obsessive-compulsive personality traits.

When Matt finally found a dentist to remove all his fillings because he was afraid the mercury in them would kill him, this was judged as "picky," but not delusional.

Had the admitting psychiatrist and psychologist seen the deficits in reality testing and the bizarre thinking associated with his homicidal attempt on his wife during sex, psychotic illness might have been diagnosed. He would have likely been treated with antipsychotic medicine and longer term hospitalization. Instead, he was discharged from the hospital after just a few days with a prescription for a selective serotonin reuptake inhibitor.

Problem 15
People With Physical Illnesses and Conversion Symptoms

People who have a serious physical illness (such as cancer, rheumatoid arthritis, or progressive deafness) may develop psychological problems associated with their physical illnesses. Chronic illnesses take their toll on people and usually require understanding, support, and sometimes advice.

Some people become physically ill while you are treating them. This presents different types of difficulties.

SHORT ANSWER

Generally, I don't try to find symbolism when people are physically ill. Reassurance, reality testing, understanding of the difficulty, and advice (supportive techniques) can be helpful. The same holds true of people in insight-directed treatment who become physically ill briefly; I avoid explanatory techniques during the period of illness.[13]

LONG ANSWER

Physical Illness Causing Psychological Problems

When people are physically ill, they may "regress." In other words, they do not use their usual abilities to care for themselves and socialize. They often feel weak in managing their feelings, and can be snappy and disrespectful. Sometimes there is also "regression" to self-centeredness in otherwise empathic people.

That is, people who are physically ill often experience weaknesses in several areas of mental functioning. They are not usually in a state of mind where explanation of conflict is terribly useful. In such cases, supportive approaches are needed, at least temporarily.

If the medical treatment does not go on for too long, (perhaps a week or two), I will hold people's appointments open but not charge them for the

---

13 Exceptions to this include people who are malingering and/or hypochondriacal. That's a "whole nuther" problem. Malingerers are usually untreatable. With hypochondriacs, their treatability depends on AIRS and affect tolerance (see Problem 101 [B]).

time that they are out with the severe illness. The reason I do not charge them is that the illness is not a resistance. Moreover, I have found that charging people for missed appointments when they have serious illnesses (e.g., when they need antibiotic treatment at home) causes them to feel that I am unreasonable and a bad parent.

Although such negative reactions are often based on factors with their own parents, that type of distortion can be impossible to explain if I have actually done something that is unsympathetic and unrealistic, such as make them feel that they are somehow responsible for an illness that they had no hand in creating.

If people develop serious illnesses that do not interfere with them coming to treatment, it is sometimes necessary for me to coordinate with the surgeon or internist who is also treating them, as far as medication goes. For example, one man in therapy developed lupus, and then had difficulty sleeping. I had several discussions with his internist regarding the type of sleeping medicine that he should use in order to minimize damage to his immune system.

People With Physical Symptoms That are Symbolic of Conflict (No Physical Illness Exists)

This is the type of case upon which Charcot (1877) based his reputation, and is the kind of case that drew Freud from neurology into psychoanalysis. Typical "conversion" symptoms are fatigue, weakness, headaches, pain during sexual intercourse (dyspareunia), premature ejaculation, and back pain.

In these cases, try to find the origins of the conflicts that are creating the pains and weaknesses and point them out to people. Usually, the hidden conflicts are found in people's present and past relationship narratives; you can also find the conflicts when people experience sudden breaks in their cooperativeness.[14]

EXAMPLE

Ellen, a 25-year-old married homemaker, presented with initial complaints of sexual inhibition, frustrations with her husband, and weakness.

After weeks of resisting his sexual advances, she allowed him to have sexual intercourse with her; but he told her, just after they had sex, that he had taken Viagra beforehand. At that point, her right arm went numb and she could not move it. The numbness lasted for several hours. By him rubbing it and her waiting it out, eventually she got some sensation back in her arm. It was still tingling when I saw her in the office, but she could move it adequately.

---

14   P. Gray (1994).

Ellen had had the same problem 2 months previously. MRIs of the brain and spine (and other studies) were all negative. I therefore felt comfortable saying to her that there must be symbolic reasons for her weakness.

We started with the idea that she was somehow protecting herself by being weak in her right arm. She responded, "Yeah, so I couldn't use the right arm to do something." I reminded her of her belief in not being violent. She then thought of guilt over the lifelong rage she had felt toward her father for ignoring her in very important situations.

While she was talking to me about her father, her right arm became weak again. I pointed out that the weakness must both punish her and prevent her from thinking or acting on a wish to punch anybody, possibly her father or her husband.

She then remembered that she had been insulted when her husband told her he had taken Viagra since he was 28 and did not have any illnesses. She felt she wasn't enough and that he was indulging himself and not paying attention to her. These feelings were quite quickly recognizable by both of us as associated with anger at her father.

Later, we could understand that her avoidance of sexual activity with her husband also protected her from guilt over angry feelings toward him, some of which were deserved, and some of which were transferred from her father.

As she learned about these various conflicts, Ellen became more affectively fluid and expressed some of her feelings to her husband. It turned out he was angry at her for having rejected him so much; he had developed a fear that he could not function during sexual intercourse, apparently because of anger over her rejecting him so much. He had taken Viagra to overcome what he felt to be an inhibition of his own.

Over a couple of years, they were able to work out their problems, and their sex life picked up. The weakness in her arms evaporated.

Problem 16
Financially Successful People

This is a relatively undiscussed problem in the mental health field,[15] since poverty-stricken mentally ill people pose a greater difficulty. However, people who have been financially successful can suffer with severe emotional problems.

People who are financially secure can experience problems with sexual perversions, obsessions, and distancing elements in relationships. They may be critical, unempathic, or hypercritical of themselves. They also have phobias, panic attacks, and insomnia, and some suffer from borderline personality or psychosis.

As with anyone, evaluation involves the factors I mention in Problem 2 (and in Problem 101 [B]). We will limit this chapter to people who are well-to-do and not psychotic.

Certain defenses are common in people who are financially successful. They tend to use more normalization and minimization ("It's not a big deal, it's just normal"), generalization ("Isn't it common?"), concretization ("Isn't this due to the economy?"), intellectualization ("I read an article about this in *The Wall Street Journal*"), and pseudoindependence. This last defense can be quite adaptive if they have not relied on anybody but are self-made and proud of it.

However, pseudoindependence can create havoc in personal relationships.

SHORT ANSWER

Quickly point out, when you see them, pseudoindependence, normalization, minimization, concretization, and generalization (defenses). Otherwise, those same defensive operations, which have helped well-to-do people become financially successful, will be used to avoid treatment.

To the extent that they have been successful in challenging other people, financially successful people will also challenge you. They may question your competence. Most successful people have been approached by charlatans who were after money; such an expectation can be displaced onto you. For this reason, having a series of consultations is a good idea before you set up a treatment contract—to let them (and you) decide whether you can really help.

---

15 Although, see Warner (1991).

Be prepared to point out projections onto you of their own ambitions for money—they imagine that you harbor the greed that they actually feel guilty about in themselves.

Emotional distancing can be hidden in wealthy people's preoccupations with time and money. They may, ironically, show more resistance to frequent sessions than some people who are less financially successful.

Finally, wealthy people can find pleasure in spending money by taking trips or buying material things. In this way, they can try to relieve any pain they are feeling.

LONG ANSWER

Wealthy people often are afraid of public exposure when they come to see us. For this reason, it is good to have "an escape door" through which they can walk privately after their sessions (without going back through the waiting room). You may need to discuss with them any shame they feel about their intense pleasure in having money.

It may be necessary to indicate your awareness of the reality of money. People who have worked for or inherited money are well aware of the ease in various areas of their lives. If they have worked for it, they are proud of it, and may misunderstand any attempt to explain its symbolism as an unrealistic criticism of their wealth or success.

The reasons financially successful people consult you usually have to do with their relationships outside of work. Showing them how they run away from relationship problems by spending money or by overworking can be important.

Well-to-do people may be accustomed to "the best" in anything, including treatment. They may feel that you are not famous enough for them to trust you. This is usually a feeling transferred from parents they could not trust and may have to be understood fairly early in treatment.

In addition, people with money have been able, often, to control other people, at least to a certain extent, by paying them. They may attempt to do this with you, as well.

Another common complication in treating people who have money is their guilt about being able to afford to see you. It doesn't make much difference what you are charging them; they may still tell you that treatment "feels like a luxury." They may proceed to "poor mouth," in other words, complain about how little money they have because they feel ashamed or guilty about their money.

They may also be afraid that people will reject them, especially you, if you know how much money they actually have. Gore Vidal was supposedly quoted as saying something like, "If the poor knew how much fun the rich were having, they would rise up and eat them."[16] Many wealthy people are aware of this antipathy and therefore speak as though they are middle class. This defensiveness poses a resistance to them being honest with you in treatment, and it is best to discuss this with them at some point.

EXAMPLE

Giorgiana commented derisively about my fee, even though she and her husband were worth millions of dollars. I was successful in showing her that her feeling toward me was displaced from and symbolic of her feeling that her mother never paid enough attention to her.

She complained that her husband was "greedy and cheap," because he only allowed her $10,000 per month to spend on herself. She admitted she never gave him an accounting of where she was spending the money. Although she agreed with me that her secretiveness no doubt caused him to feel suspicious, she liked not telling him everything.

I saw that she had "oral" desires of her own, perhaps characterizable as "greedy," which she was projecting onto her husband as well as onto me. As we understood her shame about the many deprivations she had felt earlier in her life, we could figure out the meaning of money (= mother). Her shame caused her to project—to imagine others, like her husband, were the greedy ones.

After we discussed all this, she stopped criticizing her husband for being stingy, and they got along much better. She never gave him an accounting of her spending, however.

---

16 Gill (1998).

Problem 17
Highly Intelligent People

Highly intelligent people often do not suffer from problems with intellect or skill in some particular area. Generally speaking, it is harder to pick up a deficit in the integrative (or organizing) function in very intelligent people. People who are very intelligent have frequently figured out enough that they have reasonable social skill (although this is not always the case). Because they are very intelligent, they also tend to use their intelligence defensively. This creates certain problems in dealing with them, as explained below.

By the way, very intelligent people may not have gone to college; or they may have a doctoral degree or two. Many of them have read about psychology and/or psychoanalysis, and this adds to their armamentarium of defenses.

SHORT ANSWER

Highly intelligent people can use their intellect to stay away from painful problems, but their intellect can also be very useful, so it is dangerous to "confront" their use of their intellect solely as a defense. You must give credit to them for understanding certain things. They may have conflicting wishes to be both compliant and defiant. Not infrequently, their intellect has led to a certain degree of grandiosity, since they found school and/or work easy.

When highly intelligent people are compliant, they will sometimes seem overly respectful because they are (defend against) feeling guilty about being so smart. In their defiant state, they will challenge you, sometimes subtly, by asking a question about the theory you are using in treating them. Both of these defenses (compliance and defiance) are used because they are feeling nervous, so the thought content of their anxiety needs to be discovered, along with how they protect themselves from it.

In addition, intelligent people experience more shame and guilt over not knowing the answers to their emotional problems, and this may have to be discussed in the beginning of treatment.

I have found it useful with very intelligent people to counter their challenges: I may respond professorially at first, and compete with them a little intellectually. This can sometimes help the alliance by

- reducing their guilt about being intelligent, and
- giving them a better "feel" that they are being understood—which is often a welcome relief from parents who underestimated them as children.

Very intelligent adults have frequently endured a lifetime of being misunderstood by their parents and teachers. They may have had to hide their intelligence during their upbringing as well as in adulthood and long for someone who can "match wits" with them intellectually or artistically. They tend to approach treatment with doubts that the therapist can tell them something they don't already know.

LONG ANSWER

People who have high aptitudes and/or skills in different subjects, such as art, music, mathematics, literature, and sciences bring to the treatment an enormous amount of knowledge, often far and above the knowledge base of the therapist. They may try to "study up" on treatment, but this can be used as a way of avoiding being open with you.

This "intellectualization" accomplishes several things at the same time: They are aggressively destroying you as the therapist with their mighty intellect; they are avoiding their competitive tendencies because they feel guilty about them; they are expressing a wish to be loved for their intellect; they are avoiding shame over their wish to be loved by making it intellectual; they may also be using their intellect somewhat seductively, having to do with childhood wishes with their parents; and they may be using their intellect either to establish closeness or to create distance from you, depending how they do it.

These multiple meanings[17] of their intellectual presentation can be discussed, but you should be careful first to recognize and acknowledge their fund of knowledge before talking about any symbolic meanings.

INTELLECTUALIZATION

EXAMPLE

Marty, a highly intelligent, 34-year-old man, complained of panic attacks and said he thought an antidepressant medication was indicated. I acknowledged that his awareness of antidepressants indicated that he had "studied up" on the matter. He then admitted that he had looked up panic on the Internet and found that medication is often recommended.

I first acknowledged that the American Psychiatric Association website lists medication as a first line of treatment (meeting his intellectual challenge). I also pointed out to him that I did not yet know what was causing

---

17 Called a "compromise formation" (Brenner, 2006).

him to feel anxious. I further countered his challenge by explaining that the mechanisms of action of antidepressants and anxiolytic medicines are essentially unknown,[18] but what was known included that panic attacks invariably involve guilt. I added that people are generally unaware of the guilty feelings that trigger panic attacks.

After considering this idea for a moment, Marty admitted to guilt over periodic extramarital sexual relationships with women, although he said, "none of them meant anything." I pointed out that his rationalization suggested he did feel guilty. He explained that those instances had been 1-night stands. I was able to show him that taking antidepressants would keep us away from talking about the affairs too much. He argued that he would have talked about it anyway, and still thought he needed an antidepressant.

I put him off about this, suggested we meet again, and during the second session was able to clarify with him that he also knew that antidepressant medications cause sexual dysfunction. In other words, we could see that his wish for antidepressant medication had to do with a wish to punish himself to relieve the guilt he was feeling about cheating on his wife.

A common problem in very intelligent people is that they tend to use technical terms to relieve their shame or guilt about their actual problems—thereby looking less disturbed than they are. For example, someone may say "I think I'm really O/C," hiding delusional thinking about a variety of matters.

Someone who complains of "panic disorder" may actually be using this term to relieve shame over perverse activities such as going to a dungeon to get whipped, or a foot fetish. I have evaluated a number of intelligent people who told me that others had diagnosed them with "agoraphobia," where on closer investigation they were actually paranoid psychotics, afraid to go out in public for fear of people looking at them and plotting against them.

One man described himself as "aggressive," and complained of a sick daughter and financial problems. It turned out that he was lying to people he did business with, and he attempted to lie and cheat with me. I only saw him for one session; he did not bring a check and never sent me one. He was psychopathic, but because he was highly intelligent, he often got away with it. Many people did not detect his untrustworthiness. In a similar guise, some disorganized but socially skilled schizophrenic people, particularly if they are physically attractive and sociable women, can be misdiagnosed as "histrionic."

---

18 The dopamine-norepinephrine responses constitute a theory that is currently falling into some disfavor (Sadock et al., 2009).

OTHER COMMON FINDINGS AMONG THE HIGHLY INTELLIGENT

> **TIP**
> Very intelligent people are more challenging to diagnose because their true symptoms and conditions may be heavily disguised. They can use their intellect to compensate for or conceal certain weaknesses or deficits.

Highly intelligent people frequently present obsessional defenses that minimize their problems. They generalize, quote studies, or exert control by not revealing certain thoughts to you (what Kernberg has called "psychopathic transference"). These mechanisms can interfere with diagnosis and treatment selection: If they are more disturbed, explanatory work is sometimes contraindicated and more "Bion-style" (Problem 13) supportive approaches are indicated, in spite of their intellect. If they have difficulties with distancing and closeness, at least a modicum of "relational" treatment[19] is indicated, based on "corrective object-relations"[20] concepts.

Intelligent people can feel ashamed of needing treatment until they come to the conclusion that it makes intellectual sense to them. Sometimes, I have explained certain concepts about what I am doing, "with the cards up."[21] In other words, I may admit I am looking at a defense—a type of intellectual honesty to facilitate the therapeutic alliance.

Intelligent people who have a sense of humor can respond favorably to a bit of humor from you; humor can be dangerous, but it can be helpful in reducing shame about dependency on you.

A final matter: Very intelligent people tend to respond well to early interventions. This may be a discussion of defense or exploration of the history of that defense. Intellectual people are often relieved by beginning to "work," and not just feel "comforted." Aside from some introductory work in the first session and some humor, I sometimes use De M'Uzan's[22] suggestion of a "surprise interpretation" of a defense or trait that previously had evaded their own awareness. This may reassure some intellectual "stars" that you know more than they do (at least within your field).

---

19 Mitchell (2000).
20 Alpert (1959).
21 Renik (1999).
22 Aisenstein (2007).

Problem 18
People Who Are Chronically Late to Sessions

There has been quite a bit of confusion about handling people who are late. Some therapists give credence to people's explanations. Other therapists tend to feel that any reason the person gives for being late is a rationalization and is not the true meaning. I differ with either of these rigid positions.

If someone is late once because of traffic, there is perhaps no particular meaning. However, if there is a pattern of significant lateness over a period of sessions, for whatever reasons, there may be unconscious conflict underlying their "reality rationalizations" ("acting in").[23]

SHORT ANSWER

The usual meanings when lateness has become a pattern are

- hostile rebellion (hostile transference from a parent to you);
- provocation of punishment to relieve guilt over the hostility;
- unconscious wishes to be treated specially versus shame over these wishes;
- avoidance of painful feelings, sometimes anger at the therapist;
- unconscious expression, in women, of a transferred childhood wish to have a baby by the therapist (I'm late!), regardless of the actual gender of the therapist; and
- unconscious distancing (rationalized by real-life occurrences) in borderline people.

Generally, it is best to talk about provocation of punishment and/or avoidance of painful feelings with people. Pointing out emotional distancing can be important for people with object-relations problems. After these defenses are clarified, you might discuss the symbolic meanings of being late involving dependent, hostile, and sometimes sexual wishes.

---

23 Paniagua (1998).

LONG ANSWER

There are many reasons people may be late. If people harbor latent psychotic problems with time management (a deficit in secondary process thinking), I may advise them to try plan to be somewhere 15 to 30 minutes early (supportive technique).

When people have been late chronically, I invite them to consider with me whether, in fact, their lateness has any meaning. Starting with the possibility that they could be avoiding something without wanting to think about it, I try to help them look at the problem with me (to "mentalize").

> **EXCEPTIONS**
> In borderline and overt psychosis, people are late because of their faulty time sense and disorganization of thought (deficits in secondary process and integration), not because of internal conflict. They should be encouraged to be on time—and perhaps given neuroleptic medicine if they are too disorganized.

It is easy to develop a complementary identification (unconsciously assume the role of one of the important people in their lives). One therapist, for example, started encouraging a man to be on time more, even though he was not psychotic. In this way, the therapist became more like the parent of a teenager, which caused more and more unconscious struggle between them as time went on. Working together to try to understand if there is a meaning is usually a more useful approach, in my experience.

I have sometimes been surprised. Some women with preschool children can be late because they are dependent on babysitters. Most of the time, this is due to reality factors outside of their control (babysitter does not show up), and I have been very slow to look at it as a manifestation of unconscious resistance or symbolism.

After a while, some of the mothers of young children admitted to me that they had been too lenient on the babysitter, not demanding that the babysitter be on time. In those cases, disidentifications from their own mothers were discoverable. The women in treatment did not want to be "too strict" with the babysitter, and therefore were somewhat victimized by sitters who were irresponsible. However, most of the time, they were not able to be "rough" on the babysitter because they needed the babysitter too much, and they tended to be flexible so that they would not lose the babysitter entirely. I remember that good sitters are hard to find.

Another surprise came from a man I was treating who walked in 1 minute late and said, "I'm sorry." When I asked him what he was feeling sorry about, he said, "I'm late." When I responded that he was more or less on time, he corrected me: "No, I was 1 minute late, and this represents my rebellious hostility toward you, because you are an authority figure like my father!" This led us into a fruitful discussion of his persistent adolescent resistance to advice, even if it were from a doctor, and for his own good.

I have seen another variation on lateness where people have a horribly oppressive schedule, constantly struggling to get out of the workplace to come see you. When I explored with one man whether he thought the lateness had any meaning, he pointed out to me that it was a miracle that he got to see me at all. If he was a few minutes late it was because of the multiple problems that he had in getting out of the office. These problems included being detained by superiors or meeting a deadline that was due right before his appointment with me. In other words, what looked like resistance actually turned out to be a manifestation of positive motivation.

Some people do not show up at all, and do not call. In these situations, I call them, leave a message that I missed them at their appointment time, and ask them to call back to discuss what they plan regarding the future of their therapy.

If people miss a session rarely, and call to let you know that something has come up, they probably do not need to examine "resistance." Trying to explore unconscious resistance can be insulting to them when a reality has interfered.

Finally, I have treated a couple of people who would call every day to cancel their appointment, always with a reason such as, "I have to go to a meeting," or "The IRS is at my business today and I can't leave." There is a crossover here with Problem 16 (Financially Successful People). People who can afford to pay for missed sessions may use cancellations as a way to avoid closeness with you. Even they call ahead of time and pay for missed sessions, they miss too many of them. You then want to show them their

- narcissistic defense against hostility toward you,
- avoidance of closeness,
- avoidance of painful material, and
- reality rationalizations about work.

Problem 19
Do All Alcoholics Need AA?

The usual wisdom in the 21st century is that alcoholism is an inherited disease. The alcoholic must admit to being an alcoholic and then devote a lifetime adapting to it.

Alcoholics Anonymous has their famous 12 steps, which include having alcoholics admit that they have an addiction; identify themselves as "an alcoholic"; try to make reparations with people they have hurt; turn to a "higher power" for help; receive lifetime support through group meetings with other alcoholics in the organization and a "sponsor," to whom they should turn when they wish to drink; and maintain total sobriety, meaning never drinking again.

I agree with much of what AA propounds, particularly that denial must be confronted and that alcoholics must admit that they are weak in avoiding alcohol. From there, I prefer to engage in "differential diagnosis" and make treatment decisions based on the diagnosis. In other words, I think the original stimulus for the alcoholism must be addressed as well as the physical addiction that developed. The original causes of the alcohol abuse can include, but are not limited to, the following:

- Anxiety caused by schizophrenic hallucinations of being killed.
- Paranoia due to schizophrenic illness.
- Agitation associated with psychotic level mania.
- Anxiety about close relationships in borderline personality.
- A defense against social anxiety (about being accepted by people who drink).
- Relief of neurotic (symbolic) anxiety (like a phobia).
- Relief of depressive feelings over a loss.
- Relief of frustration (e.g., in a marriage).
- Adolescent rebellion (doing what is prohibited to establish identity).
- Fantasies of masculinity (the cowboy who can "hold his liquor").
- Association of drinking with any pleasure (like foreplay, "revelry").
- Relief of chronic agitation and depressive affect.
- Emblematic relief of anxiety about social class.

The point is that alcohol can be abused for different reasons in people with divergent mental disturbances (the so-called dual diagnosis, which most clinicians recognize as just about universal). After detoxification (if necessary), these different disturbances require different therapeutic approaches.

Alcoholism, as I see it, is not simply a hereditary disease. Some people could have weaknesses in certain functions that may have genetic origins, in whole or in part, making them less able to tolerate the challenges of life without resorting to a crutch such as alcohol. I see alcoholism as an acquired characteristic that requires the brewing of alcohol, the purchasing of alcohol, and the volitional act of drinking it.

A physical addiction to alcohol can develop. Alcohol is different from some other substances in that it stimulates alcohol reductase in the liver,[24] which then physically causes the person to have to drink more alcohol in order to get the same effect of somnolence or relaxation. Because of this induction of liver enzymes, alcohol is one of the most toxic substances. After a while, the person needs the alcohol in order to maintain relative body stability.

The well-known "withdrawal" symptoms from alcohol include seizures, vomiting, hyperpyrexia (high fever), and hypothermia. In other words, withdrawal from alcohol can be a life-threatening situation. Delirium tremens is a state of hallucinatory agitation that can occur during withdrawal as well.

To my mind, however, to say that alcoholism is a hereditary illness utilizes a theory of evolution that was propounded by Lamarck, namely the inheritance of "acquired characteristics." Most scientists have dismissed Lamarck's ideas in favor of the theories propounded by Charles Darwin—about random mutation (on a genetic level) and natural selection.

The more practical problem is what to do about it, considering that the motivating causes of alcohol abuse (before physical addiction has developed) can be quite different and that the degree of addiction in different individuals can vary.

SHORT ANSWER

No matter what the mental functioning of people may be, if they are physically addicted to alcohol because of heavy consumption over a fairly long period of time, they will need detoxification.

LONG ANSWER

If reality testing, integration, abstraction, and self-preservation are intact; better impulse control exists in other areas; trusting relationships have formed;

---

24 As well as alcohol dehydrogenase and other enzymes.

and the conscience includes integrity—that what is promised will stick (intact superego), people can often be detoxified as outpatients. They (with or without a family member) agree to rid the household of alcohol and take the usual medications to prevent withdrawal. (At the time of this writing, in 2012, these are primarily benzodiazepines.)

If the above capacities are intact, and people are being (or have been) detoxified, you can begin to help them understand what makes them drink. That is, you can discuss the meaning of their use of alcohol—such as relief of painful depressive feelings, relief of anger, self-punishment, or relief of social anxiety (fear of rejection by friends who abuse or overuse alcohol.)

Once these meanings have been elucidated, you may find that copying (identifications with) important people in their lives (mother, father, siblings, and friends) has been instituted to relieve fears of being alone.[25] Sometimes, identifications with the aggressor are present or identifications with idealized parental figures who have led the person into abuse.

Some people may be using alcohol to distance themselves from others and to soothe themselves without having to turn to someone else for support (object-relations problems). Soothing themselves (without the need for others) can also guard against shame over dependency wishes which have been intensified by feelings of maternal deprivation, whether these were real or not.

Occasionally, a man will associate drinking with the "he man" alcoholic of old western movies and detective stories.[26] One man I treated associated drinking with "revelry" and with "becoming a man." He had had his first drink at age 21 with his father, who was an alcoholic. In other words, he associated alcoholism with his passage into adulthood, with masculinity, with celebration, and with fun.

Alcohol may be used as a substitute for masturbation when masturbation causes too much shame. In other words, alcohol can be both a pleasure and a defense (a compromise formation).[27]

---

25 Also called "identification with the lost object" (Blackman, 2003a).
26 In these cases, the drinking is a defense against castration anxiety ("I'm no sissy!") or castration depressive affect ("I'm not the man I used to be…").
27 Marcus and Francis (1975).

Problem 20
What Do You Do With Different Types of Alcoholics?

Many alcoholics, unfortunately, suffer with borderline personality disorder and a certain degree of psychopathy. This means that they have difficulty maintaining close relationships with other people; they distance themselves emotionally, and then alternate this with becoming annoyingly dependent; and they are not trustworthy because their conscience is unintegrated.

This common type of alcoholic probably had much to do with the original appearance of Alcoholics Anonymous and, in my opinion, remains the type of alcoholic for whom Alcoholics Anonymous is the most successful. Considering that only a small percentage of people who join AA ever maintain sobriety, the differential diagnosis then becomes much more important in selecting those who can be treated as outpatients.

ALCOHOLICS WITH AN IMPAIRED CONSCIENCE

Some alcoholics are untrustworthy, unfair, have a poor sense of integrity, and feel almost no shame or guilt. (In other words, they fall into the category of "psychopathic"[28] or "antisocial.") They may be forced by family members into a detox program, but generally they do not stay with treatment. They tend to continue drinking and use other drugs. A number commit petty crimes (or sometimes major crimes) and will eventually be incarcerated. These are some of the least treatable of all alcoholics.

SCHIZOHOLICS (ALCOHOLICS WHO ARE ALSO SCHIZOPHRENIC)

Another difficult-to-treat type of alcoholic is the "schizoholic"—schizophrenic people who drink to relieve delusional and hallucinatory activity. They are difficult to treat because they are so paranoid that they rarely develop any trusting relationship with a therapist or clinic. If the schizophrenia can be discovered, it is possible that they might be treatable with antipsychotic medication, but they have to agree to take it. Often, in these cases, the schizophrenia coexists with psychopathic features (delusional and/or disorganized thinking,

---

28 Blackman (2010), Chapter 3.

breaks with reality, and failures in conscience functioning). These people have a poor prognosis.

NARCISSISTIC ALCOHOLICS WITH A CONSCIENCE

There are people who are "near borderline,"[29] mostly with narcissistic problems; and they possess a very strong and sometimes rigid conscience.

People with a conscience generally will stick by what they promise, so they can be detoxed as outpatients as their typical narcissistic defensive operations are confronted. These defenses include devaluation, primitive idealization, reaction formations (too nice) against hostility, projection and projective blaming, and emotional distancing.

If they have sufficient abstraction ability and integration, narcissistic people can benefit from understanding these mechanisms. Once their distancing tendencies are clarified, some "relational" elements of treatment can be instituted by the therapist, gradually, to help with "secure organized attachment."[30]

GUILT-RIDDEN ALCOHOLICS

The most treatable alcoholics are people who are using alcohol to relieve guilt.

EXAMPLE 1

Doug, a male alcoholic, began every session by saying, "I know I'm still drinking too much."

We gradually understood that he punished himself by drinking to relieve guilt related to a number of people whom he loved, including his mother, his father, and his younger brother. In Doug's case, detoxification was only possible when he decided to stop hurting himself, as a result of understanding more about why he felt so guilty.

The guilt began when his younger brother got killed in front of Doug's eyes. They were both in grade school, running across the street between parked cars, when Doug's brother got hit. Doug eventually saw, with my help, that his guilt about this accident was a reaction to an earlier wish for his brother never to have been born. At the time of his brother's death, most of the sibling rivalry had been resolved, and they were close friends.

---

29   Volkan (2011).
30   Bretherton (1992).

Doug eventually agreed that he did not need punishment. He agreed to detox from alcohol (he was drinking about two six-packs of beer a night), even though he could rationalize that his drinking didn't interfere with his work. This took him a couple of weeks, with the help of a benzodiazepine.

About a year later, Doug fell off the wagon after an argument with his wife but was again able to detoxify. His psychotherapy lasted about 8 years, on a once-a-week basis, and he was eventually able to benefit from his reliance on me, stop fighting it, stop punishing himself, and treat himself more humanely. He also found other outlets for pleasure, which had been somewhat inhibited through the years by his drinking.

ABUSE OF ALCOHOL FOR SOCIAL REASONS

Alcohol is commonly abused by women, in social situations, when they are feeling needy of love and sexual activity but are ashamed of these wishes. In such cases, they may get drunk both to relieve the shame and to facilitate their aggressive pursuit of sexual gratification. In a funny episode in Season 3 of the British comedy *Coupling*,[31] we are treated to Sally and Patrick recalling the same incident involving Sally being drunk and the two of them kissing ("snogging"). The alcohol facilitated her either being sexually predatory or desperately helpless, depending on whose recollection we believe.

Teenagers commonly use alcohol to "fit in." They associate alcohol, symbolically, with adulthood, possibly because of the U.S. drinking age of 21. When I studied in Ecuador, in 1963, as a teenager, I noticed that the degree of teenage drinking was minuscule compared to the United States; this was ironic, because if there was a drinking age in Ecuador at the time, it was certainly not enforced.

Interestingly, in Germany, where as of this writing the drinking age is 14,[32] teenagers may get drunk, but they do it without the illicit quality that attaches to it in the United States. Drinking is less "attractive" as a rebellious activity, and getting drunk once or twice does not connote the breakdown in superego functioning (doing something unlawful) that it does in the United States.[33]

Treating teenagers who drink too much involves getting them to understand that they are symbolically associating drinking with adulthood, sexual

---

31 Moffat (2002).
32 Beer and wine in the company of parents; 16 – beer/wine without parents; 18 – all (McDonald's Serves Beer! 2009). In Switzerland, the drinking age is 14, and there is no drinking age in Portugal and Poland (Richburg, 2004).
33 My son, after participating in an exchange program at a German high school, said he felt teenagers in Germany could be closer with their parents because they did not have to hide their drinking. He felt the U.S. ban on drinking before age 21 caused more teenagers to engage in deception.

prowess, and rebellion against authorities who generally represent their parents. Others may be identifying with alcoholic parents.

DRINKING TO RELIEVE EMOTIONAL PAIN

There is another group of alcoholics who drink because they are depressed, trying to relieve the depressive affect.

EXAMPLE 2

Lisa, a 37-year-old woman with two small children, spent quite a bit of time telling me about her horrible relationship with her husband, which made her depressed. He was never home, took business trips, and when he was home, he paid little attention to her or the children.

Her passivity, which I showed her, relieved her guilt; she therefore had a difficult time confronting her husband about her dissatisfactions.

After a while, Lisa admitted that she was drinking "some wine" at night. It turned out that her husband was "busy" each night, staying up to the wee hours of the morning in his "man cave." The "some wine" turned out to be a bottle of wine each night; she was addicted to alcohol.

Her alcohol addiction had begun as a defense against depressive affect and frustration, along with passivity, reaction formation, suppression, and avoidance. She soon stopped therapy with me to pursue marital therapy.

In my opinion, had she not used alcohol as a defensive operation and perhaps been able to confront her husband earlier, this might have led to an earlier resolution of their problems.

Problem 21
Bullies

Bullies (people with sadistic personality disorder) are not in the *DSM*. Masochism was deleted from the *DSM* decades ago as well, although there has been a study group about it. In the psychoanalytic literature, sadism and masochism are amply covered in multiple articles about theory and the treatment of people who have such problems. Socially, bullying has become a national concern in the 21st century, and many social programs have been designed to try to curtail it.

Most often, therapists see the victims of violence. Sometimes, however, the bullies, themselves, become unhappy with their lives, particularly with the lack of gratification they are feeling, and seek treatment. Some of them feel guilty about what they are getting away with. What do bullies look like and how do we go about treating them?

Before getting to the answers, let's again look over the differential diagnosis. Bullying can be the result of varying factors, including the following:

- People who have deficits in functions; that is, their lack of reality testing leads them to try to control others and make others miserable.
- People who have no conscience but take some particular pleasure in seeing other people suffer.
- People who use bullying to ward off anxiety over getting close (such as the nagging wife).
- People who provoke punishment and create distance (such as the explosive husband).

SHORT ANSWER

Bullies may suffer with insomnia, anxiety, and some situation in their lives that is making them unhappy. As you listen to them, however, you get a picture of how they dominate others.

It is imperative to discuss your awareness of their bullying activity with bullies. You may pick it up as they describe a relationship with a coworker, lover, or child. (Bullying of children—ridiculing them and laughing at their expense—is a time-honored, rationalized behavior.) Most likely, you will see it in relation to yourself when the bully, who is suffering so greatly, makes demands that you change your fee or see them at a different time of the day.

Aggression is necessary to treat bullies. It is not enough to be "a container" (Problem 13). You must actually say something like, "I see that you are controlling me, pushing me around, and trying to get me to do something that I do not want to do."

Some "manipulative" bullies have the capacity to observe themselves. With your help, they can recognize the bullying and examine the origins of it. Often, they have identified with people who had bullied them or have disidentified from passive people they did not respect.

LONG ANSWER

As mentioned previously, there is a differential diagnosis of people who are bullies.

Psychotic Bullies

EXAMPLE 1

When I was first in practice, I treated Jill, a 24-year-old single woman who had a history of schizophrenia. She was taking antipsychotic medicine and coming to see me once a week in the office. She was also working.

One day, she insisted I help her practice shooting a new rifle she had just bought. When I asked her why she had bought the rifle, she said she wanted to kill some people, including me and herself. She wanted to do it "skillfully." I asked her where the rifle was. She told me she had just bought it and it was in the trunk of her car. I demanded she give me her car key. I also insisted she go to the hospital for treatment because she was getting sicker. She insisted she did not need hospitalization. It took 30 minutes of arguing, but I finally got her to agree with me.

I called an ambulance, which took her to the hospital. I went in my car, admitted her, and promptly arranged for her to be transferred to a different psychiatrist, since she had developed a psychotic transference to me (planning to kill me as well as herself).

When I spoke with her in the hospital, she was upset that she was going to lose me as her doctor and tried to bully me into feeling guilty by saying she would now definitely kill herself. I told her she was in danger of killing me and herself and needed to get some distance from me so that those feelings would diminish. Although she didn't like it, the last I heard, she was still alive and had not killed anybody.

It was important, in that case, for me to respond to her psychotic demand that I help her with her rifle by taking charge of the situation, myself, and making sure that nothing bad happened.

Psychopathic Bullies

EXAMPLE 2

Irene, a 29-year-old woman, came to see me, ostensibly, because of problems with her boyfriend. After a few minutes, she explained that she was a prostitute. She was having trouble with her boyfriend, she claimed, because he was jealous about her work. He had lost his job, so she no longer wanted to date him.

She looked at me in a seductive way and invited me to be her next boyfriend. I pointed out that this was a manipulative, coercive tactic on her part, and had nothing to do with her coming to see me because of her problems. She admitted that was the case but invited me to have sex with her in my office.

I felt that this type of coercion needed counter aggression from me. I pointed out to her that she was being destructive toward me as a doctor and that I would not even consider her invitation. I told her I suspected that her destructiveness was hidden in the prostitution and her relationships with other men, just as I could see that she used sexual wiles to try to coerce me into doing something illegal, improper, unethical, and destructive.

After I gave her this speech, Irene started laughing and said, "You're good!" I got a bit more history from her, and, much to my surprise, she paid for the evaluation (in cash) and made an appointment to come back for a follow-up visit. She, however, did not keep it.

Irene was a more psychopathic person, with very little conscience. She involved herself in illegal activity, was apparently shopping around for a sugar daddy, and would have coerced me into that position if I would have allowed that type of corrupt deal.

Depressed Bullies

Another common type of bullying occurs when people want something aside from treatment. It may not be as corrupt as the actions of the prior person I described, but it may be something like wanting a leave slip from work because of "depression." These evaluations are difficult.

EXAMPLE 3

Eduardo came to see me because he was getting drunk, beating up his gay lover, and failing in graduate school.

After about a month of treatment, he asked me to give him a phony bill showing extra sessions that were marked paid, even though I had not seen him and he had not paid for them. He would show this false bill to the bank where he received student loans, to persuade them to increase his loans because of medical need. He would use the extra money to take a trip to Africa with his lover.

I told him this was a destructive wish toward me, hiding behind his so-called neediness: He was trying to bully me into doing something illegal and fraudulent, and I would have no part of it. If he wanted to be in treatment with me, he must consider this coercive request so that we could see where it was coming from.

His accused me of being homophobic and "a Republican who hates poor people and gays." I confronted this manipulation by telling him that his request had nothing to do with poor people and that I didn't feel guilty about him suggesting I was a Republican. He was still trying to manipulate me into doing something fraudulent to get him more money, and "beating up on me" about it. I told him if he refused to consider what this meant, I could not treat him. He said he would think about it.

In the following session, Eduardo cried and apologized to me. He knew he was sadistic. He had gone out the night before and had unprotected sadistic anal intercourse with an unknown man on the beach. He knew he could pick up AIDS this way. He felt desperate. He said he would go by my rule.

Edward linked his bullying of me with boys who had raped him when he was in junior high school. Symbolically, he was attempting to "rape" me—to abuse me in a way that would cause me harm.

> **TIP**
> Some bullies engage in "undoing": an attempt to neutralize guilt by misbehaving. They may only be treatable if they have enough of *a conscience to want to understand and improve their behaviors.*

Eduardo's attempt to destroy my integrity needed an aggressive response. I figured when I confronted him that there was a 50/50 chance he would return to treatment, but it seemed to be effective, at least in his case.

Oral Demanding Bullies

Some people will try to extract something from you that is not part of treatment per se. Most commonly, people cancel an appointment the same day but do not want to hold to the cancellation agreement and pay for it: "oral-sadistic bullying."

Often these requests cannot be successfully confronted, but it's worth a try. Some people will respond to your pointing out how they are coercively approaching you, degrading you, condescending to you, and pushing you around.

If you are lucky, they may be interested in the forces causing them to do such things. They may also develop more guilt, or become aware of an attempt to neutralize guilt by misbehaving (undoing).

Most people with these character traits will quit treatment after you point out the traits to them, since they demand feeding. In my opinion, if you keep rescheduling appointments for them, they will reward you by torturing you further with their inconsiderateness.

> **TIP**
> Clinically, you can consider someone has sadistic, bullying traits when they are coercive, want their own way, and seem to have *a conscious or unconscious intent to cause suffering to other people or to you.*

Sadistic Bullies

There have been many definitions of sadism.[34]

Clinically, sadistic, bullying traits involve a conscious or unconscious intent to cause suffering to other people or to you.

---

34 S. Freud (1919), Brenner (1959), Novick and Novick (1996).

Problem 22
Procrastinators

Procrastinators waste time and do not get things done on time. This can be a minor issue for many people, who do not need treatment. For some people, however, it becomes a major problem. Lawyers often have statutes of limitations on a particular law that will run out on a certain date, or they must have documents filed on a certain date in court. If they are late, they will be penalized, possibly lose the case, and be vulnerable to sanctions by the state bar where they are practicing. They may also get sued for malpractice by the client.

Physicians have constraints on time, as well. Operating rooms are run on a strict schedule, and doctors cannot be late. Also, charts (hospital records about patients) must be completed (and signed) by physicians by a certain date or they can lose hospital staff privileges as a punishment.[35]

Businesspeople must complete documents by a certain time, and people applying for immigration visas also must complete certain tasks within a certain timeframe. In fact, much of life centers on time and time management, and there are gazillions of books about how to do this well. By the time people get to us, they have exhausted the usual attempts to correct their procrastination. When their classes and their resolutions have failed, it is usually necessary to help them figure out what their procrastination means.

SHORT ANSWER

Procrastination is a complex character disturbance. Its features can vary considerably with each individual.

In brief, look at how procrastination helps people avoid certain painful feelings (a defensive operation). Invariably, procrastinators will also do this with you in some fashion; for example, they may be late to appointments or ask you if they can postpone paying you.

Whenever procrastinators want to postpone something, even just talking about something they are thinking about, this becomes an entry for trying to understand the conflicts that are causing the procrastination.

Look for guilt as a motivator for procrastination. Unconscious guilt causes people to be late so that they get punished. The punishment then relieves the

---

[35] Where hospitals use electronic medical records, doctors can be sanctioned if they have not completed history and physicals, progress notes, and discharge summaries online.

guilt.[36] The next question is, what are they feeling guilty about? That is the rest of the treatment: to figure out what is causing such an enormous amount of guilt.

Procrastinators usually harbor a huge amount of hostility toward any type of authority and control. They rebel by forgetting to do things, by being irresponsible, or by being slow to complete things. Sometimes, they keep emotional distance this way, as well (an object relations issue). In other words, we again must look at areas of conflict involving wishes, superego functioning, defense, and object relations (see Problem 101 [B]).

EXAMPLE 1

George, a 44-year-old divorced surgeon, came to see me because he had just lost his hospital staff (and operating) privileges for not completing his charts on time. He hated EMR (electronic medical records), but he was also slow in doing a number of other things, including finding another wife and having children, which he very much wanted to do. He kept putting off going to social functions and dating, as well.

I first approached his procrastination as a way of getting himself punished. He was a little bit reluctant to think about this, but he eventually could see that in some way he was bringing the punishment on himself; we could then begin to investigate why he felt so guilty.

Through his thoughts and memories, we discovered that he was feeling very guilty about any decisive action. He felt guilty about doing better than his brothers and sisters, two of whom were on welfare and one of whom was still in jail. In "screwing up," he identified with his siblings' failures and antisocial behavior and got himself punished to relieve himself of his guilt over doing better than they did.

I treated him in classical psychoanalysis for about 5 years, with an excellent result. He was eventually elected president of the local medical society and was on time. He also remarried.

LONG ANSWER

Procrastinators are struggling with inner (intrapsychic) conflicts, causing them to do things that are self-destructive at the same time that they are expressing rebellious feelings. However, they can have many other unhealthy motivations.

---

36 S. Freud (1916).

EXAMPLE 2

In the case above, George had also wished to be a woman, stemming from feelings of deprivation by his father (unrequited "father hunger").[37] He thought of this in relation to a dream where he was lying on his back and I was "floating" above him. He was "kissing toward" me.

> **THEORY**
> Procrastination can involve the following:
>
> - Provocation of punishment.
> - Expression of hostility toward authorities.
> - Wishes to be loved as special.
> - Wishes to be pregnant.
> - Identifications with dysfunctional siblings.

I thought I recognized something, but to be careful,[38] I asked him what direction he was kissing. He said, "I just told you, up, toward you." I responded, "So you were kissing up." George exploded with laughter. He said "I'm always kissing up to you. I thought you were going to tell me I was gay."

That thought led to his fantasy that if he were gay, he would be closer to being a woman, and he could then have my baby. He felt that if he could have been a girl and have his father's baby, his father might have loved him better.

Being "late" had to do with a hermaphroditic fantasy that he was both a man and a woman and could become pregnant. He clearly remembered a wish to be pregnant from around age five or six, of which he was rather ashamed. The whole matter had become symbolized in his behavior of "being late" (like missing a menstrual period).

He was also pseudoindependent to avoid shame over very intense wishes for a woman to take care of him. Instead of becoming aware of these wishes, he had been "late" to dates with women, sometimes an hour or two. He expected them to be understanding and sympathetic without him having to apologize: He felt that he did not have to kowtow to any woman by being on time.

These problematic attitudes were related to his relationship with his mother growing up—both his fight for independence and his intense wishes for her to care about him. His mother had been a marijuana addict (she had

---

37 Herzog (2001).
38 Arlow (1979).

been a hippy in college) who, when stoned, did a lot of cooking. When not stoned, she was irascible and distant.

George had some difficulty with his identity, stemming mostly from difficulties in late adolescence and early adulthood. He had chosen medicine as a profession, in spite of the fact that both of his parents hated doctors. They complained of their own medical care and the medical care that their relatives had received. They saw doctors as inattentive, money-grubbing charlatans, who could not be trusted. When George was accepted to medical school, they were not happy, and refused to pay for it. He got loans.

This choice had given him a feeling of separateness from his parents, which relieved some fears that he would be "part of their agenda." George had chosen a male mentor during his residency and spent a lot of time with him. Even in the hospital where he took his surgical residency, people joked about how George was "Dr. Washington's shadow." This ingratiation and symbiotic tie to his mentor facilitated his training, as Dr. Washington did not reject him in this role.

George had a good experience during residency and was able to join a successful surgical practice afterward. He still yearned for a male mentor from whom to introject a sense of strength. Inevitably, he saw me this way.

As we learned from his fantasy life how he wished to incorporate a mentor, he was able to curtail his wish to be "saved" by a father when he "screwed up," another motivation for his procrastination.

In summary, when someone is not psychotic, procrastination is a character disturbance with meanings. If you can find the meanings, people should be able to rectify their self-destructive delaying.

Problem 23
Passive, Wimpy People

There are certain people who are doormats for others. They do not stand up for themselves and they let other people abuse them financially, morally, and in other ways. As long as they don't have too many deficits in functions, you can bring their wimpiness to their attention, understand it, and they can become more self-protective.

For decades, self-help groups have taught "assertiveness training." Assertiveness training can be of some help, but some people become "too assertive" or "too aggressive" at times.[39] Therefore, showing people their conflicts causing automatic passivity helps them make their own decisions in a more adaptive fashion.

Sometimes passivity is a good strategy and sometimes passivity is a very self-destructive strategy. The same is true with being assertive. It can be a mistake just to encourage people to be more assertive, because any assertiveness requires the use of judgment, executive function (decision making), and reality testing to be effective.

SHORT ANSWER

When people are too passive across the board, it is important to bring this passivity to their attention. Most of the time, the person's chief complaint will not be about passivity. Instead, they may complain of being depressed, anxious, and somewhat helpless.

Try to obtain the history of their current relationships to get a feel for how they handle conflict. As you listen to their story, you will hear many instances where they should have done something but did not. You will want to choose one of those points to highlight how the person did not take action when they should have.

Fear of punishment (common punishments people fear are abandonment and rejection) is often the cause of passivity; it's reasonable to tell people, when you see they are being too passive, that they seem to be withdrawing in order to relieve some guilt. If they can see this, they should reward you with memories of conflict where they tried to be more assertive and got punished or hurt. These memories may be from latency (school-age years), adolescence, or earlier in adulthood.

---

39 Mayo Clinic (2012) has a website about this.

It is tempting to try to "motivate" people who are passive. Don't do it. Passive people will be insulted by this, they will try to rise to the occasion to please you, and frequently they will fail. It is much safer to discuss how their passivity relieves guilt. Then you can look at what they imagine they might have done had they not been so passive. This approach is more likely to effect a change in the way they manage aggression.

LONG ANSWER

Passivity usually doesn't exist by itself. We see it in combination with inhibition of executive function (indecisiveness); inhibition of speech; sexual inhibition; provocation of punishment; reaction formation (being too nice); minimization; normalization; and rationalization. In other words, passivity turns out to be complex.

Passivity also may indicate people's wish for someone to take care of them without them having to risk the shame evoked by their intense wish. The passivity is designed to relieve the shame over the intense wishes to be paid attention to and taken care of.

Passivity in men is often associated with envy of women, particularly in the sexual realm. They consciously envy women's supposed "ease" during sex, since the woman "doesn't have to perform." Envious feelings, leading to passivity, can sometimes be traced to specific incidents involving siblings and parents.

Women's passivity may express a sexual wish, especially if the woman is ashamed of her own sexual desires or feels intense guilt about it. Some marital difficulties are caused by shame in both the woman and the man regarding exposure of sexual wishes and appetite.[40]

EXAMPLE

Passivity, combined with withdrawal and avoidance (by a woman), is depicted by Sandra Brown (2003) in her novel *The Crush*. In this novel, the protagonist, a female surgeon, has not had a relationship, apparently, since she was a teenager. She is seen as icy and withdrawn, although she has collegial relationships in the hospital.

The complex story begins when a male homicidal maniac develops a crush on the surgeon. She then meets a male police officer who is protective, eventually breaks the ice, and they wind up in a love affair. As they get close,

---

40 Levin (1969a, 1969b).

she eventually tells him the truth about what had happened to have caused her to withdraw from sexual activity.

She had been a flirt as a teenager, and had eventually had sexual intercourse with one of her father's colleagues in her father's study. When her father walked in and saw this, he had pulled a gun, but instead of aiming the gun at the man, he pointed it at her. To save her, the colleague jumped in front of her as her father pulled the trigger and her father killed the man instead.

Her father then put the gun in her hand and persuaded her to take responsibility for the killing, claiming she had killed this man during a rape attempt. She had gone along with this scheme, although it turned out that she also hated her father. She felt guilty over letting her father off the hook, having seduced his colleague into a position where her father killed him, and surviving, herself ("survivor guilt").

Her enormous guilt had caused her to avoid men for at least 2 decades before she fell in love with the police detective. It is only through his "interpretive" comments to her while they are dating that the reader learns the whole story.[41]

Sometimes, passivity develops as a result of being neglected as a child ("low-keyed" children).[42] These children grow up to be people who do not have a lot of motivation to do anything, are not terribly interested in engaging with other people, but may be smart enough to get a job and lead a rather perfunctory existence. If they get depressed, they may show up in your office.

Treating low-keyed people involves gradually establishing a relationship with them and letting them see that you care about them. Treatment, which is difficult, involves asking questions, expressing interest in what they are doing and allowing them then to "reintroject" aspects of your image of their capacities.[43]

People with this type of disturbance tend to avoid affect storms by staying passive, away from people, and away from entanglements. Some withdrawn people suffer with "empathic inhibition."[44] When you discuss their avoidance and lassitude as ways of staying away from anxiety and anger, they may respond by allowing more openness in themselves and with others.

---

41 Similarly, in the movie *The Lion King*, Nala saves Simba from a life of degradation by confronting him with his unnecessary self-exile (self-punishment). Simba had felt guilty because he imagined he was responsible for his father's death.
42 Mahler et al. (1975).
43 Goldberg (2002), Kohut (1971).
44 Easser (1974).

Problem 24
The Male "Yes, Dear"

These men are aggressive and successful at work but become passive with their wives or girlfriends. They are often trying to be "men of the 21st century": thoughtful and egalitarian with the women they love (ego ideal influenced by 21st-century Western culture).[45] However, they go too far to please their partners.

SHORT ANSWER

The mainstay in treating the male "yes, dear" is a two-fold approach: (a) acknowledging his assertiveness and effectiveness at work and (b) contrasting this to his remarkable passivity and compliance with his wife.

EXAMPLE 1

Adam, a man who ran his own software business, complained that his wife constantly nagged him with "honey-do" tasks. He rarely refused. He also rarely initiated sexual relations with her.

As I discussed his passivity with him, he recounted how, when his wife asked him to take out the garbage, he would obligingly do so, but on returning through the backyard, he would stop to urinate on his wife's flower garden.

I pointed out how his agreeability (in taking out the trash) was belied by this activity—which replenished his sense of masculinity at the same time he expressed hostility toward his wife.

He then recalled how, during adolescence, he had felt angry and humiliated when his mother discussed his diarrhea with doctors while Adam was in the room. He realized he had avoided any confrontation with his wife in order to avoid, similarly, any feeling of humiliation; at the same time he repeated his passivity with his mother (transference from the mother to the wife).

LONG ANSWER

In addition, "yes, dears" feel emasculated. To handle their "castration depressive affect" (Brenner, 1982, 2006), they engage in various symbolically compensatory behaviors.

---

45 K. Parker (2008).

EXAMPLE 2

Dr. Loving, a family practitioner whose wife was a full-time homemaker, had one daughter in grade school. His wife refused to cook dinner, claiming she had too much to do, and was often a bit drunk when he came home. He therefore cooked dinner for everyone, although he was quite tired and depleted emotionally. He joked to me, "Funny how my wife can always tell when we're going to have sex."

On Sundays, he played golf with male friends. He generalized, saying "all" his friends and he jokingly commiserated about how they had no choice but to answer their wives, with "Yes, Dear."

Dr. Loving had had a sister born when he was 5 years old. He was the fifth of six children, from a blue collar family. He remembered his mother being overwhelmed and cranky after his sister was born—and he was no longer the baby. Without realizing it, he had reacted to his wife by being too nice (reaction formation) because he feared losing her.

I formulated, with him, that his passivity with his wife, which was exacerbated after the birth of his daughter, relieved a fear of loss that was based on his experience of feeling left, in favor of his sister, by his mother when he was five. In addition, commiserating with his friends helped him generalize to relieve his shame and sense of emasculation (castration depressive affect). At the same time, he avoided talking to his wife about his own (shameful) wishes for attentiveness (e.g., for her to make dinner once in a while) and better sexual gratification for both of them.[46]

Male "yes, dears" are common. Unfortunately, their wives tend to see their husbands as compliant but "needing his man-cave." In treating male "yes, dears," it's a good idea to help them see how, although they are aggressive people (especially around other men), they are pretending to be nice to their wives. In the process, their wives do not obtain the correct information about their husbands' actual reactions to marital interactions.

After clarifying the specifics of the man's passivity with his wife, look for his generalizations, social humor, and avoidance of his wife as ways he uses to run away from feeling emasculated and ashamed of his own dependency wishes.

---

46 Volkan (2009).

Problem 25
Self-Centered People Who "Need a Spanking"

People who think that they are God's gift to the earth may show up in our offices periodically when things do not go right in their lives. They may have experienced a loss or a frustration of some sort, but generally they are very focused on themselves and their control over people and matters. They are difficult to treat, but you may try a couple of the approaches below.

Even if they have had some success in their careers, entitled people generally offend others unless those others are "passive, wimpy people" (Problem 23). You are likely to be tempted to give narcissistic people "a lesson" on social empathy: to advise them to stop being so self-centered or demanding. They provoke this type of punishing response from many people they encounter, unless they are simultaneously seductive.

With you, they may make some demand that is unreasonable, perhaps a boundary crossing. They may not tell you important things because they feel that it is not your business, or they may demand medication. It is important that you resist at the same time that you point out how self-centered and controlling they are. If they agree and start thinking about themselves, they may be treatable. But don't get your hopes up.

SHORT ANSWER

Don't give in to the narcissistic manipulations; instead, try a confrontation.

EXAMPLE 1

Tina, a 32-year-old married woman, consulted me for insomnia. She was happy with her work, with her husband, and with their decision not to have children. She got along with people. She had had a "good" childhood.

She just wanted me to prescribe something for sleep. I responded that I did not know enough about her to prescribe medicine. I said I saw that she tended to minimize things and keep secrets. I offered to see her again, if she wanted to discuss how her minimization was possibly connected with her insomnia. She demurred, saying she would go back to her family doctor, who had referred her.[47]

---

[47] Her family practitioner never made any more referrals to me.

Ten years later, Tina called me. When I saw her, she admitted that she had been having an affair with a married man since she had been married to her husband. She said, "You were right when I saw you that first time. I was hiding the affair. But now, he wants to leave his wife and marry me. I can't!"

Her boyfriend's request caused Tina anxiety. She had liked the arrangement pretty much as it was: She had sex with her husband every other week and met her boyfriend in secret rendezvous periodically for sexual encounters. This was now all getting messed up by her boyfriend's wish.

Tina agreed with me that her boyfriend had disturbed her sense of entitlement and specialness. She knew she was self-centered. We learned about this over the next year in intensive psychotherapy. She eventually dropped the boyfriend and stayed with her husband.

EXAMPLE 2

Bud, a 51-year-old man, came to see me under duress. He seemed grumpy, and began by telling me that he did not need treatment; it was his wife that had problems.

When I asked what his wife would say about him, he accused me of being sneaky. I said that he seemed angry, and was blaming his wife to stay away from telling me about his own problems. He responded, "Why should I talk to you? You're not worth it." I asked him what he thought I was worth. He said, "$8." My attempts to look at his bullying and devaluation of me were unsuccessful. He left without paying the fee.

Obviously, there can be a crossover between narcissistic people and bullies. However, some bullies are identifying with aggressors—a mechanism that can be quickly understood as long as they do not also manifest "malignant" narcissism,[48] like Bud did.

LONG ANSWER

People with a sense of entitlement have a problematic developmental history. There often have been losses early in life, followed by findings of corruption in their parents which demoralized them. Their ego ideals are damaged; they are pessimistic and critical of anyone who wants closeness with them. They may be involved in somewhat shady dealings, see the world as corrupt, and

---

48 Kernberg (1998).

rationalize by citing corrupt activities in the culture and famous people who have been corrupt.

Although the prognosis is not good, you may attempt the following: (a) discuss the distancing element of their behavior with them; (b) confront the way they avoid shame over dependency wishes; (c) discuss their identifications with corrupt people who have hurt them; and (d) confront their "character transference,"[49] in and out of your office.

EXAMPLE 3

Lonnie, a 25-year-old single history teacher, consulted me because his doctor had found no physical cause for his hyperacidity and lack of appetite.

Lonnie's speech was slurred and he was woozy. He reeked of marijuana. He said that even though his doctor wanted him to see me, he didn't agree. I responded by discussing his obvious marijuana use with him. He said, "So I smoke pot! So what? What's wrong with that? Everybody does it." I expressed curiosity about his reasons, since marijuana is illegal in Virginia. He then argued about the merits of marijuana usage. I said, "I feel like I'm a father talking to a teenage boy."

Lonnie laughed and agreed with me. His parents were critical of his pot smoking. His mother had always been on his side and protected him from criticism from his father, so Lonnie got away with murder. He had not worked hard in most subjects in college. He had good grades in history, which he said he could "bullshit" his way through. Lonnie returned to see me twice. I never heard from him again.

EXAMPLE 4

Paul, a 49-year-old divorced man with no children, consulted Jessica, a social worker, who asked me for supervision. Paul was depressed and frustrated. Although successful in his work, when dating he would suppress frustrations and then explode and curse at the woman. Later, he would apologize. He thought he had destroyed his marriage and was having trouble with his current girlfriend.

When Jessica had discussed his identification with his critical father, Paul replied that he had seen lots of therapists and nobody ever did him any good. Then he apologized for being critical. He paid for his session in cash.

---

49 Sandler (1981).

I explained to Jessica that Paul was self-centered. He also showed "Akhtar's sign": paying for a session in cash. (Akhtar has opined, I think correctly, that this is a negative prognostic sign.[50]) I advised Jessica not to get her hopes up. Paul had agreed to a follow-up session and had "stuck out" a couple of his relationships for a few years, so perhaps she could treat him.

I suggested Jessica look at his disidentification from his father: Paul's attempts to be nice. She could explain how he maintained emotional distance by not being honest with women and let his anger build up until he exploded. But I suspected there was more to it. Most women sense emotional distancing, even without realizing it, and then become irritable and perhaps "nagging."

The irritable responses, to the man, seem to be based on nothing; eventually he explodes, feeling criticized unfairly; he thinks the woman is "controlling and castrating." After his explosion, she will feel defeated, but when he apologizes and attempts to make things right, many women appreciate the sensitivity and could reconcile with him, at least until next time.

I suggested to Jessica that she discuss Paul's distancing, suppression, rationalization, isolation of affect, and disidentification from his father. She had some success: Paul became more thoughtful, and paid her by check. However, he only stayed in treatment for a few sessions.

---

50 The reasons for this are multiple, including poor object relatedness, problematic relation to reality, paranoid anxiety, and psychopathic trends.

Problem 26
Can You Understand the Meanings of an Obsession?

An obsession is a recurring thought that includes a preoccupation about people or activities (usually symbolic of sexual, hostile, or dependency wishes) and is usually disturbing to the person having the thought. Compulsions comprise a variety of actions (which are symbolic) that relieve people of guilt and express some wish. Since people often use compulsions to relieve the affects they experience while obsessing, the term "obsessive-compulsive" was coined.

Obsessions and compulsions comprise a controversial diagnostic area. Some of Freud's patients (the Wolf-man and the Rat-man) had obsessive-compulsive problems that were analyzed. But since the advent of tricyclic antidepressants and SSRIs, some studies suggest using these medications to treat obsessional people.

I have not seen a study that distinguishes obsessional people based on their ego functions, ego strengths, and object relations, as I do in Problem 14.[51] Like most symptom complexes, obsessions and compulsions may exist as a superstructure when basic mental functions like organization of thought and reality testing are lacking.

You must check to see if people with obsessive-compulsive symptoms also have capacities for empathy, trust, and closeness, good reality testing, and reasonable abstraction ability. If they possess those functions, you can attempt to treat them by figuring out the meanings of checking, doubting, perfectionism, rituals, and/or hyperpunctuality, hyperneatness, and perfectionism.

SHORT ANSWER

The first line of approach centers on the defenses of isolation of affect (shut-off of sensation) and rumination (thinking the same things over and over), which basically guard people against feeling guilty. You may say something like, "I notice that you seemed unaware of your reactions when you told me about your wife's crying over the miscarriage. You are concerned, but somehow what you feel is shut off, so you wind up sounding kind of emotionless."

---

51 See Problem 101 (B).

> **DEFENSES OF OBSESSIVE-COMPULSIVES**
> Reaction formation
> Perfectionism
> Hyperpunctuality
> Undoing (going against their conscience)
> Rituals
> Isolation of affect
> Externalization
> Compartmentalization
> Rationalization
> Rumination
> Intellectualization

To approach rumination, you might say, "I know that you 'analyze' yourself a lot, but really what you're doing is beating a dead horse. In other words, you are punishing yourself. I think we should try to understand why you feel so guilty you need punishment."

The other elements of obsessions should be left for later. Obsessive-compulsive people may initially resist accepting the ideas of isolation of affect and rumination. They may talk quite a bit (garrulousness as a defense) without seeming to feel too much. Still, try to discuss their isolation of affect.

LONG ANSWER

Obsessive-compulsive neurotics use "primary process" defenses of displacement (shifting feelings from one person to someone who does not deserve it), symbolization (seeing danger in specific objects—like doorknobs), and condensation (imagining death lurks in unlikely locales). They also repress (forget the thought content) of recent events, libidinally regress (fantasies of dependency or control), identify with fantasies, and transfer expectations to you (usually from critical parents).

In order to treat obsessive-compulsive persons with understanding, you explain the conflicts that produce the maladaptive constellation of defenses.

Abraham (1923) made quite a fuss over symbolic anal components in obsessions. Brenner (2006) corrected this: The thought content of obsessional people's fantasies can derive from any psychosexual phase.

People may become preoccupied with starvation, for example. Preoccupation with dirt may be a symbolic of something sexual; touch phobias often symbolize conflicts over masturbation. Conflicts about sex and competitiveness play a great role in obsessional neurotics, so the oral (dependency, trust, and attention issues) and anal (messing, cleaning, and control issues) may be a red herring. Accordingly, the target of insight-directed therapy for such cases is to elucidate the defenses and conflicts.

EXAMPLE

Stuart, an obsessive-compulsive man, called me for a consultation. He was preoccupied with the straightness of his teeth. While we were walking toward my consulting room door, he asked, "Do you mind if I bring my umbrella in the office?" I asked him why he was raising this question. He responded, "Well, it's raining outside, and I didn't want to make a big flood on your consulting room floor." Catching the symbolism, I responded ironically, "Well, not as far as you know."

In other words, I suspected that he had a wish to make a mess on my floor, but was unaware of it, felt guilty about it, and therefore was preoccupied (reaction formation) with getting permission to bring his mess into the office.

I learned that Stuart's supposed concern with flooding my office was connected to his suppressed rage, displaced from his father, who controlled him in one way or another. Stuart used suppression to relieve guilt caused by his father's financial generosity to him. He had a conflict. He liked depending on his father financially (oral gratification). But he was angry at his father because his father bullied him and he wanted to achieve a sense of separateness. To solve this conflict Stuart became preoccupied with his teeth (worried his teeth were "crooked"). This obsession represented

- his wish to take something from his father (which would feel "crooked" to Stuart, like stealing), and
- his self-criticism of those oral wishes.

Problem 27
People With Visible and Nonvisible Disabilities

PEOPLE WITH VISIBLE DISABILITIES

Disabilities include congenital anomalies and acquired limitations (illness or accident). People with disabilities can have the same problems as other people, but there are certain caveats that you should keep in mind.

> **THEORY**
> Paul Schilder[51] was one of the first people to point out that finding meanings was relatively contraindicated for people with congenital limitations or disabilities. His clinical discoveries led to an understanding that when people have a congenital disability or hereditary limitation, their body dysmorphia causes problems with self-esteem.
>
> When self-esteem is an issue, people become more vulnerable to overwhelming affects and impulses. People with disabilities usually require support of their self-esteem, not confrontations that might interfere.

Almost all people with disabilities have faced feelings of loss (of function) and some shame or humiliation. Often they feel that they are alone or "different." Although these feelings can occur in others, physical disabilities tend to inflame those experiences.

When a disability is congenital, there may be a concordant difficulty with affect regulation, so you should be cautious not to cause overwhelming affect.

SHORT ANSWER

If people have a visible disability, try to understand conflicts caused by the disability: shame, isolation, and defenses like turning anger on the self and avoidance of people. It is best not to attempt to approach whatever the disability may represent symbolically to the person you are treating.

---

51 Schilder (1939).

EXAMPLE 1

Nate, a 39-year-old divorced physician, was having difficulties with women. During his sessions, he would make references to his "gimpy arm," which was congenitally short. He could manipulate things with the shortened (right) hand, but it was not as capable as his left hand.

During one session, he pulled a pack of cigarettes[52] out of his shirt pocket with his left hand, one-handedly popped a cigarette into his mouth, replaced the cigarette pack, and then pulled out a book of matches. He used his left hand, alone, to strike the match and light his cigarette. He shook the match out and threw it in the ashtray. He then looked at me with a wry smile.

I erroneously commented to him that this activity seemed important to him. Only this much focus caused him to become agitated, shake a bit, and say to me, "Oh, no! We're not going there!"

I responded that I was impressed with his ability to get the cigarette out and light it. He immediately calmed down and said, "Thanks, I've practiced it quite a bit. Only thing now is, I need to stop smoking!" He then started laughing. I took his advice and "did not go there" regarding anything he may have been compensating for symbolically.

Problems with later-acquired disabilities were poignantly depicted in the movie *The Best Years of Our Lives* (Wyler, 1946), about men after World War II who returned to differing lives but stayed in contact. One of them was a double amputee[53] who expressed feelings of inadequacy as a man due to his disability. His impaired sense of masculinity caused him to withdraw from his fiancée.

It is of some importance that the injuries that caused his disability did not occur until he was about 30 years old (in 1944). Even so, it was a very sensitive subject, and what helped him, at the end of the movie (as would help him in life, as well) was his fiancée's support, acceptance, and encouragement. His understandings of symbolism alone had led him to feel depressed and withdrawn. Remarkably, this movie can be a lesson for therapists, who, while allowing symbolic discussion of a later-developing disability, must be sure to maintain support and understanding.

I have had similar experiences treating male athletes in their early 20s who had experienced a career-ending injury. Whatever the sport, the depressive affect was intense. It was enough to allow grief for them to improve.

---

52 This occurred before 1985, when I banned smoking from my office.
53 Harold Russell, who played himself in the movie, and later helped found AmVets.

LONG ANSWER

Freud and Schilder were aware that body image developed through proprioception (using the five senses) and memory. Later, H. Hartmann (1965) would add that integration (the part of the mind that puts memories together) also contributes.

When a congenital anomaly is visible, the integration of body image during development may not be stable. Resulting weakness in affect regulation may be hidden by obsessive-compulsive defenses (see Problem 26); if you confront the defenses, the result may be upsurges of emotions that overwhelm people's capacities to think.

Freud is often quoted as saying, "the ego is first and foremost a bodily ego."[54] Kohut (1971) later formulated that a breakdown in the self-image, for whatever reason, leads to "aggressive breakdown products." The concept a person has of him- or herself can be weakened in a variety of ways, including by perceptions of a congenital anomaly.

EXAMPLE 2

Roger, a 25-year-old man with spasticity due to cerebral palsy, consulted me for mild depression. He had graduated from college and had dates with two girls during that time. He was intensely interested in women but frightened about rejection. I expressed understanding. He told me he felt relieved that I was not "pushing" him to do better, as his mother always had. In fact, he had introjected her "pushiness" and still demanded a lot from himself.

I did not offer any explanations to him about himself. When he became too critical of himself, I argued that his self-criticism was not necessary. He said, "I wish I could convince my mother of that."

After a couple of sessions, he felt better and decided to stop therapy. He was going to get a job and ask women out when he could. During his last session with me, he gave me a book on how people with disabilities overcome them. I accepted this gift. He was thankful that I had understood some of his frustrations and said it had been helpful.

PEOPLE WITH DISABILITIES THAT ARE NOT VISIBLE

I have treated men and women who were blind in one eye. Some had had untreated "lazy eye" (amblyopia) due to parental neglect. Their problems

---

54 S. Freud (1923), Sheets-Johnstone (2002).

included shame that led to their hiding the blindness. A number of people told me no one had ever guessed, since childhood, that they were blind in one eye. Their secrecy, fear of being discovered, and the always-present self-experience of being "different and alone" were pervasive.

When blindness in one eye developed later in life due to illness (such as glaucoma) or trauma, the meanings were different. There was more grief over the loss of bilateral vision (loss of depth perception, as well), which caused people to use conscious suppression, reversals, denial, and externalization (expecting other people to be critical). When these defensive operations were pointed out, people could become briefly overwhelmed, but this was nowhere near as severe as in those with visible disabilities.

Problem 28
Counterphobic People Who Risk Their Lives

Counterphobic refers to a mental operation where people who are actually quite terrified of something will pursue that activity in order to prove they are not frightened. Sometimes, the activity in which they engage is life threatening.

Most often, people who use counterphobic operations consult you because of some problem in their relationships and/or some other psychiatric complaint. The counterphobic mechanisms have often become part of their personalities, accepted by them and by those around them to a certain degree (ego-syntonic and socio-syntonic).

What do you do when you see one of these?

SHORT ANSWER

In my book on defensive operations (Blackman 2003a), I suggest, in Chapter 6, that life-threatening defensive operations should be pointed out before all others. I try to talk to people about counterphobic defenses before I talk with them about resistance, pathological traits, or childhood and adolescent problems. Counterphobic mechanisms take front and center when you see them.

You will find counterphobic elements in daredevils (dangerous sports) and in sexually promiscuous people. Point out to people that they are doing something dangerous in order to overcome fear and to avoid embarrassment over using judgment.

LONG ANSWER

Counterphobic mechanisms, like most defenses, do not usually exist alone. They occur with other defenses, like reaction-formation (turning a feeling into its opposite), minimization (noticing danger but not reckoning with the severity), suppression (purposely putting frightening thoughts out of consciousness), and sometimes seduction of the aggressor (ingratiating yourself with, or having sex with, someone you should fear and avoid). In the following example, Bob also used sexualization of speech, avoidance, inhibition of judgment, and undoing (breaking his own rules).

EXAMPLE

Bob, a 38-year-old sales manager for a toy store, began a session by saying, "Now I've done it! What a mess…" He then became silent. When I saw the silence, I wanted to ask a question, which I realized meant that Bob was feeling defensive (Problem 77). I therefore said I saw he was hiding something, but I did not know why. He responded, "I'm embarrassed to tell you what I did." I waited.

He continued, "Well, I might as well tell you. I was with my wife and our friends at the beach, and they were talking. I got bored. So I decided to go in the ocean. You know, I'm a good swimmer. But there were no lifeguards because it was so windy, and there were signs up saying don't go in the water, et cetera.

"Anyway, I dove right in anyway. I went out a little too far because I got caught in the current. I eventually made it back okay, but everybody was jumping up and down, yelling. I think they got too worked up, but I guess if I hadn't been able to pull myself out, I could have drowned." Then he paused and said, "What do you think?"

I responded that I thought Bob had taken a chance, not just to break rules, but to prove to himself that he was not afraid. So far, the only clue about what was scaring him was the discussion between him, his wife, and his friends on the beach. He thought, "It's like they were a bunch of old women, sitting around talking. I kind of got disgusted." I could then explain that he reacted to engaging in conversation as though it were feminine. He definitely agreed. He added, "It's like my mother and my sisters; a gaggle of girls, gossiping and giggling."

We discussed his anxiety about getting close to women: fears of being controlled by women or "feminized." To guard against shame over wishing to verbally interact with others ("feminine"), he proved he was a "real man" by taking a very dangerous chance. He now admitted that the riptide pulled him miles down the beach before he could safely swim ashore. His wife and friends had not noticed until he was almost out of sight; when they saw him being pulled, they went screaming down the beach but were unable to reach him. His wife was distraught and furious with him.

Later, we were able to tie this counterphobic behavior to his previous abuse of alcohol. He had stopped drinking about a year previously, but he continued to institute "masculine" behavior to guard against his fear of being unmanly.[55]

---

[55] As you might guess, Bob was also provoking punishment because he felt guilty about various angry feelings toward women, associated with his mother. There were also other mechanisms at play: There was a bit of a grandiosity (feeling invulnerable to any danger); he felt self-object fusion anxiety about being close to his wife and then distanced himself from her by going far out in the ocean (an object relations component); he also "acted out" a wish to be closer to his mother (the "oceanic feeling"), symbolized by his going out deep in the ocean. Later, Bob had a dream about a portrait of his mother, with inaccessible bare breasts, confirming some of his frustrations about his dependent wishes toward his mother.

Problem 29
Seniors Who Feel Entitled

First, a disclaimer: Not all senior citizens become dependent on others, nor do they develop a sense of entitlement.

Nonetheless, there is a select group of senior citizens who, at a certain age, undergo a modification in superego functioning. Their values change, they begin to consider themselves "exceptions,"[56] and they demand special treatment. The basis for this "specialness" is often that they have suffered through so many things in their lives that they feel they are due some recompense.

Life is not fair. This becomes clearer the older you get. Certain elderly people become bitter as they recognize some of the unfairness—that one's wonderful spouse dies from cancer or that a con artist makes millions of dollars.

The last I saw,[57] age 65 is now considered "young old" in Western civilization and age 75 is "old old." These numbers may change with improvements in medical treatment and preventive care. Nevertheless, for now, we are considering people over age 65.

SHORT ANSWER

Sometimes, there is no psychological approach possible to people who believe they deserve special treatment because they are over 65. They can become impossibly demanding toward their doctors, therapists, and friends. Such seniors are condescending to waitresses, attorneys, and even government officials.

However, sometimes the sense of entitlement may be approachable. The therapist must express understanding of how the sense of entitlement has developed and show people how their attitude is destroying relationships with their adult children, grandchildren, et cetera, thereby causing them more pain than pleasure.

EXAMPLE

Bertha, a 68-year-old woman, stereotypically criticized her daughter for "not calling enough." Her daughter became alienated and then called her mother even less. Bertha felt entitled to respect, since she spent years raising the child.

I pointed out to Bertha that, in attempting to relieve her grief over missing her daughter, she was not thinking about her daughter's family pressures. At first,

---

56   S. Freud (1916).
57   See, for example, McCrae et al. (2003).

Bertha was angry that I did not understand her pain. But she quickly realized she had been minimizing her daughter's stresses. She then offered to visit her daughter, help out, and not criticize. She stopped making demands on her daughter about visitation, birthdays, and the like, and their relationship improved.

LONG ANSWER

As with many disturbances, entitlement during the senior years can be caused by different conflicts. People who suffer with borderline personality disorder often seek to replace their own mother with their child.[58] When the adult child becomes individuated, the borderline mother/grandmother becomes depressed over loss of identity (as a mother). You can explain this to some borderline seniors who have reasonable abstraction and integrative ability. If they can see their childish symbiotic pressures on their own children, they may be able to modify their approach.

Many senior citizens develop a sense of entitlement because they have developed physical illnesses. Autoimmune diseases (such as rheumatoid arthritis, gastrointestinal problems, and lupus), osteoarthritis, and hearing losses are common in this age group, cause pain, weakness, and frustration. The resultant depression can cause crankiness and childish directness/demandingness (regression).

In other words, instead of grieving over the losses in function, some people may pout like little children when they are not granted whatever wish they have. If they have enough abstraction ability, reality testing, and integrative functioning, you can discuss how their attitude guards against the pain of loss of function, of certain abilities, and of certain elements of their health.

Still another cause of difficulty in some seniors is a neurotic reaction to getting older. They become obsessional about death, which unconsciously is equated with punishment for any sinful destructive thoughts they have had during their lives. This type of guilt can occur in younger people as well, but it is particularly prominent in neurotic seniors, who equate the idea of death with the ultimate punishment.

In this type of neurotic structure, you may see seniors provoking punishment (maladaptive defensive operations). They may provoke their friends and/or adult children into being critical of them in a variety of ways. Or they may turn the superego outward and criticize others for minor things; this comes off as unreasonable and unempathic.

---

58 Masterson and Rinsley (1975).

Alternatively, seniors may become more paranoid: They use projection of feelings of damaged self-image (from aging) and thus see others as damaged (unable to care for the senior).[59]

Statements that no one is interested (negative mother transferences) may be made to adult children and friends, not only to induce guilt in those people but also to guard against shame the elder person experiences in conflict with increased dependency. If the seniors have been "in charge" throughout most of their lives, increased dependency may cause guilt. This guilt may lead them to provoke punishment. If seniors have become (or have always been) concrete thinkers, they probably will not improve when you explain their defenses guarding them from guilt.

---

59 My grandfather, when he was in his 80s, needed hospitalization. When a nurse asked if he "needed anything else," he responded, "I want another nurse to keep an eye on you!" Fortunately, she thought this was funny. In retrospect, I'm not so sure he was kidding.

Problem 30
Promiscuous People[60]

The word *promiscuous* has almost disappeared from the English language. Modern harlequin novels, in general, are highly explicit. Promiscuity is normalized in later shows of *Seinfeld* and the British comedy *Coupling* (2000 through 2004). It seems everybody is having sex with everybody. Many people have children without being married.

Frequently, you need to clarify the (ego) ideals of people with relationship problems so they can think about any behavior that might not be commensurate with those ideals/values.

Casual sex with someone who wants casual sex (and is not looking for commitment) may be fine for certain people. Casual sex is not against 2012 social mores: It is not "socio-dystonic."

SHORT ANSWER

If people engaged in casual sexual activity want a relationship, it is a good idea

1. to help them clarify what their own goals and ideals are and
2. to understand the meanings of their sexual activities compared with #1.

It is a cliché to say women's sexual activity is designed to relieve fear of abandonment, to solidify a relationship, or to make them feel loved and cared for (the notion that appears in the bestseller *Men Are From Mars, Women Are From Venus*). The song "Girls Just Want to Have Fun"[61] contradicted this stereotype. Feminism correctly emphasizes that women want to be cuddled and held but also wish for sexual stimulation and orgasm.

All of this said, people who consult us, who are having problems in the realm of close relationships, usually desire something stable.

LONG ANSWER

Once a person's (ego) ideals have been clarified, therapy proceeds more smoothly. People with borderline personality may not think about why they

---

60 For an interesting social account of this problem, see Clarke (2008) and K. Cohen (2008).
61 Lauper (1983).

have sex. You find problems in their self-image and sense of stability and fears of identity disintegration. In relationships, they may get close and then run away or maintain distance but hang on. Ironically, they enjoy sex more when their partner does not want a close emotional relationship.[62]

Try to find and point out patterns where people use sex as a tool to express desires for closeness but simultaneously or sequentially create emotional distance ("space").

EXAMPLE 1

Wanda, a 32-year-old divorced, attractive, and personable woman, was suicidal. Highly intellectual and feminist, Wanda faulted herself for sleeping with "cute" men somewhat indiscriminately. She half-joked, "Women can do whatever men can do." Due to an unsatisfactory relationship with one man, she had begun a sexual relationship with another man, a womanizer.

After she had sex with the womanizer, she became suicidally depressed. As I got more history, I could show her how she guarded against feeling deprived by her cold mother by having sex with men. (Her father had been warmer, but absent.)

In her 20s, Wanda had married an older, impotent man who eventually admitted he was gay;[63] he was seeing other men. This ended the marriage.

Wanda's ideal was a stable relationship with a man. To compensate for her pessimism, she would unsuccessfully "try again": have sex with another man. Her disappointment had grown to a point where she felt suicidal.

I discussed with her that she used sexual activity to overcome her pessimism (a defensive operation); she rationalized that she only wanted sexual gratification; she used denial in fantasy (sleeping with the womanizer); and she used "seduction of the aggressor" to relieve her fear of being hurt.

Though we knew her yearnings were displaced from her mother, she continued to have one-night stands. After one bad experience where a man walked out of her apartment immediately after sex, she ruminated about suicide again. The next day, she told me, "I might as well die. Nobody cares about me."

I said I noticed she now added me to the list of people who did not care about her. She upped the ante: "Well, I *pay* you!" I responded, "Thanks a lot!"

---

62   Nicely depicted in the movies *Looking for Mr. Goodbar* (Brooks, 1977) and *Closer* (Nichols, 2004).
63   If you think this is a 21st-century story, see *King Lehr*, where Elizabeth Drexel Lehr (1935/1975) describes how she stayed in an unconsummated marriage for years to avoid upsetting her mother. When her (probably gay) husband, Harry Lehr, died, she wrote a book about her travails and the "Golden Age" of the early 1900s. She later remarried John Beresford, Lord Decies.

When she expressed confusion, I explained that she was suggesting I was a prostitute, providing "services" for money.

Following this confrontation (Problem 1 and Problem 101 [A]), Wanda apologized. We discussed how she had felt like a "prostitute" when men did not love her. I explained that to relieve shame over yearning to be cared for, she had seen *me* as someone who just wanted money (symbolic of mothering). She wanted me to love her as her mother had not—but my fee symbolized her taking care of me, instead.

Wanda agreed but still complained of feeling "no good" and "pathetic." I said, "Maybe your parents never told you this, but you are a worthwhile person: smart, witty, attractive, and capable. There is no reason why you should let any man have sex with you if he is not worth it. You have to decide whether he is or not."[64] Wanda cried briefly, thanked me, and then asked, "How am I supposed to judge this?" I told her she needed to wait for several dates before she got into sex—and that her very life depended on this. It was not enough to convince herself, intellectually, that sex was not immoral.

Over the next month, Wanda reported dates where she withheld sexual intercourse. With all these men, she reported, "He's a jerk," broke up with them, and was relieved she had not slept with them. She could see the difference in herself as her self-control improved.

Neurotic people, who generally do not suffer with self-image or mistrust (object relations) problems, may develop maladaptive sexual patterns. When they are afraid of sexual activity they may force themselves into it to prove that they are not frightened.[65] Adult women who make bad choices of sexual partners may also be obsessional, overly guilty, and controlled. Without realizing it, they "break" their strict morality (undoing) by indulging in sexual intercourse when they feel they "shouldn't."

Impulsive sexuality in women may also relieve anxiety over a weakly developed image of internal genitalia. Sexual intercourse replenishes the mental image of the vagina[66] through locating it, thereby reestablishing "vagina constancy." One woman seduced her taxi driver on the way to Dr. Kramer-Richards's office in Manhattan.

Although the term "promiscuous" is not usually used to describe men, Marcus (2004) described 10 common types of this type of character pathology in men.

---

64 Kohut (1971).
65 A sort of 21st-century version of "Whistle a Happy Tune," by Rodgers and Hammerstein from the musical *The King and I* (1951).
66 Kramer-Richards (1992).

EXAMPLE 2

Jack, 42, was worried that his wife would "catch him" in one of his extramarital dalliances. He loved his wife and children but pursued women in his office. He fit the description of a "playmate":[67] humorous, smart, well-to-do, and epicurean. Although spoiled, he was proud of the money he made.

Jack seemed to be taking risks (Marcus's "daredevil") in "playing around" with women. One of his "screw buddies" was a woman who, while I was treating Jack, married a Navy SEAL. When her husband was deployed, she called Jack for a "quickie." He went.

When he reported this adventure, I told him I thought some of his panic came about because he denied the real danger of what he was doing. He said, "It isn't dangerous; she would never betray me." I argued that this woman had betrayed her husband in spite his being in Special Forces. Whether he would kill Jack if he found out, I did not know. But I thought Jack's "trust" in her represented denial: that is, he told himself it was safe but then had panicky feelings.[68]

Jack's reactions to my confrontation included shame over not being popular in high school and failures with girls during college. He had not had sexual intercourse until he was 25 and was ashamed of this. He married in his late 20s. His financial success was attractive to certain women in the workplace who traded sexual favors for jewelry. I explained that he supported his self-esteem and defended against depression from adolescence and early adulthood by engaging in extramarital affairs.

After understanding these conflicts, Jack reported a new problem. His wife informed him she had been having sex with different men for years, and some had "a bigger penis than you." Jack, at first, laughed ironically. He mused that his wife had "evened the score." She, however, was not so sanguine about the situation, and eventually they got divorced.

---

67 Marcus (2004).
68 Blechner (2007).

SECTION D

Techniques With Acting In and Acting Out

GENERAL COMMENTS ABOUT BOUNDARIES

Although we indicate the frame and the working alliance to people we treat, they do not always follow our rules. When they do something that breaks the alliance in the session, we call it "acting in." If they misbehave outside of therapy, we usually call it "acting out."

Acting out originally meant that a behavior outside the session symbolically reflected conflicts people felt too embarrassed or guilty to think of in relation to their therapists. Today, we use the term to describe people who engage in maladaptive behavior (possibly using poor judgment) that is symbolic of various wishes, emotions, and defense mechanisms.

There are, no doubt, an infinite number of ways people can break rules inside and outside of treatment. My examples only reflect the tip of a large iceberg.

Problem 31
What About Boundaries?

The idea that there is a "boundary" between the therapist and people in treatment is an abstract concept but sometimes becomes concrete and immediate.

The concept of a boundary developed over many decades; practitioners in the early 1900s had little sense of this boundary.[1] The idea began to take shape when Freud (in delineating his own technical errors in the "Dora" case) figured out that most of the feelings people in treatment develop toward their therapists are based on feelings from childhood that have been unknowingly shifted onto the therapist. These shifts, or transfers of feelings from people in the past, were named *transference*.

Once you realize that only a fraction of what people in treatment feel about you is really about you, it is easy to spot transferences. You can then understand and discuss those feelings *while people are in your office.*

Transferences threaten the "therapeutic barrier"[2] or the "frame"[3] in treatment. This "barrier" prevents action between you and the person you are treating. Talking is allowed and encouraged, but there should be no hugging, touching, kissing, and certainly no sexual activity. The "frame" refers to the person (and you) being on time, stopping on time, and not engaging in any activity aside from talking in your office. Bringing a non-silenced cellphone, a drink, or anything else to a session can be considered "acting in" —a break in the frame—and the meanings understood.[4] "Boundary violations," sometimes sexual, are the most serious and dangerous of all boundary crossings.

The following problems include several variations of boundary problems, how I have understood them, and some thoughts about how to handle them.

---
1 Makari (2008).
2 Tarachow (1963).
3 Langs (1973).
4 Malawista, Adelman, and Anderson (2011).

Problem 32
"Let's Make a Deal" and
Gifts—Boundary Crossings

There are differences in severity among the types of boundary crossings. In Example 1, below, I refused to engage in an unethical business venture with Jeff (I did not cross the therapeutic barrier—although he had read my first book).[5]

In Example 2, I accepted the boundary crossing of reading an article from Angela, because it did not involve unethical behavior. My reading her article seemed to contribute to her development of closeness; it helped her analyze negative transferences from her mother; and it did not become sexualized.

I do not usually consider it a boundary crossing if people I am treating call me after hours with a problem. I cover my own practice 24/7 when not on vacation (then a colleague covers me), and encourage people to contact me if they become suicidal. Occasionally, someone I treat gets into a crisis, and after talking to them on the phone, I decide on an emergency appointment for that person in my office. Usually, I have found that people do not take advantage of this policy, and this approach has allowed me to treat people who can become suicidal. They know I am available if they become overwhelmed by depressive affect (transient breakdown in affect tolerance).

I have treated some people who left a message threatening suicide several times a day. I had to have them committed to a mental hospital. A few women have attempted to engage me in nontherapeutic activity—"erotized" transference (Problem 33)—a severe boundary violation that posed serious technical headaches.[6]

Boundary crossings include behaviors of people in treatment who dislike the therapeutic barrier. They invade your life or tempt you in mild, seemingly harmless ways to step out of your therapeutic role. Keep in mind that their invitations are inimical to their own interests. Moreover, their (mis)behavior gives you useful material to understand.

SHORT ANSWER

If you have the data, explain the meanings of people's attempts to cross the therapeutic barrier. If you have little data to explain it, explore the meanings: Express interest in the boundary crossing and ask people their thoughts about

---
5 Stein (1988).
6 Gabbard (1994a).

it (like a dream).⁷ With certain people, at certain times, you may decide that a boundary crossing is acceptable—but be forewarned: Boundary crossings always have meanings, whether you can figure them out or not.

LONG ANSWER

Some people attempt to cross the therapeutic barrier by suggesting that you engage in activity that is unethical or improper ("boundary violation"): money-making schemes, hostility, or sexual conduct. If people attempt to engage you in any behavior other than verbal communication, you need to show them the meanings (if you know them), explore the meanings (if you don't), or stop the behavior if it is inappropriate.

Mild boundary crossings include therapists suggesting a book to a person in treatment "to help," for example. Alternatively, some therapists will accept books or articles from schizoid people who have had problems feeling warmth and closeness with other people. In supportive psychotherapy (with borderline and psychotic people), such activities may be useful at times, but these activities have other meanings and can be counterproductive.

EXAMPLE 1

Jeff, a 50-year-old tax attorney, had marital problems and anxiety. At work, he was known as "the fixer." He spent so much time solving others' problems at work, as well as his mother's problems, that his wife was threatening to move out.

After obtaining some of his traumatic childhood history, I showed him that he became overly independent and caring (pseudoindependence and pathological altruism) to guard against fears of being humiliated.⁸

In his second session, Jeff reported he had told his wife he had been distant from her because of embarrassment stemming from painful adolescent trauma. She responded favorably, they spent more time with each other, and for the first time in months they had sexual intercourse.

He revealed he had found my first book, *101 Defenses,* online and downloaded it onto his hand-held reader. He read me about pseudoindependence, which he thought fit his problems. I agreed.

He said he had a "great idea": I should put together a kit for married people who were too independent from each other. He would get this advertised as a self-help book and provide business and tax input. My response to this

---

7 Lewin (1955).
8 A. Freud (1936).

suggested boundary crossing (his offer to start a business with me) was first to acknowledge that he felt better and wanted to do something for me in return. His offer also seemed to be part of the "fixer" pattern, however (pathological altruism). Helping others through a book and helping me with income seemed to parallel behavior that had caused him to help others to the detriment of his relationship with his wife.

He saw this. I further explained how he positioned himself not to face his "need" for my help (just make a kit), similar to how he had avoided depending on unreliable people during his formative years. He concluded he needed to spend more time with his wife and less time on extra projects for others.

On follow-up a week later, Jeff reported that he and his wife planned a church ceremony to renew their marital vows. They would then take a second honeymoon for a month. We agreed that he had, as was his way, "fixed" the problem. When they returned, if he needed anything from me, he'd call.

If he calls, I may find out whether "fixing" his problems in a hurry relieved shame over relying on me further.

EXAMPLE 2

Angela, a 62-year-old married woman, suffered from depression and some deficits in self-image. She could not maintain friendships or closeness with her husband (a characteristic of borderline personality). She voiced suicidal thoughts but no plans. She avoided asking much about me; she was more comfortable knowing me as "just my doctor, with no life." Her reality testing was good enough to know that I had a life; she had heard of some of my activities in the community.

After 2 years of twice-a-week psychotherapy, she brought me a short story she had just had accepted for publication. Since she had been keeping distance from me for so long, I thought this indicated a (sublimated, although symbolic) gesture of closeness. I therefore accepted it without exploring any meanings of her act of giving it to me. I thought that Angela fell into a category of people who, when I attempted to explore the meaning of a gift (including inexpensive Christmas gifts or cards), had concretely experienced me as "spoiling" their meaningful gesture of emotional closeness. Rejected, they did not buy any explanations of transference.

I later read Angela's story, which I enjoyed, and told Angela so. She then recalled how her mother was never interested in anything she did. She now realized that her anger at her husband not only distanced her from him but was displaced from her mother. The symbolism in the story pertained to her conflicts.

Some analysts prefer to refuse and then try to understand the motives for any gift.[9] They try to understand why people might be upset if the therapist refuses it. The problem is that for some people, like Angela, a reality rejection would have been more difficult to understand as transference. Her pain would have occurred due to a reality where deprivation seemed unnecessary.

Adatto[10] commented ironically that accepting gifts caused problems for the therapist. What should we do with them? Put them on the refrigerator, frame them in the office, throw them out? And then what do we tell people we did?

---

9   Volkan (2011).
10 Dr. Adatto mentioned this conundrum during a class on dynamic psychotherapy at LSU medical school in 1974, when I was in training there.

Problem 33
Boundary Violations, Erotic and Erotized Transferences

Boundary violations are the most serious types of boundary crossings. You commonly see them in psychotic or psychopathic ("antisocial") people and/or therapists. "Lovesick" therapists are especially liable to sexual transgressions.[11]

I found in my limited experience consulting with (or about) therapists who engaged in sexual misconduct with people they treated that the therapists were defending against the concept of boundaries (rebellion against "authoritarian rules") or were grandiose and had no conscience.

SHORT ANSWER

If people you are treating "come on" to you—that is, make sexual overtures—first try to figure out what this means. They may be using sexualization (a common defense) to guard against shame over their wishes to depend on you.

They may also be a transferring onto you sexual wishes toward some figure in their past—or doing to you what abusive people had done to them. If people do not cooperate in understanding their "erotized transference," you will have to explain that there is a boundary that cannot be broken. If this does not help, you must discharge them from treatment and refer them to a colleague. This situation has occurred in my practice when I overestimated people's capacities for abstraction and integration during evaluation—often because of their intelligence and social skill.

The same principles apply if people attempt to destroy you (e.g., by demanding narcotics). Try to figure out and understand the meanings. They may be guarding against fears of closeness or may have shifted anger to you from violent parental figures ("aggressive transference"). If this is not enough, demand they desist from their destructive behavior. Finally, if they don't stop ("aggressivized transference"), refer them to someone else.

Either erotic or destructive approaches may be conscious manipulations by narcissistic psychopaths, who wish to exploit you; they are not treatable.[12]

---

11 Gabbard (1994b, 1996).
12 For an entertaining example of this genre, see the movie *Novocaine* (Adkins, 2001), where Steve Martin plays a dentist who is seduced by a psychopathic drug addict, played by Helena Bonham Carter.

LONG ANSWER

If you treat people long enough, they will become aware of both fond and angry feelings toward you. In short-term therapies, you may not see much of their reactions to you, since they are consulting you for a solution to a specific problem; once that problem is solved, that may be all they need in treatment (Problem 7).[13]

However, if you treat people twice a week or more frequently, or if you see them once a week for some period of time, they will develop reactions to you. Whether few,[14] some,[15] or all[16] of their reactions are due to defense and transference is a matter of considerable debate.

In my opinion, people's reactions to the therapist are based on the therapist's personality, degree of skill, timing and accuracy of interventions, transferences, and other defenses. The difficult task is to determine how much of each, which to mention, and when. So although it is expectable that people will have feelings about you, whether you can explain the meanings varies from person to person and from time to time.

There is a subset of people who develop either "erotic" and/or "erotized" reactions to you. Erotic transference refers to the phenomenon of people imagining being married to you, having your children, or just having sexual relations to you. Generally speaking, if they can use their self-observing capacities to think about the meanings of such thoughts, we call their reactions "erotic." If they concretely believe they are "in love with" you, and cannot or will not examine the unconscious bases for this, we call it "erotized."

EXAMPLE OF EROTIC TRANSFERENCE

Fran, a 43-year-old married woman, had resolved the sexual problems she had had with her husband and had agreed with me that we should wind down and finish her treatment. She was, however, reluctant to stop her psychoanalytic treatment because "Now that I have found a father that loves me, I don't want to leave you!" We pursued further understanding of the meanings of me as her "father." She recognized that she had continuing "father hunger":[17] a wish to be loved by her father. Her feelings toward me had been an "erotic" transference, where the symbolic meanings could be deciphered.

---

13 For an exception to this generalization, see Sifneos (1987).
14 Mitchell (2000).
15 Killingmo (1989).
16 Brenner (1982).
17 Herzog (1980).

EXAMPLE OF EROTIZED TRANSFERENCE

Jane, a 34-year-old divorced woman, decided after several months of treatment for depression that I was the only person in the world who understood her. We had understood that her (probably psychotic) mother saw her as worthless and that Jane had incorporated ("introjected") her mother's distortions.

During a session, Jane asked me to meet her later for "a drink." I pointed out (the "frame") that I was her therapist, and we should figure out why she wanted to break the barrier between us. Jane responded by complaining that I saw her as inferior, just as her mother had. I pointed out that Jane

1. was pressuring me to do something improper in breaking that boundary, similar to how her mother had treated her (identification with the aggressor);
2. was accusing me of seeing her as inferior, which represented
   a. Jane's criticism of her own self-image (split into loving and hateful elements; she projected the hateful part onto me, then criticized me) and
   b. a manipulation to make me feel guilty so I would do what she wanted.

Unfortunately, Jane could not see the identification (with the aggressor mother) or the transference (me as a controlling mother). She could not see how she split her own self-image and then projected one part onto me, nor could she see her (psychopathic) manipulation. She could not separate her wish to date me from the reality that I was her therapist. I therefore tried to refer her to a colleague.

At first, she argued with me about her treatability and suggested I tell her my problems in treating her. I pointed out how her approach was reminiscent of her mother's bizarre controls over her: Her mother used to examine her "bottom" after every bath until Jane reached puberty, to make sure it was "clean." I finally convinced her that she was not getting anything out of hating me for not dating her, and she accepted a referral.

Jane had developed an erotized transference to me, where reality testing and abstraction did not aid her self-observation and learning about herself.

Problem 34
People Who Berate or Verbally Attack You

People who suffer with depression and a variety of personality problems may eventually complain about you, your competence, and whether you are helping them.

Most of the time, personal affronts to you, your office staff, your office decorations, or your competence, reflect people

- seeing you as inadequate (projection of their inadequacy and devaluation);
- turning their criticisms (superego) onto you, as you represent their projections;
- shifting anger toward you from other people in their lives, past and/or present
    a. from a current relationship (called "displacement") and
    b. from a past relationship (called "transference"); and
- generalizing from a hated prior therapist onto a group (such as therapists).

SHORT ANSWER

Find the answer to the hostility people feel toward you. If you can't figure out where it is coming from and explain its irrational basis, refer them to someone else.

It is not usually a good idea to "contain" people berating you or criticizing you (see Problem 13); if unconfronted, people may believe their hostility to you has a real basis, become paranoid, and, in extreme situations, bring legal action against you.

LONG ANSWER

Some people express hostility toward you when you have not done anything to deserve it. We might call these reactions "hostile-aggressive" (if you can understand them) or "hostile-aggressivized" transference (if you can't).

EXAMPLE OF HOSTILE-AGGRESSIVE TRANSFERENCE

Fred, a 39-year-old hospital administrator who suffered with inhibitions at work and around women, realized he needed analysis to figure these problems out. During treatment, he averred that psychoanalysis was not "evidenced based." Contrarily, he had read studies showing that analysis might help. After about a year of working together, he presented the following dream:

"I am being kidnapped and the woman with me is screaming. There is a Black man who is threatening to shoot her and me."

Fred thought about his recent visit to his widowed father. He felt guilty over a wish that his father would die, so Fred could be free. When I suggested that the "Black man" in the dream might represent me (because of my surname), he laughed. He recalled being afraid he would be in treatment forever. That would be his punishment for hating his father.

I said I suspected he wished his father had died instead of his beloved mother, a thought that caused him guilt—this possibly was represented in the dream where the man threatened to kill Fred for preferring his mother (represented by the woman in the dream). Fred said that was "an interesting idea—my Oedipus complex?" He then recalled feeling "bad" because he was "envious" of my success. He wondered if anyone had ever "taken [me]...down a notch."

I connected those thoughts with his argument about the supposed unprovability of psychoanalysis and connected the argument to feelings he experienced toward his father as a child. Fred recalled how he had believed his father beating him as a child was normal; but now Fred felt angry at his father. I agreed, and showed him that his devaluation of my "treatment" of him with psychoanalysis was symbolic of his father's "treatment" of him as a child—against which he could not voice his criticisms.[18]

Fred understood his transferred hostility and defenses, and he overcame his inhibitions both at work and with women.

EXAMPLE OF HOSTILE-AGGRESSIVIZED TRANSFERENCE

Jim, a 27-year-old corporate attorney, was referred by his cardiologist after a workup found sinus tachycardia (normal heart beat, but too fast) possibly brought on by "stress."

Jim showed up at my office 15 minutes late, jumpy, agitated, and speaking fast. He admitted he had been snorting cocaine and told me he was

---
18   See Volkan (2009) for a similar case.

not going to quit. He had not told his cardiologist about the drug abuse. I first commented that since he was an attorney, he must know what he was doing was illegal. He didn't care. He wanted me to prescribe narcotics for his "chest pain."

I got more history from him, which included his being fired from several jobs. He thought they were all "unfair," and could not imagine, as I suggested, that they had noticed his agitation. Jim had a girlfriend whom he was "using" for sex. He had not been caught by the police for his drug abuse, yet. All told, he seemed narcissistic and at least somewhat psychopathic. He would not sign a release so I could speak to his cardiologist.

Both of his parents were physicians whom he described as very "nosy" about his personal habits and critical of his drug abuse. I told him I thought his breaking the law represented an attempt to separate from his parents. I also told him he knew his wish for me to prescribe narcotics was a hostile manipulation of me; I would not consider it. He responded that my explanations were "aggressive" and disagreed with me. He said he would not pay me if I did not prescribe narcotics for him. I told him he need not pay me. He got up and left.

In Jim's case, we could not understand his denial or his hostility. Analysts are prone to term this phenomenon an "unanalyzable hostile-aggressivized transference." He could not utilize abstraction and integration for resolution of his resistances to treatment. He seemed concrete. His insistence on pursuing unlawful activity (superego defect) also militated against him being treatable.

Problem 35
"Acter-Outers," or Impulsive People

The term *acting out* has a long history. We will use its common 21st-century meaning: acting on impulses without thinking. If the impulses are displaced from some other situation and have significance, we might use the term *symptomatic behavior*.[19] The usual problematic wishes involved in impulsive behavior are oral (eating or depending), sexual, and hostile-aggressive. We see them in obesity, sexual addiction, philandering, destructive temper outbursts, and self-destructiveness (such as cutting).

Some impulse disorders are so severe that people need to be hospitalized to stop them from acting on the impulses. This is necessary when people cannot mentalize, that is, understand that the impulse is pathological (self-destructive), or when they cannot contain it between sessions (deficit in impulse control).

SHORT ANSWER

When people know they have a problem and are self-motivated, the prognosis is better than when they deny the problem. In cases where people are concerned about their impulsivity, so-called Step 1,[20] that is, confronting their denial, is not necessary.

If you can get enough information about people's current conflicts, you can piece together the reasons for the impulsive activity—usually, defense, pleasure, and self-punishment (to relieve guilt). You can discuss those reasons with them. Be careful not to become their superego, where you tell them to control themselves—when you do that (supportively), they may see you as their conscience (externalization). Then they behave like they have no conscience at all; they "act out" their impulses and wait for you (now

> **TIP**
> Be careful not to "become" people's conscience (superego), where you start telling them to control themselves; when you try that supportive technique, they may feel like you are their conscience (externalization). Then they often behave like they have no conscience at all; they will "act out" their impulses and wait for you (now representing their conscience) to criticize them. (Many teenagers do this with their parents). See Johnson & Szurek, (1952.)

---

19 A. J. Sanchez (1976), personal communication. In other words "acting out," like most other mentally based phenomena, is a compromise formation.
20 AA's recommendation.

representing their conscience) to criticize them.[21] It is also helpful to express some understanding of their struggles with the impulses.

LONG ANSWER

People who eat, smoke, drink, and sometimes talk too much are acting out what analysts call "oral" impulses—they all involve the mouth and are pleasurable. Persistent orality is often seen in people who are morbidly obese.

EXAMPLE OF ORAL IMPULSIVITY

Patricia, a 53-year-old married woman, consulted me for overeating. She was feeling neglected by her husband, an entrepreneur who frequently worked late and traveled. Eating acted as a substitute for (defense against depressive affect over losing) his attention.

She noticed that she "pigged out" on foods she disliked; we understood that she was also punishing herself for some reason. She thought she felt guilty about imagining having an affair and about masturbating. She joked that she was "better at eating than at masturbating." In other words, Patricia used orality to avoid anger at her husband and to repress (and punish herself for) sexual wishes toward other men.

On completing 2 years of twice-a-week psychotherapy, Patricia had lost quite a bit of weight and discussed various difficulties with her husband. About a decade later, she called to say she was divorced, but that she had developed a good relationship with a different man.

In Patricia's case, overeating had had many meanings: pleasurable, defensive, and self-punitive.

EXAMPLE OF SEXUAL AND HOSTILE-DESTRUCTIVE IMPULSIVITY

Albert, a 42-year-old founder of a computer programming firm, was drinking too much and cheating on his wife. He felt guilty about both but could not stop either. He had also once hit his wife while drunk; this caused him consternation and fear of himself.

Albert had problems with oral (drinking), sexual (philandering), and hostile-destructive impulses (hitting). In his work, however, he was affable,

---

21 Many teenagers do this with their parents. See Johnson and Szurek (1952).

successful, and even honored for his contributions. In other words, he did not have impulse control problems "across the board." Also, his superego seemed more or less intact (he felt guilty), though it did not stop the impulsive behavior.

As is usual in the real world, his case turned out to be rather complicated. His wife also drank too much. When he "pushed" her, it was midnight, and they were both drunk. She had insulted him and rejected his sexual advances. She then went out on their deck, which overlooked water, stripped naked, and began to sing and dance to loud music. When he tried to stop her, she resisted, and he pushed her back in the house. She pouted and refused to have sex with him.

You might think that her rejecting him had caused him to philander, but actually, he had cheated on her since their courtship. I tentatively formulated that she might, in some way, realize he was unfaithful—one cause for her apparent misbehavior (she also acted out).

I pointed out to Albert that behaving as though he was single might be behind their altercations. He wanted to save the marriage and not hurt their two school-age children, so I encouraged him to think about why he did not stop the extramarital affairs, discuss with his wife his sensitivity to her withdrawal from him, quit drinking, stop his wife from drinking, and avoid buying alcohol.

Albert agreed to try. I expressed understanding that stopping these activities would be painful but suggested that if he desisted from any of these activities we could figure out what he was avoiding, what gratification he got, and how he was punishing himself.

In other words, Albert and I had to agree, first, on his ideals and goals, not mine. He wanted control over his various impulses. This set up the working alliance—and allowed us to understand how he wanted me to be his conscience (externalization). When he misbehaved and then expected me to criticize or stop him, we learned he tried to rid himself of guilt.

When I expressed understanding that controlling his urges was difficult, Albert felt I had more "empathy" for his weakness. He worked with me first in twice-a-week therapy for a couple of years then in psychoanalysis (four times a week using the couch) for another few years. We came to understand that his extramarital sexual behavior had many meanings: repairing poor self-esteem; displacing anger from girls who had rejected him in high school; identification with his alcoholic father; behavioral reversal of his castration anxiety.

Eventually, he only had a glass of wine once or twice a year (he insisted he did not want to give up social drinking completely). Around the time he stopped philandering, he noticed his wife was "staying late at work." She eventually admitted she had been having an affair for a couple of years, and was not sure she wanted to give up the affair or her drinking. She voiced, nevertheless, a wish to work things out regarding the marriage, and requested marital therapy. He agreed, and asked me for a referral.

In Albert's situation, we understood the following:

- Drinking had been relieving depressive affect regarding his wife's rejection of him and her exhibitionism.
- He created "distance" emotionally by drinking and philandering.
- When his wife punished him, he felt less nervous about closeness and less guilty about cheating on her (which included a wish to hurt her).

In other words, Albert's impulsivity had many meanings. As these were understood, he ceased acting out; he was then faced with his wife's acting out and the sad state of their marriage.

> **CAVEAT**
> When people come to see you, they have generally exhausted other means of solving their problems. For this reason, their lives are often in a terrible mess. What can be done therapeutically in such situations is quite variable.

Albert and his wife did stay together, no one went to jail, and they eventually ceased cheating and cut back their drinking. Their children, later, also needed psychological treatment.

Problem 36
Those Who Get to Understandings of Themselves Before You Do

After developing understandings of themselves, many people who have been in therapy for some period of time can reflect on their thoughts without much help. Sometimes this indicates that people have developed excellent self-observing capacities.

They have often developed what I call "signal defense": awareness of using defenses that were confronted during treatment. They put together new-found insights. Other people, however, use "pseudointerpretation" of an intellectual nature,[22] which essentially maintains distance from and unconsciously competes with the therapist.

SHORT ANSWER

When people figure out the meanings of their behavior before you do (or, in another variation, present you their diagnoses), take their discoveries seriously. Acknowledging their efforts to understand themselves is necessary. Sometimes they will have figured out important conflicts in their lives but need further help in elucidating the ramifications of these conflicts. You need only interject a comment, suggest a trend, or question vague areas they are discussing. In my experience, this is a relatively rare type of person, but I have treated some people like this.

On the other hand, if you are being "boxed out," where people jump to intellectual conclusions and leave you out, you must suspect they are avoiding something (defensive activity). Gently, acknowledging their attempts, I bring to their attention that although they are making some connections they are taking over the process. This excludes me—and perhaps thereby relieves fear about me getting into their private thoughts.

Often, people admit they were consciously aware of mistrusting me, so they kept distance by working alone. They were using me as a prop: "a partial person that I can bounce things off of." They were afraid to get to know me as a human being for fear that I would turn on them or turn into somebody they didn't like. I could then discuss their distancing mechanisms and "as if" playacting (transference).

---

22 Glover (1931).

LONG ANSWER

Obsessive-compulsive people tend to have conflicts with hostile-aggression. These conflicts are unknown to them; they see themselves as cooperative, intellectual, and motivated toward understanding themselves. These are difficult character problems to treat, since it is so nice, as a therapist, to work with people who are motivated and serious in their attempts to understand themselves.

EXAMPLE

Evelyn, a woman in her early 40s, was having difficulty in relationships with men. Her judgment was fairly good, but often the relationships did not work out in the long run. When she got into any relationship with a man, regardless of his personality, she would begin to doubt herself. She would begin to doubt him. She would pick on minor idiosyncrasies in the man's personality and then try to draw major conclusions from minor observations.

As she got older, and her nitpicking complaints about more functional men had led to the loss of several relationships, she developed the opposite problem: When she was dating a man who had major problems, she would minimize these and hold onto him.

By the time she got to see me, Evelyn was at least moderately depressed about her failures in these relationships, and lonely. At that point, she was holding onto men who were either financially in the doldrums, lacked capacity for stability in relationships, or avoided her after sexual intercourse. Nevertheless, she would make half-hearted attempts to keep contact with them because she was desperate not to be alone. She would then criticize herself for her desperation, connect this with her conflicts with her father and his obsessional tendencies, and verbalize to me that she thought perhaps she was punishing herself because she had hostility toward her father. Consequently, she would hold onto some unworthy man in a "transference way."

> **TIP**
> People who do their own interpreting may be avoiding closeness with the therapist.

Her telling me all this usually did no good. She would continue to cling to the man anyway. My impression was that she was intellectualizing, thereby avoiding conflicts that involved control and loss. Whether she was nitpicking or being "too nice and understanding," these (anal) mechanisms protected her from loss.

After listening to many of her thoughts that fit this pattern, I finally said to Evelyn, "I think we have to face the fact that you will hold onto a piece of shit as long as it is warm."

This first shocked her; then she began laughing. She understood immediately that she was using men whom she considered "shitty," keeping them around, just to relieve her ("cold") loneliness. She commented that making her laugh was a good thing. She felt warmer and somewhat friendlier with me.

I had decided to make a more explicit, drive-related confrontation because Evelyn was so busy obsessing, using intellectualization, rationalization, and even introspection[23] to avoid closeness with me and with other men. She certainly could get to particular understandings before I did, but her attempted "interpretations" were intellectual and allowed her to maintain ambivalent ties to me and other men. In other words, she maintained a tie at the same time that she constructed a barrier against emotional closeness.

---

23 Kohut (1959).

Problem 37
People Who Ask You to Hug Them or Want to Hug You

This is a remarkably common request from people in treatment. It is surprising how often this comes up and how frequently therapists see it as innocuous. In my opinion, people who want you to hug them are "acting in"; there is nothing innocuous about it. Responding to their request with any sort of physical contact is a mistake in technique. Hugging exacerbates erotic transferences in the person you are treating, blurs boundaries of the therapeutic barrier, and causes emotional havoc in the person.

Some literature[24] debates the pros and cons of offering physical soothing to people who are overwhelmed. Some therapists feel that holding a crying person's hand or embracing them gently can be helpful. I disagree with this approach (as does Dr. Good), because I believe touching people you are treating always has a negative impact, whether you want it to or not.

> **TIP**
> Touching or hugging people in treatment is almost never innocuous. Don't do it.

Sometimes, simple displays of affection lead to more physical activity.[25] Even if therapists do not have overt (conscious) sexual wishes toward the person they are treating, they may be vulnerable to getting involved with that person sexually.[26] Later, after those therapists are disciplined and wind up in treatment, they express chagrin, mortification, self-criticism, and amazement that they let themselves go too far.

So what do you do when a person you are treating asks you, at any time in the treatment (frequently at the end of a session), if they can have a hug?

SHORT ANSWER

The easiest way to handle this request is to tell people that their wish to touch or hug you means they feel positively toward you. Most people are aware of

---
24 Good (2010).
25 Gutheil and Gabbard (1993).
26 Celenza (2006).

this, and when you say it they will agree. They may argue, "What's the harm? It's just a hug."[27]

At that point, you can explain that they don't seem to be aware of wishes to break their agreement with you—thereby breaking the therapeutic barrier.[28] This brief explanation will usually bring to people's attention that they are doing something destructive. The usual response I have seen, particularly from women, is something like, "Oh! I'm sorry. I didn't mean to do that. I just was feeling grateful." I can then acknowledge their warm feelings but suggest that we discuss them.

I have also sometimes mentioned that they do not have to touch me for me to realize that they felt grateful or appreciative. We often find that their wish for physical contact guarded them from sadness about their mothers being cold to them or their fathers having abused them (hugging as a defense against remembering).

LONG ANSWER

There is probably one exception that I can think of to the usual rule against touching or hugging people. I have experienced this twice in my life, where, after treating a woman for some years, we have come to an end in therapy. She has been relieved of phobias, sexual inhibitions, compulsions, anxiety attacks, and/or inhibitions of aggression, and is feeling much better. We finally chose an end date, and understood the various meanings of her finishing treatment with me (the "termination phase").[29]

The woman was feeling grateful. As I walked to the door with her for the last time, she opened the door, then turned around suddenly and gave me a quick hug. Since it was at the end of treatment, and I was not going to see her again, I did not try to make anything of it. The hug lasted just a few seconds, I patted her on the shoulder, and she said thank you. I told her, "You're welcome," to be courteous, and that was the end of it.

As I mentioned, both of the people who did this with me were women. In retrospect, I have considered that there may have been some unresolved

---

27   Years ago, as a member of an ethics committee for a professional organization, I heard a complaint against a colleague from a woman who said he had hugged her while she was an inpatient in a psychiatric hospital, with the nurses watching. The (female) nurses reported that the woman had actually hugged the therapist, who at the time was too surprised and flustered to say anything or evade physical contact with her. The therapist who was accused was innocent, but he still suffered considerable humiliation in having to explain himself to the committee.
28   Tarachow (1963).
29   Firestein (2001).

issues that may not have been understood, possibly unresolved mother and father transferences. On the other hand, I considered that in Western civilization, many women hug each other and hug friends in a relatively nonsexualized way when they feel happy to see them or are grateful about something.

Keeping this in mind, I thought it inappropriate to make a fuss about those two quick hugs. I do not, however, encourage this activity. As I have gotten older, I tend to keep at least 4 or 5 feet away from females who are leaving my office, just to prevent them from suddenly embracing me.

Some female therapists I have supervised opined that a woman who expresses affection, hugs them, or requests a hug, is not breaching anything. They see it as a "natural" form of affection from the person they are treating. However, I have often heard about this after these therapists have had some difficulty with the case and called me for supervision.

EXAMPLE

Teri, a woman therapist, had been treating Lily, a 51-year-old divorced, lonely woman. At the end of the third session, when Lily left, she said to Teri, "Can I have a hug?" Teri allowed this briefly. However, Lily also requested this after the fourth and fifth session, and although Teri allowed the hug again, she was feeling progressively more uncomfortable about it.

One day at around 5:30 p.m., when Teri left her office, she noticed Lily standing in the parking lot, and nodded to her. Lily waved at her. When Teri drove home and pulled into her driveway, she stopped for a moment and looked in the rearview mirror. There was Lily. Teri got out of her car and asked Lily, "What are you doing?" Lily answered, "Well, I thought we were friends, so I might come over and maybe have a cup of coffee with you."

Teri knew there was trouble. She told Lily that this was not possible, and that she would only see her in the office. Lily started crying, said, "I know I'm a bad person," and impulsively yanked open the door of her car. At this point, Teri became terrified that Lily would kill herself driving, so she went over to Lily's car, insisted that Lily roll down the window, and talked to her for a couple of minutes. Lily did so. Teri reassured her that she liked her, but that this was a boundary problem they must talk about. She was able to calm Lily down, but Teri, herself, was quite stirred up.

During supervision, Teri discussed with me how she had minimized hugging. She had been trained in a program where hugging was condoned, but she now questioned the wisdom of this. She would never let men hug her this way because it would be too sexual, but she had denied that hugging could be problematic with women in treatment.

I advised Teri to tell Lily that Lily's wish for a hug seemed significant, representing, possibly, Lily's wishes for soothing. Teri could acknowledge Lily's loneliness, and encourage Lily to make friends with others.

Further, I suggested Teri discuss the unresolved problems arising from Lily's relationship with her ex-husband that were causing Lily to avoid any contacts with men.

Teri came back to see me a week later. She reported that limit-setting along with discussion of Lily's displacements onto Teri of unrequited wishes toward her ex-husband were useful. Lily remembered how frustrated she had always been with her ex-husband's refusal to be physically affectionate or verbally interactive.

Lily now generalized that all men were dangerous and cold; she had therefore refused a number of dates. Lily had been acting on her wish for warmth by hugging Teri (who seemed "safe"), because of her distorted thought that all men are cold (generalization).[30] Generalization of her anger to include all men had prevented Lily from facing her rage and disappointment with her ex-husband; she also avoided criticism of herself for mistakenly marrying him.

---

30 Loeb (1982).

Problem 38
People Who Try to Undress in Front of You or Attempt to Seduce You During a Session; Also, People Who Touch You

All of these behaviors are connected, although, clearly, touching is less egregious than undressing in front of you or inviting you into sexual activity during a session. During my fairly lengthy career, I can think of only three or four women who acted this way in my office, and one gay man; supervisees have occasionally reported this.

What should be your technique if someone tries to undress in front of you, invites you to have sex, or touches you on the way in or out of your office?

SHORT ANSWER

The main solution to the problem of undressing, first, is that you must forcefully stop the behavior by telling the person to cut it out. If they refuse to stop, open the door to your office and walk out into the waiting room. You tell them to stop undressing; you leave your consultation room until they are dressed and willing to speak with you about it. In the case of people who touch you on the way out, it's a good idea to indicate to them at the time that this is unwelcome, and to discuss this with them at the beginning of the following session, no matter what else is going on.

Interestingly, these types of "acting in" are not limited to females with male therapists but include occasional instances of males in treatment with female therapists and men or women who wish to seduce a therapist of the same gender.

When someone undresses, the break in the frame of the treatment is severe. In my opinion, it is impossible to treat people who insist on doing this. Treatment involves discussing and resolving conflicts, both internal and external. It has nothing to do with people taking off their clothes or having sexual relations with their therapist.

> **TIP**
> Sexually inappropriate behavior in a therapist's office is dangerous to the therapist and to the person in treatment. It must be stopped immediately. If the therapist cannot successfully impart understanding in subsequent sessions as to what the behavior meant and why it is unacceptable, the person will need to be referred to a different therapist.

EXAMPLE 1

Some years ago, Caleb, a psychiatry resident, presented his case of Zena, who insisted he have sex with her. He told her he was her doctor, that he was married and had children, and was not available. Zena argued that he was depriving her. He did not know what to do with this.

When he discussed the problem in a class of residents, I explained that Zena had developed a psychotic transference, so he should refer her to someone else on the staff. He said he had tried to do that, but she began taking off her clothes, telling him she felt unlovable and might kill herself if he didn't have sex with her. I pointed out the dangerousness of the situation and suggested that if Zena threatened suicide again, he should hospitalize her.

Caleb told me later that his therapy supervisor advised him to try to "stick it out" and become even firmer in denying her wishes. He suffered in this "therapy" until he finished his residency over a year later and then told her that he did not have time to work with her anymore. She did accept referral to another person, this time a woman therapist.

For several years after this, Zena "acted out" her anger toward Caleb for "rejecting" her by calling in anonymous bomb threats to the hospital. Actually, nobody could ever be sure that it was Zena, but sometimes she mentioned Caleb's name when she called, and Caleb was fairly sure Zena was the caller. Each time she did this, large numbers of people had to vacate the hospital, including inpatients, therapists, and other faculty members. The hospital had to be cleared, which often took an hour.

After several years, the bomb threats finally subsided.

So the short answer is that if people do not stop their seduction, and you cannot help them understand what they are doing, it is best to refer them to someone else.

LONG ANSWER

Usually, after you tell people to stop undressing or touching you (and that they must desist from it immediately), they stop. At that point, if they have enough abstraction ability and integrative capacity, it is usually a good idea to try to understand what their undressing in front of you (or touching you or being seductive with you) meant.

In the case of touching, commonly when a woman touches a woman therapist, this indicates the woman does not feel enough closeness with the woman therapist; touching her relieves frustration, disappointment, and sometimes anger (i.e., touching is a defense as well as a pleasure). You can explain these meanings to the person in treatment.

When a man in treatment with a woman therapist touches her on the way out (more threatening), it is useful for the therapist to tell him, immediately, that this is inappropriate and must be discussed in the following session.

EXAMPLE 2

Ursula told me in supervision that Will, a man she was treating, patted her on the shoulder as he left her office. She felt controlled and nervous, although Will apparently had touched her in a "friendly" way.

I advised Ursula to tell Will this was inappropriate, unwelcome, and that he must promise not to do it again; she should point out that he was breaking a barrier, and, possibly without realizing it, exerting some sort of control over her.

I also suggested she explain that what he saw as "friendly" was hiding his conflicts about coercing women into a position where he was in control.

Ursula reported in her following supervisory session that she had successfully linked Will's behavior to how he had felt controlled by his mother throughout his life, and then by both of his wives.

After these clarifications, he said to her, "I guess the worm had turned." In other words, he had developed anxiety about Ursula (another woman in his life that he cared about). He had been afraid she would coerce him, criticize him, and otherwise emasculate him. Touching her was a way he took control and scared her; but he rationalized this as just "friendly" (unconscious defenses). He later saw that the way he handled his wives had led to the demise of the marriages.

EXAMPLE 3

Lynn, a schizophrenic 22-year-old woman, described a lot of pain in her legs. She then pulled up her skirt and jumped up on the desk in my office, did a split, and started removing her skirt. Shocked, I told her to get off of my desk and put her clothes back on. I opened the door to my office, and as I walked out, told her I would come back in a minute after she was dressed.

When I came back, she had put her skirt back on and was putting on her shoes. She said, "I'm sorry. I was just trying to show you what happens when I do a split. My legs get all sore. I told you I'm a ballet dancer." I acknowledged her attempt to communicate with me, but told her it was too sexual and inappropriate and she was not to do that again. She again apologized. I completed the evaluation and referred her to the clinic.

EXAMPLE 4

Vera, 38 years old, complained of pain in her breasts during her evaluation session with me. I was listening, trying to understand the problem, when she quickly slipped off her blouse. I showed my surprise, told her she could not do that, and insisted, in a loud voice, that she put her top back on.

She laughed, argued that she was just trying to show me the problem with her breasts, and was about to take off her bra when I raised my voice even more strenuously. She became contrite, said she was sorry, and put her top back on. Again, she rationalized that she was just trying to show me the problem.

I told her she was using huge amounts of denial not to recognize that what she was doing had a sexual meaning, and added that the denial might explain her confusion about why men came on to her sexually. She then remembered a horrific experience of being date-raped in college. At the time, after she had shown her date a mole on her breast, he pushed her into anal intercourse.

EXAMPLE 5

Hastings, a gay man I treated for depression and alcohol abuse, raised a question about having sex with me. I pointed out to him that this wish to change our relationship represented his desire to relieve some sort of anxiety and to get control over me.

He claimed he just wanted to have sex with me "for fun." I insisted that his wish had multiple meanings. These included

- hidden violent urges toward his father, which had become sexualized, and
- hidden competition and violent feelings toward other men, which he also sexualized.

He then reported how he had been beating up his gay lover. Although his gay lover was a masochist (who "wanted to be hurt"), Hastings had overdone it many times, and his lover threatened to leave if Hastings continued to hurt him.

As we connected Hastings's behavior toward his lover with his attempted seduction of me, we understood that he hid, in his playfulness, anger at his mother and father because of their traumatic mistreatment of him.

Problem 39
People Who Talk to Your Secretary

Many therapists do not have a secretary, or if they are in groups, they share a receptionist or secretary.

I am in solo practice, and I have my office set up in such a way that when people enter, they walk into my secretary/office manager's work area. (See the diagram at the back of the book, p. 380.)

The waiting room is a separate room to her right with a door that closes behind people after they enter. A short hallway to the side of the waiting room leads to my consultation room. People walking in will see my office manager before they walk into the waiting room. People coming out of my office will see my office manager as they exit the office suite.

My office manager has many responsibilities, including dealing with vendors, maintaining office supplies and inventory, typing up evaluations I have dictated (and books), transcribing independent psychiatric examinations for different agencies or attorneys, and handling financial matters.

In other words, she is busy, but her duties generally do not involve direct communications with the people I treat. When people come into the office suite for the first time, she will indicate where the waiting room is, point out the coffee pot if they would like a cup of coffee, and usually indicate to them that I will be with them shortly. If I am running a bit late, I may ask her to tell people that. When people leave my office, they will pass by her again. If she is not busy, they may say good-bye to her.

My feeling is that when people have a brief, social interaction with her, this is normal. I have not instructed her to ignore the people who come to my office. She is courteous and very professional in responding to their interactions, without being excessively friendly or personal.

Every once in a while, my office manager reports that someone has stopped to talk with her about something that is not administrative. One man, for example, apparently chatted with her about their mutual interest in bird watching. A few people have been interested in whether she was married to me (she is not) and have subtly fished around in talking to her to find this out.

What should you do when a person you are treating stops to have a conversation with a member of your office staff?

SHORT ANSWER

In general, ignore this. Most staff members working in a mental health practitioner's office know that they should not engage in prolonged personal conversations with people you are treating. (This should be part of their training, when hired, along with a discussion of the strict confidentiality obligations that apply to the job.) I have asked my office manager to explain to people that if they have any questions about fees, treatment, or appointment times, they should speak with me. Issues about the "frame" of the therapy can become fertile ground for understanding.

LONG ANSWER

Occasionally, someone stopping to talk with a secretary is more meaningful. At least one man, whom I treated for a number of years, began to see the office as a new family, and very warmly chatted with my secretary for a few minutes while he was getting a cup of coffee. He would then wait in the waiting room. After his session, as he left, I noticed he would say a warm good-bye to her, and she would respond in kind. It was my impression that these simple interactions were gratifying to him, and I did not attempt to interfere with them. I could see that he felt comfortable in my office, respected my office manager and me, and his positive feelings about this reflected his positive response to his therapeutic work.

On the other hand, in certain instances, people I am evaluating for the first time may say something strange to my office manager. In these cases, I have asked her to let me know what those "strange" things might be, and this has taken a lot of pressure off of her. It also gives me an idea about psychopathology.

EXAMPLE

Belinda called my office for directions. My office manager had already given Belinda directions; but Belinda called a half dozen times because she couldn't get the directions correct. Belinda then blamed my office manager for not being clear.

Belinda's use of projective blaming, her disorganization, and her possible disorientation alerted me to the possibility of serious psychopathology. When I evaluated Belinda, I did a thorough mental status, looking for signs of brain deterioration or other organicity. Interestingly, I didn't find any. Belinda was socially appropriate but extraordinarily disorganized. She jumped from one subject to another without realizing it, and could not evaluate other people's responses to her. These and other data pointed to a diagnosis of schizophrenia.

Finally, a subset of people linger to speak with my secretary after their sessions. This behavior disturbs the confidential setup of my office, since the next person I see will pass by my secretary (and the lingering person) on the way to my consultation room. I usually bring up this behavior in the lingerer's next session. In one case, the person was oblivious to the confidentiality issue and disliked leaving my office. In another case, the person was surreptitiously acting out a wish to see others I was treating.

Problem 40
People Who Date Your Secretary

This has only happened to me once in my life, decades ago, but it was instructive. I had not known about the affair for several months. Steven, a male law student I was treating in psychoanalysis, had not told me anything about it at first.

At the time, I thought my half-time secretary was married, but it turned out that she had separated from her husband several months previously. Apparently, Steven arrived early for his appointments so he could chat with her. She was lonely, and he was frustrated. He had eventually asked her out.

At the time that he told me about their affair, I was astounded and not sure what to do about it. Then and since, I have reflected on that incident. Here's what I think.

ANSWER

When someone starts dating your secretary, they attack the working alliance[31] and break the frame (see Section E) of treatment. Steven's sexual relationship with my secretary put me in a peculiar position. Steven deserved confidentiality in the sense of me not speaking about him to anyone else, including my secretary. As a member of my office staff, however, she might be privy to some information about him.

Another problem was that, in a way, it was none of my business what the two of them, as consenting adults, did with each other. Contrarily, I thought his getting involved with her had very profound meanings, and I thought these should be examined.

Fortunately for me, a few days after I heard about this from him, my secretary approached me and explained that she needed to stop working for me. She said she had secured a full-time job with benefits, which she now needed due to her divorce. I sympathetically accepted her resignation.

Interestingly, she volunteered, "Women get a raw deal." What she meant was that, at age 35, she had not had children because she and her then husband had put it off. Some months prior, she had found out that her husband was cheating on her, and they had separated. At this point, she was afraid she would never have children. She cried as she bemoaned the advent of feminism, which she angrily said had "duped" her. I found her self-recriminations

---

31 Greenson (1972).

and societal blaming curious, and wondered if some of these complaints were connected with her affair with Steven, which she did not mention. I simply expressed understanding and wished her the best.

With Steven, who had already "confessed" about their sexual relationship, I suggested that he tell me his thoughts about dating my secretary. When he said he just found her attractive, I told him I thought his relationship with her was uncannily similar to his relationship with his mother.

He and his mother had taken frequent trips together, many times a year, without his father, to visit his mother's friends around the world. He now reported that as he got into his middle adolescence, he had had sexual relationships with a number of his mother's women friends. He had always felt peculiar about this.

We were eventually able to link this up with his "acting out" of a wish to steal my wife (symbolized by my secretary) from me.[32] He had not told me about the affair at the beginning because he had been afraid I would punish him. Breaking the boundary with my secretary repeated a wish he had had in childhood to steal his mother from his father, which he had acted out by having sexual liaisons with several of his mother's friends. Similarly, he did not go after my wife, but "competed with me" (figuratively, at least) by seducing my secretary.

Soon after my secretary quit, interestingly enough, they stopped dating. I wondered if she were no longer interesting to him because she wasn't connected to me in some way; but Steven reported that she had started dating her new boss, and he felt betrayed. She told him she needed a man who was established and could commit.

Steven's guilt about oedipal victory had been hidden from him. He at first seemed to feel entitled to choose an "older woman." I was able to show him that he was "acting out" many elements of his feelings of victory over his father: seducing "older" women who were associated with male authority figures, like my secretary, but then suffering punishment by not committing to her and by sloughing off in school. This pattern also replayed many years of social promotions he had received at school; he had gotten away with traveling around the world with his mother.

After we understood these meanings, Steven did better in school and became more responsible in his dating approach.

---

32 This was his fantasy. I was not married at the time.

Problem 41
Enactors: "Actor-in-ers"

There are people who insist on "getting into it" with you, the therapist.[33] They engage in what Sanchez called "symptomatic behavior." They usually do this in their lives outside of treatment, as well.[34]

An entire section of this book is devoted to different types of acting in. This chapter will focus on people for whom action is the main method of communication. Understanding their various actions with you becomes one of the major routes to understanding the complexity of their problems.

SHORT ANSWER

When you see people behaving (or misbehaving) with you in a persistent way, it's a good idea to bring the pattern of behavior to their attention. Their behavior, generally speaking, is laden with meaning, but the meanings are very difficult to decipher.

Nevertheless, the first order of business is to make the pattern of action conscious to them. After you and they agree that their behavior must mean something, the next step is to try to find ways their behavior protects them from knowing something about themselves (the defensive meaning).

EXAMPLE 1

Gus, a 53-year-old accountant, consulted me because he and his wife were arguing all the time over nothing. They had gotten married when he was 21 and she was 20 and had one child when he was 23. That child was now working and doing well. Their empty nest had proven to be problematic. He had a number of complaints about his wife and she had a number of complaints about him. These ranged from cleanliness to punctuality to paying attention to each other to differences about wishes for sexual activity.

I began seeing Gus twice a week. We agreed that I would bill him monthly and that he would pay me within 15 days. He was not using insurance.

I began to notice a pattern. He forgot what we talked about in prior sessions. He often went on "guys' holidays" with his buddies from college. He then was 2 weeks late in getting me a check for his third month of treatment.

---
33 Paniagua (1997, 1998).
34 Andrew Sanchez described this during his supervision of my work in 1975.

I brought to his attention that he had agreed to my billing policy. However, we could see that, in his behavior, he acted on rebellious, hostile, anti-authoritarian wishes without thinking about them. Gus had lots of excuses (the defense of rationalization) about why it was hard to get me a check on time; these excuses relieved him of guilt about his wish to "stick it" to me, which he finally admitted.

With some humor, he recalled how, when he had worked for the IRS, he had played the role of humble investigator. When he audited large businesses or firms, he would let the grandiose leaders of those firms "pontificate" or criticize him. After he had gone through all of the records, however, he would get his chance to "stick it" to them. He took particular joy in this.

His thoughts about this pattern of behavior included his relationship with his wife, where he would passively do whatever she asked him and then "stick it" to her by forgetting something important or by dragging something out. Invariably she became angry with him; thereby he got punished, which relieved his guilt.

On occasion he brought a large bottle of mineral water to his session. When I brought this to his attention, the bottle had all sorts of meanings regarding who was going to take care of whom, his sense of autonomy (by not needing me), and a regressive preoccupation about "purified" water, with symbolic elaborations about dissolving his destructiveness.

On another occasion, he took off his shoes, and commented to me that his feet were stinky. This also was loaded with meaning, most of it hostile.

In other words, Gus was a person who substituted action for verbalization. After a couple of years of treatment, we could understand more fully that one of the main reasons he engaged in these symbolic activities was that he could never get his mother's attention by talking to her. However, if he misbehaved or if he was "obedient" she would recognize and comment on his behavior.

He had been raised in a household where his mother was preoccupied with his behavior. Affection, understanding, support, and discipline were relatively absent. There had been a lack of verbal interchange between him and both of his parents. Action became highly symbolic, and had plagued him throughout his life.

LONG ANSWER

Symbolic behavior can have various causes. One of the meanings of Gus's behavior was a symbolic representation of wishes toward his mother (transference)—that is, he subconsciously expected me, the therapist, to respond to various actions. This was substituted for verbal interchange.

Generally, symbolic meanings of action can be traced through developmental stages of childhood. During the second year of life, action allows the child to experience a sense of autonomy and individuation from the mother (or primary caregiver)—for example, the toddler's thrill at running out of the room and then turning around and running back. For some people, misbehaving continues to have the meaning of expressing rebellious feelings (for autonomy) that enhance avoidance of self-object fusion anxiety. This is a common cause of extramarital affairs.

During the first genital phase (ages 2–6), action is generated by aggressive wishes, among them individuation, destructive hostility, revenge, and control. Depending on the attitudes toward gender in the household, activity may be equated with masculinity or femininity.

During latency (school-age years), activity is usually equated with either submission or rebellion. During adolescence, again, action becomes alloyed with self-esteem regulation and autonomy.

EXAMPLE 2

Becky, a 48-year-old divorced woman, liked talking to men at parties who "had an edge." She confessed to me an attraction to "men who have emotional problems," especially narcissistic men who broke rules.

She knew her preference posed a problem because she also wanted to settle down with a man she could trust in a committed relationship. She was therefore making choices based on sexual preferences and fantasies that were not commensurate with her wishes for long-term stability.

Verbal interaction was something she did "with friends" (a leftover attitude from latency) and with her mother. For a heterosexual relationship to be exciting to her, it needed to be action packed, especially with a man who did not communicate many feelings verbally. The more closed off and self-centered he was, the more she felt excited by him. This preference led her into frustrating relationships where she felt disappointed, wounded, and disillusioned.

> **TIP**
> Some people never develop the ability to verbalize their emotions and desires. If this persists into adulthood, it can result in self-destructive behaviors. The therapist attempts to help people "mentalize"—that is, think about their behaviors—but this is not always successful.

Although she wished for stability, she consistently involved herself with men who were not stable. She admitted to me that she found me somewhat boring since I had not shown her anything "weird." After six or seven sessions, she had already made some progress in that she had broken off an ungratifying relationship with (by her description) a troubled man.

After 10 sessions, she announced she was not coming back to see me. She felt she had had enough understanding; she had resigned herself to not aspiring to form a committed relationship. She admitted she was stuck with this problem but had decided that she had had enough discussion about it. When I linked her attitude with her problem with action, she could see it but she still did not want to continue treatment, which was limited to verbal communication.

Problem 42
People Who Bring Their Spouse to a Session

Some people surprise you by bringing a spouse to a session. Some ask to bring their spouse to a following session. Both of these requests are, fundamentally, manifestations of action that have meaning, and sometimes can be understood.

For decades, I have eschewed attempting to do marital therapy at the same time I am treating, in individual therapy, one of the partners in a marriage. There are too many confidences which people need in individual treatment.

For example, someone may want to discuss prior sexual relationships or masturbation fantasies involving other people; exposing this material to their spouse usually is an irritant to an already troubled marriage. I have reminded people in treatment that memories are, in reality, "dead": the people and experiences they remember are no longer active in their lives; introducing those memories may have a distancing and painful effect on their spouse. I realize my opinion about this goes counter to many current-day trends, where people "get into" "absolute honesty" with each other. Several people who have consulted me have suffered because of this penchant.[35]

SHORT ANSWER

People who bring their spouse to a session reveal something about their relationship with their spouse, but it is difficult to know what. No doubt, spouses can give you material you have not heard from the person you are treating.

From a technique standpoint, if a spouse comes to a session, I allow the spouse in, at least briefly. I ask the invited spouse to tell me whatever they want to say. The spouse frequently fears the other partner left things out or distorted history. Husbands, more commonly, tend to underestimate their wives' problems, while wives tend to overestimate their husbands' pathology.

Usually, when the spouse has finished, I ask the person I am treating to comment. I then ask the invited spouse return to the waiting room.

If there are persistent problems, and a couple needs marital therapy, I refer them to a colleague with whom I (usually) do not share information. That way, I maintain the confidentiality of the person I am treating.

---

35 See the defense of frankness (Blackman, 2003a).

These are not necessarily popular approaches to marital therapy, but I think they work out best; I would recommend handling things in these ways, as long the person you are treating is not psychotic or overtly suicidal.

LONG ANSWER

Sometimes when people bring their spouse, it aids differential diagnosis. The inviting spouse often wants you to see the cause of their suffering, and feels you will understand better if you meet the spouse, yourself.

At some times and in some places, it was routine for psychoanalysts to consult privately with the spouse of any person beginning analytic treatment. This practice has largely been dropped, and I agree with that. Years ago, when I evaluated a spouse separately, it interfered with my empathy for the person who consulted me.

What about evaluating a couple together? The problems there revolve around confidentiality. In select cases, when a spouse has requested to come to a session "for a few minutes," especially with people who are suicidal or highly agitated, meeting with the couple together can illuminate elements of the problem I had not seen. The conjoint consultation, therefore, can foster understanding, improvement of the working alliance, and better assessment of pathology.

EXAMPLE 1

Anatolio, a 47-year-old man whom I saw once a week, initially complained of anxiety attacks. He was successful financially, as was his wife. When he awakened in the middle of the night, crying, he asked his wife to talk to him. After he had seen me for a couple of sessions, his wife requested that she come to a session with him. I agreed.

I saw them together briefly. She argued that I should put her husband on antidepressants. She had read about this; she had friends who took SSRIs. She said, "I love him, but I have to work. He has to get better."

He was somewhat resistant to taking medicine, but admitted that he was not getting enough rest. I explained my understanding that they both wanted him to feel better, but he did not want to see me more frequently because it meant spending more money and thereby admitting that he needed to depend on me.

In other words, he wanted to take medication rather than see me more frequently. I said I saw that both of them wanted him to take antidepressants because she felt worried and irritated about becoming his auxiliary therapist, and he felt guilty about depending on her so much. I opined that if he wanted me to treat him, his dependency needed to be shifted to me, where it belonged—he needed to give me a chance to help him by coming at least twice a week and taking a mild hypnotic.

They were both surprised by my clarification, but after discussing it with me were agreeable. I treated Anatolio for 4 years, with considerable success.

Much of Anatolio's treatment involved understanding elements of that session, where his wife had clearly stated that she wanted to help her husband, she wanted to save the marriage, and she was deeply concerned about his emotional problems.

Periodically, when he imagined his wife wanted to get rid of him, I could explore these fantasies, aided by my recollection of the conjoint session where she had described her fervent wish for him to get better.

EXAMPLE 2

Rose, a 77-year-old married woman, had panic attacks and trouble sleeping. The panic attacks occurred when she left the house, particularly without her husband of 52 years. When I first met her, Rose and her husband, Alan, were standing in the waiting room. He shook my hand, introduced himself, and said he wanted to be present for the evaluation session with his wife. I agreed after Rose indicated that she also wanted this.

Alan began without any indication from his wife or me. He spoke for over 10 minutes. He was very worried about his wife, critical of some of her doctors, but not tangential, circumstantial, or out of touch with reality. He was worried about losing his wife to an illness. He also complained that he had to "take care" of her all the time, although he preferred to do this, in some ways.

When Alan talked about her neediness, Rose smiled; she joked that he was overprotective, as always. They bantered about this. She explained she was losing part of her eyesight due to glaucoma and therefore could not drive. Alan, who was retired, drove her everywhere. She had a number of friends.

Rose was a well-groomed, attractive woman who looked at least 15 years younger than her age. She was personable and joked with her husband. I could not clearly formulate what was causing her anxiety. I noted to myself how she reminded me of my beloved (and long-deceased) grandmother.

She wished to see me alone for her next session, which I arranged. During that meeting, she gave me a lengthy history about her family, her complex relationships with her brother and sister, and the early history of her marriage. The material was organized, fit into patterns where she felt guilt over competitive feelings with her sister, idolized her brother, and seemed to have transferred some of those idealized feelings from her brother onto her husband. She made a follow-up appointment.

During the third appointment, her husband came with her, but this time I asked him to sit in the waiting room. I had realized, during both the initial consultation and during the follow-up visit, that I had not completed Rose's evaluation. I had recognized my countertransference (from my grandmother) which inhibited me in pursuing further diagnostic information.

In this session, when Rose began talking about her childhood, I gently interrupted and told her I noticed she was avoiding talking to me about her current relationship with her husband, her current physical problems, and her relationship with her children today.

She could see that this was the case, but (as many people do) rather than responding to my comment as an observation, she took it as a direction to tell me more about her current-day life. As she began to describe this, it became painfully clear to me that she could not remember very much about her recent experiences. As she tried to tell me things, she forgot, got lost in her description, and then became painfully embarrassed. In other words, she could observe her difficulties with recent memory.

I expressed an understanding of her pain in this, and then tested her orientation with some questions. She was disoriented to the day, date, year, and the day of the week. She did know approximately what time of day it was. She knew that I was a psychiatrist but had forgotten my name.

Her husband's presence in the evaluation session, and her focus (in the second session) on her past history—which she remembered well—had prevented me from seeing her organic brain syndrome (senility). Rose's defenses (talking about the past, humor), her husband's skewed view of her neediness, and my own countertransference had interfered with my approach in approaching diagnosis.[36]

> **TIP**
> Watch out for countertransference interference with gathering diagnostic data when a person brings a spouse to an evaluation.

Once I made the diagnosis of organic brain syndrome, I referred her back to her internist for further workup, including an MRI of the brain. MRI showed decrease in brain volume, some indications of vascular disease, but no strokes or neurological syndromes. Rose was slowly becoming demented.

---

36 Blackman (2010) and Problem 101 (B).

At this point, I felt Rose needed individual supportive therapy, supportive marital work, and careful pharmacological treatment. I referred her to a colleague who was a specialist in psychopharmacology and geriatric psychiatry to help her and her husband adapt to her situation.

I learned from this experience that marital consultations cannot only elucidate but can sometimes obfuscate diagnosis and treatment selection.

Problem 43
People Who Bring Their Parents to a Session

Adults generally do not bring their parents to a session with them. When this happens, however, it can be quite interesting. Talking to parents is routine for child therapists but unusual for therapists who treat adults.

What do you do when adults show up with their parents?

SHORT ANSWER

When people bring a parent to my office, particularly without my permission, I do not immediately invite the parent into the session. I presume the parents have come as a convenience to the person I am treating; they may be planning something together after the session. On occasion, people tell me they want me to meet the parent.

In the waiting room, if I see the person has brought parents, I wait for the person to introduce me to the parents and then treat this as a social interaction, with courtesy and social appropriateness. Usually the person does not invite the parent into the consultation room. I do not preempt people by inviting the parent in.

During that session, people often tell me something about the parents that had not previously come up. Or they may ask me my reaction to seeing the parent. I may try to help people think about why they desire my opinion, although if I have an opinion I think may be helpful, I may share it.

EXAMPLE 1

Janet, 39 years old, divorced and lonely, had been contemplating suicide. After three sessions, she expressed a desire to take a vacation, "take a break" from her life, and go visit her mother (who was then in town), in Santa Fe, New Mexico. Perhaps she would get treatment there. Janet was afraid that her mother would not allow Janet to accompany her home. Janet had always been ambivalent about her mother but yearned for her company.

Janet asked me if I would talk with her mother. After signing a release, she brought her mother (who also signed a release) to the following session. I saw them together.

At Janet's request, I explained that she was suicidal and wanted to camp out with her mother while she got started with therapy in Santa Fe. Her mother responded: "Well, she just has to get her life together. I can't be there for her all the time. I have work to do, and I can't take off. The guest room is filled with stuff, although she could sleep in the bed, but I prefer that she doesn't."

I expressed understanding for the imposition, but repeated that Janet was suicidal and lonely, and that I felt her loneliness raised the danger of suicide. Her mother repeated the litany of reasons she did not want Janet in New Mexico. The mother's narcissism and lack of worry were startling to me.

When Janet returned to see me the next day, she asked what I thought of her mother. I responded that I had a clear appreciation of what Janet had suffered with for many years. I indicated that I found her mother cold, withdrawn, and full of excuses. Janet laughed. She was amused that I had felt her mother's rejection. Janet decided not to go to New Mexico. She saw me twice a week for the next year, during which she understood that much of her suicidal ideation was based on turning of anger (at her mother) onto herself.

LONG ANSWER

Allowing parents into a session with an adult can be fraught with problems. In the following example, I think you will see the difficulties with countertransference from the therapist. You will also notice how complex the therapeutic relationship became once the therapist allowed contact with Butch's parents.

EXAMPLE 2

Tim, a psychodynamic psychiatrist, asked me to supervise his treatment of Butch, a 41-year-old attorney. Butch had marital problems, sexual inhibitions (fear of initiating sex), and worries about his masculinity. He feared his wife would leave him because he was not masculine enough. His wife complained he was nitpicking, critical, and nasty. He complained that she was lackadaisical and spent too much time with the children.

Tim was surprised that Butch had asked if he could bring each of his parents, individually, to a session. Butch had complained, throughout two years of treatment, that his father was controlling, demeaning, and critical toward him.

Butch also complained that his mother was nosy, critical, and cloying. She was critical of Butch's wife and of the way they managed their children. Yet, she wanted to be present in their home frequently. Butch compared her to Ray's mother[37] on the TV show *Everybody Loves Raymond*. Except, for Butch, the situation wasn't funny. He fantasized about running away but felt guilty about avoiding his parents.

Butch envied his older sister, the favorite of his parents. She was the "good girl" who was allowed to sleep in the parents' bed. Butch, the boy, was supposed to take care of himself. At least that's the way he remembered it.

Tim had been curious about Butch's parents but hesitant to accept Butch's version of things. He had suspected that Butch felt guilty about competitive feelings with his father but invited his father's control.

Recently, Tim and Butch agreed Butch was still trying to "separate" from his mother, who had been "enmeshed" with him since his adolescence.

I did not advise Tim regarding Butch bringing the parents. I suggested Tim try to understand with Butch what this all meant. Tim was curious, as well.

In our following supervisory sessions, Tim told me he had met with each of Butch's parents in conjoint sessions with Butch. Tim was surprised how accurate Butch had been. Tim's reactions to Butch's parents were stronger than Tim had anticipated. The mother was controlling and obsessionally worried about her son. She infantilized him, talked over him, and controlled the session. She seemed disrespectful and condescending.

During their conjoint meeting, Tim pointed out some of these qualities to Butch's mother. She seemed to know her attitudes had caused Butch problems. Butch later told Tim that Tim's directness was a model Butch would emulate.

> **TIP**
> The person in treatment may want the therapist to share the pain inflicted by the parent but may be highly conflicted about this. When a therapist points out a parent's character flaws, the adult child may then feel simultaneously relieved and guilty—and may therefore become defensive about their own feelings toward the parent.

Butch's father was more critical of Butch than Butch had described. He had nothing good to say about Butch, was not pleased to be talking to a "shrink," and complained about the time and money he lost by not being at work. His narcissism and relative disinterest in Butch's problems were poignant.

Following these consultations, Tim felt more understanding of Butch. He shared some of his reactions with Butch, alleviating some of Butch's misery. However, in a session after this, Butch yawned and almost fell asleep. On exploring the yawning, Tim found out that Butch wanted to run away from his problems and felt guilty that Tim was critical of Butch's parents.

---

37 Aired from 1996 to 2005. Marie, Raymond's mother, was played by Doris Roberts.

In later sessions, Butch explained how he had wanted to love both his parents and was disappointed that Tim was critical of them. Fortunately for their work together, Tim could explain that Butch had minimized his own reactions to his parents' difficult personalities—which Tim had described, and then wanted to run from Tim (yawning). Butch agreed, and could see that minimizing their character flaws had caused him to allow them to invade and interfere with his marriage.

Problem 44
People Who Do Not Want to Leave Your Office on Time

Certain people cause difficulties in the therapist's schedule. They start talking about an emotional topic 30 seconds before the end of the session; when the time is up, they are crying and in the middle of important material, and they prolong the session.

What do you do with people who seem to control your time this way, and who make you feel guilty if you end the session on time?

SHORT ANSWER

If people are crying as the end of the session approaches, I may indicate that we'll have to stop soon and that we can take up the matter in their next session. This lets them reintegrate before ending the session (especially once a week).

If I am on my toes, I do this diplomatically. At times, I have been more abrupt when I tell people we need to bring things to a close. If I feel sympathy as people tell me something painful, I may allow them to continue for a few minutes. I try not to be compulsive about the time; empathic attunement is preferable to obsessional regulation.

Regardless of any flexibility, however, there are some people who begin getting into material, routinely, at the end of their sessions. If I see this, I bring up the issue of "endings" at the beginning of the following session. This gives me a chance to discuss the matter with the person I am treating without being squeezed by time.

In brief, I usually allow some flexibility if people are upset toward the end of a session unless this becomes a pattern. When it becomes a pattern that has meaning, it is peculiar because you cannot deal with it at the end of the session while it is happening without running over considerably and wreaking havoc on your own schedule. Better to bring it up the following time.

LONG ANSWER

Being able to understand the meanings of people prolonging their therapeutic sessions can make or break a treatment. When people do this habitually, they are unconsciously (or sometimes consciously) coercing you to spend more time with them. I view this behavior, at first, as a way people avoid the pain of being separate from me.

So why don't they want to separate from you? The answer lies, usually, in disturbances of people's self-image that derive from problems during the first 3 years of life (separation-individuation) and during the process of identity formation during middle and late adolescence.[38] Sometimes, they fear you will disappear when they do not see you—a disturbance in object constancy.[39] They may have fond feelings for you and not want to miss you.

People who stay late shade into the group of people who commit boundary crossings. As described in Problem 101 (B), the diagnosis depends on reality testing (ego functioning); capacities for empathy and trust (object relations intactness); and fairness and integrity (superego functions).

Neurotic people may dislike leaving because of symbolism. People with borderline personality[40] may fear you will go away. Psychotics may decompensate.

EXAMPLE OF NEUROTIC SYMBOLISM

Al, a 32-year-old orthopedic surgeon, saw me twice a week. He had panic attacks in the office, depressive feelings at night, and anxiety about his career. His family doctor had put him on an antidepressant, which made him feel worse.

Al was routinely 15 minutes late to his sessions. Each time, he gave a "reality rationalization": patients in the office, a delayed surgical procedure, phone calls from his wife, administrative hang-ups. Eventually, after "holding it in," he became angry when I ended our session at the appointed time; I could not discuss his anger right then, since I had another person waiting.

I began his following session by bringing up his lateness and his wish to keep me later. We were at an impasse where he broke the working alliance (coming and leaving on time) but felt persecuted when I did not prolong his sessions to compensate for his scheduling problems.

Management of his reaction was difficult. I found myself stumbling, critical, or not understanding his conflicts. When he threatened to quit, I pointed out that this was interesting, since he imagined he would deprive me (of money), punish himself, and still disobey his contract with me about time.

At first, Al insisted on criticizing me for being money grubbing (not giving him extra time). When I pointed out his pattern of being late and demanding I change, he balked. I decided to shift technique. I expressed curiosity about his intense reactions about time, and pointed out that it seemed to have special meaning. He then recalled that, because his father had been in the military, Al

---

38 Blos (1967).
39 Mahler et al. (1975).
40 Kernberg (1975).

never had enough time with him. Al yearned to play with his father when his father came home, but his father routinely got drunk and fell asleep. When sober, his father worked in his woodshop, making furniture, alone.

Al tearfully remembered how his father was warmer when leaving on deployments. The "rule" or "boundary" imposed by his father's scheduling had always infuriated Al.

I now could link Al's being late to his father's lateness with Al (identification with the aggressor). Al simultaneously enacted a wish at the end of sessions that I would stay with him and not make him leave, thereby hoping to undo the pain that he had felt when his father had left.

EXAMPLE OF BORDERLINE PERSONALITY ORGANIZATION WITH PSYCHOTIC TRANSFERENCE[41]

Barbara, a 23-year-old graduate student in history, came to see me because of marital problems compounded by displacements onto her husband from her very peculiar mother. She seemed aware of this link and wanted to understand more about it. Her father had died when she was six; she did not remember much about him. I treated her twice a week.

After she had been in therapy about a month, Barbara's husband suddenly announced that he wanted a divorce. She was not devastated. She was actually somewhat relieved, although sad. They had no children, and she thought it better to scratch the marriage sooner than later: she would find someone more appropriate.

We continued trying to understand more about how her relationship with her mother had tinged her attitudes. After four months of therapy, Barbara demanded, at the end of a session, that I meet her for a drink after work. Thinking this was a simple oedipal-style fantasy (erotic transference), I clarified that if she knew me outside of therapy, this would alleviate frustration she felt toward me for being unavailable in the way her father and her husband had been.

She rejected my explanation, became vehement that I meet her for a drink after work, and threatened to kill herself if I would not. Ironically, she was my last appointment for the day. She was still arguing with me about this 15 minutes after her session should have ended; she would not leave my office.

Because she threatened suicide, I asked her if she felt she should be hospitalized. She responded, "No you don't! I'll sue you for false imprisonment. I don't need to be hospitalized." I then confronted her manipulation of keeping me late, which she admitted was purposeful. She argued that by insisting

---

[41] Volkan (1988, 2011).

she leave, I treated her "like a cockroach," just like her mother had. I stood up, opened the exit door from my office, and insisted she leave as she argued with me. Nothing I said helped. She said I might not see her for the next session.

She showed up for her next session, however, and terrified me with threats of suicide for over a year. When I recommended that she consult someone else, she refused and threatened to kill herself if I "abandoned" her. Periodically, she became contrite, and discussed her coercive attitudes.

Every few weeks, however, she would refuse to leave my office. I would explain that her threatening to kill herself broke the "frame"[42] and therefore had meaning. Her obstinate manipulativeness was the prime concern as I struggled with her over that year. I felt I was the victim of her mother, who had been cruelly demanding and manipulative with her. Barbara did not give me "space" to breathe (projective identification): I explained that she did this because she did not want to recall being smothered by her mother.

While I tried to help her understand herself, I also remained adamant that we stop sessions on time. She managed to keep me in the office extra time, anyway; she would sit and argue with me about leaving.

After 18 months, I opined that I could not treat her any further. I gave her the name of some colleagues. She again threatened to kill herself. A few months later, I heard from a colleague that she had consulted him and was still alive.

Since that experience, a number of people have praised me as a therapist but made impossible demands. They did not respect me as an individual and would not get close. Such people were annoyingly coercive, threatened to destroy the boundaries of the treatment, and threatened to destroy themselves.

Some people with these problems were (pseudoneurotic) schizophrenics; they had psychotic transferences to many people. Others seemed to be in the "borderline" range, with better reality testing and integrative capacities but damaged capacities for empathy and trust (object relations problems) and manipulative character traits.

I have sometimes likened people with these character traits to *binary stars*. They circulate around you, never let go, but continually threaten a galactic explosion. I learned, through Barbara, that I cannot treat such people successfully. When I see this type of pathology, I no longer try. Some people like Barbara seem to do better with colleagues of mine who see them once a month for fifteen minutes and give them medication for anxiety or depression. Understanding and reintegration of their personality, at least in my hands, does not seem possible.

---

42 Langs (1973).

Problem 45
People Who Accuse You of
Not Paying Attention

This complaint from people in treatment is rather common, so it is a good idea for therapists to become familiar with techniques for handling it.

Most therapists pay close attention to what people in treatment say, listening for elements that shed light on their unconscious conflicts, defenses, and fantasies.

Ironically, this type of attention is often misread by people in treatment, who may feel that any gap in verbalization indicates that the therapist is not listening. On the other hand, when a therapist asks questions, people may also feel like they are "not heard," since they are responding to the therapist's interests.

In my supervisory work with therapists, I have found myself advising them to ask fewer questions and to pay more attention to people's verbalizations and *resistances*. When the therapist wants to ask a question, this usually indicates that people they are treating are using a defense. It is usually better to formulate about which defenses are blocking the material the therapist wants to ask about.

So, how do you handle it when someone makes this complaint?

SHORT ANSWER

When people worry that I am not paying attention, I usually first point out that this is a fantasy, and that I am actually intently paying attention. If people are not psychotic, this explanation opens the door to exploration of the reasons for their worry. Most commonly, people expect me to react as one of their parents did during some phase of their development—the parent may have been too busy working, taking care of other children, or simply nonresponsive.[43]

EXAMPLE

Sissy, a 47-year-old career woman who had difficulties in her marriage, also suffered from inhibitions of aggression, periodic jerking motions in her limbs, and tension. Her problems required intensive psychoanalysis, which she requested. She used (reclined on) the couch, with me sitting behind her, 4 days a week.

In a few weeks, after we had had multiple interactions regarding her conflicts, Sissy suddenly asked me, "Are you listening? Please, answer me!" I responded that

---

43 Gaiman (2002), whose children's book, *Coraline*, depicts unresponsive, busy parents who are part of her problem.

of course I was listening, and I thought she was having a terrifying fantasy that I was not. She responded, "How do I know? You could be reading the newspaper!"

Since I was, of course, not reading the newspaper, I said that her fantasy was coming from somewhere, but I did not know where. She suddenly recalled, "Damn it! My father used to do that. I would be sitting at the kitchen table, trying to talk to him; he always had the damn newspaper in front of his face." Her frustrations with her father also involved his withdrawal when she desired affection from him. Her fear that I was not paying attention turned out to be a productive fantasy which had many origins.

LONG ANSWER

Aside from displacements from parents, people who complain about the therapist not paying attention may have limitations in trust caused by trauma, neglect, or other disagreeable experiences in early childhood and adolescence (object relations deficits).

People with object relations problems often require "relational" technique, where the therapist, as a "container"[44] (Problem 13), allows people some personal interaction. One goal of interpersonal disclosures is to make the treatment a "safe" environment.[45] Also, a calm, nonjudgmental approach to people's affect storms seems to lead to an improvement in their capacities for trust and affect regulation.

> **THEORY**
> When people have problems with identity and object constancy, using the couch provokes identity diffusion and emotional storms. Adults with borderline personality can lose the image of the analyst, who has "disappeared" behind the couch; the combination of inflamed mistrust and being overwhelmed by affects can produce transient psychotic states in the person in treatment. For this reason, the couch is generally contraindicated for people with borderline personality, although I have seen exceptions to this rule.[46]
>
> Studies[47] of children between ages 6 and 11 have found that self-stability and affect regulation continued to develop during this stage. The stable period of latency for boys lasts from 6½ to 11½, whereas for girls the range is 7½ to 10½. The girls' shorter latency period, necessary for the development of ego strength, seems to account for the common observation of relatively greater affective lability in preadolescent girls.

---

44 Bion (1970).
45 Sandler (1960).
46 Blackman (2010).
47 Knight (2005).

People with problems in empathy, trust, and closeness are difficult to treat; the prognosis is in the fair to guarded range. They often quit treatment or stay in treatment for a long time without getting much better. People with these problems generally require sitting-up psychotherapy and should not be treated with psychoanalysis.[48]

The idea that you are not paying attention may not be due to object relations problems. Women's sexuality often includes being noticed. When they accuse you of not paying attention, this can easily have meanings regarding narcissism and sexuality. Karme (1981) described the psychoanalytic treatment of a professional woman who consulted her because Dr. Karme was a woman. The female analysand did not want a male analyst telling her that she had penis envy. Ironically, the analysand eventually expressed envy of Dr. Karme, and imagined that Dr. Karme had a penis!

In other words, a *neurotically disturbed* woman's feelings of incapacity or worthlessness may be traced to a childhood fantasy of not having male equipment.[49]

In addition, people who think the therapist is not listening may be projecting onto the therapist a wish not to pay attention to the therapist. This is often traceable to adolescent rebellious feelings.[50]

---

48 Levy et al. (2006).
49 Also, see Lewin (1948).
50 Malawista et al. (2011).

Problem 46
People Who Don't Let You Get a Word in Edgewise

Garrulousness is commonly used by early adolescent girls and sometimes boys when they are nervous (defense against social anxiety). They call it "motor mouth." This may have developed into a character trait in adults and may show up in their relationship with the therapist. When it does, it is often a gratifying relief from working with people who withhold information and are silent (Problem 48).

Actually, though, talkativeness can be a resistance to treatment and this often needs to be discussed somewhere during the first few months of work. Talkativeness is not usually a treatment-busting resistance like missing sessions or not paying the fee, but it can be useful to examine, especially if you feel yourself boxed in by it.

SHORT ANSWER

If you feel you can't a word in edgewise, and the people you are supposed to be treating seem to be doing all of the work on their own, something is afoot. The defenses of garrulousness and pseudoindependence often work together. Bringing them to the attention of the person you are treating should go something like the following successful interaction (as you already know from reading other problems in this book, not all interactions are successful...):

Therapist:	You have been doing a lot of work on yourself lately. But I notice that you have somehow also possibly been doing this all on your own, almost like you were afraid to hear what I might say.
Person in treatment:	Well, I've been trying hard. You think too hard?
Therapist:	Yes, something like that.
Person in treatment:	Well, maybe. My mother always said I talked too much. But then, when she did talk, it always made me feel guilty, like she was too overprotective, you know? That made me want to shut down.

LONG ANSWER

Often, garrulousness has many meanings besides preventing people from feeling anxiety or guilt. Sometimes, speaking is equated with aggression, invulnerability, and at times, ideas about gender.

EXAMPLE

Holly, 30 years old, an attractive, married employment lawyer with a large firm, felt frantic about her marriage. She was not yet a partner, since she had taken time off from her practice after giving birth to her son 2 years previously. Her "part-time" work week was fairly predictable, about 35 hours a week in the office.

Her husband was also an attorney with the firm. He had already made partner in the business litigation section and was working 60 to 80 hours a week. Their children, ages 3 and 5, were doing okay, but Holly was very worried about having enough time with them, having enough time with her husband, and somehow felt her world was falling apart—in spite of their being relatively affluent.

Holly was an engaging person with many interesting things to say. Her ability to observe herself was excellent, and she spent the first three or four sessions telling me many of the things that she had figured out about herself, her husband, and her children. She related much about her upbringing and her husband's. She reported levels of symbolism in her interactions at work and with her husband based on relationship problems between her and her parents over the years.

In spite of this rather optimistic presentation, after three or four sessions, I found that I was not speaking very much. Aside from my own personality tendencies that led to certain reactions, I began to consider how Holly boxed me in, or at least caused me to feel that I was boxed in.

Because I am not a gestalt therapist, I did not reveal my reaction to Holly to her. Rather, following Arlow's (1979) recommendation, I tried to integrate my reaction to her with some formulations that she had suggested about her own problems. I therefore said to her that I thought all of the information she had given me about herself, her family, and her upbringing was very important and useful. I also stated factually that I could see that she had excellent capacities to observe herself and that this was also a positive prognostic sign.

Her initial response to these clarifications was to chuckle and say, "Good. So I'm not hopeless!" She then looked at me quizzically and said, "Is there a *but*?" I told her she was right: There was a *but*. I explained that I had noticed, as she was talking to me, that she seemed to be filling the time and talking as though she was nervous about what I might say. She then laughed out loud, and told me that she had been glancingly aware of this anxiety but not quite sure what to do with it. She had also been somewhat aware of how talkative she was, but wasn't sure what to do about that, either.

I suggested she tell me her thoughts about it. She quickly told me that she knew that she was a talkative person and that sometimes her husband had complained about this. However, most of the time, they interacted pretty well. Lately, though, they had not been having as much fun when they were with each other, and they had not had sexual relations in over a month.

She rationalized that he was working very hard. She was also tired and working pretty hard and taking care of the children; she did not particularly feel sexy. When I did not respond, but paid attention, Holly became aware that she was making excuses about all this (the defenses of rationalization and normalization).

In the next session, Holly reported a dream:

"I am in an office, and it's something like this office. Except that there is a huge something in the room, maybe like a tree trunk, and it's kind of like coming up from the floor between us. I'm not sure what it is exactly. It was sort of a bland color, or something…"

I suggested she tell me what came to her mind about this object in the room, and she then gasped. She said, "I don't believe it!" I then looked at her in a querying sort of way. She continued, "Don't you know what it is? You're the analyst!" At the time, I remember thinking that a tree trunk was something like a stable mother, or perhaps represented a defensive "bark" connected with her talkativeness. I told her I was not sure what she was thinking, but I could tell that she was thinking something.

She responded, "It's a penis. It's one big penis. It's between you and me. It's what's keeping us apart." I expressed interest. She then thought that perhaps this had been the problem all along with her father. He was a man, and she now thought that he wanted her to be a man, like him. He, also, was an attorney, whereas her mother had been a homemaker. She quickly associated that she was a lot like her father but then commented that in some ways she was "obviously like my mother, also."

In a later session, she had a dream where she was somehow holding onto the top of a long flagpole and being blown by the wind. She was holding on for dear life. Again, her associations had to do with the flagpole being a phallic symbol and how she had clung to ideas about being masculine in order to please her father but that it was not working in her marriage.

The various elements Holly considered "masculine" were then elucidated by her. Unfortunately, she had developed an idea, throughout development, that femininity meant passivity and "not having a brain." She began to understand this. Her standoffishness with her husband evaporated and after a year of treatment she was functioning very well.

Problem 47
Women Who Bring an Infant to the Session[51]

Mothers with infants in the first year of life often depend on sitters to get to your office on time. The sitter may not show up; this is not the women's fault; they are victims of their sitters' capriciousness, irresponsibility, or illness.

At such times, a mother may, in desperation, show up for her appointment with her infant in a car seat, hopefully sleeping. Usually, the session is limited because the baby wakes up when the mother talks. The mother must tend to the baby.

SHORT ANSWER

When a woman brings a young infant with her, be attentive to the realities of her life. Women therapists who have children will immediately understand, as will most male therapists who are fathers.

In many cases, there is not much to understand. The mother got stuck, could not change the appointment, and did not want to stand up the therapist, so she brought the baby with her. Acknowledging the reality of the mother's travails will go a long way toward furthering the therapeutic alliance, especially when the therapist, like me, is male.

In following sessions, if women express shame and apologize for bringing the baby, you can understand more about the visit with the infant. Many "modern" women expect themselves to have more control over their lives than is possible once they have an infant. They may be embarrassed because their expectations of themselves are too high. Their expectations of their infants may also be too high; a savvy therapist can allay the mother's shame by discussing the reality strain of taking care of an infant.

A change in the mother's perfectionistic ego ideal (exalted expectation) about herself or the baby can be effected through her identification with the therapist's attitude. If a woman feels guilty because her sitter did not show up, excessive self-blame may be traceable to experiences where she felt too guilty over hostile feelings toward siblings, rebellion toward parents, or narcissistic ungratefulness.

---

51 I have not, as yet, seen or heard about a father who brought an infant to a session. In the future, I look forward to that variation.

When you see the woman's guilt, discuss the apology (the defense) with the woman first. She apologizes, hoping to make you feel better, but why is that necessary? It must be that she feels she has committed a transgression by bringing in the baby.

With two women I treated, apology was connected with guilt over having abortions, although the abortions were rational at the time—when they were single teens. That guilt, in turn, arose in response to the meaning of the teen pregnancies, often involving anger at their mothers during adolescence (acted out through sexual activity)[52] and wishes that their mothers cared about them more.

LONG ANSWER

When a woman brings an infant to the therapist's office, realities must be taken into consideration before interpreting symbolism. However, the symbolism may be discoverable in the following sessions. A woman who brings her infant is "acting in," and the infant causes countertransference reactions in the therapist (almost automatic).

EXAMPLE

Dr. Aileen Kim,[53] when she was a psychiatry resident, presented a case to me in supervision which seemed to be prototypical of the 21st century. She was treating Hillary, a 27-year-old married woman who had worked in an administrative job before having her son. Hillary had consulted Aileen when the baby was about a month old, complaining of "postpartum depression."

Hillary was an intellectual, self-sufficient woman, who prided herself on her abilities. Initial work on Hillary's depression centered on her guilt and shame over needing help from her husband. Hillary's father had drilled into her head that it was bad to be "dependent." Hillary recently had reinitiated contact with her mother, from whom she had been distant for years because of her mother's controlling personality. Now, Hillary asked her mother for help but often quarreled with her.

After months of once-a-week treatment, Hillary showed up in Aileen's office with the 4-month-old infant in a car seat. She apologized to Aileen, made excuses about child-care problems, and whispered that she hoped the baby would stay asleep.

---

52 Blackman (2011).
53 Dr. Kim gave me permission to use her actual name. The identifying information about the woman she was treating is heavily disguised.

Predictably, within minutes, the infant started screaming. He also vomited on Aileen's desk. Hillary was embarrassed, and ineffectively tried to soothe the baby without removing her from the car seat. Aileen suggested they take the child out of the car seat and clean up the mess. Together, they unbuckled the child, and Aileen instructed Hillary to pick up the baby, hold him, and feed him while they cleaned up.

Aileen noticed that Hillary propped her son on her knee to feed him, facing Aileen. The baby kept crying. Aileen suggested that Hillary cleanse the baby's face, cradle the baby in her arms, hug the baby, and look at him while giving him a bottle. Hillary seemed awkward, but did so. Between the two of them, over the next 15 minutes, they got the child to stop crying. After another 5 or 10 minutes, he was asleep again. Soon, the session was over. Hillary apologized and thanked Aileen.

In discussing the case with me in supervision, Aileen expressed some feelings of shame, herself, that she had helped Hillary with the baby, worried that she had done something untherapeutic. First, I found myself reassuring Aileen that there was no other course of action with screaming, vomiting babies, who generally take precedence over almost anything else. Aileen's response to the child was maternal. I said to Aileen that her own intact capacities had helped her in advising Hillary about how to soothe a crying child who was attached to the mother, already in the "symbiotic" attachment phase.

This also gave me a chance to review, with Aileen, the importance of Mahler et al.'s (1975) conceptualizations about the symbiotic-like phase—where the child is intensely attached to the mother—which begins around 2 months of age and reaches a height around 5 months of age or so. Other studies have focused on mother–infant attachment when infants are 4 months old.[54]

In addition, I invited Aileen to think about what had happened in her interaction with Hillary. She realized she had acted as a mother to Hillary. I agreed with her, and added that some interesting facets of their interaction included Hillary's shame and guilt about the crying baby, Hillary's resistance to cuddling with the child, and Hillary's identification with Aileen.

Aileen then filled me in on the rest of the story. Hillary was raised in a family where her father insisted that dependency was a weakness. He instilled in Hillary the concept that she should never rely on anybody for anything and that she should take care of herself. Interestingly, this had led Hillary to a period of some promiscuity between ages 18 and 22.

As Aileen discussed this with me, it became clear to both of us that Hillary, in denying her dependency wishes because of shame, had also used sexualization for two purposes at once:

---

54   Beebe and Lachmann (1988).

- to relieve her shame about dependency wishes (a defensive operation) and
- to gratify dependency wishes (physical contact).

Hillary had not become aware of shame about wanting love, sustenance, and attention from her mother and father, or from anyone. Instead, she unconsciously saw her baby as herself, and turning to Aileen for help indicated her own wishes to be "mothered."

Hillary's complex conflict, I thought, fit with her apologies to Aileen for bringing the baby. It seemed to me that Hillary felt ashamed about her need for help with the child and ashamed about her wishes to be close to the child and to allow the child to depend on her.

I discussed the possibility with Aileen that Hillary might have more severe object relations problems, with failures in her abilities for empathy toward the child and closeness. Aileen was more of the opinion that Hillary was defensively identifying with her father's ideals. We decided that the strategy in the following sessions should be for Aileen to discuss some of the defensive operations with Hillary and to elucidate some of the transferences and countertransferences that had been "acted in" during the session.

Over the next several weeks, when I met with Aileen for supervision, she reported remarkable success in elucidating the various conflicts with Hillary. Hillary readily saw that her sexual activity before marrying her husband at age 23 had been largely defensive in nature.

Hillary had not stopped to think that she wanted someone to pay attention to her and be understanding. Instead, she had seen herself as a "player," who knew the ropes of sexual interactions with men. This type of savvy, however, did not help after the birth of her child. Hillary was needy, and it turned out, disappointed with her "player" husband, who did not seem to feel the same conflicts she did. He was disgusted by the dependency of the baby, by his wife's need for him, and returned to "playing" by cheating on her with other women. A number of months later, Hillary insisted that the two of them separate.

For a while, however, Hillary used considerable denial about her husband's infidelity. In another way, she did not seem to mind: She could not be critical of him for being "independent." This was also elucidated by Aileen, so Hillary came to understand the pathological nature of her own pseudoindependence, minimization, and inhibition of judgment.

During the session with the baby, Hillary had unconsciously appealed to Aileen to be a mother and father to Hillary. She wanted a husband who was thoughtful about the child. She also wanted a mother who supported her needs as a mother.

Aileen, an empathic physician, had responded automatically by providing some help. That help, it turned out, was based on a countertransference toward Hillary as though Hillary were Aileen's daughter and her son Aileen's granddaughter. Aileen taught Hillary how to be a mother, encouraged object relatedness, and Hillary responded by apologizing.

Hillary saw her inhibition of her need for help. Aileen was right about Hillary's defensiveness. As they discussed Hillary's avoidance of dependency in herself and her criticism of any dependency in her infant, Hillary allowed the infant's dependency to grow, allowed the symbiotic attachment, and began to enjoy holding and singing to her child. The child laughed with her.

Hillary's child's crying was readily relieved by cuddling and soothing from the mother. Hillary also felt more gratified and realized her father's "ideal" of independence was misplaced and exaggerated. By the end of her treatment, Hillary was able to set out a plan to take care of the child and to work part time until the child could function more autonomously. Then she planned to return to work full time and to arrange some sitting during the day with a trusted neighbor.

Hillary finished treatment when Aileen left for Washington, DC.[55] At that point, Hillary was not yet dating. However, her depression had lifted, she was no longer suffering with a husband who was cheating on her and would not pay attention to their child, and she had a revised plan for her life.

---

55 Dr. Kim now practices in Washington, DC.

Problem 48
Silent People

Whatever the chief complaint, be it anxiety, depression, compulsions, phobias, personality problems, and/or relationship conflicts, explanatory therapy is greatly complicated if people have difficulty talking. In most situations, silences of more than a minute or so are counterproductive to the therapeutic progress. Since most silence is volitional in adults, silent people are "resisting," that is, breaking the working alliance.

> **THEORY**
> The working alliance is established between people and their therapists, and consists of a contract whereby the person in treatment agrees to
>
> - attend sessions at the scheduled time,
> - pay for the therapist's time in the manner the therapist requires,
> - pay for missed appointments as is the therapist's policy,
> - agree they have a problem, and talk
>
> In return, the therapist agrees
>
> - to listen carefully, and
> - to offer ideas about the problems that may help people in treatment better understand themselves.

Generally speaking, a resistance such as *reticence* needs to be pointed out and the conflicts and affects engendering such a conscious refusal to cooperate understood.

SHORT ANSWER

Confront silence as a resistance ("guardedness") unless severe object relations problems are present and/or the person is severely depressed (object relations damage and melted-down ego functions).[56]

---

56 When there is regression in ego functions and object relations, as in severe depressions, I "force the object relation" by talking to the person who is depressed and insisting that that person respond to me. (Also, see Lorand, 1937.)

EXAMPLE 1

Jyoti, a 38-year-old homemaker and mother of two children, was anxious and depressed. In her 15th session, she stared at the floor and said nothing. I said I noticed her guardedness (confrontation), but I had no idea what was causing it (clarification). She first responded, "I have nothing on my mind," and became silent again. She then commented on the pattern in my carpeting. I gently confronted her silence, again, by saying I could tell there were things she was thinking that she, for some reason, was having problems sharing with me.

She laughed, which surprised me, and barked, "Ask me a question!" I decided to work from "within the metaphor" and asked, "Okay, what were you just thinking about?" She laughed again, and said, "Pretty clever. Do you recommend this sort of thing to your students?" I responded that her joking around was also clever, but that it avoided whatever she was troubled about. She finally said that her husband had been smoking pot again. She found a pipe in his closet, and it still smelled. She had no idea what to do about it.

Jyoti had been using *humor* in addition to *reticence* and *suppression* as defensive operations. These protected her from troubling material. She and I spent some time figuring out the many conflicts she had in her marriage and about her husband's periodic substance abuse.

In some scenarios, however, silent people have problems with closeness, trust, and empathy (object relations damage). In those instances, the therapist usually attempts to draw the person into a discussion, and will self-disclose to help the person gradually develop a relationship. Getting a silent person to talk may be the goal of treatment.

EXAMPLE 2

Audrey, a 25-year-old married woman, was referred by her mother, a loquacious socialite who found me through mutual friends. The mother related on the phone that Audrey was too shy even to call to me. The mother would be paying my fees and wanted to meet me.

I agreed to see Audrey. When I met her in the waiting room, her mother was with her, as planned. I mentioned to Audrey that her mother wanted to speak with me, she agreed, and they both entered my consultation room. The mother explained her concerns to me. Thereafter I met with Audrey alone.

Audrey had graduated from college and married a year later, but she had always been "quiet." Her mother was a not-so-secret alcoholic, as was her father, and her father had had several affairs that her mother knew about. She did not know if her mother had been unfaithful, but suspected so.

Audrey had women friends from college with whom she had periodic phone contact. She was close with her husband, who had a successful job. She was a homemaker but had no children and no immediate plans for them.

As long as I asked Audrey questions, she would relate to me. If I self-disclosed, she had hardly any reaction. When I tried to confront and/or explore her quietness, she would acknowledge it, but have no thoughts about it. It was difficult to get her to mentalize.[57] I could not find any deficits in her abstraction, integration, reality testing, or self-preservation. She had no impulse problems and did not get overwhelmed by affect. For a while, I thought most of her problems seemed conflictual: I formulated to myself that she was disidentifying from her mother, who talked too much and was annoying. Further, I thought Audrey was quiet because she did not want to face anger, guilt, or separation anxiety in relation to her mother, whom she saw frequently. In other words, she seemed to have a mild schizoid personality disorder, based on difficulties with separation-individuation, plus reticence as a character defense that managed guilt and anxiety.

I saw Audrey once a week for about 2 years. If I attempted to draw her attention to her defensive activity, such as control (of her thoughts, emotions, the environment, etc.), suppression, or inhibition of observing ego, she would generally remain silent. When I would try to understand her (especially regarding quietness being a protective response to her invasive, controlling mother), she would usually either say, "Probably," or "I don't know."

She seemed to "do better" in sessions if I did not attempt to understand her problems. If I asked questions and responded to whatever she told me in a reality-oriented way, she would become interactive.

After 2 years, her mother called me to say Audrey was feeling much better and had been talking! Her mother related to me that Audrey did not wish to pursue treatment any further. I told the mother I was glad to hear there had been improvement.

Five years later, her mother requested a referral for marital treatment, at Audrey's urging. I then found out that Audrey was still fine, and that she and her husband had had a son, apparently doing well at age 2.

This case is, no doubt, representative of a class of disturbances where insight is neither achievable nor even a goal. Although there were no severe deficits in Audrey's major functions, her object relations deficits were so great that just a bit of a "new relationship" apparently gave her enough feeling of

---

57 Fonagy, Gyorgy, Jurist, and Target (2005).

separation from her mother that she was less despondent and more communicative. She was not capable of sharing such observations with me[58] and did not seem capable of much mutual empathy with me. The best I seemed able to do was to express my interest in her as a human being, ask her questions, and offer my opinions about what she would bring up.

There was no doubt transference of some sort, and resistance based on this. My attempts to clarify these during treatment, however, were fruitless. In retrospect, I have at times wondered if I should have handled things differently, but have come to the conclusion that, at least within the scope of my abilities, Audrey's silence seemed to be only slightly available for treatment and resolution through mostly supportive interventions.

---

58 This is similar to the attitude described by Wilson, Hogan, and Mintz (1992). They explained how certain people who suffer with anorexia withhold positive feedback to the therapist because their positive feelings toward the therapist give the therapist too much "control" (engender too much self-object fusion anxiety).

Problem 49
People Who Stand Up and Walk Around

For many years, I thought that people standing up and walking around in a therapist's office occurred only in the movies.

However, as I was in practice longer, I saw, both during evaluations and sometimes during treatment, that some people would occasionally stand up and begin pacing around the room as they were talking. When people did this, I noticed that they were overwhelmed by affect, usually anger.

It wasn't until last year, when I was teaching a course on Freud's cases, that I ran across Mark Kanzer's paper on Freud's report of the "Rat Man's" treatment.[59] Kanzer astutely pointed out that the Rat Man, early in treatment, jumped off the couch and started pacing around. Kanzer understood this, in retrospect, as father transference to Freud, which Freud missed.

In other words, somebody jumping up and pacing around has meanings—in the case of the Rat Man, of transference. Kanzer thought that Rat Man reexperienced the terror of being beaten by his father, transferred onto Freud. The Rat Man relieved his fear symbolically by running away and (my addition) "standing up" to his father.

In other words, people pacing around may be representations of an ego deficit and/or have symbolic meaning that can be understood.

Additionally, there are those who stand up and walk around in order to manipulate the therapist into believing they have a mental illness. These people usually have financial motives: They may be involved in a lawsuit, a pension dispute, or a disability determination.

SHORT ANSWER

When people stand up suddenly, while they are talking, and begin pacing around, it's wise to discuss this particular bit of behavior with them. You may wait a minute to hear what they have to say while they're pacing around, but you certainly want to discuss the fact that their standing up must mean something. The average person will probably admit to being "full of anger" or "full of fear" and leave it at that. If they do, it is probably best to express understanding, wait a minute, and then ask them to sit down again.

---

59 Kanzer (1952).

People pacing around the room usually make the therapist anxious. Some therapists would actually say to a person that they are feeling anxious because of that person (projective identification). But in my experience, most of the time, the pacing is due to agitation overwhelming the person's function of psychomotor control.

LONG ANSWER

If you can think of the symbolic meaning, you may mention it. Confronting body behaviors or body activity is always tricky and requires a lot of translation of symbolic thinking on the part of the person you are treating, as well as yourself. It is hard to figure out exactly what the symbolism may be. In his paper about the Rat Man, Kanzer, acting as a latter-day supervisor, easily could spot the transference elements. It is, of course, much more difficult while you are sitting in the room with a person who is upset.

Furthermore, as I have noted previously, trying to explain symbolism when people are very upset may be a mistake, because it leads them to feel that you do not understand the overwhelming nature of the affect they are experiencing. You could argue that if people have a negative reaction to you trying to explain something about their behavior, like pacing around the room, that their negative reaction is further explicable.

This has not been my experience. If people begin to think that you are unempathic, unreasonable, and unrealistic, I have found it to be very difficult to try to understand meanings. One tenet of understanding transference reactions is that the people you are treating need to realize that their reactions to you are displacements from other people and not *really* about you.

EXAMPLE

Connie, a 37-year-old married homemaker with two young adolescent daughters, started treatment because of phobias of horses, airplanes, and, to a small degree, of driving. Of some curiosity was that she had developed these phobias suddenly, after her husband fell off a horse and broke his leg.

The phobia of airplanes prevented her from going on business trips with her husband, which she had supposedly enjoyed previously. Her phobia of horses prevented her from engaging in an activity she enjoyed with her husband and children, namely horseback riding.

During her analytic treatment, she connected her husband's injury with the death of her father when she was 12. She and her father had been in a sulky (a sort of buckboard), riding through the country, when the wheel of the sulky hit a rock, and the vehicle tipped over and fell. Her father apparently hit his head on a rock, unfortunately experienced a cerebral hemorrhage, and died within a day or two. Connie got thrown off the sulky. She had not lost consciousness but was bruised and apparently had urinated on herself. At the hospital, with her father, she remembered urinating again and feeling embarrassed. At the time of the accident, she vaguely remembered bleeding somewhere, or maybe menstruating.

About 6 months into her treatment, she reported to me that she felt an urge to urinate when she arrived at my office and was sitting in the waiting room. She would often use the facilities briefly and then come back and sit in the waiting room again. I asked her for her thoughts about it. She immediately compared this behavior with the accident when she was 12 and thought that perhaps she was worried about urinating. It was as though in preparing to see me, she was afraid there might be an accident; she did not want to have the embarrassing experience of urinating on herself.

Her motor behavior (going to the restroom) occurred just before the session while she was waiting for me. Further thoughts included material that led us to understand a variety of conflicts that she had regarding her husband, which had been displaced from various fears that she had about her father. When her husband became injured in the horseback-riding accident, this had triggered a whole series of reactions that unconsciously were connected with her father's death from that accident, also involving a horse.

In her case, the standing up and walking around occurred before her session. It turned out to be symbolic of many conflicts ("highly overdetermined").

Problem 50
People Who Check Their Watches

People who check their watches are generally obsessive-compulsive. They fear loss of control, which is symbolic of a variety of conflicts throughout their lives. Because they fear this, they act in ways that are controlling, especially about time, neatness, and perfection. They may preoccupy themselves with aesthetic interests.

Many people in treatment check their watches toward the end of the session. This common defense is called "turning passive to active." They do not like being told to leave; they would prefer to time the session, themselves, and then tell you when they are leaving. This restores their sense of control and sometimes relieves guilt.

SHORT ANSWER

When people check their watches during a session or toward the end of a session, it is usually a good idea to notice this, verbalize something about it, and invite their thoughts about it. People may already have had thoughts during the session that they don't like spending money, and/or that they feel people mistreat them or cheat them and are angry about it. They hate being controlled.

You want to "link"[60] these thoughts to the particular aspect of their thinking that they have just told you. In other words, they may fear being cheated by you (out of time), and they may want to ensure that they get their money's worth. They may be controlling the time at the end of the session because they dislike being rejected and/or they dislike endings of anything.

People's watch-checking may indicate reluctance to work with you, which may be unconscious. Especially in obsessional people, who tend to be overly nice (reaction-formations), their mistrust and/or hostility toward you for billing (taking money from) them and their fear that you are taking time from them can lead them to become controlling about the time. They complain if you are a few minutes late or you end the session on time whether they were on time to begin with or not.

My policy throughout my career has been to try to be on time; but if I'm not, I will add the number of minutes that I am late to the predicted ending time of the session. That way, I do not penalize people, time-wise, if I am a few minutes late. However, if a person I am treating is late, I do not generally extend the time

---

60 Volkan (2011).

of the session to make myself late. If they are late, it's their problem; we may investigate the meaning of it at some point, but the "frame"[61] remains intact.

LONG ANSWER

There are a variety of conflicts that cause people to check their watches. People may have worries about wishes to be loved and taken care of (oral wishes versus shame). On the one hand, they try to be independent, but on the other, they yearn for maternal love.

EXAMPLE 1

Shelley, a 53-year-old woman, checked her watch as a session ended. She criticized me for ending "a minute early." Actually, this was a distortion: I had ended a minute late, at least by my clock. (After dueling with obsessional people for decades, I eventually got an atomic clock so that I always know the exact time. This put an end to any doubt in my mind about whether I was late or not, or whether I had "shorted" anyone.)

Armed with my knowledge that I had actually spent an extra minute with her, I suggested we discuss it the next time I saw her. She was still a bit suspicious. This issue came up again. It had mostly to do with her feeling that her mother had never spent enough time with her, which she displaced onto me.

However, she also felt that her father had looked down on her as a girl and had thereby somehow given her "short-shrift." We realized that her anger at me was actually targeted at her father for condescending toward her. In addition, she thought I was retaliating against her (by shorting her on time) for having reduced her fee—which she imagined made me feel deprived by *her*.

EXAMPLE 2

Richard, a 58-year-old vascular surgeon, was having marital problems. He complained that when he came to a session he lost "thousands of dollars." He paid me and lost money by not being in the office or operating room.

I pointed out that his complaints were laden with symbolic meaning, not the least of which was a challenge to me as to whether his treatment was worth it. He acknowledged he often thought it was a "waste of time" just to

---
61 Langs (1973).

try to understand himself, although he was concerned about his lack of sexual interest in his 45-year-old wife, Ginger.

Ginger seemed to be tolerating him. However, she was depressed; a psychiatrist had started her on an SSRI. Although she was not quite as moody when taking the SSRI, it interfered with her sex drive toward him. This was a handy rationalization for him, since he felt very little sexual interest in Ginger. Richard preferred to masturbate while looking at Internet pornography that showed women with large breasts.

I showed Richard how his wishes to be taken care of came into conflict with shame and therefore were sexualized. That is, he saw himself as macho and masculine while masturbating, looking at pictures of women with big breasts, which actually represented his unconscious infantile wish to suckle. He then began looking at his watch at the beginning and the end of each session. When I said to him that I noticed it, Richard responded, "Time is money!"

He wanted to make sure I started on time and ended on time so that he could get back to work. Sometimes he rationalized this by telling me, "People depend on me, too." I had some success in explaining to him that he was projecting his own neediness onto his patients and then complaining to me that I stopped him from taking care of them correctly, which was a reflection of feelings he had had about his own parents. He felt his parents ignored him, in favor of a younger sister, and could see his displacement into our relationship of his competitiveness with this sister.

He had also developed a reaction formation, where he was too nice to his patients, and put them ahead of himself and his wife. He used his own workaholism as a rationalization for feeling he wasn't getting enough from me.

Another meaning of Richard's insistence about time had to do with competition. I pointed out to him that his "big" income made him feel more masculine. In part, this compensated for terrible feelings of inferiority, especially sexually. When I brought these meanings up, and connected them with his checking his watch to prove that he was somehow masculine, Richard gave this some value, but then said to me, "I've never been cavalier about sex."

He recounted how he had loved one girl in high school and one girl in college, but neither of them would sleep with him. When he finally did have sexual intercourse, at age 23, the woman with whom he had relations complained to him afterward about his premature ejaculation. He was unhappy about that.

He still had premature ejaculation periodically but blamed this on his lack of sex drive. I told him that I thought he was making excuses for an inhibition. After this confrontation of his defensive activity, Richard responded, "Well, I don't know if it is an inhibition. I don't want to fuck a woman to death or anything."

This gave me an opportunity to remind Richard of his descriptions of his mother as a cold person who often beat him. I suggested that the idea of "fucking a woman to death" combined some of his anger at his mother with some of his fonder feelings toward her and got associated, during adolescence, with more generalized sexual feelings.

It sounded like he felt guilty about the hostility that went along with viewing his penis as a weapon that could kill somebody. Richard's fantasies of phallic killing later became associated with any of his criticisms of his wife, which again caused guilt. He had then avoided her sexually and experienced premature ejaculation.

Richard's checking of his watch had provided the stimulus for our understanding of his inhibitions, compulsions, and finickiness.

Problem 51
Parting Shots

This phrase was first suggested to me by my friend Dr. Albert P. Koy, a psychoanalyst in New Orleans. A savvy therapist, Al pointed out to me, during numerous discussions, that some people did this: As they were walking out of his office, they would say something hostile and then escape. Sometimes, the (transference) hostility was directed toward him.

One characteristic of "parting shots" is that people who use them can escape. They run from their fear of retaliation, before they can face just how hostile they are, themselves. They escape an understanding, but simultaneously "act in."

The escape can be symbolic of wishes they had to escape from volatile, hostile parents. You will also see identifications with parents: they do to you what their parents did to them, namely, leave you with some critical comment that burns you up.

What should you do?

SHORT ANSWER

Sometimes, a parting shot can be met with a countershot. In other words, you can respond immediately to set the stage for understanding in the following session.

EXAMPLE 1

Melissa complained of feeling irritable and depressed after the death of her third husband from a heart attack. She was 55 years old and felt deprived.

After a couple of sessions where I was able to clarify some of her guilt (for not noticing his illness sooner) and avoidance of grief, Melissa felt a bit better but was still crying a lot. I recommended she see me three times a week so we could better understand things. She was feeling weak, over-whelmed, and ashamed, but she agreed it might be helpful if we had more time together.

In the next session, she told me that she was proud that she had enough money put away that she did not have to depend on her two children to support her. We made some useful links between her divorce from her first husband, the death of her second husband from lung cancer, and the death of her third husband recently. As she left, she said, "Oh, by the way, I don't think I'm going to keep that Tuesday appointment that you set up for me for the third day a week."

I immediately countered this by saying to her, "I think that you're running away because you're ashamed that you have exposed a wish to depend on me." She responded quickly, "Well, I don't know if I can afford it." I responded with another countershot: "My fee reinforces your shame about depending on me."

> **TIP**
> Handle parting shots, if you are ready, with a parting countershot. If you are not quite ready or in an awkward position (like outside your consulting room), absorb the parting shot and bring it up in the next session.

I did not make any changes in her schedule. The next time I saw her, she smiled as she walked into the consultation room. As she sat down, she said, "Where were we?" I said we had been talking about money when she left. She smiled again, and said, "I guess I'll stay with you three times a week. But you were wrong: I'm not ashamed. It's just that I don't want to get all involved and then have another loss. I really try not to spend money on myself. I feel like it's not my money. Does that make sense?" I connected her using the life insurance benefits she had received with her guilt; she agreed.

My parting countershot to her parting shot, although slightly off (she wasn't ashamed of depending on me, she felt afraid of loss if she let herself depend on me), seemed to help her think about the meanings of her resistance.

LONG ANSWER

It is sometimes better to withstand a parting shot and address it in the next session, to be more accurate. Also, if someone makes a parting shot when you are not ready, or you are in an awkward position (such as outside your consulting room), giving an immediate response breaks the "frame," disturbing the working alliance.

EXAMPLE 2

Bill, a Jewish, 59-year-old general contractor and roofer, consulted me about panic attacks that had begun 5 months previously, about the time his wife developed rheumatoid arthritis. His reactions to his wife's illness, including guilt over his wish to find a healthy woman, were causing anxiety.

Bill was trying to be thoughtful toward his wife although she was irascible because of the pain from illness. Recently, a female interior designer he knew had made it crystal clear to him that she was available sexually if he was interested. He felt guilty about that temptation, causing more anxiety.

Bill's father had been unfaithful to his mother—he learned this while he was in college. His parents had been born in Austria, and although they were Jewish, one grandmother had been married to a distant (non-Jewish) relative of Emperor Franz Josef. His grandparents left Austria before it was invaded by Germany during World War II but were unable to persuade the rest of their relatives, who later perished in Nazi concentration camps.

At the end of one session, as Bill left my office, we saw a stack of mail lying on the floor, where the mail carrier had put all the mail through the mail-slot in the outer door to my suite. As Bill left, he quipped, "You've got a little Holocaust here." We were outside my consultation room, so I did not respond.

In the next session, as Bill and I delved into the links between his childhood and his current symptoms, I said I thought his parting comment about me having a Holocaust, although a joke, represented something. He connected his wife's illness with his grandparents' stories of loss. His panic attacks also included his overreaction to potential loss of a family member. Thus, he was worried about his wife's illness: "She'll never escape it."

Further links were to be found between his grandparents' "story,"[62] the parallel that his wife was not Jewish, and other conflicts between Bill and his parents when he was an adolescent.

In this case, my patience in handling his "parting shot" allowed us a more in-depth discussion of the bases for his anxiety in the following session.

---

62 Volkan (2009, 2011).

Problem 52
People Who Ask How You Are Feeling

This is an element of technique that I have had to handle frequently. Some people, when you see them in the waiting room, say to you, "How are *you*?" This is a standard greeting in the United States and sometimes means nothing except for saying hello. In Chinese, the phrase for "hello" (ni hao), means "you good." To ask someone how they're feeling, the question is *ni hao ma*? This means, "You good (word that means a question)?" The phrase is the same, except for the word that means question.

In English, someone asking "How are you?" may be more like ni hao ma. It is difficult to figure out because the social convention usually means very little except a greeting. The usual response to "How are you?" is, "Fine. How are you?" The problem with this response from the therapist is that it begs the question of why people are coming to see you.

Of course, the whole question is how they are. Not only that, but when you respond with the same question, you are breaking the "frame" by discussing their problems in the waiting room.

Based on some worries like this, when I first went into practice, I felt squeamish about answering this question from people.

EXAMPLE 1

Clem, a salesman, started each of his once-a-week sessions by asking me, "How are you, Doctor?" Because I was trying to maintain the frame, I didn't answer his question. In my office, we would work to understand his problems.

After about 4 or 5 months, something good happened to me (I can't remember what), and I was in a good mood. When I went to meet Clem in the waiting room, he said, as usual, "How are you, Doctor?" I responded, offhandedly, "Fine. How're you doing?" He said, "For God's sake! I can't believe that you finally answered that question. For the past four months, I thought you weren't human...." He laughed, and I laughed, and therapy proceeded.

Considering the social convention but also considering the frame of the treatment, what's the best policy if someone repeatedly asks you how you are?

SHORT ANSWER

Here is my current solution. When I open the door to the waiting room and people ask, "How are *you*?" I respond, "Fine." I do not counter other than that. This lets people know I am responsive to them, but I avoid starting the session until we are in the consultation room and the door is shut. I sit down and let people begin; but in some instances, I may, after we are seated, ask, "How are *you*?"

Most of the time, I don't ask that because that is the issue. It is redundant to ask people in your office how they are doing. They are not doing well or else they would be done with their treatment. Sometimes they feel better, but you want to try to understand connections between their thoughts and their resistances to treatment.

If they have trouble talking, that's a defense which you bring to their attention. Asking how they are doing also sets a social tone, and can derail the work if they respond socially or superficially.

LONG ANSWER

> **TIP**
> The seemingly innocuous social convention of asking "How are you?" can have other meanings when the question is posed to a therapist before a session. Consider whether the question bears a relationship to the person's problems when deciding how to respond.
>
> Most of the time, it's easy enough to answer, "Fine." Sometimes, however, if the person repeatedly asks you this question, it may have some meaning.

EXAMPLE 2

Leslie, a 42-year-old married woman with two teenage children, consulted me for difficulties with her husband. He wanted more sex, although he was frequently not home. She did not understand why she had lost interest in sex with him. She knew it was causing trouble. She loved her husband; they did not fight.

I treated Leslie four times a week for 4 years. During the first year of treatment, when I went to greet her in the waiting room, she would always ask me how I was feeling. By this time, I had devised my short solution, would answer with one word, and then we entered the consultation room.

After getting to know her, I suspected her question had other meanings. I therefore decided to do something a little different with her. The next time I saw her, before Leslie stood up to walk into my office, she asked, as usual, "How are *you*?" I wondered aloud if she were for some reason, worried about me.

She hesitated for a moment. In my office, as I was closing the door and she was heading to the couch, she said, "You're right. I have been worried about you." I said this sounded important, and we should spend some time on it. She agreed.

Leslie realized she was afraid I would suddenly get sick. When she asked me how I was feeling, she was reassuring herself that I was okay. She first associated to her brother becoming alcoholic when she was a teenager.

Then she thought about her mother. Her mother was still living, and they had frequent conversations by phone. Although she was friendly with her mother, she remembered, as a teenager, that her mother was unpredictable and unresponsive. Her mother got depressed when her father was busy with "homework," sat for hours watching television, and did not speak with Leslie. Leslie was expecting me to act like her mother (transference). She asked how I was feeling because she was afraid I would be inattentive to her on any given day.

An even deeper "layer" of symbolic meaning involved Leslie's problems with object constancy. She was fearful that I was not stable and that I would change from day to day. She was, without realizing it, checking whether I was "there" emotionally for her or had "changed." Asking me how I was feeling was also a way of relieving her anxiety about this.

EXAMPLE 3

Neil, a 49-year-old general surgeon, consulted me because he was losing control of his temper in the operating room and yelling at attendants. He began his sessions, in the waiting room, by asking me how I was feeling. In his case, I first pointed out that he had some difficulty accepting the role of a patient. He was used to being the doctor, and asking people how they felt, and I suspected he was turning the tables on me (unconsciously) because he was nervous about being in a situation where he did not have control. He laughed, and agreed that he was a bit of a "control freak."

This understanding led to a fruitful connection to his yelling at people in the operating room: When they did not do exactly what he wanted he would feel that he had lost control, and he would then fear that everything would go wrong. As Neil further reviewed this with me, he argued that in the operating room, things can go wrong, and that he needed to be "the captain of the ship" (the legal term for this is *respondeat superior*), meaning that the surgeon in charge is liable for any mistakes that are made by other personnel in the operating room.

Although I acknowledged to Neil that he was, of course, right about his responsibility, I also pointed out to him that he was using this as a rationalization to relieve his guilt about verbally abusing people who were helping him in the OR. He had not thought of this but recalled how much he hated it when his father yelled at him and criticized him.

His other interesting association was to a couple of mentors during his surgery residency who had ridiculed him and "called him on the carpet" when he made any error. He had also become like them (identification with the aggressor) instead of recognizing his anger at them for their rather churlish attitudes in general.

Problem 53
Adolescents Who Sit in Your Chair

For the first 15 or 20 years of my practice, I treated large numbers of adolescents. I still occasionally treat a few. It is my habit, when bringing people from the waiting room into my consulting room (which requires a walk down a hall of about 6 feet—see Figure 3, 380), to allow people to go in ahead of me. After they enter my office, they sit in the seat I have set aside for people I treat while I close the doors and then sit down, myself. Occasionally a teenager may, on entering, purposely expropriate my chair.

I had to figure out what to do with this. Since I was dealing with a teenager, my technique had to be different from what I would do with an adult—since teenagers, not far from school age (latency), can play games that are meaningful. When they do this, they are challenging authority, being disobedient, expressing wishes for individuation, and not "going along with the program" as far as treatment goes (a resistance).

SHORT ANSWER

When teenagers sit in your chair, you must know that they are playing a game. What I have usually done is play with them (sometimes latency-age children will do this, also). In one variation, I walk over to my chair (where they are sitting), look down at the teenager, who is usually, by this time, giggling, and say, "So you're the doctor today!"

Usually this is enough to move teenagers out of my chair back to theirs, at which time I can speak with them about how much fun it is to be the doctor and how awful they feel about being in treatment. They really don't like it, and would like to turn it around.

LONG ANSWER

In a more complex approach, I do not go over to my chair, but stand near (or sit in) the teenager's chair. I accept the gambit that the teenager has started, and "interpret from within the metaphor." I say to the teenager, "Doctor, I have a problem."

Usually, the teenager, who is already playing, will respond, "Tell me all about it!" I then say, "I have emotional problems, but I really hate it. They suck. And not only that, I'm embarrassed I have to go see this doctor who wants to examine every piece of my mind, and I don't even want to do it. So

I don't even tell the doctor about this, but I pretend that I'm good. He doesn't know how much I don't want to do this."

Most teenagers who have reasonable abstraction and reality testing understand this immediately. If this approach does not move them out of my chair, and they keep giggling or asking me more questions, I may go along with the game a while longer. What I "play at," in reverse, is a description of the teenager's problems as though they are my own, interspersed with my formulations about their feelings and actions.

For example, if a teenager asks me to elaborate on my wanting things my way, I may say something like, "It all stems from my relationship with my mother. She's so nice; you wouldn't believe that I get pissed off at her. Very often, I feel so terrible that I want to kill myself or run away. Then I told my mother and what did she make me do? She made me go see this doctor. I don't even want to think about it!"

I am sure you get the drift. This second technique is to play along with the game but to use it in such a way as to communicate an understanding of the teenager's wish to dominate, escape, and individuate.

Problem 54
People Who Bring Their Own Drinks to the Office

Drinking anything during a therapy session is, at least to some degree, a form of acting in, or possibly a break in the "frame." People are supposed to be serious in your office and focused on their problems, and so are you.

Nevertheless, while sitting for 45 minutes, people often get thirsty. I sometimes drink tea or coffee during the workday. Over the years, I have decided to be flexible in having a cup of tea or coffee while I'm working with someone; I also make coffee, tea, and water available to people entering the waiting room. I do not object if they bring a drink into my consulting room. What people do with their drinks becomes interesting.[63]

EXAMPLE 1

Olga, a woman in her middle 20s, had borderline personality problems: She kept emotional distance from me. During the course of treatment, I noticed a pattern in her cycles of trust and mistrust.

When she would take a cup of coffee from the coffee pot, she was feeling more trustful and would open up more. If she did not get a cup of coffee, I braced myself for a session in which she was likely to attack me for allegedly not caring about her, complain that the world did not love her, or sometimes express suicidal feelings.

Olga used distancing defenses when she was feeling mistrustful. Her attitude toward my coffee sometimes gave me a clue about how "receptive" she was feeling, in any particular session, especially toward depending on me.

Obsessive-compulsive people may fuss about their drink or accidently spill it and then apologize. This sometimes gets interesting, particularly with people who have good observing ego and symbolic functioning. Sometimes they will say, after the spill, "Well, I guess I was feeling irritated with you."

---

63 I do not provide food, candy, or cookies. In 1985, I removed the ashtrays and have not permitted smoking in my office since then. I have treated several physicians and therapists who insist they leave their mobile phones on when they are "on call." In those special situations, I have allowed this—and it has not caused much trouble—although I understand my colleagues who request people turn off their phones during sessions.

When they clean up the mess, I may comment on how they are relieving guilt, and this often leads to understanding of (transference) expectations that I will be critical. Sometimes, they project onto me their own self-criticism over making messes, or turn their self-criticism around onto me. Like women who bring their infants to the office, however, they can make a real mess. (See Problem 47, where the woman Aileen Kim was treating brought an infant to the office; the infant threw up all over Dr. Kim's desk and also gave Dr. Kim a viral infection which lasted over a week.)

My late residency supervisor, Dr. George Caruso, a seasoned psychoanalyst, once told me that he might have a sip of coffee after he had made a clarifying comment to someone or if they had expressed feelings toward him, either positive or negative. While waiting for the person to integrate and respond, he would take a sip of his coffee, look at the person, and thereby subtly encourage the person to think further. Thus, he used it as a timing tool in face-to-face psychotherapy..

Even more interesting are people who bypass having a cup of tea or coffee from my supplies; they bring their own drink to the office. This can have even more meaning than someone who just wants a little tea around in case they get thirsty.

SHORT ANSWER

When people bring their own drinks to the office, I tend not to comment right away. It is a type of acting in and usually represents the person having conflicts about depending on the therapist. Rather than depend on you, they depend on "their own bottle." (The same dynamic is common in alcoholics—see Problems 19 and 20—although most of the people who bring their own drinks to the office are not alcoholic.)

You may notice people holding back or avoiding talking with you (or talking too much) to avoid depending on you. You can bring their reluctance to depend on you to their attention; you connect it with relevant material about their upbringing—especially problems depending on their parents; then connect those problems with their bringing their own drink to the office. In other words, the drink symbolically means they are avoiding anxiety about depending on any authority figure.

It is safest to view this type of acting in as "oral." If people are in more intensive therapy, the orality may indicate that they are acting on oral conflicts rather than facing conflicts over control or sexuality.

LONG ANSWER

There are many ways in which people use drinks.

EXAMPLE 2

John, a 40-year-old man who ran a women's clothing business, had an addiction to using prostitutes. His wife did not know. He had sex with his wife about once every 2 weeks, which was what she preferred. He would often sneak out of his office for a few hours and meet with a prostitute.

One of his business associates would fly expensive prostitutes in from Las Vegas. John would just say he would be "out for a while," and leave his office to meet them for a mid-day rendezvous.

John brought a large latte with him to his therapy sessions. He placed it on the side table by his chair, and would proceed to discuss his problems. For a couple of months, once a week, I discussed the problems in his marriage as well as his conflicts with his mother and father when he was a teenager, and we made many useful links concerning his inhibitions of assertiveness with his wife. Much as the male "yes, dear" (Problem 24), he was passive with his wife, but then, a few years prior to seeing me, he began cavorting with prostitutes.

When he reached a more advanced stage of treatment, I explored with John what he was looking for when he saw prostitutes. He ironically responded that he was looking for "sex." I pointed out his vagueness, which I thought was shielding him from some shame about something.

He became a little bit red in the face and responded that he liked to "perform cunnilingus." He, in other words, requested the prostitute allow him to do this, which he enjoyed. He would then have sexual intercourse with her. He liked that the prostitutes did not give him any "lip" (resistance) but he was not interested in them performing fellatio on him.

I explained to him that his activity with the prostitutes was an enactment of a masturbation fantasy. In this fantasy, he was very sexual, but sexuality was protecting him from shame over his wish for his wife to be more attentive to him (his "oral" wishes). He stayed away from guilt over expressing any anger he felt toward his wife. That is, in performing cunnilingus, he was acting out, in sexual form, an "oral" wish for a woman to love him and "feed him," and in cheating on his wife he was secretly expressing anger. I showed him how the oral and hostile wishes were connected to his bringing a latte with him, which relieved his shame over "sucking" or depending on me, and expressed rejection of my coffee.

This was a very fruitful discussion. John laughed as he considered what he had been doing with his drink. He then had bitter memories of his mother's invasiveness and neglect, and his father beating him as a school-age child. These experiences with his parents had caused him to be overly independent, to fear losing other people if he became too aggressive, and to suppress his oral wishes because of shame.

EXAMPLE 3

Laura, a Jewish homemaker, had problems with her husband. They were having sexual problems. She did not enjoy sex, and he had premature ejaculation. They had a 2-year-old son and collaborated in their parenting.

Laura was raised in an Orthodox Jewish household, where sexual discussion was avoided. She did not date during high school, an Orthodox school for girls (Yeshiva Girls Division). She met her husband during college at a function for people who were "shomer Shabbat" (strict observers).

They dated for 6 months but did not have sex before marriage. They did not have sexual intercourse on their honeymoon; he was impotent. They eventually had sexual intercourse after being married a few weeks, but she did not enjoy it. After their son was born, she lost interest in sex.

Interestingly, Laura was a strikingly beautiful 27-year-old woman. Her husband was 29 and had an excellent job as an accountant, which made them comfortable financially. Although she had a college education, Laura preferred being a homemaker.

Her upbringing in a small town in New Jersey had left her quite deprived. Although her father had provided for the family, she had seven younger siblings, the closest being 11 months younger than she was.

Her mother was overwhelmed taking care of the children and brought Laura into child-care duties. In addition, her mother disciplined Laura, as a young child, with "time out" for hours. Laura could not remember why her mother had punished her but recalled crying, alone in her room, feeling no one cared.

Laura was sexually inhibited, but because of her physical appearance, she was voted the "sweetheart" of a Jewish fraternity in college. Being "zaftig" (voluptuous figure) bothered her; boys were "all over me." She had once considered breast reduction surgery, but her parents would not allow it. She got married just after college partly to avoid the "sexual stuff." She was disgusted by any ideas of oral sex, which her husband wanted.

As I got more material from Laura, I could help her understand that she felt like sexual relations involved "taking care of the man." She equated relations with a man with (a) taking care of her seven siblings when she was a child and (b) "giving in."

She was disgusted by fellatio: It symbolized dependency, which caused her shame. Being "passive" during sexual intercourse went against her wish to be in control and not "give in."

As Laura understood these conflicts, she felt available for sex with her husband, and they had sex more frequently. During a later session, she came to my office wearing a low-cut, red miniskirt outfit. She was carrying a Big Gulp, an oversized beverage cup from a convenience store. While she was talking about her husband, she sat back in the chair and placed the cup between her thighs. This gave me an obstructed view, which I did not want, up her skirt. After a minute, I said to her, "Do you have any idea how you are sitting?" She then looked at the Big Gulp between her thighs, and shrieked, "Oh, my God! I'm so sorry!" She grabbed the Big Gulp, crossed her legs, and sat up straight. She kept apologizing.

The Big Gulp represented her wishes for dependency gratification that derived from her feeling neglected by her mother. She drew my attention to her sexually, a sexualization of (defense against) those oral wishes. And she had denied how the way she was sitting expressed oral or sexual wishes.

Regarding her sexual inhibition with her husband, we could see that she was interested in sex but ashamed over the intensity of her displaced oral wishes, which translated into her disgust about fellatio. She "acted in" sexual wishes toward me, representing oral wishes as well. When I pointed out her denial and "acting in," she felt guilt and shame—identification with her parents' values.

By understanding the origins of her sexual conflicts and inhibitions, Laura made considerable progress in her sex life with her husband.

Problem 55
People Who Don't Hang Up Their Coats

When I was in practice in New Orleans, where it was often too warm for coats, I did not see this type of "acting in" very often; when it was raining, people would bring their raincoats into the session. In Virginia Beach we have four seasons, so we get some genuinely cold days in winter and even occasional snowfall. For several months, therefore, people need to wear coats; it is interesting what they do with them in my office.

Sometimes, people just are not thinking about this very much. They have more serious things on their minds and therefore it does not occur to them to take off a jacket and hang it up on the coat stand in my consultation room. When people are wearing heavy coats for winter, it is more striking when they do not use my coat stand. They may keep their coat on in my 71 (Fahrenheit) degree office; more commonly, they take their coat off, hold it on their body, or put it on the floor next to them.[64]

It is difficult to make therapeutic use of this behavior in explaining people's problems. Many people are resistant to examining this, since it is easily normalized: It is cold outside and they need their coats. Under certain circumstances, however, this type of behavior may provide useful information.

SHORT ANSWER

If someone who is holding a coat in your waiting room then enters your consultation room and walks past your coat rack without using it, this may indicate something about the person's resistance and/or conflicts. When you see the coat is still in someone's lap (this is a little bit more common with women) it is an indication, usually, that the person is feeling defensive, guarded, and resistant to explanatory comments.

> **DEFINITION**
> "Negative hallucination" refers to the phenomenon where someone looks right at something but does not see it.

---

64 For practical reasons, I keep a coat stand near the door in my consultation room and not in my waiting room. To protect the privacy of my next appointment, I do not want people to have to return to the closed waiting room after a session to fetch their coats. See Figure 3, 380 for my office layout.

Generally, when I see someone is doing this, I do not comment on it but use it as a guide to be careful about the timing of any comments about symbolism. I wait and watch even more carefully for other signs of resistance. These resistances may take the form of superficial socialization, discussions about art and music (aesthetics as a defense), asking me how I am (to avoid thinking about how they are), or silence.

When I want to ask a question, this can be an indicator that the person I am treating is using defensive operations. At that point, I will try to discuss some element of the person's guardedness, but not necessarily connect the resistance to the behavior of holding the coat "close to the vest."

LONG ANSWER

In more complicated situations, people who keep their coats on are manifesting a type of "insulation defense" (pun intended). Commonly, they are terrified of emotional closeness and/or terrified of angry feelings. They keep all of this "cloaked" symbolically.

When people hold coats over their bodies, and I think this indicates object relations problems, I may point out to them that I have a coat stand, should they wish to use it. As a form of *negative hallucination,* some people may not have even seen my coat stand despite its conspicuous presence at the entrance to the room. This is often an indication of reluctance to letting me take care of them. Sometimes, there is a mild integrative weakness, where they are not terribly cognizant of their surroundings.

I usually wait until I have enough data, so that if I bring up the issue of the coat, we have enough working alliance that people already understand something about symbolism. Therefore, if I point out the existence of the coat stand, and people respond, "No, that's all right," I might bring their attention to how they are covering themselves in my warm office. I may add a speculation that they are somehow feeling guarded about something. This can be a useful approach, as people who are hiding under their coats can then discuss their guardedness over emotional closeness or shame over sexual matters. The meanings (compromise formations) of holding onto their coats may also include

1. use of it as a transitional object,[65]
2. unconscious provocation toward me (to make me ask), and/or
3. wishes for me to somehow break through their resistance.

---

65 Transitional objects are the teddy bear/soft objects used by toddlers as a transition between symbiosis with mother and independence (Winnicott, 1953). They often help toddlers sleep alone at night in their cribs without the presence of their mother or caregiver.

At times, people just say they feel "cold." These people, often women, are yearning for emotional warmth from the therapist but are afraid to ask for it. This is another dimension of their object relations problems, and may derive from difficulties they had in early childhood; more frequently, they lacked support from parents during adolescence.

Problem 56
People Who Ask to Borrow a Magazine

Many people who ask to borrow a magazine from the waiting room insist that it is a minor issue. According to Langs (1973), however, it is a break in the frame of the treatment and, according to Greenson (2008), it is a break in the working alliance, since the person is doing something that is not part of the contract with the therapist.

So is it a minor thing that you shouldn't fuss about or is it a highly symbolic piece of behavior that should be understood?

SHORT ANSWER

Volkan (1988, 2011) suggested that when people ask to borrow a magazine, you should always raise some question about this. He explains to people that if they simply take the magazine without discussing it, he will not be able to understand what it means. This is a fruitful approach much of the time.

With some people, exploration of the request can reveal narcissistic character problems or dependent transferences to the therapist.

LONG ANSWER

Decisions about whether to allow people to "borrow" a magazine are complex. As Lord Polonius advised his son, Laertes, in *Hamlet*, "Neither a borrower nor a lender be."[66] This advice is useful most of the time in treatment settings. It avoids the inevitable problems that arise when people forget to bring the magazine back or when "their dog eats it."

In my practice, I have made a couple of exceptions to the practice of questioning the motives of magazine-seekers, and they turned out okay.

EXAMPLE 1

Beth, a 37-year-old woman who was having marital problems, asked me one day, when I met her in the waiting room, if she could borrow a magazine. It was *The Atlantic*. I inquired about the content, and she explained that it was an article on modern mothering. There was a debate in the article about

---

66 Shakespeare (1602). Polonius explained further that if you lend money to a friend, you will lose both the money and the friend.

whether mothers could handle full-time work and at the same time raise children. The article also included contentious arguments about whether men should be more involved or not.

I indicated to Beth that it was okay if she borrowed the magazine, as long as she was willing to bring up the article's content and her interest in this matter with me in her sessions. She laughed, and said, "I plan to!" She borrowed the magazine and brought it back the next time I saw her. Since I was only seeing her once a week, we never did get to what transference meanings this must have had, but I did help her understand some of her conflicts that had to do with her exalted ideals about being a both a superworker and a supermom.

> **THEORY**
> Borrowing a magazine strays outside of the formal frame of the treatment alliance. Exploring the meaning of the request can reveal character problems, such as narcissism, or conflicts about depending on the therapist. In rare instances, fulfilling the request can facilitate trust, which may be helpful with people who are reluctant to trust anyone.

EXAMPLE 2

George, a lonely man in his 50s, had few friends. I saw him for therapy once a week. Occasionally, he would bring in an article he had cut out of our local newspaper or one of his own magazines. I considered this a form of expression of emotional closeness, and accepted these articles, which I kept in his chart.

When my first book came out, he expressed interest in reading it. I decided to give him a complimentary copy. I signed it and inscribed it to him with a personal message. He appreciated this sentiment.

I considered our swapping of intellectual material an indication of mutual trust, mutual interest, and mutual affection. This was one element, in a relational context, that allowed George to progress in treatment and understand some of his withdrawal from other people.

Problem 57
People Who Don't Pay the Bill

There are actually two different, though related, problems. Some people forget their check for the current session. Others do not wish to pay for a missed session. In the first instance, they play on the therapist's sympathies. The second, not wanting to pay for missed sessions (even if they agreed to do so previously), often involves an argument that, since they were not present, the therapist should not be paid.

It may sound unsympathetic (just what people who don't pay you count on), but unlike people who want to borrow a magazine, people who don't pay your fee are doing something overtly damaging to you. Borrowing an article might have that meaning, but it might have many other meanings, up to and including simple mutual trust.

However, when people don't pay the bill (either for sessions they attended or missed), they are brutally breaking their contractual agreement with you. This is also a break in the working alliance.

(Reminder: the working alliance includes people coming on time, paying their bill, talking to the therapist, and agreeing that they have a problem about which they and the therapist are going to speak in order to understand the bases for the problem.)

A growing challenge has evolved over the past decades as more therapists have accepted assignment from insurance companies and federal programs. In these cases, the insurance companies do not pay for missed sessions. In addition, many of the people who use their insurance are required to pay a copay at the time they come for their visit. Many people "forget" the copay or claim that they don't have the money that day.

Although I have not accepted assignment for over 20 years, I have treated and supervised many therapists who do, and these types of breaks in the treatment alliance are extremely painful, frustrating, annoying, and disappointing to them. Therapists inevitably have negative reactions to people they are treating because of not getting paid.

I have noticed that many therapists institute the defenses of reaction formation and rationalization: They are too nice and make excuses for people who did not bring a copay or pay for a missed session. Under some insurance agreements (including Medicaid), therapists are not allowed to bill for missed sessions, which means engaging in psychotherapy with Medicaid beneficiaries involves unfortunate limitations.

So what is the therapist to do when people do not bring their copay or do not pay for a missed session? Or, in the case of therapists who use direct billing, what can the therapist do about people who do not pay their bill, either at the time of the session or at the end of the month when they are billed?

SHORT ANSWER

People who do not pay their bills require attention to their use of money. "Letting it go" is almost always a mistake. The person is not thinking about what it means. They are simultaneously expressing hostility toward therapy and showing a powerful need to be taken care of like a baby. You should discuss their

- "oral dependent wishes,"
- hole in their conscience (unfairness),
- self-centeredness (object relations disturbance), and
- letting themselves off the hook (minimization, rationalization, and/or normalization defenses).

Otherwise, the person in therapy will get no benefit and the therapist will lose money. This is bad for everybody.

LONG ANSWER

Therapists, under usual conditions, are not working for charity. They want to help people, but need to be compensated. If they are not compensated in the manner agreed upon with the person in treatment, then the work can be effectively destroyed.

You do not have to be critical to bring this to the attention of a person who is making excuses and/or not paying. Gentle firmness (as parents often exercise with teenagers) is indicated. You might say, "I understand that you are having problems, or that you forgot your payment, but you and I have an agreement, and I think it is very important that you stick with our agreement, as I do. If you want to break the agreement, then we should understand why you want to do that and why you give yourself license to do that. I think this attitude is connected with your problems in your close relationships, so I don't think we should ignore this."

If people in treatment fight with you, do not want to pay because they don't have the money or they used the money for something else, it is best to discharge them or refer them to a free clinic. As my brother, Cliff, once told me, "You can work and not get paid, or you can not work and not get paid." Keep that in mind.

The situation becomes more complex when dealing with insurance or government agencies that will not compensate therapists for their time when someone misses a session. A slightly different problem occurs in any setting where the therapist is on a salary and people in treatment either do not pay their therapists or do not pay a fee at all.

I have advised therapists that I supervise, in those situations, to have a discussion with the people they are beginning to treat, where they make it clear that

- they are setting aside valuable time for the sessions,
- they cannot do anything else with that time,
- it is important for the person in treatment to show up for sessions, and
- if people do not want to come to a session, that is even more reason why they should show up and discuss their negative feelings and wishes to run away.

I also suggest that therapists in these positions use both a "carrot and a stick."[67] The carrot consists of reminding people they are getting treatment for free and that the therapist will spend a lot of time thinking about people's problems. The "stick" in this preliminary lecture should be advising people that if they miss an appointment, they may be discharged from the clinic.[68]

Some people ask if there are any "exceptions." I first answer that this is an interesting question which we ought to examine: Right away, they request exceptions to the rules, which must mean something. Secondly, I admit that under certain circumstances, I make exceptions, but they should not count on any. People attending free clinics frequently miss sessions anyway.

---

67 For non-American readers who are not familiar with this idiom, the carrot represents an inducement, the stick a punishment.
68 Discharging people from treatment is a bit complex. It's usually best to write them a letter stating that they are discharged, documenting how they have missed sessions but offering to help until they find another therapist. The letter should provide names of other therapists they can call for further treatment.
   If people you are treating are not suicidal or homicidal, this should be enough. If they are suicidal, homicidal, or overtly psychotic, you are best off telephoning them to assess their status and making decisions from there. If they don't need hospitalization, one way of minimizing the risk of legal "abandonment" is to offer to make an appointment for them with a community clinic or another private practitioner. Once you have done so, you should let the person know in writing, e-mail, and telephone when the new appointment is and how to get there.

> **TIP**
> People who do not show up for sessions or do not pay the bill should not be allowed to get away with such behavior. It is bad for them and for the therapist.
>
> The meanings of the behavior will vary from one person to another. The therapist should be polite yet firm in demanding compliance with the ground rules of the alliance.

Typical exceptions to paying for missed appointments include hospitalization for medical reasons, being caught in a snowstorm, having a severe illness that is keeping the person at home, and requisite military duty.

Situations where young mothers' babysitters have been irresponsible and not shown up are more complicated and usually need to be dealt with on a case-by-case basis. Sometimes you can make an exception for such a mother, but if it happens all the time, you have to consider possible passivity or poor judgment on the mother's part as far as choosing babysitters—often the mother is being "too nice" (an inhibition of critical judgment with reaction formations as defenses) so as not to feel guilty.

Problem 58
People Who Miss Many Appointments

Some people pay their bills but miss appointments anyway. This is a break in the working alliance, which needs to be addressed before anything else.

> **THEORY**
> When people miss appointments, the therapist should investigate what this has to do with money, control, self-esteem, competitiveness, and the defenses of undoing, minimization, and avoidance.

As therapists get busier and develop a reputation, more affluent people are likely to consult them. Affluent people present certain problems (Problem 16). One is that your fee is often quite minimal to them (no matter what you are charging). Unless they have a rather firm conscience (a "well-structured super-ego"), where they honor their agreements, wealthy people can take the "hit" of paying for missed appointment.

What do you do in these situations?

SHORT ANSWER

When people miss one appointment, and they pay for it because they have agreed to, sometimes there is nothing to understand. People may have had to go to court suddenly or had to attend an important meeting or a real estate closing where the time was changed. In these and similar instances people call you and let you know they cannot make it. If this happens before their appointment, and I'm able to reschedule their appointment within 1 work week, then I do not charge people for the missed appointment. However, if they do not let me know ahead of time or I cannot reschedule it, they must pay for the missed appointment.

Some people pay for missed appointments—but start missing a bunch of them; some change their appointments frequently. They are usually manifesting some type of resistance (due to character problems), and they are not aware of this. The evidence of their problems arises in the way they are behaving with you.

LONG ANSWER

Being able to understand people's missing appointments, even if they pay for them, can be a make-or-break issue in treatment. If the problem is not addressed, people will likely continue to miss appointments (and pay you), but you will feel frustrated and you will be wasting your time. Moreover, people's character problems will go unresolved.

EXAMPLE 1

Randy, a 41-year-old man, consulted me because he was having terrible problems in his marriage. He'd been married for 10 years, and he and his wife had two children. His wife complained that he was always working, but he countered that to make the money that he had made, he needed to work this hard.

Randy had made millions of dollars in business and was quite pleased with himself. He had come from a rather poor family, paid his way through college, and then started his own company. After 22 years, he was worth an enormous amount of money. In fact, he no doubt did not have to work as hard as he did, but he was quite opaque to his wife's pleas for more attention and more time spent with family.

When I noticed that Randy was using too much diplomacy (reaction formation) in describing the marriage, I pointed this out to him. He broke down crying, and said, "I don't want to hurt my wife!" He had been neglected by his mother, who was an alcoholic, and beaten severely by his father, also an alcoholic. He left home at 15, lived with a friend, and eventually was accepted to college and paid for it himself. He was not a drinker but was a workaholic. He knew this.

I suggested Randy come frequently to work with me on his problems. He was at first agreeable. After about a week of sessions, however, he began missing sessions almost every day. For the next 3 weeks, he saw me twice and missed his other sessions. At the end of the month, I sent him a bill; he paid it promptly.

On reflecting on the whole situation, though, I suspected he was "keeping me," the same way he treated his wife. Each time he missed, he called and left a message that he was tied up in a meeting. I didn't have an opportunity to discuss his character issues with him because he was never there.

After he missed the next two sessions, I spoke with him by phone, and told him that if he did not come to sessions, there was no point in me holding the times open for him or taking his money. Reluctantly, he agreed. I said if he ever had time to make appointments, I'd see him; he thanked me for what help I had given him, and apologized for having kept me waiting. He paid for the final two missed sessions and I never heard from him again.

Ten years later, I saw in the newspaper, by chance, that he had remarried. He had sold his business, and there was a big celebration.

Randy had posed an ethical dilemma. I felt it was improper for me to take his money when he wasn't coming to his sessions. He may have been trying to prove to himself that everybody can be bought; I also suspected that his payments to me were used as a ruse to calm down his first wife, who was concerned about the marriage. Whatever the reason might have been, Randy was being deceptive with me—so we could not understand his behavior. I did not like his deal with me, although unstated, so I broke it off.

EXAMPLE 2

Bruce, a 32-year-old sales manager, came to see me because of a series of problems at work. He had been put on probation for forgetting several appointments. He was not drinking or using drugs; his doctor had given him a stimulant for attention-deficit disorder, but he still "just forgot." In addition, his wife, a medical oncologist, was busy in her practice. Together, they were well-to-do, but he felt inferior to her.

She was a bit of a schedule freak. Over the 5 years of their marriage, they had one child, and she had organized things by the hour, 7 days a week. They had four babysitters who came at different times when they were working.

There was some mutual distancing between Bruce and his wife. He often went to different cities for baseball games. She, on the other hand, went on tennis vacations with her girlfriends. There had been no infidelity on his part, and he thought there had been none on hers. However, their sex life had suffered; they were having sexual relations once every 4 weeks. He was dissatisfied with this but could not tell if his wife was.[69]

Bruce and his wife both seemed ashamed about dependency wishes, projected blame onto the other for being irresponsible, and seemed to feel stoic about not needing sexual satisfaction. Unfortunately, they were becoming distant.

Bruce often "forgot" to do something his wife put on the schedule. This was similar, I pointed out to him, to the pattern at work, where he had been forgetting things. Bruce agreed to see me twice a week.

Almost stereotypically, he forgot an appointment. I showed him that he was now doing with me exactly what he did at work and with his wife. Bruce could see this. He then started crying, and yelled, "I'm a fuck-up!" I took this as a good prognostic sign: his irresponsibility, repression, and procrastination were now unacceptable to him (ego-dystonic). I did not interrupt his self-criticism.

---

69 Interestingly, this case showed a lot of the dynamics that were originally described by Levin (1969) in his study of marital incompatibility.

When he stopped crying, he asked me if there was any hope. I told him if we could understand the causes for his irresponsibility, the prognosis was good. We figured out, later in treatment, that much of his irresponsibility (apparent "superego defect") seemed to be designed: to get him punished; to obtain love that he never had from his mother; and to express hostility toward his father, which he had never even thought of. (He had always idealized his father.)

I treated Bruce for about three years, twice a week. He became responsible, got his wife to become more flexible, and stopped hiding his aggression and then getting himself punished. He and his wife mutually developed a schedule that they both found acceptable.

Problem 59
People Who Demand Medicine

Psychotropic medication is currently used by an enormous percentage of the populace in the United States. Whereas Valium (diazepam) was once the biggest seller, today, selective serotonin reuptake inhibitors are a multibillion dollar industry.[70]

There has been controversy about whether these antidepressants are even effective. Some metastudies suggest that they are no better than placebo.[71] Many other studies of people with both anxiety and depressive disturbances suggest SSRIs are effective.[72] As of this writing, SSRIs and SNRIs are being used to treat obsessive-compulsive disorders, phobias, panic disorder, depressions, PTSD (posttraumatic stress disorder), adolescent impulsivity, attention-deficit disorder, and adjustment disorders associated with affective reactions (American Psychiatric Association, 2000).

In Problem 2, I summarized my thoughts on when to use psychotropic medications and when not to. There is still much dispute about the indications for medication versus the indications for dynamic therapy, CBT, and supportive therapy.

A further complication is that the U.S. government has removed the ban on pharmaceutical advertising of prescription drugs to the general public. Since the ban was lifted, and the average U.S. adult watches 5 hours of television a day,[73] many people believe that what is ailing them psychologically has a medicine to fix it.

Primary care doctors are bombarded by people wanting medication. All therapists must be prepared for questions about medication from people who are beginning treatment.

SHORT ANSWER

First of all, there are liability and ethical issues in the United States surrounding the prescription of any type of treatment. Once you have selected the appropriate treatment for anyone, more discussion is necessary.

---

70 According to the Centers for Disease Control and Prevention (2011), "Eleven percent of Americans over age 12 take antidepressants" (¶ 1).
71 Kirsch, Moore, Scoboria, and Nicholls (2002) and Fournier et al. (2010).
72 Pizzi et al. (2011).
73 Semuels (2009).

For example, an adult presents with agitation and sleeplessness associated with severe problems in a marriage. You see that the person is worried the marriage may break up, is critical of the spouse, is contemplating an extramarital affair, has already consulted an attorney about a separation, and is upset. Nevertheless, the person is continuing to work, to take care of children, and poses no threat to self or others.

Furthermore, you see no evidence of breakdown in abstraction ability, integration, relationship to reality, or self-preservation. The person forms a relatively trusting relationship with you during the first session and seems to be ethical. In other words, psychotherapy seems indicated.

Even if you think psychotherapy is indicated, you still need to tell people about other types of therapy that are also available, including, at this time: CBT, medication, supportive therapy, group therapy, and marital therapy.

You need to explain the pros and cons of each of those and your reasoning as to why you are recommending which treatment. I suggest to most people that we first have a follow-up session to see how it goes. After we've had a couple of sessions, we will have an idea whether treatment that aims to understand their conflicts is the best choice.

> **TIP**
> You need to be prepared for some people asking you to give them antidepressants or other medicines. It is your job as a therapist to develop a methodology for determining when medication is warranted (indicated). I offer some advice on the indications for medication in Problem 2 and Problem 101 (B) in this book, and in the book *Get the Diagnosis Right*, Chapters 3 and 6.
>
> These medications can have serious physical side effects as well as powerful psychological meaning and impact. The decision should be made by the therapist (either alone, or in conjunction with an MD for nonphysician therapists). The person in treatment should not be allowed to push or bully you into giving medication if you feel it is not the best treatment for that individual.

This gives people an out, should they decide that they don't like the therapy or that they don't like me. It also gives me an out if I find something I don't want to treat or I don't like the person consulting me. In either case, referral to someone else is comparably simple if you have only had a few sessions.

What should you do when a person, after just a few minutes, or after half an hour of evaluation, or later during therapy, asks you for medicine?

LONG ANSWER

If you think medication is indicated (Problem 2, Problem 101 [B], and Blackman, 2010), certainly go ahead and prescribe some (or refer the person to an MD for medication if needed). On the other hand, if you think medication is relatively contraindicated and that the person should be receiving individual psychotherapy, you should say so.

I usually add a comment about their request. Since people have been bombarded with advertising about medicine, I explain that I understand many people are taking them, but I think that focusing on medication is kind of a red herring. The person who has marital problems needs to think about those problems and make decisions about the marriage. They may go through a period of some turmoil as they think through this. In my opinion, it may be ethically problematic to prescribe medication for people who need to make important decisions.

EXAMPLE

In 2003 I reported a case which I had supervised, where Dr. X, a psychiatry resident, had been asked by a man she was treating to change his antidepressant from Wellbutrin to Prozac. He badgered her about this for 20 minutes, after which she gave in. As she examined this interaction with me, we both realized that she had been bullied by him into prescribing a medication that he knew caused him to have sexual dysfunction. This was even more curious because he was cheating on his wife and felt very guilty about it.

What Dr. X and I were able to figure out was that she had been "too nice" (reaction formation) because of guilt over quite a bit of anger toward him for pushing her around. She also realized in further discussion with me that, at some unconscious level, she felt he deserved to be punished in the form of losing his ability to function sexually, due to his misconduct in cheating on his wife.[74]

---

[74] Blackman (2003b).

Problem 60
People Who Move Your Furniture

Three people come to mind when I think about this interesting behavior. There were two men and one woman.

> **THEORY**
> Depending on the psychic structure of the person you are treating, you can monitor what they do with your furniture as an indication of their thinking, or you can bring to their attention that they are doing something that is meaningful. They may not know what it is, but it is interfering with their ability to understand their conflicts.
>
> Usually, the meaning refers to the therapist, especially as the therapist symbolically represents a member of the person's family (transference resistance), especially someone who had interfered with the development of the person's autonomy.

SHORT ANSWER

The more the person you are treating has disturbances in tolerating emotions or in maintaining trust and empathy, the less you should mention minor adjustments they make to your furniture. When you bring this kind of thing up, they will feel attacked, pushed away, and agitated. It is arguable that you might bring this to their attention to "set limits" on their "boundaries," but in my experience, confrontation is countertherapeutic.

On the other hand, if the person has better affect tolerance and abstraction ability, bringing their moving of your furniture to their attention can be quite revealing regarding symbolic features of their relationship with you. You can then put together that behavior with their symptomatology, which can lead to resolution of their conflicts.

LONG ANSWER

EXAMPLE 1

Kelly, a 62-year-old married woman, presented with psychosomatic complaints. She knew they were caused by emotional conflicts (psychogenic). Within days of beginning treatment, she criticized the plant in my office. I have a silk ficus tree in a corner of my consultation room; she noticed it was artificial. When I invited her to tell me more about this, she said, "It's cold. It's dead. You don't nurture anything. You should get a real plant!"

I immediately told her three things about this: She somehow gave herself license to attack me, which she had not realized; she was shifting her wish to attack me for not being a "good nurturer" onto my plant; she shifted some frustration onto me (and then onto my plant) from her mother. She confirmed that her mother had never taken care of her properly, never played with her, and was now dead—like my plant.

Kelly used the table next to the couch for "show and tell." For years, that table told me a lot about what she was thinking. She would put cups of water on it when she was feeling distant from me, her handbag on it when she was worried about money, her jacket on it when she felt open, e-mails on it when she wanted to discuss interactions with people in her family, and photographs that were meaningful.

After I pointed out the hostility in her supposedly "helpful suggestion" to get a new plant, and she saw it, I approached her use of my table. At that point, Kelly felt comfortable relying on me; so my musings about her use of the table were timely. She replied that my observations were accurate and used the symbol of the table to delve into various problems.

EXAMPLE 2

Harold, a 65-year-old man who had never felt secure with women, although he had had a number of long-term relationships, was lonely and depressed. He was curious about why he could never sustain a relationship and blamed himself. He was still physically healthy and working, and felt he had some good years left that he would like to put to better use.

As we explored his relationships and his personality traits that contributed to his problems, I noticed that each time he came in for his twice-a-week therapy session, he would do a number of things ritualistically. First, he would sit down and then adjust the angle of his chair. He would then relax his 6'6" frame and stretch out his legs. Next, he would untie the shoestrings in his shoes. Once he did all this, he relaxed and told me his thoughts.

For the first 8 years that I treated him, I did not comment on this behavior, although after a number of years, he commented on it. He told me he liked his ritual of readjusting the furniture and loosening his shoes before beginning to talk. He commented how "safe" he felt talking to me and how much he learned when he relaxed and did a little free association.

Since his ritual afforded him a degree of safety he had never experienced during childhood, and preserved his independence by allowing him to move the chair in his own way, I spent more time helping him understand his conflicts with women, which often involved struggles with autonomy, him pushing away, or the woman breaking some ritualistic pattern that he preferred.

Finally, after he had discussed these patterns, I opined that the ritualistic behavior he went through in my office might be linked. He was surprised, but curious. At that point, he thought he had recreated a situation with me similar to what he had created as a child because of his neglectful mother. He had taken care of himself, rearranged his furniture, and "made a special space" for himself in his room where he kept things that were prized. Interestingly, he continued his ritual with me, and we never discussed it again.

During the period that I was treating him, he developed a gratifying relationship with a woman about 10 years younger than he, although he never saw her more than once or twice a week. She seemed satisfied with this, and they were dating when he stopped treatment with me.

EXAMPLE 3

Bo, a 38-year-old successful computer programmer, came to see me during a divorce. He had found another woman he loved and was leaving his wife of 3 years, but he felt agitated. He had no children with his wife, but she was devastated by his revelation of his affair. The new girlfriend had two children by a prior marriage and was several years older than he was.

Bo's mother objected to his new girlfriend, to him leaving his wife, and to him moving in with his girlfriend. He argued with his mother, who was in her 60s and divorced. He felt that this was "weird."

As we looked at his ways of protecting autonomy, his struggles with masculinity, and the differences between his wife and his girlfriend, Bo linked his childhood resentment about his mother's control to reactions to the women.

One day, Bo moved the table next to the couch about a foot away from where it had been sitting. Because he did not suffer with weaknesses in containing emotions, I asked him, "What are you doing?" He said, "I'm making space for myself." I said to him, "You didn't ask me for permission."

Bo found this curious, and moved the table back to its former position. He asked me, "Is that better?" I suggested he tell me his thoughts. He told me I must be a nitpicking idiot to fuss about him moving the table. He just wanted "space."

Amazingly, Bo did not see the connections between his behavior in my office and his behavior with women. I showed him how he made attempts to find "space" because he hated being trapped and wanted a quick escape. He felt his identity was being "taken over" and he was being controlled and emasculated.

He knew this feeling was connected to his father, who constantly criticized him, was pessimistic about him, and had not attended Bo's first wedding.

In a following session, Bo was 30 seconds late. He said, "I'm late." I responded, "Not much." He answered, "I'm one minute late, and that's my hostility to you as a father figure!" We connected his hostility toward his father with having moved the table: provoking punishment and rebelling.

The act of people moving your furniture turns out to have meaning. How you understand the meaning, and what you decide to say about it, will vary, depending on people's problems and their ability to examine the meanings with you.

Problem 61
People Who Fall Asleep in Your Waiting Room

Every few months, when I go to my waiting room to greet people, I open the door and find them sleeping. It is quiet in my waiting room. I do not have music, and the consultation room is soundproof. When my secretary is there, she is in a separate area, not in the waiting room. (See diagram on p. 380). What do you make of this, and what do you do about it?

SHORT ANSWER

Most of the time, I take this as a sign that people are feeling comfortable with me and unconsciously react to my waiting room as though it is the warm arms of a mother. They somehow feel cradled, and they fall asleep. When I open the door, if they suddenly wake up, they may say something like, "I hope you don't mind if I was sleeping." My usual response is, "No, that's fine." And we go into my office to work. In other words, I do not try to "interpret" something about this, unless people say something that makes this necessary.

EXAMPLE 1

Frieda, a 50-year-old woman, woke up from her snooze as I opened the door to the waiting room. As she walked into my office she made a joke about my waiting room being a "holding tank." On another occasion, she referred to the evaluation sessions I required before accepting her for treatment as her "audition." Although she was funny, and I laughed at both of her jokes, the meanings were interesting and had to do with her frustration in waiting for me.

This frustration also could be found in various instances in her life, where she had been too nice (used reaction formations) and kidded rather than discussing her irritation with the person with whom she was frustrated. Problems like this had led to the demise of her marriage some years before she met me, so it turned out to be a serious issue. We could trace her impatience to her relationship with her mother, who never seemed to be in tune quickly enough.

LONG ANSWER

> **THEORY**
> Although it is best, usually, to consider somebody sleeping in your waiting room as a sign of "positive, pre-oedipal mother transference," there are times when the sleeping may either be highly symbolic of other things or may constitute a resistance.

EXAMPLE 2

Eileen, 42, was snoozing in my waiting room when I went to get her. She entered my office, proceeded to recline on the couch in the usual way, and then told me she wanted to go to sleep again. She started yawning and felt like sleeping. She was not sleep deprived because of practical issues, such as a demanding schedule. It turned out that she had some problems sleeping, but this was due to her frustration and irritability with herself because, as she remarked to me, she was "lonely and horny, a bad combination."

Her sleeping and her wish to sleep were not only due to her sleep deprivation but were connected with a dream:

"A man, I think a professor was there. He looked like you. I'm there too, but I'm younger. My clothes are falling off. I was embarrassed that the professor was watching, but he didn't stop me."

Her thoughts about the dream included musings about what it might be like to be married to me. Those fantasies, in turn, were protecting her from massive rage toward her ex-husband because of the way that he was holding back child support payments for her child in college.

In other words, Eileen's sleeping in my waiting room represented her wish to "sleep with" me, and this was a defense against her massive anger toward her ex-husband.

Problem 62
Suicidal People

> **WARNING**
> At any time in their treatment, people may kill themselves. What I recommend here is not, in any way, foolproof. People can kill themselves even if they are in a mental hospital. Prisoners have three times the suicide rate of the general population.
>
> If you undertake treating people who have been seriously suicidal (or those who have hurt themselves previously), you may be in for a nasty surprise no matter how careful or skillful you are. People who have not attempted suicide, but who are ruminating about it, pose a somewhat reduced risk of a completed suicide, but, again, there are no guarantees.

Many people have either attempted suicide or have ruminated about it. If their suicide wish is "imminent" (different definitions by law according to state), they will need to be hospitalized for their safety. Inevitably, they are discharged from the hospital after several days, and outpatient treatment is recommended.

Although some guidelines[75] recommend antidepressant medication for suicidal people, the obvious complication is that suicidal people can overdose with it. Antidepressant medications, in an overdose, are dangerous, so it is a bit of a conundrum to give them to suicidal people.

Let's consider how to approach suicidal people who have not attempted suicide but are ruminating about it; let's include, in this mix, people who possess reasonable integrative capacity and self-preservation, some self-esteem, some ability to trust the therapist, and some honesty (superego functioning) about what they tell you.

SHORT ANSWER

Discuss Turning of Anger on the Self

If people possess the above functions, you can unearth what they are angry about. They shut anger out of awareness (defenses of isolation of affect and repression), and are too nice (reaction formation). So this enraged person is

---

[75] American Psychiatric Association Practice Guidelines (2012).

not aware of anger, which includes homicidal wishes. People harboring anger and guilt may use *turning on the self* (defense against anger) and therefore may contemplate suicide.[76]

If you can find out who they are angry with and why, and can sort out their guilty feelings in relation to the anger, it may be possible, even in a consultation, to show them how turning anger against the self relieves guilt and avoids anger but produces a suicidal thought. This explanation, when effective, can save a person's life.[77]

EXAMPLE 1

Jill, a 37-year-old vice-president of a national company, was referred by her dermatologist. Upon learning of a small patch of psoriasis in her scalp, Jill banged her head on the table and threatened suicide. I arranged to see her right away, expecting to meet a psychotic person who needed to be hospitalized.

Rather, Jill was poised, thanked me for seeing her, and expressed embarrassment over her "incident." She was still feeling out of sorts. She and her husband, Jack, had just been transferred. They were satisfied with the move, liked their situation, and Jack was relieved to be in the same city with his elderly, ill mother.

They had been happily married for 10 years. They had resolved a number of problems, decided on having two children instead of three, and arranged to move together. Jill was glad Jack would be nearer his mother, so he wouldn't have to fly to visit her. I commented that I suspected Jill was overlooking negative things: moving is usually an ordeal (I confronted splitting, reaction formation, and rationalization).

She responded by admitting, "The tough part has been John's mother living a mile away." Jack's mother was "really nice." He spent 2 hours with her every day.

I told Jill I thought she prided herself on adaptation and did not like getting angry. She responded: "Absolutely. My mother raved for years; I never want to be like that!" I said, "So, it has been important for you to be different from your mother" (confirming her defense of disidentification).

Jill agreed. I said she seemed overly nice about her husband and his mother, but I suspected she would be mad at herself if she got irritated about him or her. She agreed and was curious. I added that, without realizing it, she had shut off her irritation to be different from her mother.

---

76   S. Freud (1917), Menninger (1933), and many people since have emphasized that suicide attempts often (but not always) involve massive rage that the suicidal person is not aware of.
77   Blackman (1994, 1997).

Jill laughed, "Oh, I've been aware of it. I had a thought, the other day, that Jack's mother would die. Isn't that terrible?" I clarified her guilt over the death wish. The guilt, I said, made her too nice, but it wasn't working. Instead, she had turned her anger on herself: the suicidal thought.

The patch of psoriasis, she added, "was just one last thing I had to handle. I think you're right, I was just angry."

The dermatologist called about a week later to report Jill felt better, had a discussion with her husband, and Jack now limited his contact with his mother.

LONG ANSWER

People who are seriously thinking of killing themselves have lost their connection to those they love. It is central, therefore, to establish an empathic tie with them if you are going to treat them. I call this technique, "forcing the object relation," which is useful if people have enough abstraction, integrative functioning, and reality testing available.

Precautionary measures in treating suicidal people who are not psychotic, in addition to examining turning on the self of anger, include the following safeguards.

THEORY

The assessment of suicidal people is a complex process. I describe it in detail in Chapter 8 of *101 Defenses*.

Schizophrenics' suicide rate is 15,000 times the general population. If they are also suicidal, their risk of suicide is about 50/50. Treating suicidal schizophrenics is risky. Medication, support, and frequent monitoring are necessary. Still, they have a higher suicide rate.

Alcoholics who are suicidal (and likely have borderline personality) run a 45% chance of suicide (Blackman, 2003a, Chapter 8). In my opinion, if borderline people cut themselves, they are in a psychotic state (breakdown in relationship to reality [hopelessness], in self-preservation, and in self/body image) during the period of self-harm, and need treatment for this.

Contract for Safety

Get suicidal people to agree not to kill themselves but to call you instead: "contract for safety." Statistically, this has been shown to be fruitless, but the statistics do not consider certain factors.

Sometimes, you can help suicidal people if they agree not to attempt suicide. I usually ask people to promise to call me, day or night, if they get close to killing themselves. I cover my practice 24/7. They have my home and mobile phone numbers.

Contracting for safety in this way may be effective if people have

- a sense of reliability, fairness, integrity, and reliability (an intact superego)
- impulse control and affect tolerance, sufficient to stop them long enough for them to call you
- empathy for the therapist

Force the Object Relation (Empathy for the Therapist)

People must realize the risk the therapist is taking. Many suicidal people have lost their attachment with others. Therefore, I insist that people agree to call me, without exception, partly out of consideration for my willingness to treat them. I call this process of establishing a therapeutic bond "forcing the object relation." If people have empathy for you, they are less likely to renege on their contract for safety.

EXAMPLE 2

Kevin, a 29-year-old insurance defense attorney, was married to Wendy, an estate and tax lawyer. They had met in law school. Wendy called because she was afraid Kevin would kill himself, as he had threatened. She wanted to be seen with him because she was "part of the problem."

Kevin was working, but was irritable and sleeping poorly. I decided to evaluate him promptly, knowing I might need to hospitalize him if he was psychotic or imminently suicidal.

In my office, Kevin said he had found out Wendy had a sexual affair with a law school acquaintance before he met her. He knew she had had a relationship in college (with someone Kevin did not know), but she had not previously told him about the law school affair. On hearing that she had had a second lover, Kevin became overwhelmed. He said he felt like shooting himself. Wendy gave his pistol to his mother.

Wendy said obviously the relationship with the other man in law school had not worked out. She hadn't mentioned it because she wanted to forget it. Kevin had a prior marriage for one year when he was 21. He also had other girlfriends before Wendy.

When I met with Kevin, I learned about his relationships with his parents and his sister, his education, and his cocaine abuse "a few times" in college. He had a number of good friends, but would not turn to them concerning personal matters, such as his current distress.

I decided to try to treat Kevin, but he had to agree: (a) to see me three times a week, and (b) to promise not to attempt to kill himself and to call me if he felt he was coming close. He argued he could not afford to come that often and that he "might get out of control." Wendy persuaded him that they could afford it. Kevin finally agreed he would rather have treatment than be dead.

On the second issue, I felt encouraged. Kevin was honest, and would not make an agreement he could not keep. He would not agree to avoid suicide out of mere compliance. He debated with me about it, which made me think we could eventually understand what he was angry about.

Kevin was integrated, his abstraction ability was good, and his relationship to reality seemed fair. His self-preservation function was working. His conscience (superego) bothered him; he did not lie. The remaining treatability question was whether he could develop an empathic tie to me.

I argued that suicide attempts were volitional; he could catch himself if he got suicidal, and call me. He responded, "You don't want to be bothered." I told him I wanted to be bothered; we would have to understand why he felt he needed to protect me from "being bothered."

He could see my reasoning, but argued that he was "trapped." He said, "I guess I have no choice." I was not satisfied. I wanted to see motivation to work together, not "mere compliance."

> **THEORY**
> When suicidal people are simply acting compliant, and you don't have the impression that they "mean it" when they agree to contract for safety, this usually means they are just saying what they think you want to hear ("dedifferentiating").[76] It's best to challenge this defense mechanism and try to get a genuine agreement that actually involves them participating in their own treatment.

I challenged his statement that he had no choice. He had plenty of choice: Other therapists might not insist on my parameters. Some psychiatrists might medicate him and some might hospitalize him.

---

76 Dedifferentiation, first described by Mahler (1968), refers to people giving up their identity to become exactly what another person wants them to be—to guard against loss of the other person's love.

Kevin did not want hospitalization. He argued that I was the only one who could treat him; he did not want anyone else. I repeated that he was not trapped. He finally agreed that: he was not trapped, he would not attempt to kill himself, he would call me if he felt suicidal, and he would see me three times a week.

I treated Kevin for 3 years. He was harboring rage toward family members, but had always been the "golden boy" growing up, who "did everything right." His drug abuse had been a secret, but he had had a few one-night stands. His first marriage was to his college sweetheart. He was proud of his controls.

Learning of his current wife's prior sexual relationship had triggered many conflicts he had with his mother, idealizations of his mother, and some idealizations of his wife. His disappointment (which he had hidden from himself) and his anger about having to be "the good boy" was now turned on himself. Other conflicts caused him poor self-esteem, inhibition, and guilt over violent wishes toward Wendy's other lover and toward his own father.

After 2 years, we agreed that he was doing well enough to come twice a week. We gradually reduced his session frequency to once a week and he finished in the third year.

While I was attending a lawyer's meeting with my wife (who is an attorney) about 5 years later, Kevin approached me and shook my hand. He thanked me and told me he was doing well. He and his wife now had a child, who was also doing well.

The story of the rest of his treatment is also fascinating, but the point here is that I needed to "force the object relation" just to get started.

EXAMPLE 3

Linda, a 31-year-old office manager for a group of pediatricians, complained of obesity, depression, and marital problems. She had three children. She had gotten married at 19; her husband had been 23. He now worked for the city, at night, and she worked during the day for the pediatricians.

The doctors were pleased with her and paid her well. However, her job was taxing: She kept tabs on support staff, assisted in making appointments, handled complaints from upset mothers, and did accounting. The doctors prized her capacities and allowed her flexibility in her work time. She was able to get off from work twice a week to see me during the day.

Linda had become suicidal when her mother sent a Christmas card to her children telling them that they should hate Linda. Linda had gone to the boardwalk in Virginia Beach and considered walking into the ocean to drown.

Linda's mother had been angry at her for years because Linda hadn't called, had forgotten her mother's birthday, and had gone on vacation without telling her mother. Her mother's inappropriately vicious response made Linda despondent.

In addition, she hardly saw her husband; he slept while she took the kids to school. Their sex life had dwindled. In addition, one of her children was having emotional problems, and she didn't have time to help the child.

From her history, we could see that her depression derived from suppressing anger at her husband, somewhat displaced from anger at her mother. Linda turned anger on herself. She could see this.

I "forced the object relation" by insisting she agree that she would not attempt suicide. She struggled with this agreement. I argued that I was not in practice to help people kill themselves; if she wanted to die, she could do it without me. If she wanted my help, we had to agree that suicide was not the goal; so if she felt suicidal, she needed to give me a chance to help her.

Linda said, with sarcasm, "So you want me to call you if I get suicidal; that would help you sleep better at night, wouldn't it!?" After a moment, I realized that she was partially right, and said, "Yes, part of it is for my comfort, that's true." She thought for a few seconds and then said to me, "All right, I'll do it for you." I responded, "Good enough."

We had a productive treatment relationship for the next 5 years. During that time, she got divorced, lost 150 pounds, met another man she enjoyed, and quit her job with the pediatricians. Her new 9:00 to 4:30 schedule allowed her to spend more time with her new husband and her children. Her troubled child went to college and got some therapy there. The other two children became independent.

In an 18-year follow-up phone call from her during one Christmas, Linda told me she and her second husband were doing well. She continued to work, was engaging in a number of extracurricular activities, and had not gained back the weight. She was happy.

THEORY
Kohut (1971) theorized that when people's self-esteem is impinged upon and they begin to feel like they don't know themselves (or like they don't like themselves), they experience "aggressive breakdown products."

Discuss Self-esteem

When people's self-esteem is lowered, they become irritable and may lash out at others and themselves. This may be the result of a feeling of dissolution of their identity.

A drop-off in self-esteem occurs in business people who retire, who no longer have their "business identity." They can become irritable and critical of themselves. Some of them have suicidal feelings, which arise because of problems with their identity. Part of the treatment is to get them to think about their identity, to recognize their grief about losing an aspect of it, and to help them create new elements of identity.

Hunt for "Secondary Depression"

"Secondary depression" occurs in people with personality problems who get themselves in trouble. Once they are in trouble, they see no way out of it, or their suffering is great, and they become very unhappy. They may have suicidal thoughts.

I refer to this as secondary depression because the primary culprit is the character problem that led to such difficulties. Such common character problems include (a) procrastination, leading to being punished for lateness in some important matter; (b) obnoxiousness, causing people to feel ostracized (often in reality) and lonely; (c) impulsivity, leading people into sexual liaisons that are almost routinely disappointing; (d) workaholism and rigidity, limiting the amount of interpersonal pleasure people are experiencing in their lives; (e) chronic passivity, leading to missed opportunities and sadness because of those losses; (f) "needling" (picking on other people's weak spots), leading to others looking to punish the needler; (g) paranoid traits (people who imagine that others are against them, which makes them feel unhappy, when actually this is not the case); and (h) symbiotic attachment to a mentally ill family member, whose lack of response causes people to feel worthless due to their ineffectiveness in relieving the relative's mental illness.

In these situations, untangling the origins of the character disturbance is the treatment of choice.

EXAMPLE 4

Walt, a 31-year-old engineer, had quickly risen in a large company to a six-figure salary. However, when he came to see me, he was on administrative leave and would be fired in 6 months, as per his contract. He also had problems maintaining relationships with women, although he had attempted some, and valued emotional closeness. He had never been married.

As Walt described how he interacted with people at work, it slowly became clear to me that he was highly critical in situations where criticism was necessary. You wouldn't think this could be a problem, but the way he spoke was so hostile that people saw him as an obnoxious ass. He was reported "upstairs," and his superiors disapproved of his behavior.

As Walt complained about people, he was unaware of the hostile, condescending way he expressed himself. When I pointed out his character trait of obnoxious criticism, he was surprised but could see it.

We traced this trait to his mother, who had "cursed like a sailor." She belittled his father. His identification with his mother and disidentification from his passive father caused Walt to get into trouble at work. When he was put on leave pending dismissal, he became depressed and had suicidal ruminations.

The bulk of his depression was based on disappointment in losing his job. We also saw projective blaming of others, denial of certain realities, inhibitions of social skill, and unconscious provocation of punishment. All of these defense mechanisms, plus his anger at his mother and father contributed to his self-destructive character trait of obnoxious criticism.[77] It was this character trait that got him fired. Getting fired caused the depression.

I have not always been so fortunate in treating suicidal people. Some have attempted suicide while I was treating them, even though they had agreed they would not.

Today, if people I am treating attempt suicide, I hospitalize them and refer them to someone else. I think a suicide attempt during therapy is too severe a breach in the alliance and shows too much mistrust toward me (object relations deficit) to sustain outpatient psychotherapy.

Many psychiatrists treat suicidal people with antidepressants and see those people every few weeks or months. Some depressed people may also have a supportive session once every week or two with a social worker or psychologist. My colleagues who do this have my profoundest respect, as they are willing to take great risks to help very sick people.

An irony about suicidally depressed people is that even if they meet many of the risk factors for a suicide attempt, most people do not actually kill themselves. It can be many years before therapists, engaged in any type of treatment of depressed people, have an experience where someone actually succeeds at suicide. This is always a tragedy, and often a surprise. Frequently

---

[77] By the way, I have also seen this characteristic in women, who often feel even more justified about it and may be more aware of their criticism. They tend to see themselves as less dangerous, thereby denying the intensity of their destructive-aggressive wishes and their angry affects.

the risk factors were not even present—but people in treatment had adopted a sort of "as if" approach to their social life[78] that made it difficult to see the suicide coming. This can occur even when you have explained meanings, when people are seen frequently, when there is a contract for safety, and when people are taking antidepressant medication.

As I mentioned in my prior books,[79] you should never consider a suicide attempt, no matter how mild, unimportant. Even in adolescents, who are more impulsive because of their developmental stage, suicide attempts involve a breakdown in their

- body image
- self-preservation
- relationship to reality
- self-esteem leading to rage and turning on the self

---

78 Deutsch (1942).
79 *Get the Diagnosis Right* and *101 Defenses*.

Problem 63
When CBT Alone Is Not Working

People who are in cognitive behavioral therapy may also benefit from the inclusion of supplemental techniques when certain issues arise. Some people hit a roadblock because they do not follow the instructions given by their CBT therapist. Others need additional understanding of the conflicts that are causing their dysfunctional emotions or maladaptive behavior (Problem 1).

How can you handle this?

SHORT ANSWER

First, a little background about CBT:

Therapists who follow Beck's (1967) original formulations and recommendations for CBT will generally focus on people's current life events and what Beck called the "negative cognitive triad." This involves pessimistic beliefs about the future, beliefs about immutability of emotional problems, and a view of the world that is filled with hardship. In CBT, the therapist generally tries to identify these, confront them, and correct the distortions through cognitive exercises, including homework.

Later CBT theory became more complex (1980s), and involved what Beck called the SAS (sociotropy-autonomy scale). "Sociotropic types" need emotional intimacy, dependency gratification, and nurturance, and without these they become depressed. To address these problems, Beck suggested that a warm, empathic tie with the therapist was needed.

Beck differentiated the sociotropic personality type from the "autonomous" personality type. Autonomous people are concerned about independence and reaching goals, and if they do not reach the goals they become self-critical: "endogenous" depression. Treatment usually involves encouraging people to work toward realistic goals.

When behavioral techniques are added, the therapist may suggest that people change their behavior in some way that will be more adaptive. At times, "flooding" (making people think of their worst fears) or other desensitization techniques are added, along with relaxation techniques and exercises to promote "mindfulness."

I have supervised a number of CBT therapists who explained that many people they treated would not do the required homework. In addition, when the therapist attempted to get people to reconsider their ideals, sometimes CBT would go awry. In these situations, CBT was more successful when the therapist attempted to understand how it was that people were "resisting." That is, people did better when they could face anti-authoritarian feelings toward the therapist, how they provoked punishment from the therapist, and what the childhood and adolescent origins of these attitudes were.

LONG ANSWER

Considerations when doing CBT:

- CBT can stir up more depression after problems with reality perceptions are clarified. When CBT therapists elucidate people's distorted versions of reality, this "reality testing" as a technique may also act as a "confrontation" (Problem 1) of denial of reality (a defense mechanism). When this occurs, instead of feeling less depressed, people may feel some increase in depression for a while. This does not mean CBT is failing. However, if people then blame the therapist for their increased depression, the therapist must be ready to explain people's wish to blame the therapist for having corrected their sense of reality, a reality that has turned out to be painful (projective blaming).
- Some people who have high ideals may be capable of reaching those ideals if not for symbolically based inhibitions. Therefore, only some people with high ideals need to rethink their ideals (or lower their expectations of themselves). Those who are capable of great achievements should try to understand what is inhibiting them.

> **THEORY**
> Kohut (1971) theorized that people with low self-esteem needed to take in ("introject") a more positive image from the therapist. This supportive (self-psychology) technique is often needed in addition to the CBT interventions.

- CBT is geared toward people's realistic assessment of themselves, which may be distorted by a number of features. Distortion of the self-image, when it is part of people's problems, often requires affirmation and validation of their strengths, when possible.
- As I have noted (Problem 33), establishing a warm, empathic tie with people you are treating, although sometimes a valuable asset to the treatment, can become problematic when people in treatment develop erotic transferences. A CBT therapist who reassures people about their abilities needs to be ready for this complication.

EXAMPLE

Amber, a CBT therapist, consulted me for supervision on Joel, a 36-year-old single high school English teacher, who complained of depression. Joel was overweight and had been rejected by a number of women. His self-esteem was low.

Amber ran into some problems in treating him with CBT. She had tried to help him adjust his ideals of finding the "perfect woman" and given him homework to write down positive things about himself—to try to relieve his self-esteem problems.

After a few months of once-a-week sessions, Amber's pregnancy became visible. Now Joel expressed self-denigration. He compared himself unfavorably to Amber's husband—Joel felt he could never find a woman as nice as Amber to marry and bear his child. Amber had tried to reassure him that he was valuable as a person, but to no avail.

Lately, Joel had been asking about Amber's pregnancy, and when she gently tried to "redirect" him, he got more despondent.

I agreed with Amber that she would have to alter her technique. First, I suggested she find out more about Joel's family. She told me he had actually already filled her in on his childhood, but she had not focused on it because CBT does not emphasize this. What she knew was that Joel had a sister 2 years younger than he was and a brother 4 years younger. After his brother was born, Joel had gained a lot of weight.

Joel described his mother as "great but stressed out" by the children. Joel had helped her with his younger siblings. His father and mother had separated when he was 11, and his mother became very depressed. He then helped her more. She had never remarried. He decided to go to college locally and lived at home throughout college to help her.

There was much to understand. Over a period of months, I helped Amber discuss Joel's problems with him with more success. Part of what they came to understand included the following:

- Joel felt guilty about his anger at his mother for having two more children that deprived him of her attention. Because of the guilt, he had been "good" (a reaction formation) and shut off his anger. His guilt also made him depressed.
- Because of sibling rivalry, Joel was angry at Amber—he had transferred his anger about his mother's two other pregnancies onto pregnant Amber. However, he felt guilty because Amber was so reassuring to him. So unconsciously, he turned his anger on himself and got more depressed.
- Joel felt competitive with Amber's husband much in the way he had felt competitive with his father. His sense of loss because his father left the home when he was 11 complicated the guilt Joel already felt

because his mother used him as a surrogate husband and father to his siblings. Joel therefore also felt guilty about his competitiveness with Amber's husband, and this caused him more depression.

- To relieve his depressive feelings, Joel ate too much. This caused many women to reject him, which also (unconsciously) had alleviated much of his guilt.

As a result of his understandings, Joel felt better, reduced his calorie intake, and lost weight. He could then compete more successfully in getting dates, which further enhanced his self-esteem.

Problem 64
Those Who Have Had a Bad Experience With a Prior Therapist

In this section, we will cover prior therapists who (a) fell asleep, (b) charged people inappropriately, (c) forgot a lot of things about people, (d) broke the usual therapeutic boundaries, (e) were incompetent and/or had bad judgment in advising people, and (f) overtly seduced people they were treating into sexual activity in the office.

SHORT ANSWER

Briefly, people who have had any of these experiences tend to minimize their emotional reactions, and instead may expect you to be the same as their prior therapist. It's a good idea to watch for any evidence that people expect you to be inattentive (or sleeping). I have met some people who expected me to charge them when I had to be out of the office (!) because they had seen therapists previously who did this. Some people had seen senile therapists who forgot a lot of things that had been discussed.

Some prior therapists had been too "chatty" or disclosed too much about themselves. In my office those people had become silent or cautious, expecting me to use them as my therapist.[80] Some people's prior therapists were psychotic or psychopathic; such people may have been manipulated in bizarre and illegal ways. Finally, if they had sexual intercourse with a prior therapist, they are very likely to be terrified of expressing any sexual fantasies about you, since they will be afraid that these will be reenacted.

When people withhold information, have difficulty talking, arrive very late for their sessions, miss sessions, or even talk too much, you should have an "index of suspicion" that they expect you to be like a prior therapist. You can explore this possibility. If people confirm it, this can clear the air and lead to more productive therapeutic work.

EXAMPLE

Bradley, a 36-year-old man, was in the process of getting a divorce. He was very upset about this, critical of his wife, and fearful that he would be lonely.

---

80 Searles (1965).

When he called for an appointment, he asked for directions to my office. I gave him some. Nevertheless, when I went to get him in the waiting room, he was not present. A couple of minutes later, he telephoned and told me he was lost. He had written down the directions I had given him, but had misplaced those directions and was trying to find me without them. He asked me to give him the directions again, and I did. He arrived about 15 minutes late.

When he entered my secretary's area, he expressed self-criticism about losing the directions, and said he wasn't quite sure why he had done that. I quipped to him, "Well, you almost didn't have to come today." His response to this was to laugh heartily, and he admitted that he agreed with me.

After he sat down in my office, he thought of his prior experience in treatment with a woman therapist who had fallen asleep, even though they were facing each other, while he was talking. When he woke her up, she told him that his way of interacting was so dry that she had fallen asleep. He felt criticized by this but believed it was the case. He stayed with her for about a year. In addition, she seemed to forget the things that he had told her. He tried to compensate for this as well. Finally, he told me that he had forgotten her name. I expressed some interest in this forgetting. After a minute, he laughed again, and said, "It was Cutler, Ms. Cutler."[81]

I asked him why he was laughing, and he said, "I guess she cut me down to size, or something. I always felt small and inadequate when I saw her." In a few minutes, we could understand why he had forgotten the directions to my office. He had not wanted to face these feelings about her, and for that reason, he had expected me to be uninterested in him, to criticize him, or to demean him.

LONG ANSWER

Seduction Victims (and Perpetrators)

The special situation where a prior therapist has sexually seduced someone is quite complex. I have treated a number of women who were seduced by a prior therapist. In addition, two woman therapists I treated admitted to me, during their treatment, that they had previously seduced men who were in treatment with them. The meanings of this severe misbehavior varied. They included (a) passivity, (b) turning passive to active, (c) sexualization of dependency wishes, (c) provocation of punishment, (d) unconscious expression of hostility and contempt, (e) undoing of the usual superego prohibitions against boundary violations, and (f) enactment of various childhood fantasies.

---

81 This was not the prior therapist's real name. I have substituted a name that expressed the same kind of fantasy that this person told me in this session.

It is particularly difficult to treat people who have been seduced, as they harbor so much rage that has never been examined during treatment; it is often kept unconscious through the so-called love that they acted out with their therapist (or that the therapists acted out with people they treated).

I have not been able to treat any male therapists who had seduced women who had consulted them. I am too critical of those therapists, and feel more like a prosecutor than a therapist about the issue (Problem 66). When this has been the chief complaint, and the therapist is in trouble with his professional licensing board, I have simply declined to treat him. I realize that this is a personal limitation concerning who I can treat effectively. I do not wish to treat someone that I have a strong negative reaction to (Problem 71), and it would not be fair to the individual if I cannot give him my best effort.

In contrast, Gutheil and Gabbard (1993) have written extensively about their treatment of seductive therapists. But unless you have had special training in handling therapists who have abused their roles, I would recommend not attempting to treat them because of their superego deficits.

People who have been seduced by their therapist are more likely treatable. But their expectations of you ("transferences" from the prior therapist) must be illuminated fairly early in the work or they will usually quit (transference resistance).

Those Unfairly Billed

Some people have been charged a session fee when their therapist was absent. In this almost unthinkable situation, they have passively allowed themselves to be bullied, and passivity should be examined as a defensive operation. In addition, they may have been using inhibition of critical judgment (a defensive operation) so that they did not judge the therapist as "bad," because to do so made them feel guilty.

Those Who Were Forgotten

People who have had a therapist who forgot things often saw their therapist as a mother or grandmother and therefore forgave them for being "a little senile" or "a little ditsy." This should also be elucidated during your work with them.

Victims of Other Boundary Violations

Breaking of other boundaries that were less egregious may still have had some negative impact on people. I have treated a number of trainees in various mental health disciplines who complained to me of supervisors who were too invasive about the trainee's personal life.

When I was in training, a new supervisor asked for the name of the person I was treating because he thought his daughter had dated that person. I demurred and stopped the supervision.

Other Problems

I have also seen a number of people whose prior therapist gave them very bad advice. Such advice included, "Stop talking to your mother," "Don't let your husband get away with that!" and "You should be more assertive with your boss." This advice was given in contexts where it appeared to me that the prior therapist was not objective and had jumped to conclusions based on some preconceived bias. The therapists sometimes acted more like an advocate, lawyer, or friend than an objective mental health practitioner.

Often, the person in treatment has idealized the prior therapist, been passive, and experienced the therapist as a better parent. It can be useful to explain these types of reactions when you see them and, as I noted earlier, to see if such expectations are directed toward you.

Problem 65
People Who Ask You Questions

What to do with this difficult issue depends on the nature of the question and the timing of when in the course of treatment the question arises.

> **WARNING**
> What you should say depends on whether you know the answer to the question!

We can break the types of questions people typically ask into three categories: Questions about (a) you, (b) themselves, or (c) something else.

SHORT ANSWER

Answer most questions about you where the answers are publicly known or not terribly invasive. Otherwise, people may feel you are playing games with them and insulting their intelligence. Also, answer most questions to which you know, to a high degree of certainty, the answer.

Don't answer questions about yourself that are too invasive; instead, confront people you are treating with the invasiveness of their questions and look for

- identification with an invasive parent (identification with the aggressor) or
- fantasies about you and your family (shifted from their own families of origin).

Don't guess at answers where you are not sure of the answer, whatever it's about. Finally, remember that many people ask you questions to avoid thinking or revealing things about themselves (a character defense).[82]

---

82 Robert B. Parker (2009) presents one of the few realistic descriptions of an interpretive therapeutic approach found in fictional works in his book *Night and Day*. The main character is a chief of police who sees a psychiatrist for therapy once a week. The psychiatrist repeatedly confronts the chief concerning his character defense of asking the psychiatrist questions to avoid discussing the chief's own issues. The chief of police then adopts this approach with people he interviews.

LONG ANSWER

Category 1: Questions About You and Your Training

In early sessions, questions about your professional training are reality based, and you should answer them. "Public domain" information about you that people can get from your website, from Linkedin.com, from Facebook, or from knowing people in the community should be acknowledged. For example, if someone says to me, "Aren't you Susan Blackman's husband?" I simply answer, "Yes." Depending on the circumstances, I might add, "Do you have some thoughts about it?" or "Do you know my wife?" For the past several years, I have also had to answer, "Are you Ted Blackman's father?" Same responses.

People I treat who have had training in medicine or a mental health discipline frequently inquire about my clinical training at the start of treatment. I usually respond matter-of-factly, with a brief answer. I sometimes add a bit of humor, depending on the personality of the person I'm treating.

Category 2: Questions About Themselves

What Is Wrong With Me and When Will I Get Better?

Questions about diagnosis and prognosis are fair game, and you should answer them to the best of your ability. But don't set expectations you may be unable to fulfill.

If people who have trouble with empathy, trust, and closeness (ETC—object relations problems) ask me how long therapy will take, I explain that it is a difficult, though treatable, problem—but it will likely take more than a few months.

Often, I am not sure how long treatment may take; I admit to this uncertainty. I usually try to clarify one major conflict during the initial consultation if I can see it and if the person consulting me is in a state where the clarification might be helpful. This gives people an idea of how the process works and what insights we might be able to achieve.

Should I See a Doctor (About Some Physical Condition)?

EXAMPLE 1

Leo, a 65-year-old married real estate executive, had been in once-a-week psychotherapy with me for several years, understanding his passivity at work, passivity with his wife, and a critical temper. One day, he told me he had fallen down the stairs at home a few days earlier and hurt his shoulder. He went to the local emergency room, where he was examined by an orthopedist. No X-rays were taken, and his arm still hurt. He said he could only raise his arm to shoulder level and demonstrated this to me. He asked my opinion as a doctor, laughingly saying he was putting me in yet another role (!).

I reminded him that I was not an orthopedic surgeon, but that I thought he ought to get a second opinion; I suspected a problem with his rotator cuff. I referred him to an orthopedic surgeon I know and trust. Leo was seen that day, and had rotator cuff surgery a few days later. Following surgery and several months of physical therapy, he regained the range of motion in his arm.

We never did get to the meanings of him having asked me that question, although my correct diagnosis of his rotator cuff injury caused him, briefly, to idealize me.

Should I Quit My Job or Sue My Employer?

EXAMPLE 2

Selford, a 36-year-old theater manager, complained of "paranoia." He described a situation at the theater where he worked. Apparently, two actresses had been sending e-mails complaining about him to Carla, the owner of the theater. They copied him on most of the e-mails, but Carla showed him other messages that Selford felt were untrue, hurt his reputation, and might be grounds for dismissal.

He gave me examples of interactions he had had with the two actresses. He felt the two women were recalcitrant, so he had raised his voice "a bit"; they accused him of screaming and unprofessional conduct. In another memo, they claimed that he was leaving the theater early. He described many memos and showed me a few of them. They were dripping with acid.

He was afraid these women were "ganging up" on him, and that Carla was leaning toward believing them; he might get fired. He wondered if he was "paranoid" and asked me what I thought. My problem: Should I analyze his "paranoia" or recommend he take action to defend himself?

We agreed that there was a way he was antagonizing the women concerned; however, it seemed to me that there was an unanswered legal question. I explained that I did not know his rights, exactly, or what procedures he should take. My understanding was that employment lawyers knew this type of thing. He talked to me about whether he needed to consult a lawyer. I clarified that the reality of his problems eluded me and no doubt needed legal input.

In the following session, he said he had consulted an attorney, and he was going to fight the theater. That would use up his discretionary income for a while, and he would not be able to afford me. I wished him the best. I wondered to myself if his spending money on a lawyer might be a resistance to treatment, but even if that were the case, he had an apparently career-threatening problem.

About 2 years later, Randy approached me at a social function and thanked me for my "advice." With the help of the attorney, he had ironed out the problems at the theater and then resigned and found a teaching position with a local private school, which he said he loved.

Questions people ask you after the initial consultation, in the early phase of treatment, are often more difficult to answer. Some people will ask for advice concerning difficult decisions they are facing, such as the following:

- Should I admit to my teenage child that I smoked pot when I was young?
- Should I get a divorce or leave my mate?
- Should I go to graduate school or make a career change?
- Should I tell my spouse about the affair I had?
- Should I talk to my mate about prior sexual partners and experiences?

There are several ways to handle these (obviously) very complex decisions:

- Point out that the question means something. Invite the person in treatment to think about the question with you (exploration plus encouragement of mentalization).[83]
- Point out that it is a "loaded" question and/or that people are avoiding revealing their own thoughts about the complicated issue by questioning you.
- Link the question with other material in the session (e.g., "You asked me what I thought of Hitler just after you were complaining about how your boss is a tyrant. There may be some way you would like me to reassure you that I understand how you feel about irrational authorities like your father.").
- Find the people's wishes for you to act as an idealized parent (transference); for example, "When you ask whether I spanked my children, I think you are afraid that I might criticize (and thereby verbally hurt) you; your fear of me seems due to a fear of punishment (to relieve your guilt) regarding your reactions to your mother spanking your brother, which you hated overhearing."[84]
- Answer the question.[85]

---

[83] Volkan (2009) recommends this.
[84] S. Freud (1919).
[85] Sheldon Bach (2006) commented that it may be preferable to answer questions from people you are treating about where you are going on vacation. If there is some meaning to their question other than simple human curiosity, you may get to it later. He felt it was artificial to withhold simple answers and caused more trouble for the therapy.

SECTION E

Your Reactions to People in Treatment

GENERAL COMMENTS

One of Sigmund Freud's earliest papers on therapy technique[21] suggested the therapist should be neutral, sort of a mirror, and not reveal personal material to people in treatment. One hundred years later, there are many conflicting attitudes about that idea. Attachment theorists,[22] interpersonalists,[23] intersubjectivists,[24] and relationalists[25] suggest this should not be so rigid. Freud, in his own case histories, reported many activities with people he treated that were not so neutral.

Throughout the history of treatment for emotional problems, we find debate about how personal therapists should be with people they are treating.

> **TIP**
> If you try to be too neutral with people, you will wind up missing a lot and irritating them. However, if you are too interactive and "open" with people, you will also miss a lot and will also wind up irritating them. I often tell my students to start with common sense; that is, don't do things that could be even construed as sexual or manipulative, and don't deny that adults have a sex drive. Don't advise people about things you don't know about, and don't presume that what people tell you is entirely undistorted. Courtesy is fine, but being a sap is not. That's the same type of judgment you would use in dealing with anybody, anywhere.

---

1 S. Freud (1913).
2 Bretherton (1992).
3 Bonovitz (2011).
4 Renik (1998).
5 Mitchell (1990).

My study and experience indicate that good therapists were humane (and not cold) with people in their offices 100 years ago, and they are not cold today. In fact, empathic experiences by the therapist turn out to be of considerable importance no matter what kind of therapy you are doing. (People even complain that they do not get enough understanding from surgeons and radiologists.)

But what is empathy? Simply, you feel something of what someone else feels (for more detail, see Problem 66). More technically, what you feel facilitates your efforts to help people understand themselves. If your emotional reactions to people interfered with their understanding and improvement, originally your reactions would have been defined as "countertransference."

Starting with Jung (see the movie *A Dangerous Method*), followed later by Ferenczi, there have been therapists who had sex with the people they were supposed to be treating. Today, in the United States, this is considered antitherapeutic and highly unethical. As noted elsewhere in this book, Celenza, Gutheil, and Gabbard have written extensively on the different types of psychopathology found in therapists who might be receptive to a complaint from someone in treatment that "If you really understood me and cared about me, you would have sex with me!"

Aside from sex, when therapists become "overinvolved" with someone in treatment, they are often interacting symbolically—based on trying to somehow solve their own problems and not the problems of the person in their office. Sensitive therapists watch out for this type of interference.

I have learned that aside from the therapists' emotional interferences, their technical errors often have to do with inexperience, lack of enough training, awkward timing of interventions, and unfortunate phrasing of an explanation or suggestion. Even in those situations, though, the therapists' feelings, of which they may be relatively unaware, can constitute part of the technical difficulty

Problem 66
What Is Countertransference and How Is It Different From Empathy?

This section is most useful when therapists are not having the same problems as the people consulting them (!). Many therapists elect to avail themselves of their own personal treatment to avoid seeing themselves in the people they treat.

Throughout this section, you will find the term *countertransference*. This term has been used to mean many things. I am using the definition suggested by Irwin Marcus (1980)[6] that countertransference is a phenomenon that

- is a reaction to people in treatment or to what they say,
- has its roots in the therapist's thinking or history (of which the therapist may be more or less aware), and
- interrupts or disrupts the treatment.

This definition of countertransference allows us to distinguish it from many other reactions to people we treat. In particular, our feelings and thoughts in relation to others may indicate empathy—where we think of our own parallel experiences, imagine theirs, formulate their conflicts, or "resonate" and feel what they are feeling.[7]

---

6 I am paraphrasing his definition a bit.
7 Buie (1981).

Problem 67
Countertransference to Unfaithful People

Unfaithful people stir up reactions in their therapists.

> **THEORY**
> Boys' fantasies of male domination arise during the first genital phase (phallic narcissism). Women's fantasies of domination (the "princess") also arise in the first genital phase. Such grandiose fantasies in an adult can affect the therapist and interfere with empathy for the symbolic defensiveness and severe depressions unfaithful people are often experiencing.[8]
>
> The therapist's wish to protect the "victimized" spouse ignores the adult executive functions of the victims of the cheating. The situation of a woman whose husband has cheated can trigger protective feelings the male therapist had toward mother and/or sisters, or projections from a female therapist from her own experiences.
>
> Too much focus on the sadistic aspects of unfaithful behavior may interfere with your understanding the suffering of the person in treatment.
>
> (I am presuming that you are not making the mistake of trying to treat a person who does not feel guilty; see Problem 101 [B].)

SHORT ANSWER

Watch out for envy of, criticism about, or overidentification with people in treatment as well as possible protectiveness toward the victim spouse or partner.

LONG ANSWER

Keeping in mind that there are as many countertransference reactions as there are therapists, generalization is perilous, but here goes.

There are typical countertransference responses to be wary of when you treat a guilt-ridden cheater. Heterosexual male therapists may find themselves envious of a heterosexual philanderer who seems to be having more sex than he deserves. Countertransference envy can occur in male therapists who have not had as much sexual experience as the philanderer or who are frustrated in their personal relationships.

---

8 Marcus (2004).

Homosexual male therapists may become frightened by the frenetic sexual activity of some homosexual men who engage in unsafe sexual practices.

In addition to experiencing envy, both male and female therapists can find themselves critical of male cheaters. The way cheaters tell their story may arouse critical reactions in the therapist. Actually, cheaters may unwittingly induce you to criticize them to relieve guilt (defenses of provocation of punishment and externalization). If you see this, show the cheater how he strives to avoid guilt. Female therapists have a tendency to identify with a wronged wife.

EXAMPLE

Joan, a psychologist I supervised, reported that Eddy, a depressed male philanderer, had expressed guilt over an affair and desperation and confusion about what to do. She had responded, "You know the right thing to do. You should just do it: Be faithful to your wife, then we can discuss your ambivalence."

Joan was concerned because Eddy agreed but then never returned to treatment. I told Joan that she may have unwittingly identified with Eddy's wife ("complementary" identification).[9] Joan readily saw this and then related an awareness of her values of the importance of fidelity—she could imagine her mother talking to her the way she had interacted with Eddy.

Countertransference to women who are cheating on their husbands has a couple of typical variations (I will again belabor the point that countertransference is often specific to the therapist). Male therapists may find themselves fantasizing about the apparent sexual availability of these women. (Heterosexual men's most common sexually stimulating fantasy is that of a sexually "omniavailable"[10] woman).

If you find yourself with such fantasies, you can miss the severe problems with emotional closeness, trust, and guilt-ridden yearnings for maternal attention[11] (object-relations conflicts) that underlie these women's supposed sexuality.

Women therapists can become frightened (through identification or because of maternal feelings) for the safety of women who are cheating on emotionally or physically abusive husbands; become overly "understanding" of the

---

9 Racker (1953).
10 Person (1986).
11 Goldberger (1988).

women's (oral and attachment) "needs" and therefore experience interference in treating women who harbor conflicts between guilt and sadism/hostility toward men. Sadomasochistic characterological features are often warded off from consciousness by such women's apparently "loving" sexual behavior (reaction-formation: consciously feeling loving while unconsciously hating someone).[12]

---

[12] Raphling (1989) and Blackman (2003a).

Problem 68
Compliant Talkers

Some people respond to being in therapy by talking freely. They develop trust quickly, know that you would like them to talk, and fill you in on hundreds of details. While you are trying to understand them, it can be difficult to see the threads in their thoughts because they are talking about so much.

Even though some freedom of associations is usually helpful, these people seem to lack focus, though they follow your wish to hear about their problems. Sometimes, they repeat things they have repeated previously, perhaps trying to master them by somehow simply saying them again.

What do you do with this?

SHORT ANSWER

It is a relief to be working with people who talk to you, and it is difficult to interrupt their verbalizations. In general, therefore, when people are compliant and talk to me, I do not confront them about this character defense. It is so facilitative of treatment that it is counterproductive to say they are repeating things, talking too much, and flooding the session with minutia. Moreover, they may feel criticized when they are "trying hard" to cooperate with the program.

My solution is to listen to the multitude of facts they present, to interrupt them periodically to clarify certain problems, and to find threads in their thoughts that can be helpful in elucidating their conflicts. When I am able to do this, people experience a sense of accomplishment about what they learned, and their verbalizations helped.

Only when people are seeing me at least three times a week, and their compliant talking has been going on for some time, might I hazard a comment that their detailed account of everything seems to be a defense against mistrust or maybe a way of controlling the session. This type of intervention, of course, invites people to discuss their reactions to you based on parents who did not pay attention to them (transference).

In the process of speaking to you, they hope you respond in a helpful way, wanting you to be different from their parents. Mostly, it's good to gratify that wish.

LONG ANSWER

Sometimes, compliant talkers are compliant with so many things in their lives that this character trait must be confronted and discussed.[13]

EXAMPLE

Alice, a 47-year-old divorced woman, desperately wanted to get over her anxiety attacks (panic attacks) and mild agoraphobia. In particular, she was terrified of dating men. She was lonely and missed being married, although she did not like her ex-husband.

As she told me the details of her childhood and adolescent experiences with males, I was able to help her see various threads where she alternatively felt competitive, guilty, passive, and punished. Oftentimes, there had been inhibition of her executive function and judgment leading her to be hurt mentally, and sometimes physically.

She had been raised in a home where she was supposed to obey her mother and father and occasionally got a spanking if she didn't. She had learned to be "good," and put on a facade of compliance and helpfulness. This particular character trait fit in with the personalities of many of her women friends, who were almost invariably trying to help one another, be "nice," and disliked any semblance of aggression or violence in life, movies, or shows.

After about a year of intensive treatment, we had examined a number of instances where she had been very compliant and passive in situations where she should have said something. She actually had been conscious of disliking certain elements in relationships but had not taken action. She remained passive and "did what I was asked."

In this case, I brought to her attention the possibility that she was also doing that with me. She responded that she actually was quite aware of this, but had been shy about telling me that she did not like paying me and found the frequency of her sessions an inconvenience. She would have preferred to play tennis with her friends, get her nails done, or any other gratifying activity. She had withheld saying anything about this for fear of offending me because she felt grateful that I was helping her.

Once we saw this conflict, we could trace it to the various dates that she had over the past year, where she either had not questioned a potentially negative trait of a man she was dating, or passively accepted a suggestion from the man that she attend some event that she intensely disliked.

---

13 B. Wolfe (1985).

Invariably, she wound up in an unpleasant mood, and those relationships went nowhere.

After the clarification of these character traits, which were intimately connected with her childhood experiences, she was able to reintegrate and handle things quite differently.

Problem 69
Those Who Have Figured You Out

People in therapy reveal much of their thinking. Sooner or later, they become very curious about the person with whom they are sharing intimate information about their hatreds, masturbatory fantasies, and suicidal ruminations. Their curiosity is predictable, and useful in figuring out conflicts from childhood (transferences).

Some people, however, spend quite a bit of time trying to "figure out" your personal conflicts, practical problems, financial situation, and even your personal history.

What do you do with this?

SHORT ANSWER

People who do this have often been emotionally traumatized during formative stages of their lives and have developed a policy of being vigilant about others' responses to them. Technically, it's usually best to answer some of their questions honestly, so that they will not begin to believe that you, like others before you, are lying, perverse, dangerous, and narcissistic.

EXAMPLE 1

Ira, whose alcoholic mother frequently embarrassed him, asked me if I drank; when I hesitated, he said, "I can tell. You aren't much of a party animal." I answered that he was correct about that. I admitted that I drink rarely. He kidded me about not knowing how to have fun. I said he was wrong about that.

Ira remembered how, as a young man, he had been a heavy drinker, and how he still thought getting drunk was necessary for "revelry" and for sexual pleasure. My disagreement with that philosophy, he said, caused him to begin rethinking whether he could actually enjoy himself without becoming the "drunken fool." We then discussed how he had become like his alcoholic mother (identified with her) to avoid intense anger at her and that he mastered his fears of humiliation by provoking humiliation (controlling the timing—called "turning passive to active").

LONG ANSWER

Sometimes, people who figure you out are acting on enormous curiosity, envy, and/or competitiveness. How much to disclose to people who have already "figured out" something about you then involves a delicate balance. On the one hand, they seem to "know," but on the other hand, they don't really know.

It's occasionally possible to show people that what they think they have figured out is a fantasy, reflecting things about them (projection) or about family members (transference).

EXAMPLE 2

Jackie, a 46-year-old divorced woman with no children, had just gotten married again and regretted never having had children. She had just heard of some of my son's successes from a woman friend who knew about my family. She exclaimed to me, "You must be so proud!"

I expressed, gently, my understanding that although I could tell she was happy for me, I also suspected it was hard for her to face her own painful feelings that she had not had children. She responded, "Well, of course I'm envious." She then explored, at length, the miserable history of her first marriage and why she had persevered in it for so long in spite of the severe difficulties.

Problem 70
Countertransference to Marital Arguments

Countertransference (a reaction that disturbs treatment) is a liability at any time but is particularly a potential when you work with people who argue with their spouses.

> **THEORY**
> Countertransference[14] has its roots in the unconscious or preconscious functioning of the therapist, is responsive to some aspect of material from the person you are working with, and interrupts or disrupts the therapeutic process.
>
> Some comments facilitate the therapeutic relationship ("empathic"), whereas some disrupt things (countertransference). In the 21st century, some authors refer to all the therapist's reactions as countertransference, but this dilutes the study of reactions that facilitate versus interfere with treatment.
>
> Important sources of disruption include when the therapist (unconsciously) takes on the attitudes of people in treatment ("concordant identification") or sides with a person in the lives of people in treatment ("complementary identification").

How to handle this?

SHORT ANSWER

Most marital arguments are based on projections. That is, one marital partner blames the other one for something that is present in the blaming partner. When you hear people complaining about a spouse, you must consider that (a) they may be right, (b) they may be projecting, or (c) they may be shifting feelings onto a spouse that they originally had toward a family member (a transference reaction).

---
14 Marcus (1980).

For example, if a woman complains, "My husband doesn't listen to me," you might say, in an empathic way, "That sounds painful." But such a supposedly empathic comment may be a concordant identification (see Theory box) with the woman, and not consider her projections and her transferences.

On the other hand, if a woman complains that her husband does not listen, and you respond, "Are you doing something to annoy your husband?" then that simple question may indicate a complementary identification with the husband, and the woman may feel you are siding with her husband and blaming her.[15]

A good way to avoid these difficulties is to steer clear of asking too many questions[16] when people complain of marital arguments. You can notice people's defenses, such as having a hard time (a) giving details, (b) being critical—especially when people are too critical of themselves for having arguments, and (c) accepting blame.

If you don't ask questions or "express empathy" you maintain better neutrality. Further, if you are married, you no doubt have resolved arguments with your spouse. If you are divorced, you are familiar with unresolved issues. In either case, it is easy to project onto the people you treat—and want them to resolve problems your way.

LONG ANSWER

To make life complicated, marital arguments often have points on both sides. Comments you make to people who are having arguments are bound to sway them in their thinking about their marriages. This is a very serious responsibility for the therapist.

I have heard complaints from men and women about prior individual and marital therapists who "sided" with one partner. I have no idea how true these complaints are, but they are frequent.

The few times I attempted to do marital therapy, I found it exceedingly difficult to stay neutral. I therefore have the utmost respect for therapists who do marital therapy. Skilled marital therapists avoid the countertransference traps, and clarify people's conflicts. People who need marital work usually need individual therapy so they can sort out their problems without the spouse listening.

One perennial problem in marital therapy is that most couples do not seek marital treatment until the marriage has about expired. There is so much contaminated water under the bridge that it is well-nigh impossible to untangle the conflicts so that the two people who hate each other can resume helping and loving each other.

---

15 Racker (1953).
16 See Problem 77.

In individual therapy, I try to clarify with the person who is making the complaints what the origin of the argument may have been.

EXAMPLE

Skip, a 46-year-old master carpenter and contractor, complained that he was depressed. His 49-year-old wife, Tiffany, felt their marital problems were due to his depression. He agreed with her and requested medication.

I first explored what had been going on in their marriage. Skip didn't want to talk about it and acknowledged to me that he never liked sharing his difficulties with anyone. He had never been close to his mother, and his father was constantly working. Skip was athletic, fit, and enjoyed skiing.

His wife preferred to go to bars to dance and drink, sometimes with strangers. Skip disliked bars but accommodated Tiffany. She was in sales for a boat dealership and made a larger income than he did. They had no children.

Skip's wife went on skiing trips with girlfriends. Since he loved skiing, he grudgingly admitted to some frustration that she went without him. She would take planned vacations without consulting him, although he thought she was faithful.

Not facing their emotional distancing, he normalized her behavior by telling me he also went on sailing and golfing expeditions with male friends, sometimes for a week or more, that did not involve her.

> **THEORY**
> Depression can be caused by two typical conflicts where people do not reach their (ego) ideals:
>
> - People's goals are unreasonable considering their actual capacities, so they cannot reach their goals. Here, use CBT techniques to clarify the reality of limitations and help readjust the goals.
> - People's goals are reasonable, but they are unable to reach the goals because of emotional conflict and inhibition. Here, try to understand the conflicts that are causing inhibition of their abilities to attain the goals.

Since depressions are often caused by conflicts between reality and ideals (see Theory box), I asked Skip what he wanted in a marriage. He began to cry, but stopped quickly. He wanted to have a wife to do things with, who loved him.

He and Tiffany, although in excellent shape, only had sex once a month. Some of it was his disinterest. He loved her and did not cheat on her; he had turned down opportunities.

Based on his difficulty talking to me, I wondered whether Skip was inhibited in discussing scheduling and sexual matters with his wife. He generally avoided it. When he brought up a dissatisfaction, she accused him of being depressed and wanting everything his way. She then recited a litany of upsets from the 10 years of marriage. He pled innocence and forgetfulness.

As is so common, Skip came for help after years of misery. The tangled marital conflicts seemed unsolvable. I decided to ask about Tiffany's complaint that he did not take her seriously enough and interact with her enough.

Those complaints comported with Skip's presentation to me. He seemed to be a physical type of man who didn't talk much. Since he wished to stay married to Tiffany (his goal), I suggested we discuss his inhibition and its origins.

Skip had yearned for his father's attention and was furious about not having it. Skip had become aloof like his father (identification with the lost object), and critical like his father (identification with the aggressor). Skip also tried not to be critical (disidentification from his father).

As he understood these mechanisms, he reported that he had spoken to his wife about their disagreements. She suggested they take trips together. He encouraged her to talk with him, and she took him to happy hours after work.

After 10 sessions, Skip felt he had made as much progress as he wanted and was glad he had not taken antidepressants. He was pursuing interaction with his wife and thanked me for my help.

A corollary point about Skip is that very often we are only able to do as much as people will let us. Many times, people consult us in situations where there is only a limited amount of progress that can be made.

The amount of modification of both his and his wife's narcissism was limited; how much closeness they could actually establish in the marriage also seemed limited. I was satisfied that I was able to help him understand enough about his problems that he was no longer severely depressed, and that was about it.

Problem 71
People You Don't Like and People Who Don't Like You

PEOPLE YOU DON'T LIKE

All therapists have likes and dislikes of character traits in others. In psychotherapy, people reveal many personal details they would not tell anyone else. They trust us to understand, empathize, and clarify their maladaptive behaviors, emotions, and attitudes. For people to do all this, they must feel warmth, understanding, and concern from us.

Once in a while, we don't like the people who consult us. What to do?

SHORT ANSWER

The usual reasons therapists do not like people involve countertransference (also see Problem 70). Countertransference means that what people say touch off in you unconscious, symbolic reactions that interfere with treatment.[17] One solution to not liking people, therefore, is to get treatment yourself to learn why you don't like certain kinds of people.

A simpler approach is to check your empathic attunement to people during evaluation. If you dislike people, refer them to a colleague. Twice I have attempted to treat people that I very much disliked; they have been treatment failures.

LONG ANSWER

Akhtar[18] has pointed out that depressed people can cause a therapist not to like them. Through behavior and speech patterns, they stimulate in you their own angry or self-critical feelings ("misery loves company"). If you pick up negative feelings (or if you feel critical), you can use your reaction, like a barometer, to formulate an intervention. For example, you could say, "I think

---

17 Marcus (1980).
18 See Blackman (2003a), Chapter 8.

you are struggling not to feel very painful, perhaps critical feelings toward yourself."

Commonly, we run into a stretch of treatment where people express hostility, criticism, or disappointment with us. We often can connect those feelings with reactions they had to parents during their upbringing. Their negative reactions may be due to guilt over getting better ("negative therapeutic reaction"). Or, we may have to face the hard truth that we are not helping people, and be ready to refer them to a colleague.

PEOPLE WHO DON'T LIKE YOU

I get disheartened by people who say, after a few sessions, "This therapy isn't working." If I have been doing what I consider to be an adequate job, including (a) giving a preliminary formulation to people and (b) showing them some defenses and resistances, and they have not responded with integration and improvement, I worry about their ability to integrate. Even more, I worry about their response to my personality.

When I hear these kinds of complaints early in treatment, I explain that there are other competent therapists in town and that I would not feel right continuing to treat people if they are finding it unhelpful. Many of them have accepted a referral. They may never tell me they did not like my personality. They'll tell their next therapist.

EXAMPLE

Tom, a 65-year-old retired Navy captain, was referred (initially together with his wife) by a faculty colleague at the Naval Medical Center–Portsmouth. Tom could only function sexually when his wife allowed him to have anal sex with her. This had been going on for a couple of years, and they both agreed that he should try to free himself of this fixation. He wanted to work with me individually. His wife was already in therapy.

After 4 months in twice-a-week therapy, Tom had figured out that he had suppressed anger at his much-adored mother. Although they had been "close" during his childhood and adolescence, she talked to him while moving her bowels and had involved him in helping her put on her underwear and hosiery.

He recalled being sexually stimulated by those activities and felt guilty. After we understood this, Tom got more depressed, and there was nothing I seemed to be able to say that helped. He felt ashamed having told me about his mother because he saw me as "a strong, successful man who would never have been his mother's servant." My colleague had told him the psychiatry teaching award was named after me, and Tom compared himself negatively to me.

My attempts to tie his idealization of me to transference, where he felt small compared to his father and frustrated by his mother, failed. Pointing out his successes in the Navy failed, as well; he had been passed over for admiral.

After a couple of weeks of Tom complaining that therapy was not helping, I suggested that perhaps he would rather work with a different therapist. He accepted the referral, and was relieved that he did not know anything about her.

Several years later, Tom's wife approached me in a supermarket. She volunteered that Tom had done very well with the new therapist, and she was glad I had referred him to her.

Alternatively, people who complain, "therapy is not working," may be forgetting (repressing) much of the work you have done with them. Point out that they seem to have forgotten what they have learned, and they may become aware of competitive, rebellious feelings toward you based on prior experiences with their parents (negative transference).

During the early part of my career, I spent 10 years as a consultant to the State of Louisiana Child Protection agencies. During that time, I evaluated over 5,000 heinous child-abuse cases (perpetrators and victims of rape, murder, sadism, and severe neglect). I realized, after a period of time, that the child protection agencies were referring me their most difficult cases, so I was witnessing severe psychopathology. I also became aware that I did not like the majority of the adults I evaluated where a "founded" case of heinous child abuse existed. They lied to me or were completely shameless about very, very severe abuse of children.

At first I felt guilty about disliking them but eventually saw that I actually disliked their untreatable psychopathology—which was responsible for great harm to children. They had severe damage to

- their capacities for empathy
- their relationship to reality (and sometimes poor reality testing)
- their superego (no guilt, shame, or fairness)

Unfortunately, these damaged areas of mental functioning usually made them unreachable by any mental health technique.

I have also found it impossible to treat professional people who have indulged in sexual relations with people they were treating. There have been reports of success with some of these practitioners.[19] In contradistinction, I have routinely felt, after evaluating these therapists, that they should have their licenses revoked and find another job. I disliked them so much that I could not treat them. I do not now accept referrals of people who have admitted to their professional licensing board that they engaged in this type of boundary violation, even if they claim to feel guilty about it.

A final thought: Most therapists (including me) do not want to be around people whose personalities involve malignant narcissism and antisocial traits. First-degree murderers, felony rapists, and felony thieves deter most therapists from wanting to help. Although therapists in the United States correctional system are attempting to rehabilitate criminals, I have been ineffective and thus have declined to work with criminals.

In a word, I don't like them; I am pessimistic about correcting the deficits in their object-relatedness and their superego once they have reached a certain phase of adolescence. However, I am grateful that some of my colleagues are interested in and willing to treat the selected number of heinous criminals who may be rehabilitatable, since this is good for those particular people and potentially good for society.

---

19 Gutheil and Gabbard (1993).

Problem 72
People Who Do Not Respond to Your Explanations About Their Problems

It is a freakish experience to figure out people's problems, show them, and then have them reject or forget all of it. The first thing to do is get over your narcissistic injury (wound to your self-esteem) because your excellent understanding (a) did not help them, (b) caused them to come late or miss the next session, or (c) led them to forget what you had discussed.

You are in good company. Freud ran into this issue in the early 1900s when he was treating Dora, about whom he had formed many brilliant conclusions (really; it's a great read).[20] He had shared some of these ideas with her and they seemed to help, but then she abruptly quit treatment. He handled his depressive affect about his apparent mistake in technique by writing up the case. Since then, there has been much written about Dora, transference (people's unconscious reactions to you when you are trying to help them), and autonomy.

The "negative therapeutic reaction"[21] refers to people not progressing because they feel guilty about getting better. They punish themselves (thereby relieving their guilt) by not allowing themselves to be affected by what they have figured out.[22]

In short, what do you do if people do not respond well to your interventions?

SHORT ANSWER

The most likely reasons people do not respond to your attempts to help them are that

1. you have been incorrect in your formulation,
2. you are focusing on the wrong part of the material,
3. your timing in making the intervention was incorrect,
4. they shifted to more maladaptive functioning, and/or
5. transference.

---

20 S. Freud (1905).
21 M. Cohen (1993).
22 For a complete dissertation on this type of masochistic functioning, see Novick and Novick (1996).

First of all, figure if you've made any error in numbers 1–3. Some errors are caused by countertransference (see Section E "General Comments").

When you cannot formulate the problems or time interventions correctly, you may want to consult with a colleague you respect, check the literature, or join a study group.

Countertransference usually[23] is not clear; you notice it when someone has a bad reaction to something you said. The simplest of the bad reactions is that they don't understand what you tried to explain to them. Check to see if you were feeling irritated with them, sorry for them, critical of them, or even somewhat seduced by them. If you can relate any of those feelings to your own adolescence, or even current life,[24] you may be able to catch yourself before you make another mistake.

You can also look to what's going on in people you are treating. It may be that you were on target when you explained something, but it was too painful and they therefore forgot about it. This is common when you have confronted denial of a painful reality.

When people forget, comment on the repression: "I noticed as you told me things today, you seem to have forgotten about the things that we discussed last time."

If people agree they forgot, and ask to be reminded, first discuss how their mind shut off painful things. If they can become aware of how their mind prevents them from being aware of feelings, they may be able to extend that insight into their lives.

LONG ANSWER

Some people experience a change in behavior after you explain their problem defenses. They may, however, shift their defenses to produce different but equally pathological behavior.[25]

EXAMPLE

Rod, a 38-year-old middle manager of a large corporation, was behind in his work, unhappy in his marriage, and unable to delegate responsibilities to his secretary—he was too inhibited to tell her if she had made a typographical error.

I learned from Rod how, without realizing it, he was making a strenuous effort to be unlike his father, who was dictatorial and physically abusive: He

---

23 Using Marcus's (1980) definition, you will not be aware of a countertransference until after you make a mistake that disrupts treatment.
24 Dewald (1982).
25 Fine et al (1995).

> **THEORY**
> When you show people they are denying, projecting, forgetting something, or acting like their mother acted with them, you are disturbing a mental equilibrium that has existed, even though that equilibrium was maladaptive.[26] After being disrupted by your intervention, they may not integrate the new material; rather, they go back to their old ways. When they do this, you can
>
> - point out the return to old defense mechanisms or
> - reexplain what they have forgotten.
>
> After showing people how they use maladaptive coping mechanisms (defenses), they may (a) understand, (b) agree, (c) become aware of new emotions, (d) begin exercising better judgment, and (e) *change defense mechanisms*!

severely beat Rod's sister. His sister eventually dropped out of high school and wound up living on welfare with a drug addict. He never saw her again.

As Rod remembered this, he became depressed, grieved over his sister, and recognized that he had suppressed rage toward his father for years. Any time Rod had to "discipline" an employee, even asking them to change a dictation, he felt he became like his father had been with his sister. He felt so guilty that his mind immediately stopped him from acting. After understanding his inhibition, Rod spoke to his secretary and others, several of whom confided about their own financial problems. He lent money to them.

His most egregious error was lending one woman $5,000 because she had not been able to pay bills. This loan was not tainted by sexuality, bribes, or other factors. Rod had voluntarily offered her money and lesser sums to a few others. Rod wondered about this, thought maybe he was doing something foolish, but he said it felt "so good" to be able to be nice to people.

Although Rod could now ask his secretary to change something (he was no longer avoiding her due to transferences from his sister and father), he now guarded against grief, guilt, and anger at his father by being too nice. He still shifted his concerns from his sister to the women who worked for him. They became his "daughters" and he became a much better father than he had ever had.

In other words, Rod had changed defenses. Instead of being inhibited, passive, withdrawn, and unlike his father (disidentification), Rod now was too giving (pathological altruism), projecting, and continuing to disidentify

---

26 Schlesinger (1995).

from his father. He also added identifying with idealized parents and "acting out" (Problem 35).

We discussed these mechanisms, and he was eventually able to get back most of the money. However, it turned out that the woman who had borrowed $5,000 from him was a cocaine addict and wound up turning to him again, this time asking him for an extra $10,000 which she supposedly owed to coke dealers. With much grief, he explained to her that he could not give her that kind of money. She eventually quit work. He associated her demise very much with his sister's and still felt guilty that he could not have done more to help her. He never got the $5,000 back, but this seemed to relieve his guilt.

Problem 73
People Who Want Your Advice

We try to help people understand themselves, but we also advise people about a variety of matters. Even if we are just sorting out options, we often imply opinions about people's judgment of danger, organization of thought (integration), and reality testing.

Advising people is tricky; it is difficult to know the vicissitudes of their lives, so advising them is fraught with danger that you do not have enough information. You may be responding as though they were someone in your personal life. Or they may remind you of some part of yourself that you would like to change.

With all of these caveats, typical types of advice that almost all therapists give to people they are treating include the following:

- Communicate more with your spouse (or significant other) about what you are feeling about them, both positive and negative.
- Be more self-protective in situations where people are actually attacking you.
- Stay out of arguments that have nothing to do with you.
- You should talk more with me about some particular subject.

Many therapists have good common sense, and their advice can be based on years of experience as human beings who have listened to other people's problems.

So should we offer people solid, common-sense advice?[27]

SHORT ANSWER

Giving advice is always a double-edged sword because, beginning at 2 years of age, people hate being told what to do. This attitude gets modified as people get older, and hopefully they become amenable to education. Nevertheless, much of what people learn comes from their own

---

[27] This is even a bigger problem for general physicians and pharmacological psychiatrists, who are constantly advising people and constantly running into patients who are "noncompliant." (See Dr. Gregory Warth's excellent website: http://www.art-of-patient-care.com/)

experience.[28] It is said that good judgment comes from having made mistakes, which in turn came from having poor judgment. Parents of teenagers know about this problem.

Some therapists attempt to get around people's natural resistance to advice by subtly manipulating people into coming to conclusions that the therapists prefer. I have not found this to be a viable solution. First of all, it goes against my own nature, and secondly, since I encourage people to be honest, I feel I should be, too.

People who come for treatment expect us to be experts that have solutions to their problems that they have not found. Sometimes, we have a solution and offer it to people. It's good to qualify any advice by admitting that most problems are complex and that one solution may not be enough. Furthermore, it's useful to admit your idea may not work.

LONG ANSWER

The most useful advice I have given people involves adult dating or information about the developmental struggles of their children (Problem 88).

My usual approach, when I want to advise anybody, has been to catch myself and then to figure out what motivated people to make mistakes (the mistakes that made me want to advise them).

To a large degree, I still follow this approach. If someone is making a terrible mistake, I may bring it to their attention, but I usually do not suggest alternate decisions. The mistake may be at work, in their love life, or with their children, but it is a glaring error that is almost guaranteed to produce pain for everyone involved. In those situations, I point out that a terrible error is in the offing, and suggest people discuss their conflicts about the self-destructive decision.

---

28 Rothfuss (2009), in *The Name of the Wind*, describes the development of a boy, named Kvothe, through early adolescence and young adulthood. Kvothe must think his way through incredible reality challenges, surreal threats, and his own foul judgment about danger and consequences. He makes a huge number of errors in judgment, but each time he learns something new about people, aggression, and how to handle himself.

When I met Mr. Rothfuss at a book-signing, I asked him whether in the sequel, Kvothe would develop better judgment and finally get the girl he loves. Mr. Rothfuss laughed but was noncommittal. I have it on my to-do list to read the sequel, *The Wise Man's Fear* (2011). My wife and son have already finished it.

EXAMPLE 1

Zach, a 30-year-old man, consulted Lauren, a therapist. Lauren then turned to me for supervision in the case.

Zach was in the middle of a terrible divorce. His estranged wife had moved in with a professional pornographer. Zach suspected his estranged wife's new boyfriend of involvement in child pornography, but he had no proof. The divorce involved a custody battle over their 5-year-old daughter, whom Zach feared was being exposed to pornography or might be used for it.

Lauren mentioned that Zach had a new girlfriend, Gabrielle, who was "between jobs and into astrology." Gabrielle was setting up an astrology center to sell potions and do séances.

I remarked that Zach seemed to be making another mistake. He was trying to extricate himself and his daughter from one psychopathic woman, but it sounded like Zach's new girlfriend was a con artist, also psychopathic.

I could not quite understand what was impairing Zach's judgment. The differential diagnosis included schizophrenia, where Lauren should advise Zach to dump the new girlfriend. If he was masochistic, unconsciously inviting women to hurt him (to relieve guilt), Lauren might bring his intent to suffer to his attention. Or, if he had impairment of judgment because of guilt over being critical, she should point this out.

Lauren had wondered if Gabrielle were "antisocial": Zach had acceded to Gabrielle's requests for a new refrigerator and laptop computer after they had been dating for 3 weeks.

I suggested to Lauren that she bring Zach's mistakes to his attention and see how he responded. Lauren did not think Zach was psychotic, but she was curious about what impaired his judgment.

When Lauren returned for supervision, she reported she had told Zach that he seemed to be making another mistake. Zach responded, "Thank you! I thought I was, but then I kept blaming myself for being a hard-ass." Zach could see he had been (a) inhibiting critical judgment to relieve guilt; (b) trying not to be like his mother, who had always criticized him and made him feel terrible; (c) too nice (reaction formation); (d) too passive; and (e) minimizing the reality he saw.

In a later supervisory meeting, Lauren reported that Zach had broken up with Gabrielle, asked her to return the laptop, but let her keep the refrigerator.

Some people are not as responsive to explanation of conflict as Zach had been. In those cases, sometimes advice is necessary.

EXAMPLE 2

Gwen, a 38-year-old divorced, attractive woman who owned a women's clothing store, was depressed. She described losses throughout her life, including her father, a number of boyfriends, a husband, a live-in lover, and an abortion in adolescence. She told me this emotionally and was responsive to my understanding of how she had borne (defended against) painful losses.

Over several sessions, once a week, Gwen reported difficulties with dating. Men sought her out, and some had propositioned her, but she joked, "I'm not that easy!" She was lonely without a partner, wished to be married and possibly have children, although she realized that might be limited by her age.

Gwen asked me, "Where could I find a decent man anyway?" She recited a litany of complaints that "all the good ones are married" and so on. I responded that her socializing seemed adequate: She met men who "came on" to her, but I wondered about the criteria she used to assess them. She laughed and said, "What criteria?" I responded that most adults, when they are dating, assess the other person. She again laughed, ironically, and sardonically asked, "Like are they good looking? Are they cheating on their wives? Do they have a job? Is that what you mean? They all want sex!"

I first addressed her apparent inhibition of critical judgment. I said I thought something stopped her from making other assessments of men aside from their sexual interest, their looks, and their job. She looked at me quizzically, and again asked, "Like what?" I then realized that perhaps she did not know how to assess men, even though she had dated and had once been married.

I told her I could not determine whether she was blocking out her judgment or had a developmental delay in her thinking. When she asked me what I meant by a developmental delay, I explained that she might still be functioning like a teenager, preoccupied with the man's looks and whether he had a nice car. She again laughed, this time heartily, and said, "I'm a teenager! Tell me what I should be doing! I really don't know!"

I was surprised but decided to give her some advice if she actually wanted it. She encouraged me, and as I described various points of assessment, she actually took notes. I did not discourage this, but we both laughed about it a little bit.

I told her that, first of all, she needed to assess whether the man was reliable: For example, was he on time? Aside from this conscience function, what were his values: How did he treat other people, how did he view money, and what did he value in a relationship?

Then, how organized was he? Could he keep things straight? How smart was he? Did he remember things that were important to her? Did his abstraction ability match hers and her quite-good sense of humor?

As I listed these off, she laughed again and told me she had never thought to categorize these factors.

I continued that she should check the man's impulse control. Did he push for sex, drink too much, use drugs, or have a bad temper? Did he have any highly irrational thoughts?[29]

Finally, she needed to know if a man was warm (as she was), was trustworthy, and could maintain a close connection to her without running away.

She then realized that she had run away since she had found her ex-husband cheating on her. She thought maybe she had accepted men who showed no capacity for closeness. This had been counterproductive since she wished to get married again.

I explained that object constancy meant the man could be consistent in his attention to her and increase their frequency of contact fairly quickly. She joked, "You mean I should not play hard to get?" "Right!" I answered, but not about sex. She should withhold sex until she was convinced the man

1. was reliable and honest
2. had proven himself trustworthy
3. showed concern about her
4. matched with her socially
5. shared her sense of humor
6. had a decent value system
7. was understanding of what she felt
8. liked being close with her, meaning
   a. talking with her
   b. listening
   c. getting to know her
   d. letting her get to know him
   e. sharing stories and events, and
   f. socializing with other people

---

29 Too much primary process in consciousness (Blackman, 2010).

9. seemed capable of sustaining closeness with her, by
    a. seeing her frequently
    b. eventually being willing to stop seeing other women
10. solving problems with her.

If those things were positive, she might introduce sex into the picture. She should then request an agreement about exclusivity before planning a "big night." She sneered that this would kill the spontaneity. I (supportively) argued, with irony: "Spontaneity is overrated." My sarcastic remark brought forth a laugh from her. She agreed that she had had too much pain in her life to be spontaneous anymore. Spontaneity about conversation, joking, and interaction were all fine. Spontaneity about sexual intercourse led to emotional trouble in the past, and predictably would do so in the future.

Over the next couple of months, as she dated men, she actually carried the list of criteria around with her and laughingly referred to them when she came to see me. Remarkably, she exercised better judgment. At the time she stopped treatment about a year later, she had chosen a man to live with who seemed to have most of the qualities she wanted. They were exclusive, having a good time, and thinking about marriage if things worked out.

Gwen appeared to need advice because of a developmental delay in her critical judgment function. I was never quite clear about why she had not developed this better. One factor seemed to be that she had hung around pessimistic, single women who had brief affairs with unsuitable men, something like in the television show *Sex and the City*.

Some of her friends scoffed at her criteria list, but a number of them took notes from her. During her last session with me, Gwen suggested I write a book about adult dating. I'm thinking about it.

Problem 74
Questions About Your Theoretical Orientation

Sophisticated people will have read about psychological theories in college, graduate school, in the *New York Times* or *The Atlantic*. From an intellectual standpoint, they may want to know what they are getting into and question which theories you are using to try to help them. On the face of it, this is a reasonable inquiry.

On the other hand, everybody you see will be different in some way. People have different stories, experiences with their parents and others growing up, and different people in their current lives. The mental health field is both appealing and frustrating in that no two people are alike and one size does not fit all as far as individual therapy goes.

Some people will not bring up a question about this for several sessions, and in one case I recall a person bringing up this question after a number of years of treatment.

Is there a good answer to this very complicated question?

SHORT ANSWER

Yes. Just as people who come to consult us have a right to know about our training, they can also know which theories we use in trying to understand their problems. My way of viewing mental problems is available in my first two books. I have included a summary of mental dysfunction in Problems 2 and 101 of this book.

If asked about my theoretical orientation, I will generally respond that I am first of all concerned about whether there are any weaknesses in basic mental functions, problems with close relationships, or disturbances in values and conscience; I am also concerned about the reality of people's lives and the impact that this has on them (what is often called "stress") as well as whatever conflicts may be present, of which people are unaware, that may be creating their problems. Usually, this brief explanation will suffice.

In his iconoclastic book, Rothstein[30] described making deals with skeptical people, where he would treat them at a reduced fee for a number of

---

30 Rothstein (1998).

months to prove to them that treatment was "worth it." They would agree that if they found it useful, they would the pay his usual fee.

I have not tried this particular approach. Instead, if I think I can treat someone, I suggest we meet for a few sessions and see how things go. I do not set up a treatment schedule until I've had follow-up sessions to see how people respond to my initial attempts to help them understand their resistances and some meanings of their presenting problems. If we are working well, and I think the prognosis is good, I will discuss this openly with people, and recommend whatever frequency I think is appropriate to them.

In short, I think it is best not to be defensive about your theoretical orientation, but to share this with the people in language they can understand.

I also follow the usual wisdom of describing other approaches to the problems, including cognitive therapy, behavioral therapy, and psychobiological therapy. If I feel one of those approaches is best, I refer people to the appropriate therapist, since I mostly do dynamic psychotherapy (to help people understand themselves) and psychoanalysis (to help people *really* understand themselves).

If I feel that an approach geared toward understanding their problems is best, I will recommend that on a trial basis. Making people aware that there are a variety of approaches available tends to make them less pessimistic about their problems. If things don't work out in their attempts at treatment with me, there are other viable options.

LONG ANSWER

A major complication of getting into theoretical discussions with people is that you introduce intellectualization as a defense. Frequently, questions about theoretical orientation are generated by mistrust. I have sometimes made a mistake in answering questions about theory rather than discussing with the people how they protect themselves from mistrust about me by asking me for a lecture about theory.

Moreover, theoretical orientation is not as certain as any theoretician, including myself, thinks. Here's an experience I had with a man a number of years ago:

EXAMPLE

John, 55 and married, complained of lifelong problems with his 85-year-old mother, who lived 3 hours away. The problem had been nagging at him for 30 years, and he finally decided to consult somebody about it. His family had descended from the signers of the United States Declaration of Independence and belonged to the First Families of Virginia (FFV).

John complained that his mother, descended from the founders, was fastidious, aristocratic, cold, critical, and obsessed with social niceties. In spite of that, he loved her. However, since he had started his own business in his 20s, his mother had criticized (a) him as a father (although his adult children were doing reasonably well); (b) his wife's clothing; (c) him as a son; (d) his manners; (e) his attitude; and (f) the way he expressed himself.

After John described these problems to me, I said I could see that he had controlled himself because of conflicts about his irritation. He responded, "I know that. I'm not coming here to get analyzed. I'm coming here because I want you to tell me a solution to my problem with my mother. I don't want years of treatment. I just want to know what I can do about it!"

I was surprised, and John saw this. He became more diplomatic and said that if I could not give him advice, he would understand and pay me for my time. I thought, based on his attitude, that he would not be treatable long term, so I decided to try to help ("supportively") by giving him advice (Problems 1, 9, and 73).

I said if I were him, I would, on the next visit to his mother, tell her that he was fed up with her ridiculous criticisms. I suggested he tell her that he is 55 years old, has had a successful business, has a successful marriage and children, and that the only thing bothering him is that his mother keeps nitpicking and criticizing him for things as though he were 5 years old, which he resents.

I also suggested he tell her that he had withheld telling her this for years because he did not want to hurt her feelings, but that he could no longer put up with her criticisms, and that he wanted her to stop it. He should also tell her to stop it because he loves her and does not want to stop seeing her; that he had considered not seeing her again because of how irritated she makes him with these unnecessary and irritating remarks.

John's response to this lecture was: "That's a great idea. I'm going to do it. Thank you. My father never would have told me to do anything like that. He was always such a wimp! He always caved in to my mother; he always let her have her way and took all of her crap! I don't have to be that way, and I'm not that way, and there's no reason for me to put up with her bullshit any longer. Thank you for your time."

John's response to my advice (supportive technique) was to come up with his own interpretation! Even though he had told me he did not want "analysis," my advice acted as a confrontation of his identification with his passive father. When John realized this, he reintegrated and rethought his approach to his mother.

In other words, what I considered to be "supportive" technique turned out to be a confrontation of John's identification with his father, leading to an interpretive result: a reintegration of John's thinking and a freeing of his speech and self-protective mechanisms. He could now attempt to establish a secure object tie to his mother, even though they were getting up in years.

Another confluence of theories occurs when a psychotherapist refers people for, or prescribes medicine. The therapist is often using a combination of insight theories and biological theories of affect regulation.[31]

In Blackman (2003b) I reported how a psychiatry resident had changed her male patient's antidepressant under pressure from him. He was cheating on his wife and feeling guilty about it. During supervision, she and I figured out that when she prescribed the antidepressant, she was being too nice to relieve her own guilt over retaliatory wishes she had developed toward him for cheating on his wife and for bullying her.

In other words, no technique is actually "pure."

---

31 Roose and Stern (1995) and Roose and Johannet (1998).

Problem 75
People Who Read Your Professional Articles and Books

People in the mental health field who come to see you for treatment may well have googled you, at least. If you have written articles or books, they may have read some of them.

What then to do with someone who brings your book or article to a session and wants to talk to you about some passage in it?

SHORT ANSWER

Although in years past I have heard many therapists discourage people from reading their theoretical and other published material, in my experience people reading what I have written has not been negative.

If someone is interested in something I have written and they find it on their own (easily discovered on the Internet), I am happy to talk with them about it, at least for a while. Very often, people apply some part of what I've written to themselves. I have been surprised by how much accuracy they have had in doing so. Anyway, when they do this, I will acknowledge their self-interpretation, and this often acts as a stimulus for further discussion and further understanding of their problems.

LONG ANSWER

So far, no one I have treated has disagreed with things that I have written about (in *101 Defenses* and in *Get the Diagnosis Right*); I have a feeling that the response to this current book may be different…(there's no doubt a reason why books on technique tend to be rather vague).

Unlike some therapists, I do not generally recommend any books to people I am treating (except for Kliman and Rosenfeld's 1983 book on child rearing). People trying to find answers in books has a point, but often is a way of taking up their problems without relying on the therapist. At other times, people's skepticism and mistrust regarding the therapist are masked by their supposed interest in other people's theories.

Stein (1988) described in detail some of the techniques that he has used in handling people who wanted to discuss his writing. His findings support my observation that people who read your work do not usually pose any particular problem.

Ironically, my first two books include material about defense mechanisms. Most of my printed articles and book chapters also do. When people bring in material from these books, therefore, it often has to do with their own defensive operations. Discussing one of the books or papers, therefore, can be a useful segue into learning more about their conflicts, does not bypass their defenses, and does not seem to disturb the treatment.

On the other hand, when people I am treating get angry with me, they may accuse me of just seeing them as material for my next book. These accusations generally concern transferences from mothers or fathers who never viewed them as important as human beings. One was a woman who felt "abused" by her mother; her mother had forced her and her sister to clean up the house while allowing the males in the household to get away with avoiding household duties.

Problem 76
People Who React to Any Intervention as an Invasion

If you are not doing "Bion-ic" treatment (Problem 13), you try to show people various things about themselves. You may ask them questions, comment on their judgment, confront them about defenses, express understanding, advise them, and make other interventions (see Problem 1). Whatever your good intentions, however, there are a number of people who will react negatively to anything you say.

Although they are not psychotic, these people are sensitive to anyone controlling their thinking. They have often had extraordinarily controlling parents or experiences with authorities or mentors who manipulated them. They may have been abused.

How can we approach people who are sensitized to any type of intervention?

SHORT ANSWER

This group of people requires an "exception to the rule against questions."[32] Most of the time, we try to find the problem behaviors and attitudes that cause people difficulty and then explain the conflicts that are causing these. Asking questions can be counterproductive, since it interferes with the flow of people's thoughts and makes it more difficult to formulate accurately. When people are sensitive to being told what they are thinking, however, explaining formulations to them can backfire.

When treating sensitive people, I ask questions (usually directed toward "mentalizing," i.e., thinking about themselves). The questions are usually broad based, such as, "What do you think about your husband's attitude?" I might also ask them about the past: "How do you think your relationship with your father affected your brother?" In this way, I attempt to help people develop an alliance with me—and not feel I am so much of an authority who is giving them the word of God. Although not perfect, this type of approach tends to obviate some of their sensitivities to being invaded.

LONG ANSWER

A more complicated approach to the whole difficulty with invasion is to observe the way people guard themselves against it. First, I will make a statement

---

32 Blackman (2010), p. 216.

regarding the meanings of people's conflicts. Later, when such people react angrily to being invaded, I will engage them in understanding their sensitivity, anger, and defensiveness about my "invasion."

EXAMPLE

Jeff, a 47-year-old sales manager for a medical equipment company, consulted me because of lack of attraction to his wife and constant arguments with her. He was depressed about all this. For several years, he had "steeled" himself to his feelings by "armoring up," but lately, he found himself more irritable and unhappy, and wasn't sleeping well.

Jeff's mother had been quite a bother to him when he was a teenager. He wound up having to hide his pornography on a high shelf in one of his closets, because if he left it in a drawer in his dresser, his mother would find it and throw it all out. She also berated him for even having pornography.

In addition, she frequently took him to doctors when he was only mildly ill and requested a variety of invasive tests.

At one point during his early work with me, Jeff was describing his wife's nighttime routine of washing up around 9:00 p.m., getting in bed at 9:15, and then waking up at 5:00 in the morning to do yoga and meditation for an hour before they woke up the children. Her habits had interfered with their sex life for about 6 months.

I pointed out to Jeff that he had some inhibition about saying anything about his frustrations to his wife; I suspected, from what I knew about him, that he did not want to hurt her and felt overly guilty about saying anything. He responded angrily: "Maybe, but why are you always second-guessing me? Do we have to analyze everything? I don't need you to tell me to talk to my wife! I know how to talk! I'm sorry, I'm just a little sensitive about this."

I then commented that I agreed with Jeff, that he was sensitive. He apparently reacted to any observation I made as though I were controlling him. I clarified that I had been trying to figure out what was causing him to feel inhibited, but I was certainly not trying to tell him what to do with his wife.

He could see this, and again apologized for his "overreaction." Since we were discussing this intimately, I told him I thought his sensitivity had to do with the years that he put up with his mother invading him.

He responded in the affirmative, and added that he thought he was probably avoiding saying anything to his wife because he didn't want to be like his mother. (He was disidentifying from his mother; if he made any type of invasive comments, he would feel guilty.) In other words, we eventually got to an understanding, but not without him getting angry at me (transference), which, fortunately, was explicable.

Problem 77
When You Find Yourself Asking Too Many Questions

I spend much of my time in teaching (and supervising) trainees admonishing them not to ask too many questions. Dorpat (2000) made a scholarly argument against the asking of questions during therapy. The name of his book sort of sums it up: *Gaslighting, the Double-Whammy, Interrogation, and Other Methods of Covert Control in Psychotherapy and Analysis*. Dorpat pointed out that any time a therapist asks questions, people in treatment feel (a) pinned, (b) pushed to perform, (c) invaded, (d) disrespected, and (e) distracted from what they were going to tell us.

Although there are "exceptions to the rule against questions,"[33] usually we allow people to tell us their "story."[34] We listen carefully to understand the multiple factors that have caused their problems. We then try to explain what will help them.

Considering that we are not interrogating people and that we are not trying to "lead" them into a direction according to our own "agenda," what can we do when we notice that we are asking them a barrage of questions during a therapeutic session?

SHORT ANSWER

Therapists tend to ask too many questions for a variety of reasons. Here, I describe the most common cause.

1. People are using defensive operations. Their defenses, such as reticence (being quiet), halting in speech, minimizing things, and forgetting important information, cause the therapist to want to know more. When we want to know more, we ask questions (!). We do it every day with acquaintances, in business, and in our personal lives.

In therapy, we can use our urge to ask questions as a red flag that tells us that people are using defenses. We then search around in our thinking to figure out which defenses, and instead of asking questions, we explain ("confront") the defenses.

---

33 Blackman (2010).
34 Volkan (2009).

LONG ANSWER

Other reasons therapists tend to ask questions in a countertherapeutic fashion are:

2. Therapists are confused about what is happening with the person they are treating.

I have been in this situation many times: I cannot understand who is doing what to whom, who forgot to do what, who said which hateful thing to whom, who was crying, or who ran out of the house. The person's antecedents are unclear.

Revealing my confusion can act as a clarification.[35] In other words, I may say to people I don't understand, to wit: "I'm confused. I can't understand who the players are in the description that you're giving me." Pleading ignorance, when true, is much less invasive than asking barrages of questions.

> **TIP**
> If you find yourself asking too many questions, think to yourself: Are people confused, defensive, or do they have deficits in their organizational ability?

Sometimes I ask questions, but if I can remember to plead ignorance (clarification) instead, the person will integrate better and be less resistant.

When you confess confusion, people try to clarify their thoughts and feelings. If they are still confused when they leave, they may request another session that week. Contrarily, when a therapist pelts people with questions, they can become more resistant, miss a few sessions, or not pay the fee.

3. People in treatment are highly disorganized.

If I allow people to speak uninterrupted for 5 or 10 minutes, they may manifest grossly loose associations (disorganized thoughts) indicative of psychosis. A gentle question from me about delusions or hallucinatory activity is then answered more honestly. I have discovered a fair number of schizophrenic cases in surprising situations. Prior therapists, who asked many questions, may have missed the integrative deficit or the breaks with reality.

---

35 The "Columbo" style that I recommended elsewhere (Blackman, 2003a, Chapter 6).

I have learned that many people suffering with a mild schizophrenic illness keep quiet. If they are asked questions, they answer, but do not reveal the bizarre, symbolic[36] thoughts they are harboring consciously. Such people's guardedness can cause the therapist to ask many questions, which they then "answer." These sessions go "smoothly," but the integrative defect can be missed.

4. In more intensive therapies, the therapist may be nervous or depressed about some of the material presented by people in treatment.

In these situations, the therapist's questions can represent an unconscious way of avoiding upsetting material (countertransference).

---

36 Primary process (S. Freud, 1900).

Problem 78
People Who Threaten You

The longer you are in practice, the more likely you will evaluate someone who threatens you. If you work on an inpatient unit or with prisoners, this will happen more frequently. Of course, those situations require special security measures.

Let's discuss situations where someone threatens you while you are treating them. For forensic evaluations, see Problem 85.

SHORT ANSWER

Threats from people you are treating come in different forms: (a) threats to your physical being, (b) threats to your integrity, (c) threats to your reputation, (d) threats to your practice, and (e) threats to your mental health.

1. As a rule, if somebody threatens you physically, you should refer them to someone else. Once a physical threat has been made (this is a crime called "assault" in the United States), you are dealing with somebody who, at best, is having a severe regressive transference reaction to you, which is probably not workable. That person will probably not improve, and you might get hurt.

When I evaluated heinous child abusers for the State of Louisiana, several evaluees threatened me. I had decided to take that risk and confronted threats by pointing out to those people that I knew they were trying to control me because they were afraid of what my opinion might be. This would usually stop the threats, and no one actually tried to assault me physically during those years.

Early in my career, when I treated psychotic people, in the hospital and out, a few came to my office with a gun. I had to convince them to be hospitalized, after removing the gun from their possession. I've been lucky. No one shot me.

LONG ANSWER

2. Threats to your integrity are a bit more common. "Drug-seeking" individuals may try to pry narcotics out of you. Others attempt to manipulate a leave slip from work for "depression." Most of us will not cave in to these manipulations; but occasionally, such people may take outrageous steps to discredit you. Keep good written records of exactly what occurred and your reasoning about it.

3. Threats to your reputation can be more subtle. When people you are treating suddenly request a second, outside opinion, this may indicate that they are planning to sue you for malpractice or to lodge a complaint with your professional licensing board. In those situations, explore why they desire a second opinion.

You can protect yourself by having people who request a second opinion sign a written release for you to speak with the professional who will furnish the new opinion. That way, you can explain to the other professional how you see the problem in the treatment. You also show you are willing to cooperate, for the benefit of the treatment, by talking with the other evaluator.

Frequently, a person's request for a second opinion suggests they want to try treatment with someone else. Often, you can discharge them and offer to speak to the new therapist if people will release you to do so.

I've had the hair-raising experience having someone quit treatment who would not release me to speak with anybody. In a situation where people have distorted ideas about your attitude, what you have said to them, or your intentions, it is likely that they will share those distortions with their new therapist. You can only hope that the new therapist will be neutral. Remember, when you see people who complain about another therapist, how distorted their complaints may be.

4. Regarding threats to your practice, when people complain that treatment does not work or that you have said something that has caused them "harm," you should consider referring them to someone else.

In the cases where this has happened to me, I explored how people felt they had been "harmed," and often found they imagined I wasn't listening. On occasion, I had asked a question that inadvertently wounded their self-esteem.

When people have better abstraction ability and integrative capacity, they may be able to see that their sensitivity is based on paranoid fears. Some people have said, "Oh, I'm getting paranoid again." Often there are projected elements, where they are blaming you for things about themselves they actually don't like.

5. Finally, you must consider referring off people who are dangerous to your own mental health. These people torture you somehow, cross-examine you, refuse to cooperate with the working alliance, and/or persistently try to get you angry.

You may want to show people how they are provocative, much in the way one of their parents (or other important people) provoked them as children. If people persist in provoking you, the prognosis is poor.

People who constantly threaten to kill themselves fall into this category (Problem 62). So-called "severe borderlines" or "flaming borderlines," who cut themselves between sessions, will worry you to death and cause you agitation, which can make it hard to maintain empathy and neutrality with other people you are trying to treat.

No doubt, some professionals should try to treat disruptive, argumentative, and threatening people; there are various behavioral and medication programs, (at this time, dialectical behavioral therapy seems to do this) who may welcome people with these types of problems. In outpatient individual therapy, they can be dangerous to your mental health.

6. In more complex situations, someone may complain about a mistake you have made and be correct but be overreacting to it.

EXAMPLE 1

Kerry, a 27-year-old man, had marital problems. He was frustrated with his wife, depressed, and drinking too much. He was on a tight schedule but was always on time for his appointments.

On two occasions I was about 15 minutes late for his appointment, which is unusual for me. On both occasions, I apologized to him, asked if he could stay for 45 minutes, and he responded in the affirmative. However, the second time this happened, he accused me of "repressing your hostility."

I had thought about this possibility, but realized that my lateness was not due to countertransference but to situational factors "beyond my control." I therefore tried to reassure him that his feeling about this was not correct. Again, I apologized for having made him wait. He continued to be angry, however.

Although I understood he was aggravated, I thought that the anger might have other roots. He immediately said, "It's from my father!" Kerry's father had been an attorney. When Kerry was in grade school, his father made him sit in his office while his father did paperwork. Kerry hated waiting.

After his parents got divorced, his father kept him waiting for hours at his mother's house before he got picked up. Kerry could see that he had been displacing rage from his father to me; Kerry had loved his father and had never told his father that he was angry. He was afraid that he would lose his father even more.

Similarly, Kerry was reluctant to tell his wife things he was upset about, but then weeks down the road, when she criticized him, he would explode.

Although Kerry got some benefit out of these discussions, he said my two late arrivals had caused him so much anger that he could not get over it, and he did not want to see me. At his request, I referred him to a colleague. Kerry sent me an e-mail a few months later, thanking me and revealing that my colleague reminded him of his grandmother, who was always attentive to him.

EXAMPLE 2

Max, 41 years old, had suffered a subarachnoid hemorrhage at work. The resulting hematoma had required neurosurgical excavation. Max's life was saved.

Later, Max complained about his memory. Neurologists could find no cause for this, thought Max was depressed, and therefore referred him to me.

After I saw Max twice in the office, he complained of marital problems. In his third session, his wife came to say Max had been threatening to kill himself.

At that time in my practice, I was doing hospital work, so I hospitalized Max, voluntarily. I noticed that he persisted in blaming his subarachnoid hemorrhage for all his problems. I began to suspect Max wanted to settle his legal case against his company based on a claim of psychiatric disability.

After a couple of sessions in the hospital, I became concerned about whether Max was using me. When I tested his memory, I saw he remembered things after a pause. I wondered how much this memory problem was caused by the hemorrhage versus how much by his depressing marital problems.

To test his treatability, I said to him, during his third hospital day, that some people had memory problems for reasons other than brain pathology. Max's response was: "Were you in Vietnam, Doc?" I replied that I had been in the Army during the Vietnam War, but I had not been sent overseas. He said, "Well, do you know what *fragging* was?" I said I did.[37] I wondered why he asked. He said, "Well, Doc, I know where you live."

I suspected that Max was threatening me. He did not want me questioning the cause of his memory problems. I thought I was not going to be able to treat him and could be in danger. I therefore asked Max if he would prefer a different psychiatrist. He responded, slowly, "Yeah. I think that's a good idea."

A few minutes later, I told the hospital administrator that Max preferred a new psychiatrist. I honestly said Max had become suspicious of me, and I of him. Under those circumstances, I did not think I could treat him any further. Dr. Lewis was on call. He was willing to take over Max's care. I explained to Dr. Lewis my worry that Max might be exaggerating his symptoms and had made suicidal and homicidal threats including a veiled threat toward me. Dr. Lewis was willing to take the case, and did so.

---

37 "Fragging" was the activity of enlisted soldiers shooting their own lieutenant. They would do this because the fresh, young lieutenant was ignorant, condescending, uncooperative, or unprotective toward his troops.

SECTION F

Modifications to the "Frame" of Treatment

GENERAL COMMENTS ABOUT EXCEPTIONS

Most of the time, we try to maintain the frame of treatment. This means that we

- talk to people,
- do not touch them,
- do not reveal much about ourselves,
- start and end on time, and
- require they pay for sessions.

Also, there is the matter of the alliance, which is reviewed in Figure 1, below.

REMINDER

The working alliance means that people in treatment with you:

- Attend their sessions
- Arrive on time
- Pay the fee the way you have requested
- Pay for missed sessions according to the policy you maintain
- Agree they have specific problems for which they want help
- Only talk (and nothing else) with you
- Give you feedback about your comments to them

You, reciprocally:

- Focus entirely on their problems (and not your own or someone else's)
- Try to figure out what is wrong
- Make comments designed to help them cope or understand the problems you and they have identified
- Also are on time
- Take them seriously

Figure 1.

There are times, however, when either we or the people we are treating make allowances or exceptions to the frame.

There are usually ramifications of doing so. In this section, I share with you some of my thoughts and experiences with these issues.

Problem 79
Bumping Into People Outside of the Office

As long as I have supervised people, they have asked me about this issue. One colleague told me that he avoided going to functions because he was concerned he would cause anxiety in people he was treating should he be there with his wife. I have heard the same types of concerns from male and female therapists.

People I treat have asked me how they should behave if they see me outside the office. Some hated seeing me outside of the office: They had to think of me as "human."

> **A TIP FROM MY WIFE TO OTHER SPOUSES OF THERAPISTS**
>
> If we are at a party or at an event and someone I don't know approaches us and begins talking with my husband, I do not ask, "So, how do you know my husband?"
>
> If the person turns to me and seems unsure what to say, I will just bring up a safe topic, such as, "Isn't it a great show?" or "Have you tried the crab dip? It's really good."
>
> Sometimes they seem relieved they did not have to identify themselves to me.

This can be a delicate issue.

SHORT ANSWER

At this time in history, confidentiality is in the hands of people you treat. You have no right to say anything about knowing them at all in any situation outside your consulting room. However, they have complete choice about whether to talk with you in public or to expose that they are in treatment with you. This does not completely solve the problem, so here's some more advice.

My general policy, which I tell people on occasion, is if they see me or I see them outside the office, it is 100% up to them whether they want to communicate with me. I will not acknowledge them unless they acknowledge me, and I will not make any effort to speak with them.

However, if they want to chat with me in a social setting, usually where I am present with my wife, I'm happy to introduce them to my wife and to chat with them briefly. I do not expose that I know them from treating them.

Over the decades that I have been married, on several occasions people I was treating (or had treated) approached my wife and me to chat socially. Sometimes they mentioned to my wife that they had been in treatment with me.

Usually when I see people I have treated outside the office, they have avoided contact with me (which is reasonable). I have not avoided any activity or event because I knew that someone I was treating was involved in that activity.

A special case has arisen periodically where a trainee consults me—typically, social work students, psychiatry residents, psychology interns, or psychoanalytic candidates. If trainees want treatment with me, I must avoid situations where I have to grade them or assess their functioning. In those unusual situations, often the trainee does have to expose their therapeutic relationship with me to someone on the faculty of their training center so that they can be freed from attending my classes.

Usually, the class material can be made up with another faculty member or a different class, and sometimes only the director of the training program needs to know. Those directors usually keep the confidentiality of the person I am treating and may find some other reason to excuse the trainee from my class, such as a project or placement.

LONG ANSWER

There has been at least one situation where I was sorry that I was present in the same situation as someone I had treated. The situation occurred over two decades ago, at a time when I was doing some general psychiatry in mental hospitals.

EXAMPLE 1

I had briefly treated Shana, a catatonic schizophrenic; she had recovered from the catatonia, was taking antipsychotic medicine, and had been discharged from the hospital to a clinic, still delusional but improved.

Later, I was asked to give a presentation to the general public as part of the hospital's educational community outreach activities. The evening I gave that presentation (on depressions), Shana was in the audience. During the question and answer period, she began a delusional diatribe about the hospital, although she said she compared me to "a god."

She had to be ushered out by attendants. There was some murmuring in the audience of 100 people. I was, of course, constrained from saying anything. I went on with the presentation. After the talk, several people expressed curiosity or sympathy. I explained that I could not say anything; they seemed to accept this.

At other times, when I have bumped into people in social settings, the contact took on symbolism. After I have seen someone at a concert, opera, or sporting event, if they do not bring up our meeting during their next session, I will, with a comment that I had noticed they had not mentioned it.

Sometimes they had thought it was insignificant, and if there is no mileage to get out of pursuing the whole matter, I may drop it. But people may have a number of reactions to meeting me with my wife and/or my son. When they tell me their thoughts about it, I can better formulate about whatever symbolism the meeting had.

EXAMPLE 2

Chet, a 29-year-old physics graduate student, had trouble finishing his dissertation. He distracted himself, took girls to karaoke, or read something else instead of preparing his dissertation. True, the deadline was years away, but his dallying around with it was a chronic source of frustration to him.

During that time, my wife and I attended the Virginia Opera on a regular basis, and we were socially involved in the opera organization. In one of his sessions, Chet told me, "I saw you and your wife at the opera!" I acknowledged that we were involved with the opera and asked him what he thought. He said, "You are pretty sociable. But I think you're too old for that young girl!" Chet thought my wife was closer to his age than to mine. Quickly, he apologized for making fun of my age; it was just that he found my wife attractive. He then became silent for a minute.

I explained to him that his silence reminded me of his inhibition studying. He seemed to feel guilty about competing with me, so he stopped talking to me.

Chet started laughing, made some more sexual remarks about my wife, and then felt guilty again. He thought how he "played around," taking girls to karaoke or having sex with them instead of doing his dissertation. He then recalled our other discussions about his competitive feelings with his father, a successful attorney.

Chet's father thought there was no money in being a physicist and had tried to dissuade Chet from getting a degree in physics. Chet had felt demeaned by this and simultaneously had suspected that his father did not want him to be successful. He had internalized this feeling from his father (whether it was true or not) and blamed himself for being smarter than his father. His guilt interfered with him finishing his doctoral dissertation.

In this case, his bumping into me and my wife at the opera had stirred competitive feelings in Chet. His reactions facilitated our understanding of elements causing his study inhibition.

Problem 80
When You Lower Your Fee

Discussing fees is controversial and laden with emotion. Even mentioning your fee to colleagues could be considered improper. Nevertheless, questions about what to charge are invariably asked by people I supervise. I will therefore attempt to address this issue as diplomatically as possible, staying within ethical constraints.

As of this writing, the highest fee I have heard for a 45-minute psychotherapy session is $700 (about $933/hour)—charged by a therapist in New York City in 2010. In the Hampton Roads, Virginia, United States, area, where I live, some master's level social work positions pay less than $40,000 a year, which equals about $20 an hour. Gauging others' fees and selecting an out-of-network fee (if you don't contract with insurance) is difficult.

No matter what you have set as your "regular fee," several factors may convince you to lower it at times. You may like to do pro bono work, or you may want to treat a particular person who cannot afford your regular fee.

What to do?

SHORT ANSWER

I bill people (directly) a fee I have selected and may lower it for several reasons. About 25 years ago, I did not have enough of a practice. So I dropped my fee, thinking that would increase referrals. In retrospect, I think it had a slight effect.

The second reason I have lowered my fee is that I would like to treat someone who cannot afford my regular fee.

Third, I have lowered my fee, when I was in training, to allow some people to be in analysis four times a week. More recently, I have treated some people in China using Skype, pro bono (per the China American Psychoanalytic Alliance, capachina.org).

Most of time, people are grateful when you lower your fee, and there's not too much difficulty. In 1958, a study was done at the New York Psychoanalytic Institute on analysands who were paying nothing.[1] It was workable.

Certain people may feel guilty about the reduction in fee, and if this happens, you can usually reassure them that you don't mind, reducing their guilt. For some people who are in training or just embarking on a career, we

---

1 Lorand and Console (1958).

may agree to raise their fee after they finish training or obtain a higher paying position.

LONG ANSWER

Although it is "nice" to reduce the fee people pay you, there are several situations where I found this to be counterproductive:

- The reduction in fee is too severe. You need to be able to cover your expenses, so you need to know what those are. If people cannot afford my reduced fee, I may refer them to the psychiatry resident clinic or the Psychology Intern Program at Eastern Virginia Medical School, where the fee is negligible. They don't have to fuss with insurance coverage or have their therapist send reports every few sessions. Also, their confidentiality is completely protected.
- I find out, later, that people have a large trust fund and could easily have afforded to pay my regular fee. It is difficult to avoid irritation with people who have "deprived me," while knowing they could afford it, but I don't make an issue of this immediately, nor do I try to recoup the lost income. Yearly, when I usually raise my fees a bit, I will discuss the issue with people who fall into this category, renegotiate the fee, and try to figure out the meaning of their initial deception.
- People in intensive treatment two to four times a week begin to feel conflicted about the reduced fee, regardless of whether they could afford more or not. Usually they cannot, but they feel enormously guilty.
- Obsessive-compulsive people become preoccupied with the reduced fee.
- They (a) worry I am angry at them, (b) imagine I feel deprived the way they did as children, (c) feel guilty they are doing something destructive to me, (d) become inhibited about expressing anger directed at me (this inhibition occurs outside their awareness as a response to guilt over hostility toward others that is transferred onto me), or (e) become passive, compliant, and humbly apologetic as well.

It is tricky when people paying a low fee miss a session. Again, if all this can be handled through understanding people's conflicts about money, the meanings of it to them, and the meaning of you lowering your fee for them, usually people can gain insight into their problems.

Problem 81
What About E-mail and Skype?

E-mail is a wonderful invention. It allows people to communicate instantaneously over large distances, send pictures and greetings, and verify appointments. The well-known downsides of e-mail include that e-mail lasts forever (you cannot throw it out), that emotions are exceedingly difficult to judge, nuance is entirely lost, and that people using e-mail tend to be impulsive and not scrutinize what they have written closely enough before sending. Another frequent problem is that the "Reply to All" button can spray an e-mail to many people to whom you do not wish to send a particular e-mail.

In spite of all the problems, we live in an age of electronic communications in the 21st century, and large numbers of people all over the world use them.

If you have provided an e-mail address or a cell phone number, sometimes people you are treating will send you an e-mail or text about a problem with an appointment time. This may be a convenient way to handle scheduling adjustments. But people in treatment may also e-mail you about their problems, worries, and even feelings about you.

What should you do about these?

SHORT ANSWER

Regarding substantive matters that pertain to their emotional problems, I discourage people from using electronic communications and request they contact me by phone.

I keep a record of people's phone numbers and e-mail addresses. If I suddenly have to be out of the office, I will first attempt to phone them. If that fails, after leaving a voicemail, I may send them an e-mail as a backup.

I have also received referral e-mails from people, who described their problems and asked me if I could treat them. They may ask me to schedule an appointment by e-mail. My usual response to these referrals is to send back an e-mail acknowledging the referral and requesting their telephone number and a time when I can call them in the evening. That way I can hear the person speak, assess their synthetic (integrative) function, and judge something about their symptomatology. I do not directly discourage them from using e-mail, but, by requesting their phone number, I indicate the frame and introduce verbalization as the main means of communication and perhaps resolution.

When people who are in treatment send an e-mail concerning their problems, I will not respond to the substantive issues via e-mail. I acknowledge receipt by e-mail and then call them to talk about what is upsetting them. I consider their e-mail as part of their work with me and therefore think it is a break in the frame to communicate substantively outside of my consultation room. During their next session, I put the printed-out e-mail on the table between us; we can go over it and discuss their thoughts about their problems.

LONG ANSWER

The Electrified Mind: Developmental, Pathological and Therapeutic Problems in the Era of Email and the Internet (Akhtar, 2011) contains chapters on how electronic media are abused by teenagers as well as adults. The chapters cover autistic withdrawal that is possible when teenagers get stuck in websites such as Second Life.[2] Issues in Skype treatments are also deliberated, including emotional distancing and resistance to treatment. One point is that Internet teaching and treatment can promote impulsivity. Impulsivity is a big problem on the Internet: 350 million pornography Web pages are an enormous lure for adolescents and can cause them (a) to avoid sublimation, (b) to avoid establishing object relatedness with the other gender during adolescence, and (c) to fail to channel hostility into competitive and ambitious activities.

Treating people over the Internet also poses many legal issues. As of this writing, in many states in the United States, it is not legal to treat somebody who lives in a particular state if the therapist does not have a license to practice in that state. Of course, you should consult an attorney to find out if such laws apply or if exceptions are made for "talk therapy" that does not involve other medical intervention. It would also be advisable to consult your professional liability insurance provider to verify that they do not exclude such treatment from coverage.

A second major difficulty that I have run into in the bit of treatment that I have attempted with people via Skype (or telephone) surrounds the matter of time. If the people I am treating are late, or if I am, one of us winds up sitting, waiting, wondering if the other is "there." A third problem concerns where people you treat are sitting. A man I treated by telephone, because he was traveling, would often be at a worksite in a room. Although the door was closed, he was concerned that somebody might be listening to what he was saying; this had a chilling effect on his openness. When he was in town and came to see me in my office, he noted a difference in his trust and openness because of the stability and absolute confidentiality in my consulting room.

---

2 See www.secondlife.com.

In people who have object relations problems, it is difficult to work with issues of closeness and distance while using Internet programs. Emotional distance is somewhat built in because the two of you are not in the same room. Distractions that may arise include a child crying or the phone ringing.

Treating people in China[3] over the Internet also introduces a difficulty regarding the 12- or 13-hour time difference. In addition, the 7,000 mile distance opens up the communication to interruptions in Internet connections. Usually, it is not possible to understand the meanings of any reactions to these interruptions, since they are realities of the treatment setup. The "frame" of the treatment is more fragile, and more disturbed people will have more difficulty with the whole matter.

A substantive e-mail may be a defense that manages anxiety people experience in talking to me personally. Nevertheless, I have rarely discussed this with people I have treated. I take the e-mail as material that needs to be brought into the session. In rare cases, the *ex parte* communication (the e-mail) symbolized a wish to have an extratherapeutic contact with me. That is a boundary crossing that I sometimes will discuss.

On the other hand, I have found e-mail or texting particularly convenient when people are in a crisis and would like an extra appointment. They can text me on my cell phone, and I can text them back my availability. This can be useful for people sitting in a meeting where they cannot use a phone; they can quietly send a text and receive one without disturbing their milieu. I have not attempted to figure out any symbolic meanings of texting as yet, although in the future I might.

---

3 Fishkin and Fishkin (2011).

Problem 82
Bosses Who Have Their Assistants Contact You

Periodically, I am treating someone who has a position of authority in a medical practice, law practice, accounting practice, or business. Whatever the problem may be, I have sometimes run into an interesting and somewhat delicate difficulty with such people when they instruct their assistants (secretaries) to call me about a change in appointment time.

This time-saving approach seems just an administrative matter, but when this has occurred, I felt insulted. Years ago, when this first happened, I blamed myself for being too sensitive, since I was glad to have anyone to treat at all. As I went on in my practice, I realized when the person in treatment had his assistant call me, this usually meant something about the boss's personality problems. So I decided to try to address the behavior in a variety of different ways.

SHORT ANSWER

The one approach to this I have not taken is to refuse to deal with the assistant. Insisting that I want the boss to call me puts the secretary in the middle and causes a disturbance outside of my consultation room—not within it.

For these reasons, when a secretary calls to change an appointment time, I look in my appointment book and see if this is possible (assuming I get verification that the caller really is the secretary of the person I'm treating and is calling with authorization). As per my cancellation policy, as long as the change is requested before the appointment time and I'm able to reschedule the appointment within the following work week, I offer the secretary a time. After talking to the boss, the assistant gets back to me, and usually the second time works. If it doesn't, I suggest the boss call me.

If the appointment can be changed, the next time I see the boss in my office, if this behavior is not mentioned (and it often is not, since it is ego syntonic, meaning it is natural), I will point out that we are not discussing how he went about changing the appointment time with me.

Usually this is a bit of a shock (it is built in to the character). People who are bosses often get defensive, saying that they were rushed that day and knew that they had to change the time. Sometimes, I'm not able to get enough traction to help them understand this "reality rationalization." At other times, I have been more successful in showing them that there are elements worth discussing because (a) they were not aware of them and (b) they had a lot to do with their difficulties.

If we have a meeting of the minds that the behavior is significant, we might understand the usual meanings of the secretary calling: (a) creating emotional distance by putting a third party in the way, (b) avoiding shame over needing to ask me for something (a dependency gratification), (c) avoiding guilt over hostile manipulation toward me, and (d) demonstrating their own importance to relieve conflicts over their self-esteem.[4]

LONG ANSWER

When people have their secretaries contact you for any reason, be it to discuss payments, appointment times, or anything else, it is best to try to accommodate this request and to take it up with them during the following session as a part of the treatment.

EXAMPLE

Kirk, age 53, the circulation manager of a local magazine, consulted me because of ambivalence. He didn't know what to do about his marriage of 22 years. His 17-year-old son was doing well in school but was spoiled. His wife, Melinda, a financially successful dermatologist, had not had sexual intercourse with Kirk in 10 years. She lost her interest after the birth of their son and more so after the death of her father a few years later.

Kirk had thought he was impotent, anyway, so he didn't bother arguing with or putting any pressure on Melinda. Much to his surprise, his sales manager, Tina, had begun offering solace and friendship to him about a year prior to him seeing me. By the time he consulted me, he and Tina had been

---

[4] Throughout this book, I mention periodically how I may or may not be able to find the explanations for people's problems or behaviors. Edward H. Knight, one of my supervisors from analytic training, once told me, "One of the lessons of analysis is that you can't analyze everything."

In a related vein, some people have asked me something like, "Do we have to analyze everything?" My general answer is that we try to understand however much we are able to. People seeing me are suffering quite a bit, and the more clues we can get from any of their thoughts, their behavior, their verbalizations, or other sources, the more accurate we can be in trying to understand what is causing them to have difficulties.

My impression is that, even though you try your best, sometimes even your best is not enough—and something that should be understandable is blocked from awareness. People who get the most out of treatment are those who are receptive to new ideas, are able to use abstraction ability, and are able to "play with" various concepts about themselves without becoming overwhelmed, insulted, or otherwise agitated. Often, people have some difficulty with thus engaging in treatment; this was one reason I decided to write this book.

having a sexual affair for a few months. Tina had, one day at lunch, invited him to a motel. The first time they attempted intercourse, Kirk had been impotent. But after Tina's reassurance and playfulness, Kirk was able to perform and felt great.

Tina's husband was dying from amyotrophic lateral sclerosis (Lou Gehrig's Disease). She had mentioned the possibility that after her husband died, perhaps Kirk should leave his wife and marry her. Enter his ambivalence.

Kirk had been raised by his aunt and uncle since the age of 3. His father, a government official, had been sent to Saudi Arabia; his parents did not want to raise him there. He never felt close to his parents, although they reclaimed him after 8 years, when he was 11. He hadn't thought about that history for years; he remembered being terrified of being alone at night, crying for his mother. That depression continued into high school until he "got" a girlfriend.

Kirk and I figured out that he had been afraid to discuss closeness with his busy wife due to anxiety over loss and rejection. That anxiety had its roots in his childhood loss of his parents—especially his mother.

After five weekly sessions, Kirk had his secretary call me to change an appointment time. I found a time, which she called back to say was workable.

In his next session, Kirk did not mention the change of appointment time. He launched into a discussion about his trouble asking his wife for a separation. He questioned how much of their marital distance was his fault.

At that point, I said having his secretary call me was a possible clue to the answer to that question. Kirk was suspicious, but intrigued, and asked me what I meant. I told him I knew he thought his secretary calling was a simple administrative facilitation. He immediately, and I thought too defensively, said, "It didn't mean anything negative. It was easier. She always does that stuff for me."

I explained to him that, besides the convenience of relying on his secretary, Kirk was defensive because it was a bit condescending toward me; and it certainly was impersonal—that is, he handled his relationship with me from a distance, and put a third person between us. Kirk, quick on the uptake, immediately questioned, "You mean you think that I'm doing those things with Melinda? You think I'm using Tina to put distance between Melinda and me?"

I agreed I thought something like that. Kirk paused, and thought it could be possible. He had been avoiding Melinda and admitted he had not tried to have sex with her for at least 5 years. She had gone to some medical conventions without him; he wondered if she had had any extramarital sexual activity, herself.

A week later, Kirk reported that he had told Melinda that he was afraid their marriage was not working out. He did not mention Tina. Melinda grabbed a knife and slit her wrist in front of him. He became panicky, wrapped her wrist, and took her to the emergency room at a local hospital, where they sutured her wrist and referred her to a psychotherapist for outpatient therapy.

After that, Melinda became a virtual sex nymph with Kirk. She seduced and teased him into sexual intercourse, performed fellatio on him, and invited him to have anal sex with her. She also began cooking complex, tasty meals for them. She became more involved with their son. All this had happened in the week since I had last seen him. He had not yet discussed the situation with Tina.

Kirk and Melinda decided to stay together. Kirk eventually recognized that he was seeing Tina as the aunt from his childhood (someone who tried to save him from his loneliness and abandonment, whom he did not want to hurt or leave). He talked to Tina; they decided, with much sadness, to stop their affair.

Kirk never told Melinda about Tina, although Melinda was suspicious. Over the next few months, Kirk's ambivalence abated, and Melinda's refound sexuality did not dissipate.

Tina obtained a job with a different company in Switzerland, where her husband died. Kirk decided, with my agreement, to stop therapy after he and his wife had "straightened things out"—as he joked, "in more ways than one."

In retrospect, it seemed that Kirk's understanding of having his secretary call me to change his appointment time had given us an inroad into understanding his distancing, condescension, and avoidance of conflict. That understanding helped him reintegrate and rethink the way he had been avoiding his wife.

Problem 83
People Who Want to Be Your Friend—Use Your First Name

Generally speaking, it is best to retain an authoritative position as a therapist and not *tutoyer* (the French term for speaking familiarly) with people you treat. This helps maintain the "therapeutic barrier"[5] and prevents boundary violations. You should introduce yourself with your title: Doctor, Mister, or Ms. I generally greet people coming for evaluation with their title and my own.[6]

I apply this rule to people, generally, who are out of college and/or who are working. I use the first names of college students and teenagers.

I do not encourage people to use my first name or my nickname. People are coming to see me for therapeutic help, not to make a social acquaintance.

Considering this general principle, what do you do if someone wants to (or does) use your first name or uses their first name during therapy? Or ask to be your friend?

In the past 2 decades, our culture has become less formal. It is commonplace for people in positions of authority to go by their first name, even in professional settings. However, in this area, I prefer to stick to the more traditional approach.

SHORT ANSWER

In once- or twice-a-week psychotherapy, if adults request that I use their first name or their nickname, I generally do. The majority of the time, they still insist on calling me Dr. Blackman, which I accept. I know this is a transference of some sort, but I usually don't confront it unless necessary. One man, a professor (who held a PhD) at a local university, consulted me because his father, a physician, had referred him. When I went to the waiting room to get him, I said, "Dr. Smith, I'm Dr. Blackman." He responded, "It's Gary. Dr. Smith is my father." I accepted this at first, but eventually, as you would predict, it turned out that Gary's problems had a lot to do with his feelings about his father and his problems in identifying himself as an adult.

---

5 Tarachow (1963).
6 In this book, I use people's first names in examples to avoid the awkwardness of the usual textbook style, "Mr. A" or "Ms. Z."

Much has been written about "relational"[7] techniques, "intersubjective"[8] techniques, and corrective object relations techniques. All of these procedures, recommended for narcissistic and borderline people carry serious side effects and complications. Using these techniques, the therapist exposes certain elements of his or her personality, background, opinions, and affects during the therapeutic process and in this manner attempts to form a "secure-organized attachment" with the person in treatment. Some people appreciate this and feel closer to the therapist. Others become anxious, for a variety of reasons, and will quit treatment. Still other people attach a sexual meaning to the "friendliness" and develop unresolvable erotized transference.

For most therapists, keeping a benign, empathic, and yet "close to the vest" approach to people in treatment is safest. This does not mean being cold or aloof, but revelation of personal material ("self-disclosure") is often problematic.

LONG ANSWER

The issue of titles often arises in long-term psychotherapy, especially if more than once a week. A special issue of the *Psychoanalytic Quarterly* (Renik, 1996) was dedicated to the question of the "authority" of the therapist.

In instances where the "authoritarian" quality of being a doctor has proven difficult for treating people, I have sometimes modified my position and carefully watched to see whether people have negative or positive reactions, or defensive or transference reactions to me generated by my closeness with them.

To treat narcissistic, borderline, and schizoid people, you may need to self-disclose. Narcissistic people make presumptions about you, project onto you, and idealize or devalue you. Sometimes, explaining those defenses is not sufficient; you have to bring a reality about yourself to their attention. Then you show them their projections and idealizations (or devaluation).

EXAMPLE

Peggy, a 50-year-old postmenopausal, divorced woman with no children, consulted me about a specific problem. She had recently been diagnosed with fibrous dysplasia in one of her breasts by one laboratory. Another laboratory had read a biopsy as ductile carcinoma in situ. The treatment for these two different entities is quite dissimilar, and different physicians had different opinions.

---

7 Mitchell (2000).
8 Stolorow and Atwood (1989).

On the one hand, she wanted to ask me what I thought she should do. I considered that this was an idealization about me, since I am not a general surgeon, breast surgeon, or oncological surgeon. When I did not answer her question directly but asked to know more about her concerns, she immediately responded, "Well I guess you wouldn't know. You're just a psychiatrist." At this point, she was devaluing me.

I decided not to confront Peggy about either of these defenses (idealization and devaluation) but instead to share with her some of my thinking about her situation (a bit of a self-disclosure). I told her if I were in her situation, I would probably get an opinion from someone in a major cancer center, and I might get more than one. She thought this was interesting. I then mentioned her avoiding this option. (Instead of confronting her narcissism, I confronted her inhibition of using her executive functioning.)

She responded by crying. She remembered how her mother had always accused her of being a hypochondriac. Peggy didn't feel she deserved to go to a major cancer center, because this would make her feel like she was a "special case," trying to get attention from her mother, and feeling guilty about it. We could understand that shame and guilt, induced by Peggy's mother's attitude toward her, had led Peggy to inhibit judgment. She stayed in a quandary where she continued to suffer (to relieve the guilt).

Following just a few sessions, Peggy made appointments at two different major cancer surgery centers, and within weeks had obtained consultations from different surgeons. She compared their approaches and their opinions about her diagnosis. She could then make an informed decision on her own.[9]

The point here is that I made a decision to disclose something of my own thoughts about serious illness when there is a problem with diagnosis. "Temporizing" ("wait and see") has always scared me when someone is seriously ill; I lean toward doing something fairly quickly. This has been my approach about myself and my own family for many years, and I allowed this attitude to become clear in my discussion with her. This, fortuitously, led us to discuss her inhibitions; the relief of those inhibitions allowed her to be able to use her executive functioning to make better choices.

When people want to use my first name, I usually explore this. Henry Kissinger, when he was secretary of state under Richard Nixon, was once asked by a journalist how he wanted to be addressed. The journalist asked

---

9 Peggy eventually decided to have surgery. As a result, she was much relieved and called me to discuss this on the phone. She did not feel she needed any further therapy and expressed quite a bit of gratitude to me for helping her think through the problem.

something like, "Should it be Professor Kissinger, Doctor Kissinger, Secretary Kissinger, or Mr. Kissinger." Kissinger, as I recall, replied (this is a paraphrase), "I prefer Your Highness." I may joke with people about the name issue to allow them to think about their conflicts regarding authority.

In long-term therapy (more than a year), the therapist gets to know people in treatment well. When I have treated people for more than 10 years, whatever the frequency (between once and four times a week), it is common for us to eventually use each other's first names in addressing each other.

However, in looking back, I saw that this has happened more when I am treating fellow mental health practitioners or people in training to become psychoanalysts. I think some of these professionals, as they resolve conflicts about competition regarding authorities, feel closer to me. We become collegial and refer to each other with our first names.

Professionals who are in analysis or supervision with me as part of their training may, after their treatment or supervision is finished (and they have completed analytic fellowship), develop a professional friendship with me. In those cases, even when social friendships do not develop, the cordial, professional relationships include first names.

Other people with whom I use first names include those I have met through boards of directors of organizations, my neighborhood, or faculties where I have been active in teaching. In these settings, although we are not close friends (whom I usually will not treat), often we have been on a first-name basis even before they consult me professionally. It would therefore be awkward to move to more formal terms of address during evaluation and/or treatment, and I don't try to do so.

People who immediately want to be your "friend" may be harboring more severe mental illnesses. They may be defending against hostile feelings toward authority, or may be more desperate for any type of support.

When people therefore bring up the idea of becoming your "friend," it is usually best to maintain some professional distance and explain to them that the therapy relationship can have a warm, understanding quality, but it is not the same as being friends. Therapy is more of a one-sided situation, where they will be telling you many problems and secrets and you're going to be trying to help them think through those. It is not a situation of mutual sharing as in most friendships. For an exception to that particular idea, see Mitchell (2000) and Renik (1999).

Problem 84
Elevator Phobics Who Must Take an Elevator to Your Office

Phobias involve fears of things that are not "really" dangerous. To diagnose a phobic illness, however, you need to make sure there are no deficits in reality testing; no deficits in integration; no deficits in abstraction; no deficits in capacities for warmth, empathy, trust, and closeness; and no severe deficits in impulse control or containment of bizarre fantasies. If there are deficits in those functions, the diagnosis slides from phobia into borderline psychosis or overt paranoid psychosis.

In spite of their reasonably good reality testing, people who have a (neurotic) phobia of elevators (where the target of their projections and fantasies is an elevator) will not get in an elevator. The anxiety they experience in elevators is so overwhelming (due to the symbolism—which is unconscious) that they avoid the elevator. During treatment, you will help them figure out the unpleasant symbolism (usually of being punished for some nasty wish of which they are only slightly aware), and the phobic symptom should fade and then disappear.

What do you do in the meantime?

SHORT ANSWER

I have been faced with this problem a couple of times. In both situations, an accommodation was necessary for a while.

Phobic people, when they are afraid, tend to think like babies who need their mommies (oral phase).[10] They fear being in the phobic situation alone. The presence of another (trusted) person (symbolizing a good mother—like Glenda, the Good Witch of the North in *The Wizard of* Oz) will allay the fear transiently. Sometimes, nothing allays the fear, and they must work around it; the therapist must also, for a while. They must be able to access your office, for a while, without getting on an elevator.

LONG ANSWER

For many years, my office has been on the second floor of a three-story office building that has an elevator and a stairwell. One elevator-phobic man, who worked downtown in a 20-story office building (on the 20th floor), asked me

---

10 That is, they have regressed libidinally (Blackman, 2010).

on the phone during his initial contact if my building had stairs, and what floor I was on. He took the stairs.

An elevator-phobic woman had a problem when the stairway was locked in the morning. So I had to check to see that the stairwell door was unlocked so she could walk upstairs. After 6 months of treatment, she and I entered the building at the same time. When I got on the elevator, she decided to ride it with me. After a year, she took the elevator alone. My "parameter" (unlocking the door for her) was needed in the early phase of her treatment.

In both situations, I did something to reassure people consulting me. The side effect of me doing so, however, had to be understood as my providing a caring, mother-type figure to guard them against both hostility toward mother and sexual conflicts.

The man had felt guilty about anger toward his mother about her doting on an ill brother. (Later he experienced guilt over anger at his wife for caring for their children.) The woman felt guilty about hostility toward her husband for being jealous and controlling. (Later she realized she experienced guilt over her hostility toward her peeping father.) Both wished for a soothing mother, partly as compensation for feelings of deprivation, and partly to allay their fears over their sexual and aggressive conflicts.

The moral to the story is that a supportive approach (accommodation) may be required at the beginning to make treatment possible.

Problem 85
Lawyers Wanting Evaluations for Their Clients Versus People Who Call at the Suggestion of Their Attorneys

If you are not interested in offering expert opinions in the legal arena, you would think this section might be irrelevant to your practice. There are people, however, who see you at the urging of their attorneys, which exposes you to being subpoenaed to court.

The question is, what do you do in these circumstances?

SHORT ANSWER

First, during telephone triage (if you have the opportunity to speak to someone on the phone before you see them in your office), if there are any marital problems, it is best to inquire as to whether there is, or may be, a child custody dispute. People getting divorced, who are having problems and are worried about their children, may want advice or wish to have their children counseled. I have never accepted this type of referral.

Testifying in criminal cases usually requires specialized training. When someone is involved in civil litigation, already, be it personal injury or marital, a therapist's opinion will eventually be requested by one of the lawyers. Child custody cases are the most complex (and most dangerous to your health).

If you agree to evaluate a plaintiff in a civil case, I recommend you obtain a signed contract *with an attorney* involved in the case, detailing your services and fees.

LONG ANSWER

If you get a call from people involved in civil litigation, ask them to have their attorney contact you. In cases where my expert opinion is requested in a legal case, I speak to the attorney, first. I then e-mail the attorney a written, contractual agreement about my activity in the case, my fees, and how they are to be paid. The attorney must sign and return a copy of the contract before I become involved.

Ethically, in most states, attorneys are not allowed to pay for the treatment of the people they represent; they are, however, ethically permitted to pay for expert evaluations and opinions. As long as I have a written agreement with the attorney, it is unusual for me to run into any difficulty with remuneration. And cases where there has been difficulty have been resolved fairly quickly. Years ago, when I made the mistake of contracting with individuals who were involved in litigation, the situation became muddy, and I sometimes did not get paid for a lot of difficult work.

People going through a divorce often need help. They may be able to maintain confidentiality if they are not involved in a custody battle. However, if the divorce is not "amicable," standard discovery procedures such as requests for admission and requests for production of documents will likely require the person you are treating to list you as a treating therapist. You may then receive a *subpoena duces tecum* (subpoena of all your records in the case), and it may be impossible for the people you treat to maintain "privilege" (meaning not having to reveal confidential therapy records in court).[11]

For most therapists (who do not want to have their records subpoenaed and/or do not want to testify in court), it's probably best, if people call you while they are in a lawsuit, to avoid treating them. I have, on occasion, decided to treat someone going through a divorce, but I have been fairly certain that the person is not involved in a custody determination. Even so, I have taken a risk in even evaluating the person, since custody (or other legal issues in the divorce) can be raised at any time.

Expert testimony must be neutral. Experts don't take sides; they evaluate people who have various types of claims (in civil, tort litigation) and render independent opinions, no matter who is paying them. But brace yourself. Other lawyers will no doubt attack you for being biased, and engage in any number of legal manipulations to discredit you. This is not particularly pleasurable, so unless you think you might experience some satisfaction in doing diagnostic work, in backing up your opinions, and in being grilled about these opinions in depositions and in court, it's probably best not to do this type of work.

For the past 35 years, starting with evaluations of alleged perpetrators and victims of heinous child abuse, I have involved myself in various types of civil cases, although I have avoided expert testimony in criminal cases. In civil cases, I may do an evaluation, but usually do not treat people while they are in litigation.

---

11 Unless it is a federal case, where the *Jaffee v. Redmond* (1996) U.S. Supreme Court decision confers an absolute "therapist–patient privilege." In most U.S. state cases, privilege is left up to the judge, who can review all materials and decide what may be relevant to any proceeding.

Problem 86
People Who Want You to Give a Second Opinion While They're in Treatment With Someone Else

Various agencies, such as Workers' Compensation, request independent evaluations when they question the appropriateness of mental health care for someone who has been injured and is covered. These second opinions are important for the Workers' Comp system: to get an unconflicted opinion from someone who is not treating the claimant as to whether the treatment is appropriate and work related.

These cases are like expert testimony in private, civil cases, and bring with them the same risks for the expert witness of attacks about credibility and heightened exposure to malpractice suits and professional complaints of various kinds.

In other cases, people (or their spouse or children) in treatment with someone else may feel dissatisfied, and request a "second opinion" from you.

What should you do?

SHORT ANSWER

Although most professional boards in the health professions look favorably on second opinions, these are difficult to render, and the primary therapists are generally sensitive about the people they are treating getting a second opinion. Most of the time, when I am asked for a second opinion, I talk on the phone with the person requesting the second opinion to ascertain the problems. If I hear they are having negative feelings toward their therapist, I may advise them to tell their therapist about them, especially if they also have positive feelings about the therapist. I do not see them in my office.

If the person, on the telephone, expresses dissatisfaction with their current treatment, and asks if I am accepting referrals, I will ask if they have stopped their previous treatment. If they have, and they are looking for a new therapist, I will consider setting up an evaluation interview, *not* treatment. After I evaluate them, I will give them my opinion about what treatment might be necessary and whether I am able to do it.

Sometimes, on evaluating people, I find they are severely mentally ill and need medication. Since I do not practice psychopharmacology, I refer them to colleagues who do. At other times, I find that there was a mismatch between the person and the prior therapist; this may be due to personality clashes or unresolved transference. In those situations, I may accept the person for treatment.

LONG ANSWER

On many occasions, I have been asked for a second opinion by a therapist who wanted guidance. These referrals may come from people I am supervising or others who would like a "hands-on" opinion from me regarding diagnosis and selection of treatment. I have found these referrals fascinating and rewarding. Usually I evaluate the person once, dictate a report and send it to the therapist. I usually speak with the therapist as well before and after the evaluation. Release forms are signed. I try to find an area where the therapist may focus and offer advice about formulation and interventions.

People who are highly dissatisfied with a prior therapist pose more serious difficulties. Some do not want you to communicate with that therapist but may be suicidal, agitated, or having a crisis in their marriage. With such cases, I am very selective, as I have "an index of suspicion" that the negative feelings toward the prior therapist may easily be transferred to me, as well.

On a few occasions, people explained themselves clearly enough and the problems with the prior therapy sounded clear enough that I thought I would risk going ahead with an evaluation. It is best if those people give me a release to speak with their prior therapist, in any case. When there has been a lot of difficulty and they are unhappy with prior treatment, however, they often do not want me to speak with their prior therapist.

Telephone triage (assessing treatability on the phone before agreeing to evaluate someone) is extremely important in these kinds of cases. I may spend a half an hour or 40 minutes on the phone in these kinds of situations.

EXAMPLE 1

On the phone, Gilda seemed to feel guilty about criticizing her prior therapist. She then began to express mistrust in all therapists, would not tell me her last name, and predicted I would not see her because "all therapists talk with each other."

Hearing this paranoid pathology, as well as the concreteness of thought, it sounded to me like Gilda was extremely ill and would not benefit from psychotherapy aimed at understanding conflicts. I gave her the name of colleagues who do psychopharmacotherapy. She immediately became angry and warned that if I breathed a word of her having called me, I would be in trouble. I reassured her that I would not speak with anyone, especially since I did not know her name and knew very little about her.

EXAMPLE 2

Jane, a woman who had lost her father in a traumatic accident, had been in therapy for a while with a psychiatrist who treated her with antidepressant medicines. These medicines were not helping, Jane was resistant to taking them, and she and her husband argued about whether she should take the medicine.

On the phone, Jane logically explained that she was not through grieving over her father, with whom she had had some difficulties as a teenager, and she described herself as "too picky" with her husband. Based on her self-observing capacity regarding her personality and her unresolved grief, I thought psychotherapy was indicated and psychopharmacology was relatively contraindicated, in any case.

I asked if I could speak with her psychiatrist, and she gave me permission. When I spoke with the psychiatrist, she was relieved to have Jane come see me. She was tired of struggling with her. She also gave me details of Jane's history and marital difficulties.

When I saw Jane, she showed intact functions (the various factors that I list in Problems 2 and 101 [B]). I thought she would be treatable with an approach that would help her understand her conflicts. I accepted her for treatment and saw her for intensive therapy for the next 4 years with a considerable amount of success.

Problem 87
People Who Consult You Because of Third-Party Pressure

The concept of a working alliance requires that people agree with you that they have a problem; a working alliance does not exist if they are appeasing someone else.

So how do you handle it when someone is referred to you by their spouse, a professional ethics board, a court, a company, or a hospital?

SHORT ANSWER

In general, when someone is referred by any of these entities, the best you can do is an evaluation. In situations where hospitals have requested I evaluate a problem doctor, or the State Bar has asked that I evaluate a problem attorney, I usually only offer to evaluate the person and give an opinion regarding their treatability.

The reason for this approach is that usually the agency or hospital will be using the evaluation to determine the competency of the person referred. To avoid any conflict of interest, I do not make myself available as a treatment resource, even if treatment is indicated. In those instances where psychotherapy seems warranted, I recommend other therapists and advise the agency not to request information about the psychotherapy. After a while, an impartial professional can reevaluate the person for another opinion.

In situations where I opined that a doctor or lawyer was psychopathic (did not show integrity in medical or legal ethics), I recommended disciplinary guidelines be followed by the licensing authority and emotional factors not considered—just the facts.

When an adult is referred by a court, the problem is greater. If the person referred has used mental disturbance as a mitigating factor to lessen a sentence in a criminal trial, that person has a vested interest in "beating the rap." Especially if your records can be viewed by the court, that person will have a hard time telling you things that might lead to your knowing anything that might have damaging consequences.

LONG ANSWER

The majority of the time, people who consult you to appease a third party (including a spouse) will not form an alliance; but there are exceptions. Some people may be "convertible"—the first reason they seek help is to please the third party; but they may, during evaluation, find, with your help, a serious problem for which they wish treatment. Although rare, I have treated at least two people in my career where the original projective blaming was understandable in the first session. They then admitted they were suffering and not just the agency or spouse was upset.

How can the conversion take place?

- You say to the person something like this: "Your wife/hospital board/licensing agency/lawyer thinks you need help. What do you think?" And the answer satisfies you that the person is feeling guilty and conflicted.
- You point out to people that they are "projecting" blame: Although their wife/hospital board/licensing agency/lawyer thinks they need help, you see personal problems they wish to blame on that third party. People may integrate that explanation but may "go along to get along." Watch out for the "you're probably right" type of response, which usually means no alliance.[12]
- People feel guilty; they have "brought the house down" on themselves to punish themselves, already. They may be "criminals from a sense of guilt"[13] who misbehaved in order to get themselves punished, at least in part. In 40 years, I have only successfully treated six people who were "criminals from sense of guilt." Three were attorneys and three were physicians. Four had committed petty, victimless crimes, which they knew could get them in trouble, and the trouble happened. Two had committed minor ethics violations. They were all self-referred after they had been punished. All were receptive to understanding both their motivations to break rules and to get caught.[14]
  - After people admit they have only come to see you to appease a third party, you explore how they agreed to this. Sometimes, you can clarify their passivity, dedifferentiation (attempting to become what the other person wants), or "taking their beating" (by seeing you). If people see these as problems, then you have clarified a "chief complaint" and may have something to try to figure out with them. Try one follow-up appointment before getting too optimistic.

---

12 Abend (1975).
13 S. Freud (1916).
14 I have also evaluated psychopathic male and female lawyers and doctors who were entirely untreatable. (The vast majority of the people I have evaluated who had committed crimes had no conscience, tried to manipulate me, and were untreatable.) During my 10 years as a consultant to State Child Protection agencies in Louisiana, I evaluated over 2,000 alleged heinous child abusers. Out of that group, I saw one I thought was treatable (I did not treat him).

Problem 88
Child-Centered Counseling

Child-centered counseling is a procedure where the parent(s) see a therapist for advice about their children. After gathering a developmental history and a history of the family's current behavior, the therapist advises the parent(s) about how to handle various situations with the child.

Anton Kris (1981) urged therapists to help people in treatment with information about their children's developmental phases and advice about management. He felt there was very little danger of this disrupting the therapeutic process.

How does this happen, and how accurate can you be?

SHORT ANSWER

A mother of a 3-month-old child has been reading pop literature on child rearing. Her baby wakes up two or three times a night, crying. She asks, "Should I pick up the baby or let him cry it out?" The answer: "Pick up the baby!"

The mother of a 2-year-old is spanking the child for potty "mistakes." The answer: "Don't!" Use gentle persuasion and rewards, if necessary.

The parents of a preschool child are walking around naked. Answer: "Don't; you're overstimulating the kid."

The parents of a school-age girl are punishing her for not doing her homework by not allowing her best friend to stay over Friday night. She is getting more resistant. Advice: "Don't punish the child by taking away conduits (sublimations) for aggression and socialization. You'll wind up with a kid who runs away or attempts suicide."

LONG ANSWER

Human infants require cuddling as well as feeding.[15] In "anaclitic depression," babies who are not held will refuse feeding. Second, they become inconsolable and do not respond to the breast or bottle. Finally, they move into an

---

15 Spitz and Wolf (1946).

irreversible position of emotional shock, stop sucking, and may die from failure to thrive (a current term).[16]

Some behaviorists believe you should not pick up a crying infant because, as one of them told me, "You reinforce the crying behavior. Then the baby will just cry more." But basic trust[17] is established when the baby cries and the mother responds with feeding and soothing. "Basic mistrust," key to the development of reality testing, develops as the baby gradually realizes the mother cannot get there instantaneously. However, purposely not soothing a baby sets the stage for the child to have fears, throughout life, of depending on anybody for soothing.

Fear of trusting another person for soothing often underlies severe alcoholism in adults, who choose "the bottle" before they turn to human beings. Alcoholics Anonymous has intuitively understood this; they provide a "sponsor" for all new members, who are encouraged to turn to the sponsor rather than to the "bottle."

Advice to mothers about toilet training is also quite useful. Many do not know that they should not toilet train the child before 18 months of age because innervation of the sphincter muscles that control waste is not completed until the child is 18 months old.[18] On the other hand, mothers and fathers who wait until a child is 3 or 4 years old to begin training may have a difficult time because there is a conflation of autonomy with the hostility of first genital phase conflicts (Blackman, 2010). In other words, advice to parents to begin toilet training around 18 months of age is useful.

You can also help parents of children between ages 2 and 6 who notice their children engaging in masturbatory play. Since this is normal, the parents' attitude should be one of patience and advice to the child to limit that behavior to the bedroom or bathroom, where it is private (to help the child with social development).

When a child between ages 2 and 6 years is having a problem, it is a good idea to ask at least the following questions.

---

16 Recently I was faced with the question of what to answer a woman in analysis when she asked if she should pick up her 4-month-old baby each time he cried. I told Gilbert Kliman and Robert Emde, both specialists in early childhood development, of my technical dilemma about whether to search for meanings or first advise how the situation with the infant should be resolved. Before I could tell them how I had handled the case, they responded, in unison, "Pick up the baby!" (Their opinion coincided with what I had done.)
17 Erikson (1950).
18 Brazelton et al. (1999).

1. Where is the child sleeping? Really? (If with the parents, there will be sexual overstimulation, perpetuation of symbiosis, and inexplicable destructiveness.)
2. What are the parents doing about their own nudity?
    a. Are they covering up, or do they believe in "not hiding their bodies"? (Nudity is overstimulating, causing ADD-like symptoms.)
    b. Do they shower or bathe nude with the child? (Again, overstimulation.)
3. What discipline are they using when the child misbehaves? (The more bizarre, the worse; but "time out" can leave the child with no support.)

A brief series of consultations I had with a father about his obstreperous 8-year-old son elucidated the value of child-centered counseling.

EXAMPLE

Erwin, a 39-year-old attorney, reported a rather harmonious marriage, except for problems they had with his 8-year-old son, Jeremy. Jeremy was punching his 4-year-old sister, ridiculing her, excluding her from games, stealing her toys, and talking back to the parents.

In the midst of this, Jeremy was doing well in school and had a number of male friends. Erwin had tried spanking Jeremy, cajoling him, bribing him, and yelling at him.

I advised Erwin that Jeremy was in the "latency phase" of development.[19] He was doing his homework and participating well on sports teams; this suggested that Jeremy had a conscience but that it had not yet grown enough to incorporate ideas about his sister. I told Erwin that he and his wife's punitive approach to his son's misbehavior was probably backfiring because in punishing him so stringently, they effectively relieved whatever guilt Jeremy might be feeling about misbehaving. Erwin was nonplussed. He asked, "Well, what the hell can we do? Are we helpless?"

Rather than addressing the dynamics of his question to me (Problem 65), I engaged in child-centered counseling. I explained to Erwin that during the latency phase, parents need to get the child to feel guilty about misbehavior: to get his conscience "internalized." To do this, Erwin and his wife needed to stop punishing Jeremy so much. I explained that by overpunishing, Erwin and his wife set themselves up as Jeremy's conscience, which allowed Jeremy to continue to act out hostile-destructive impulses.

---

19 Sarnoff (1975).

To fix things, I advised Erwin to do a number of things. I suggested he have a long talk with his son, in private, during which he should tell Jeremy he was unhappy with Jeremy's behavior. Erwin was surprised. He asked, "You mean, I'm supposed to be nice to him? And let him get away with all this?"

I told him that was not the point. The father's efforts should be aimed at helping his son develop a value system like his father's. Erwin said, "I thought the child should develop his own identity." I explained that this was an issue for adolescence, less so during latency. Jeremy needed to identify with Erwin. Disidentifications came later. Erwin nodded.

I advised Erwin to ask Jeremy if he wanted to be a criminal. I predicted Jeremy would say no and rationalize that he couldn't help being mad. I also suspected that Jeremy would use projective blaming: claim his sister was starting the trouble. Erwin noted that these interactions had already happened.

I suggested Erwin tell Jeremy that excuses were not manly. Being a man meant he should (a) develop control when angry and (b) protect his sister—Jeremy should act toward his sister as Erwin acted toward his wife.

Erwin should say he wanted Jeremy to be a real man[20] and not a wimp: Real men protected sisters. I also suggested Erwin make impersonal, intellectual arguments about how hitting people was a crime (assault and battery) that people go to jail for. I reminded Erwin that, as an attorney, he carried particular weight about laws.

Erwin noted my suggestions. As he repeated them during our consultation, I saw that he had absorbed every one, although he expressed pessimism about his ability to get through to his son. Nevertheless, he said he would try.

A week later, I saw Erwin for a follow-up consultation. He was pleased. He had discussed all the matters with his son. Jeremy was suitably shocked, depressed, and apologetic after first arguing with his father for several minutes. Erwin said he had not argued with his son before; this was a new experience. His impression was that Jeremy gained respect for him and agreed to pattern himself after his father.

Some hours after they had had their long discussion, Erwin overheard a conversation between his son and daughter. Jeremy was teaching her, "Do you know they have jails for kids?" Erwin also noted that his son turned around and became more protective toward his sister.

---

20 Ideas about masculinity are critical for boys during the school-age years; value systems are developing. Ideas about masculinity are important for teenage boys, too. A great danger developing over the past 25 years is the notion that masculinity involves impulse discharge and defiance. If this symbolism penetrates into adulthood, men can become "sex addicts" (Goodman, 1998).

Erwin realized this was not a cure. He would need more discussions with his son from here on out. I said if he ran into trouble, he could feel free to call me. Erwin was grateful, said his son had been okay for 4 or 5 days, and he felt equipped to handle the situation should it arise in the future.

Erwin at first had a hard time convincing his wife that they should take this approach. She thought more punishment was needed. After the shift in Jeremy's attitude, even she came around and was utilizing the same techniques.

One final note. When you teach people about their children's developmental phase (the "calamities of childhood"),[21] you do something else simultaneously. You subtly suggest speculations about what happened to the parent during that developmental stage during their development. I have treated many people who recalled the results of overstimulation, themselves, once we discussed their handling of their own children.

---

21 Brenner (1982).

Problem 89
People Who Travel a Long Distance to Sessions

With the advent of videoconferencing (Skype and others), many therapists now treat people via the computer. Although people thereby avoid the inconvenience of traveling long distances to your office, I've noticed that when people are in my office they feel more relaxed and confidential. I think therapy is a bit more effective "in person."[22]

I consider it a "long distance" if someone has to travel more than 45 minutes to my office. The usual length of my sessions is 45 minutes, so if someone is traveling 45 minutes each way, they spend over 2 hours for each session. If they see me frequently, the total number of hours is daunting. (In larger cities, such as New York and Los Angeles, many people routinely travel 1 or 2 hours to work. They will need to find a therapist proximate to their work or home, unless they can take off as much time as they want.)

SHORT ANSWER

If people must travel to see me from a distance, I usually spend 60 minutes with them instead of 45. I have done this with a number of people for a number of years, with quite a bit of success.

The longer individual session, usually once a week, is different from a 45-minute session. We clarify more and go over the conflicts in more areas of their lives. To benefit from this approach, people must have good integration and affect tolerance.

Usually, if you point out one or two conflicts (maybe one about the person's resistance) during a session, that is enough. When therapists try to tie more than three or four elements together in 45 minutes, people tend to become overloaded. They may forget connections, or experience increased resistance (may miss a session).

During a 60-minute session, humor can sustain the therapeutic relationship. People in treatment (or I) may make ironic comments about what we learn about them; this supports the greater amount of therapeutic work that they do during the session.

---

22 Although one person I had treated via Skype in China remarked, on having a "live" session with me in China, that it felt "exactly the same" to her. It felt different to me, though.

People I have treated this way have had control over their schedules. During periods of heightened upset, they may Skype me, but usually prefer coming to my office.

LONG ANSWER

I have been involved with cases where people found ingenious ways of managing sessions from even a greater distance from the therapist's office.

EXAMPLE 1

Cao Lingyun,[23] a therapist I supervised via Skype in Shanghai, China, presented a problem with Li Yong, a suicidal 13-year-old boy. His family consulted her in Shanghai, though they lived 2 hours away by plane, because they appreciated her knowledge about adolescent individuation and identity formation.[24]

The family consulted her monthly for advice; the boy saw a therapist in his home town. She engaged the parents in child-centered counseling. Here is an excerpt from a recent e-mail from Cao Lingyun:

"I meet the whole family for a two hour session each day…they stayed in Shanghai. The 13-year-old male patient is diagnosed with depression by a psychiatrist…in his home town…

"He tried committing suicide several times by taking an overdose of medicine. His relationship with his parents was terrible. He was [too]…close to his mom and often slept with his mom in the same bed. His mom wouldn't let him sleep alone…when his father was out of town.

"His relationship with his dad was hostile. He had suspended his schooling for a while before our first meeting.…

"I suggested that his mom not sleep with him…and try to repair the relationship with her husband. Everything was getting better. He went back to school last September. He…developed a…relationship with some girls in school. He and one girl texted each other.…

"[But] his parents print[ed] out all of his texts…he felt…humiliated and tried to commit suicide again…He often has the thought that he wants to kill his parents and kill himself."

I think this is a good example of the difficulty of treating families where symbiotic ties prevail between mother and child. The well-known side effects

---

23 Cao Lingyun, who had trained through CAPA (capachina.org), asked me to use her actual name, as she was pleased to contribute to the question of long-distance treatment. The name of the family is fictitious.
24 Blos (1960) and Erikson (1968).

of "co-sleeping" are (a) perpetuation of symbiotic ties, leading to suicide attempts (as a means to individuate by expressing hostility at parents and to relieve guilt), and (b) sexual overstimulation, leading to overwhelming frustration (that interferes with academics and concentration).

Co-sleeping is common in other countries in Asia and in some places in the United States. Cao Lingyun has continued to advise the family to desist from adhesive control, to stop the overstimulation, and to allow better individuation (friends outside the family).

EXAMPLE 2

My first experience with long distance treatment was decades ago.

Wilma, a 27-year-old married woman, was hospitalized for alcoholism. I saw her for psychotherapy 7 days a week for several weeks. As she was detoxified, she and I developed a good working relationship, and I was able to help her understand a number of the conflicts that had led her to abuse alcohol.

Wilma and her husband had one child. She was working for a family business about 200 miles from the hospital.

When Wilma was discharged, I suggested she find a therapist in her city, but she had a different idea. She could stay in treatment with me, she figured out, since she was a pilot who owned her own twin-engine plane. She wanted to see me four times a week. So on Monday afternoons she flew from her town to mine, which took her about an hour, for an appointment with me at 5:00 p.m. At 8:15 the next morning, I saw her again. She then flew home. A relative let her stay overnight.

Wilma flew back for a session Thursday afternoons at 5:15 p.m., saw me at 8:15 a.m. on Friday, and then flew home again. We worked together this way for 2 years, with very productive results.

Ten years after finishing treatment, Wilma called for a follow-up visit. I was interested in seeing her. She again flew in from her hometown.

She was now CEO of the family business. She had divorced her alcoholic husband and her child was doing well, keeping some contact with his father. Now 37 years old, she had been dating a man for a year and was considering getting engaged to him. She wanted to talk this over with me.

I spent 60 minutes discussing her situation with her, and together we tied her concerns to older conflicts with her parents and first husband. Those conflicts, in part, had led her to identify with her first husband and overdrink.

At the end of the session, Wilma told me she had decided she was going to get engaged. I later received a wedding invitation.

EXAMPLE 3

In 2004, Ann, senior vice president of a wholesale food company, consulted me for panic attacks on the job. She had been hospitalized for a workup for a heart attack, but she was physically normal and diagnosed with anxiety.

Ann was an attractive woman in her late 40s. She had been divorced three times and for the past 6 months had been dating Chip. She had no children. She felt some sorrow about this, but since none of the marriages had worked out, she felt this was best. She liked her job and seemed happy with Chip.

It soon became clear that she was denying negative aspects of Chip's personality, especially his "continuing friendships" with prior girlfriends. He claimed they contacted him. Ann had put up with this. Chip did not hide his phone calls with the "women friends," and Ann did not think he was cheating on her. Chip mentioned getting engaged just before she had her first panic attack.

Part of Ann's anxiety stemmed from her denial about her feelings about Chip's "friends." Her denial, I explained, relieved guilt over angry wishes to leave Chip, the way she had left her three husbands. She then insisted Chip stop his contact with former girlfriends; he agreed. She shamefully admitted she had enjoyed breaking up her marriages; she felt "in control." Although she had liked being married, she felt "trapped," found fault with her husbands, and then broke up the marriages. She almost did the same with Chip.

Feeling trapped was connected to guilt over rebellious feelings toward her parents during adolescence. She slept in her mother's bed until she was 10 then, during adolescence, their fights were severe. Ann did well in college but drank too much. She frequently used the phrase, "I'm not proud of it, but...."

She had used pseudoindependence (not needing anyone) to avoid shame but also got plastered, so people took care of her; that is, she acted out wishes (a) to be taken care of and (b) to be punished and humiliated. Then she became "independent" and forgot all about her dependency needs. Ann eventually stopped drinking and did not have panic attacks. She became dependent on me and pleased that she was not ashamed, trapped, or having to run away from that feeling.

After 6 months, Ann was promoted, requiring travel. Simultaneously, she was making plans to get married. Because of her work, she was rarely in town. At her request, I agreed to treat her by phone while she was traveling. When she was in town, I saw her in the office. We did this for 2 years. She was never suicidal, so it was relatively safe to work with her on the telephone part of the time. Also, her residence was in Virginia, so I had no licensure issue.

She and I both noticed, however, that she disliked the phone. She might be in a room at work where the walls had ears. She preferred seeing me in my office.

Problem 90
What If You Opt Out of Medicare or Are an "Out of Network" Provider?

Although most people in the 21st century use private or government insurance to pay for treatment, occasionally you will see someone who prefers to pay you directly. Some years ago, I was asked by a 67-year-old man if he could simply pay my fee and not file for Medicare benefits. I found out (and this still holds true) that, in the United States, physicians are automatically included in Medicare and must use Medicare's fee schedule. I, therefore, could not do what he requested.

The only way to bill Medicare recipients directly is to "opt out" of Medicare. This must be done in writing, using a special form, every 2 years. If you sign a contract with a private insurance company, agreeing to fees and billing procedures ("in-network provider"), usually you cannot "opt out" unless you cancel your contract with the insurance company. After people's insurance benefits for the year are totally used, you may be able to charge what you like—but check the contract you signed.

In 1989, I resigned from all insurance contracts and since then have billed people directly. I do still put *DSM* codes and current procedural terminology (CPT) codes on bills if people wish. My employer ID, address and phone number appear on each statement. So if people want to file for reimbursement from their insurance company, they can (but not with Medicare or Medicaid).

Since I am not a contracted provider, insurance company representatives cannot enter my office and demand records of people I have treated. They must obtain a court order if they do not have people's written permission. If an insurance company asks me for documentation, a narrative summary will usually suffice. After I dictate the summary, I show it to the person I'm treating; they redact what they choose so this is not disruptive to treatment. I do not charge for the time to dictate up a narrative summary.

ANSWER

The reasons I have abandoned insurance-based practice are many. Besides the disruptive effect on me, I realized that the confidentiality of the person I was treating could be compromised.[25] The request for narrative summaries is understandable, but many insurance companies request them every three

---

25 Bollas (1999).

to six sessions, so this becomes onerous to both me and the person I am treating.

If people ask me during "telephone triage" if I accept insurance, I explain that I bill people directly and ask them to bring a check when they come for their consultation. I am happy to put diagnostic and CPT codes on the bill and indicate their payment if they wish to file for reimbursement from their insurance company. Some people do, but many don't.

Regarding Medicare, in 2012, as a physician I sign out every 2 years. Once I sign out, Medicare-eligible people I see cannot file for reimbursement for my fees. They remain able to use Medicare for other doctors.

Direct billing gives people freedom to decide whether to make their diagnoses known to the insurance industry. I believe that in psychotherapy, people should be able to tell me anything without fear of it being repeated.

Mental health practice groups may require members to be "contracted" with insurance companies to foster referrals. When large groups do this, they hire billing clerks who specialize in electronic insurance reimbursements: refiling lost and delayed forms and calling and waiting on hold while insurance companies inform them regarding people's deductibles, copays, and the like. I have one colleague who is "in network" for many insurance carriers; he has hired a billing company to handle all his billing; he simply submits the codes and dates for each person he treats.

SECTION G

Special Issues

GENERAL COMMENTS ABOUT UNUSUAL SITUATIONS AND BEHAVIORS DURING TREATMENT

This section concerns unusual things that happen during treatment—phrases people use, the way they dress, and complications of their relationships with other people.

You may see some of these, or not, but I hope you can find useful information, even about situations that are not exactly the same.

Problem 91
People Who Say "You Know" Repetitively

At this time in the 21st century, "you know"[1] is a common, habitual verbal punctuation in American English. Although this phrase is often used as a comma, I have treated people who utter "you know" every four or five words, which makes what they are saying difficult to follow. In addition, their repeating "you know" can be annoying.

What can you do when people interrupt themselves with the phrase "you know"?

SHORT ANSWER

First, I don't make much of this sort of thing unless it becomes prominent. Younger people tend to start a sentence, "So,..." in response to any question. They also say "you know" fairly frequently. Essentially, this is a verbal way of handling anxiety (a defense). When I see it, I understand that people are feeling anxious about something and that the anxiety is producing the phrase. However, when the frequency interferes with the intelligibility of what someone is saying, I may bring this verbal peculiarity to the person's attention.

When I do that, people may argue that it is just a habit. Their argument is a hint that this verbal comma partly expresses hostility toward me or any authority figure who resembles their parents. Saying "you know" can also relieve guilt. Therefore, as you comment on this phenomenon, it is wise to be gentle about it, since what is being avoided (defended against) is usually rather painful or frightening.

LONG ANSWER

Oral phenomena include "snout-hand" gestures that were first described by Adatto (1970). One of his male analysands had a habit of wiping his hand over his facial area (nose and mouth) as he was talking. Dr. Adatto brought this to his attention, which led the analysand to have a series of thoughts about dependency, hostility, guilt, shame, masturbatory fantasies, defenses, and his relationship with his analyst (transference). It's a fascinating *tour de force* and a great read.

---

1 Other more recent additions to the list of punctuation phrases are "I mean," "Dude," and "Know what I mean?"

Almansi (1960) discovered the reason that so many men stare at women's breasts. His scholarly article includes material from analytic cases, archeological icons, and art images from various parts of the world. He concludes that men's interest in women's breasts derives from a downward displacement from and sexualization of interest in her eyes. The search for eye contact, in turn, develops out of pleasurable early attachment to the mother (Beebe, 2004). As men develop, their early-developed (oral) wish for pleasurable eye contact and attachment becomes unconsciously associated with sexual stimulation. If you treat somebody long enough and deeply enough, you may find that oral phenomena, including figures of speech and gestures, are connected with dependency conflicts, closeness, and thoughts about sex.

One final note: Men who say "you know" frequently experience identity diffusion anxiety; they are therefore unclear in their expressions. They may also be afraid you will not understand them, so when they repeat "you know," they insist that you understand. Young adults also say "you know" due to identification with friends.

Problem 92
Loud Throat Clearing and Globus Hystericus

Periodically when people are speaking they may need to clear their throats. This normative biological activity occurs automatically. When it happens once in a while, throat clearing probably has no meaning and does not need to be addressed. On the other hand, when you are treating people who clear their throats frequently or vociferously, or if the clearing is prolonged, then it probably has many meanings, which will vary from person to person.

SHORT ANSWER

Like many symptoms, first consider the defensive use of this particular activity. Most people who engage in raucous throat clearing are not aware of (i.e., are unconsciously blocking) some emotion, often discomfort or anger.

After I pointed it out to him, one man thought about "roaring like a lion." His thoughts about a lion's roaring included territoriality, self-protection, masculine aggression, hunger, and scaring off all of the competition for his girlfriend. In fact, he revealed a fantasy that if he told me too much about his girlfriend, I would talk him out of dating her, much as his father had tried to do for the past few years (transference).

People who loudly clear their throats may also wish to draw attention to themselves but are embarrassed about doing so; because of this conflict, they develop a gag in their throat and start clearing it.

You can discuss throat clearing with people you are treating. Once they see it is problematic, the next step is to obtain their thoughts about it and put those together. Consider symbolism and avoidance of shame and you probably will have some success in resolving the problem.

LONG ANSWER

Sometimes throat clearing is associated with globus hystericus. This symptom, first described by Charcot in the 1870s, is a bit more common in women than in men.[2] It has multiple meanings but often represents conflicts about pregnancy and sexuality.[3]

EXAMPLE

Wendy, a 29-year-old single respiratory therapist, was referred by her endocrinologist because of gagging and inability to swallow before and during her menstrual periods. Endocrine workup had ruled out any hormonal or other physiological cause.

Wendy was a slender woman who wore her hair short without style and had on no makeup. The first time I met her, she was wearing a long skirt suit and sensible shoes. She was intelligent and engaging. I found out, as had others who had evaluated her, that the "lump in the throat" occurred during her menstrual period, and sometimes a day or two before.

I mentioned to Wendy that menstruation was an obvious sign of not being pregnant. She responded that she had always wished to get married and have at least one or two children, but she had had terrible relationships with men. She had had sexual relations with two men, each an affair that lasted 3 years. One began in college, and the other had started somewhat after she got dumped by the first man.

Both men left her without a satisfactory explanation. She became so bitter that she had not dated in 2 years. Later in her treatment, I learned that she had been watching pornography (sexual intercourse) alone, to masturbate.

I treated Wendy once a week for 18 months. First, we linked her avoidance of men to avoiding anger at the men she had dated. As she spoke about them, she suppressed anger and blamed herself: "Anger has no purpose."

That attitude began in her relationship with her father, an alcoholic. She remembered him taking her to bars when she was in grade school; he left her sitting at a table while he chatted up women. She hated it but put up with it. She never knew why her mother allowed this; she thought her mother was a sap.

Wendy felt men did not find her interesting. When I gently raised a question about her knowledge of what attracted men, she admitted she purposely avoided making herself look "alluring." She refused to act like the "slutty" women her father talked to at bars; she also avoided going to bars to meet men.

---

[2] Most studies have found that from 62% to 75% of people who suffer with *globus hystericus* are women. See, respectively, Harar et al. (2004) and Moloy and Charter (1982).
[3] For a full description of oral libidinal regression as defense, see S. Freud (1926) and Blackman (2003a), Chapters 3 through 6. Interestingly, Charcot (1877) originally thought globus hystericus was more common in men.

She thought of wearing makeup or being alluring as being "a whore," which she despised. She complained that being alluring took too much time, whereas men could get dressed so quickly. She also wanted be the "real Wendy," without all of the phony "warpaint."[4]

We spent many sessions discussing this interesting and controversial topic. Wendy realized she was putting up a wall, denying her own sexual wishes toward men, and making it difficult to meet anyone because she did not do anything to make herself "alluring."

Ironically, she worked in a hospital department with many single men: residents, surgeons, and pulmonologists. However, she sidestepped the coffee shop in the hospital lounge, hid in the corner of the cafeteria during lunch, and avoided other contact with men.

I clarified with her that she avoided men because of (a) guilt over rage toward the men who jilted her and (b) high sensitivity to ever being rejected again. Her masturbatory activity indicated that she was interested in men and sex, but her reactions to her bad experiences had caused her to avoid men.

After several months of treatment, Wendy started dressing differently. She grew her hair out, began wearing makeup, and looked "attractive." Several men approached her while she was working, and she went on several dates.

The question about her "lump in throat" had remained somewhat unsolved, although it had become attenuated. We took up the matter of that symptom and were able to find several meanings. In summary, she gagged herself during her periods because (a) these were the times when she wished to have a man in her life, (b) she got depressed that she was not pregnant, and (c) she experienced conflict about children because of anger at the men she had dated.

She hated being angry, felt guilty about it, and had therefore shut off the anger (isolation of affect) and repressed the memories. The inability to swallow also expressed her reluctance to say what she wanted, which turned out to be "Go fuck yourself!" Once she "got that out," she then felt guilty about the anger.

Following the "Go fuck yourself!" exclamation, she revealed a wish that men should be women for a while, "to see how it feels." She thought, "If they were women, they wouldn't want to be treated this way." Her wish to turn men into women (so that they would understand her better, not hurt

---

4   For readers outside the United States, warpaint was the colored stuff Native Americans put on their faces before "going after" the enemy. By using the word "warpaint" to describe women's makeup, Wendy referred to a common American joke, but she did so in a disparaging way.

her, and know how she felt) made her feel guilty; we understood how she had suppressed these wishes as well because of guilt. The lump in her throat stopped her from expressing hostile-destructive feelings toward men, and she was punished.

She also symbolically "stopped the flow" into her body (mouth), which was the reverse of stopping the flow out of her body (as in pregnancy). Her rage at men led her to "close up" and let "nothing in."

Finally, Wendy recalled a childhood fantasy of getting impregnated through her mouth by eating special foods. The lump in her throat during menstruation symbolized her control of her wish to be pregnant: She wanted to be pregnant at the same time she wanted to avoid the process of getting pregnant to avoid the conflict she had about men.

I suspected Wendy had other conflicts about control, but we never got to them. We saw oral features, sexual and pregnancy conflicts, guilt, rage, inhibition, and avoidance. After 16 months of treatment, Wendy was dating; at 18 months, she had settled in with a man and had sex with him. They decided to be exclusive for a year, then consider marriage. She was happy and free of globus hystericus; we ended her treatment.

Problem 93
Women Who Wear Ultra-Short Skirts and/or See-Through Blouses

The degree of exposure allowed by any particular style of feminine attire has varied by culture (and situation) over thousands of years. In the 21st century, variety is the norm, and most criticism of how women dress is considered inappropriate.

Cole Porter deftly captured the social problem in his song from 1934, "Anything Goes." The well-known lyrics begin, "In olden days an inch of stocking was looked on as something shocking, But now God knows, Anything goes …"

Although women who dress provocatively pose a perennial difficulty for male therapists, it can be an issue for women therapists as well. We are talking about adults here, not teenagers. Teenage girls pose different problems regarding the way they dress and must be approached somewhat differently because of their developmental stage.[5]

Women who wear sexually provocative clothing cause overstimulation and conflict for heterosexual male therapists, no matter how the male therapist denies or rationalizes this. Sometimes, the women know they are being sexually stimulating and enjoy this (a narcissistic or sadistic trait), but often women who dress this way are unaware of their sexual effect on men. The unawareness involves projection of their own views onto men. That is, women may expect men to merely admire them; men's ease of visual sexual stimulation is either unknown or denied.

How can you approach a woman who is dressing in a highly provocative way, especially if it is on the "edge" of social acceptability (varying with the era)?

SHORT ANSWER

It is usually necessary for male therapists to tolerate their own visual stimulation for quite some time before discussing a woman's dress in therapy. An exception arises when the woman's dress is so provocative that it is too distracting.

---

[5] Teenage girls are exquisitely sensitive to control, especially about how they dress. They are experiencing the recrudescence of separation-individuation and struggling to resolve their oedipal heterosexual wishes simultaneously (Blos, 1960). Usually much time must be first spent discussing their problems with separation of their identities from their mothers. Discussion of girls' dress will inevitably cause the girls to react to the (especially female) therapist as a critical mother. Insurmountable resistance may ensue.

EXAMPLE 1

Bonnie, a buxom, 33-year-old divorced woman, showed up for her evaluation at a male therapist's office wearing a see-through blouse without a bra. She proceeded to complain that men were hitting on her all the time; she was fed up with men who had "just one thing on their minds."

After obtaining more history, the therapist gently asked if Bonnie was aware of how she was dressing. At first, Bonnie made excuses, claiming she was just being stylish. When he pointed out that she was minimizing the effects of her almost-bare breasts, she was shocked, and put on her coat.

Some women wear such a short skirt that when they sit down, they reveal their underwear. Although common recently, flappers "kicked up their heels" doing the Charleston in the 1920s and British women wore "microskirts" in the 1960s.

The best way to handle issues about dress is to gather data from the woman to correlate her difficulties with the way she dresses. Women with self-esteem problems may dress exhibitionistically to compensate. If, like Bonnie (above), women deny the sexual element of dress, you can point out the denial.

LONG ANSWER

Nine times out of 10, I do not say anything to women I treat about how they dress, as long as this is within the "standard of wear."[6] The way women dress is normally part of their identity as female[7] and reflects socially conditioned feminine tastes. Although choice of attire may be meaningful, the meanings are often unconscious and not particularly helpful in aiding women in understanding their problems. Commonly, attire simply expresses wishes to conform with fashion (identification) or not (disidentification).

Women therapists have a somewhat easier time discussing dress; a male therapist can be perceived as a "dirty old man" by a woman in treatment, no matter how he phrases his comments. However, women therapists may

---

6 Again, some of you reading this may not be familiar with the American legal principle that is applied to doctors. Physicians must practice within the "standard of care," which usually is defined as the manner in which similarly trained doctors would operate in a similar situation, given certain information about a patient. Doctors are at risk of losing a malpractice suit if they are not practicing up to the standard of care. In the phrase I just used, I was trying to make an ironic joke.

7 Kramer-Richards (1992). Also, many mothers are surprised their 3-year-old daughters insist on wearing dresses and skirts.

be seen as critical, "sensible" mothers who dictate the girl's wardrobe. Even women therapists who are trying to be helpful can easily stimulate adolescent rebellious attitudes in adult woman they are treating.

Actually, the meanings of women dressing provocatively are numerous. In more intensive treatment, issues about sexuality usually arise. Numerous case reports reference meanings of seductive behavior with both male and female therapists as well as outside the treatment.[8]

"Progression" (as opposed to regression) as a defense is common: Women can engage in sex (a later-developing function) to avoid conflicts over dependency and control (earlier-developing wishes); at the same time, they unconsciously gratify the dependency and controlling wishes ("compromise formation").[9] Dressing provocatively often has these same meanings.

The most common type of progression as a defense is *sexualization* to guard against shame over wishing for a mother to take care of her, especially when dependency wishes are strong. Women who sexualize will engage in sexual acts to (a) avoid facing their dependency wishes and (b) gratify their dependency wishes unconsciously.[10] Their seductiveness toward men masks (and secretly gratifies) a wish to obtain a mother.

Provocative dressing may also reflect controlling wishes: an object-coercive[11] element toward men that includes hostility toward mother.

EXAMPLE 2

Fern, 43, was having an extramarital affair (of which her husband knew nothing). When she worked out at the gym, she wore clothing that was eye catching. She was a pretty woman and, when she dressed that way, she said she knew men would ogle her.

She took pleasure in this, but it was not "normal narcissism."[12] She imagined (and this was likely true) that the men looking at her were frustrated. This idea gave her sadistic gratification: She suspected they were tortured by their inability to attain orgastic release to relieve the tension caused by her stimulation of them.

Fern showed characteristics of "Rat People":[13] Her father had peeped at her and walked around naked during her adolescence. She was not frankly abused but overstimulated and frustrated.

---

8 Malawista et al. (2011).
9 Brenner (2006).
10 The so-called mother-breast-penis equation (Marcus, 1971).
11 Kramer (1983).
12 Kohut (1971).
13 Shengold (1967).

Her seductive behavior as an adult was partly based on identification with the aggressor father; she also became the cause of the man's frustration (reversal). Her sexual provocativeness relieved anxiety about closeness with her husband, as did the affair.

Rarely, women may have a fetish about clothing,[14] where a good part of their treatment centers around the meaning of sexual teasing, including how they dress. If you wait to mention women's dress, when a woman brings up the issue, you can discuss it without encountering the predictable concordant and complementary identifications in the countertransference.

EXAMPLE 3

Gina, in her early 40s, was a sexpot. I did not mention her attire for over a year, however. Finally, she asked me what I thought of an outfit she was wearing.[15] I could then explore the nature of her question, the way she dressed, and what it meant. In her case, dressing seductively was closely linked with hostile-destructive rebellion toward her mother from adolescence.

Her mother had forbidden her to wear miniskirts to high school. Gina had purposely worn a miniskirt under a longer skirt so her mother would not know. At school, Gina went to the restroom to remove the longer skirt. Before she came home, she put the longer skirt on again.

Recently, when I was describing this type of behavior to a group of psychiatry residents, one of the women residents laughed and commented that she had done exactly the same thing with her mother.

---

14 Raphling (1989).
15 Similar to a case of Renik's (1999).

Problem 94
Wiseguys

In English, this colloquialism originally referred to men who knew less than they pretended to know. The current-day usage suggests that the man is self-centered, condescending, irritating, sarcastic, immature, offensive, and not willing to take serious matters seriously.

The origin of the word seems to be from German, particularly the Yiddish version, *wisenheimer,* meaning the same thing. Other English equivalents have included the more or less anachronistic terms *wiseacre* and *smart-alec*. The last of these has nothing to do with Alexander the Great but most likely was based on somebody named Alec.

In my decades of working with people, I have rarely run into a woman with this type of character issue, so this section concerns the problem as it occurs in men.

Verbal brutality is a common feature of boys' socialization during the latency and adolescent phases of development. Boys tend to mock each other, condescend to each other, and even hit each other in play, but the pain or damage is usually minor.

As boys develop abstraction ability during adolescence, they may incorporate elements of brutal play into their verbalizations with each other. For example, I overheard my son, at age 18, answer a cell phone call from a good friend. He picked up the phone, and on recognizing his friend's voice, said, "Hi, asshole!" It is hard to envision an 18-year-old girl doing that with a best friend.

I also recall picking up my son, at age 7, from a birthday party. I arrived toward the end of the party; there were about 10 boys left in a room with a horseshoe-shaped table that probably had handled about 20 or 30 boys originally. After I chatted briefly with the parents, I entered the party room to get my son.

For a few minutes, I observed their play. Half of them were under the table. The boys sitting at the table were kicking those underneath. The boys under the table tried to grab the kicking legs of the boys seated at the table and pull those boys under the table. After a boy was pulled under the table, he and the other boy switched positions, so the "kickee" became the "kickor." The new kickor kicked the boy under the table; and the game repeated itself. In the many times I have been at birthday parties for 7-year-old girls, I have never seen this type of game. It is the beginning of wiseguy-ness.

A wiseguy can be brutal in his verbalizations with others and with the therapist. If the wiseguy is also depressed because of difficulties in personal relationships, he may be amenable to understanding his noxious character trait.

SHORT ANSWER

Wiseguys may suffer with "secondary depression" (see Problem 7) due to difficulties sustaining closeness in relationships (object relations problems). They often respond to a "counter-wiseguy" comment designed to bring light to their almost ubiquitous hostility in social, personal, and even work situations.

> **TIP**
> Confrontation of a wiseguy's sarcastic, condescending traits can be done with a bit of counter-wiseguy sarcasm to be more effective.

EXAMPLE 1

Rob, a depressed 49-year-old manager, consulted me because of depression in relation to his wife. She complained she could not get a straight answer out of him and was fed up because he ridiculed things she thought were serious.

As he described instances where she criticized him, I noticed that he saw her as foolish, stupid, and oversensitive. He mocked her and made "wisecracks"; this irritated her; she nagged him and had lost sexual interest in him. They had sex sporadically, and he complained that she "laid there like a board."

Rob's favorite TV program was HBO's *Curb Your Enthusiasm,* an outré farce that is overtly offensive. At work, Rob was in danger of being demoted due to offensive remarks to women, minorities, and superiors.

Since Rob was not condescending toward me, I could not at first figure out what was so troublesome to others. I asked him for examples. He laughingly explained that when he was critical of people, he said things like, "You lily-livered idiot!" (paraphrasing Shakespeare), particularly at work.

> **THEORY**
> H. Hartmann (1939) termed certain reactions "preconscious automatisms," behaviors or attitudes that get mobilized periodically, somewhat outside of awareness, to relieve fear or depression.

At home, when irritated with his wife, he would mumble, "Shit-for-brains." When she was irritated with him, he would say, sarcastically, "I can see you haven't taken your Premarin today!"[16]

---

16 Premarin is the trade name for a conjugated estrogen product that women sometimes take during menopause. It sometimes helps them, among other things, avoid being irritable.

He volunteered that these put-downs "tried to offer constructive criticism in a humorous sort of way." Rob was surprised when I told him I thought his offensive, condescending attitude provoked difficulty in all spheres of his life.

Rob got fired from his job but because of his high level in the company he was given a 6-month payout. He was not allowed back in the building.

After clarifying that his obnoxiousness caused difficulty, he observed that he was not that way always. After some discussion, I pointed out how he became this way when nervous, depressed, or feeling guilty about something.

Rob's understandings helped him at work, but the "contaminated water under the bridge" in his marriage caused him and his wife to separate.

He made amends with his teenage daughters, who had previously rejected him for being a "loser." When he finished treatment, he was getting along better with them. He found himself a new girlfriend and was not as sarcastic. She seemed to respond to him better.

In summary, when a man has a responsive character trait (preconscious automatism), the therapist tries to explain how he becomes a wiseguy to guard against feeling helpless, frightened, unhappy, or depressed.

LONG ANSWER

If you are seeing a wiseguy frequently, he will eventually misbehave with you: not-so-subtle sarcastic remarks. Try to understand the meanings of those remarks early in a session.

The reasons causing men to be severely obnoxious wiseguys include

- identifications with one or both parents, who may have been sarcastic and needling toward them during childhood;
- transferences, where they repeat what they said or wanted to say to their parents;
- reversals of their passivity with their parents, turning the tables on you; and
- guarding themselves from remembering just how much they hated their parents.

Obnoxiousness often provokes punishment, to relieve guilt.[17] If you can get a man to see how he provokes punishment, you may learn what he feels guilty about.

---

17 Blackman (2003a).

EXAMPLE 2

William, a male neurosurgeon in his 50s, was referred after he had been disciplined by a hospital for verbally attacking a nurse during surgery. When he asked her for an instrument, she gave him the wrong one. He responded, "Did you ever learn anything!? Where did you get your training, in Bolivia!?" Since the nurse was of Latin American background, she resented his condescending criticism and felt it was prejudicial.

William was on a 1-month suspension when he came to see me. He knew he had been "sarcastic" for years and wasn't quite sure how to shake it. Understanding his wiseguy trait took about 2 months, twice a week. William was astute, kind to his children, but acerbic with his wife. He had been married four times; his wives got sick of his attitude.

His wiseguy expressions were partly based on identifications with mentors. His residency had been in a "pyramid program," which lasted 5 years. Each year one of the residents was dropped, so by the time he was chief resident in neurosurgery, the others had been dismissed and had to find training elsewhere (sometimes in an affiliated hospital). He admitted he hated that process, but it had "got into my system somehow."

Also, many mentors brutally embarrassed him about his lack of knowledge. I showed William how he became like them, doing what had been done to him—which shielded him from anger at his "loved" mentors. He was surprised. William had thought he was "just the way I am."

His wiseguy attitude had other roots in his frustrations with his grandiose and presumptuous father. His father had said to William, as a teenager, that William was "not so smart after all," and "You think you're hot stuff, just because you're going to college. You don't know squat about real life!" When I pointed out how William had become like his father, he understood. He readapted, becoming polite to people at work, and thanked me for the insights. I believe he had no more work troubles.

EXAMPLE 3

Scott, a 47-year-old CEO of an auto dealership, had cheated on his wife for 15 years. He did not have "relationships" with his extramarital "babes." His wife was suspicious, but he never admitted the dalliances. Things were getting tense in the marriage; he thought he had a "sexual addiction."

I first explained to Scott that diagnosing himself with sexual addiction let him off the hook for betraying his wife. I suspected his use of rationalizations meant he was avoiding guilt. He knew if she found out, she would be "hurt.

So what. Hell hath no fury like a woman scorned, but Hell also hath no fury like a woman who nags. I might as well do something if she's going to bitch at me."

Scott glibly argued, "What Brenda doesn't know won't hurt her. In fact, I think it's better for our marriage, because I don't get into so many arguments with her. I can relieve myself with a 'babe.' So it's probably better for Brenda in the long run. Also, when I screw other women, it's good for them, too, right?"

I thought Scott was glib and mocking me. So I responded, "Bullshit!"

He laughed and almost cried it was so funny. He joked, "'Bullshit!' Well, that's empathic…" I said, "I failed empathy during training" (confronted his rationalization). This time he laughed for more than a minute.

This wiseguy interchange set the stage for Scott to consider the meanings of his misbehavior. I think it also gave him confidence that I could handle his hostile aggression. For a number of years, he idealized my abilities to see through him, which he both enjoyed and feared a bit.

Problem 95
People Who Are Friends With Other People You Are Treating

Whether you live in a city, a small town, or something in between, if you do a good job, people you treat may refer their friends to you.

This presents a certain awkwardness. What should you do?

SHORT ANSWER

In years past, there has been hypocrisy about this issue—as though it was a conflict of interest or breach in confidentiality for a therapist to treat a friend of someone already in treatment. Nevertheless, throughout history, therapists have often built their private practices by accepting such referrals.

In my own experience, treating people who are friends with other people I am treating has rarely caused a problem. As long as both people realize they may talk about each other with me, and that I may hear many sides of stories, the situation has been easily workable.

A caveat is that confidentiality must be maintained by the therapist. If the therapist does not see either of the people frequently enough, the therapist can get confused about which person told him which story.

But most of the time people have their own personal problems, and even if they're close with another person, the other person does not know the secrets of the other's masturbation fantasies, obsessions, phobias or inhibitions. In other words, the "stuff" of psychotherapy is generally not part of friendships, though there are exceptions.

In those exceptional cases, usually among certain women, people know an enormous amount about each other's feelings, and have been "analyzing" each other for years. It is sometimes best to have a colleague as a referral source for the friend.[18]

---

18 For a whopping good story, I recommend Donald V. Stevenson's (2000) book *Not So Innocent*, a psychoanalytic-style murder mystery where four people who are all in analysis with him become embroiled in sexual relationships with each other as well as a murder. Don, who was a friend of mine, wrote this story based loosely on his experiences working in Hampton Roads, Virginia (about 1.3 million people). In this size area, it is not uncommon for people who know each other to consult the same therapist.

LONG ANSWER

Although there is generally not too much difficulty in accepting these types of referrals, at times it may become complex. One danger is that the two people may "act out" conflicts rather than discuss them with the therapist. In other words, if you treat people who are good friends, they may talk about things with each other and then forget to tell you. In those cases, it's necessary to point out these displacements, especially if they act as a way of keeping secrets from you, the therapist.

The meaning of the referral may be significant, but I have found it difficult to approach. People in treatment with you, who are doing better, feel grateful and logically assess you as a good therapist. When their friends have problems, they naturally think about referring them to you, and are not terribly worried about what the friend tells you. Some issues, though, become clearer after you evaluate the friend.

EXAMPLE 1

Carol, a 51-year-old woman, consulted me because of marital difficulties. She had made progress in understanding her contributions to their problems, had gotten her husband interested in treatment (he consulted a different therapist), and was happy that her marriage was becoming more fulfilling.

Over a couple of years of treatment, she referred me two friends of hers, who were both having marital problems. In those situations, I found out later, Carol was planning on dumping them as friends and was feeling guilty about it.

Part of her motivation for referring them was to relieve guilt about jettisoning them. Partly, she hoped they would not hate her for giving up on them. Interestingly, both women were highly narcissistic, and each only came for one consultation. Neither was interested in treatment but had come at Carol's suggestion.

Carol's guilt stemmed from conflicts in her family, particularly competitiveness with a sister who was 3 years older. Growing up, she consciously wished her sister had never been born. She pulled pranks on her sister as a teenager that had distanced them for a number of years.[19]

---

19 For an excellent depiction of these types of conflicts between sisters, see the movie *In Her Shoes* (Hanson, 2005).

EXAMPLE 2

Nick, a partner in a large law firm, consulted me because of worries about his 13-year-old daughter. His daughter was rebellious, dressing "like a whore," refusing to do her homework, and talking to friends on her cellphone late at night. He had been critical, and punished her by taking away her cellphone. None of the punishments or criticisms had any effect. She simply used the house phone in the middle of the night, stayed up later, and still did poorly in school.

I treated Nick for over 10 years, once a week. The story of how I helped with his daughter and his marriage is possibly the topic of another book. The point is that about 2 years into his treatment, when he was feeling better and having some success with his daughter, he referred me a friend of his who worked for the same law firm, but in a different section.

Whit, older than Nick but equally smart, was also having trouble with his teenage daughter. Whit's teenage daughter knew Nick's, and they were somewhat friendly. Nevertheless, Whit's marital problems were entirely different from Nick's, although each knew the other had problems.

I treated Whit for 5 years, once a week, and was able to help him resolve his distancing, passivity, irascibility, and neurotic criticism of his wife and children. Neither Nick nor Whit mentioned each other very often. When they did, they would usually make an aside such as, "I know you can't talk about this." I agreed.

Both of them had successful treatments.

Problem 96
People Who Are Involved With Someone Who Is Driving Them Crazy

Calef and Weinshel (1981) described "gaslighting." The name for this noxious mechanism was derived from the movie *Gaslight,* in which a husband tries to convince his wife that she is going crazy. It can afflict either gender. The person who consults you is often the victim of a gaslighter. In such situations, the therapist must strike a delicate balance. First, you want to point out how people take in and believe (introject) the accusations made by the gaslighter. Second, you must steer clear of criticizing the apparent villain.

> **TIP**
> When people are being conned into criticizing themselves, be careful not to criticize their tormentor. Instead, discuss their minimization and inhibition of being judgmental about other people.

ANSWER

Although it is best to stay neutral, sometimes you are faced with someone reporting a relationship that has a tragic quality. As you get to know people you are treating, you may see that their relationship to reality is good, their abstraction ability is good, they can organize their thoughts, they have a reasonable conscience, and their capacity for trust is relatively unimpaired. Notwithstanding these positive features, as they describe the people with whom they are involved, you see that they put themselves in jeopardy based on the character traits that they are, no doubt accurately, describing in the other person.

Such people may see reality but not give it enough weight (minimization). They equate judging people with being cruel or evil, and therefore the simple act of judgment creates guilt. To relieve (defend against) guilt, some people become "nonjudgmental" (inhibition of critical judgment) or even laudatory toward someone who is a scoundrel (reaction formation).

EXAMPLE

Hannah, 42 and divorced, had a daughter who was a freshman in college. She was financially successful and her daughter was doing well. Nevertheless, she experienced severe panic attacks whenever she considered breaking up with Reggie, the man with whom she had lived for 2 years. The reasons for the panic attacks were rather complicated and took about 3 years of twice-a-week therapy to untangle. One glaring feature was her acceptance of her lover's criticisms of her.

After a day skiing at Lake Tahoe, they had drinks at the bar in the lodge. Reggie took some digital pictures. As they chatted with other people at the bar, she noticed that he was taking pictures of a voluptuous, seductive woman sitting next to him. He also got her name and home address. This bothered Hannah, but she put her suspicions aside until she looked at the pictures on his digital camera later that evening.

She noticed that among the pictures of the other woman, there were many only of the other woman's breasts. After she integrated this with her memories of Reggie coming on to the woman at the bar and even finding out details about her, Hannah asked him what was going on. He told her she was imagining things and blamed her for being "too jealous." This struck a nerve in Hannah.

After Hannah recounted this story, she said, "I need you to help me with my jealousy." This remarkable phenomenon occurred in a woman who was not psychotic, not psychopathic, and not intellectually challenged. I had to consider why Hannah had accepted her boyfriend's opinion that she was "too jealous."

I asked her to tell me more about this supposed hyperjealousy of hers. She said she also got "jealous" when she and Reggie were in the checkout line at Macy's, and she heard Reggie getting the name and telephone number of an attractive woman cashier. When she later asked him about that, he said he was only getting the other woman's number for a sales campaign he was running for his business (he was in sales). Hannah had believed him.

On another occasion, Reggie had obtained the name and telephone number of a woman waiting on them at a restaurant. He said he wanted to give her name and phone number to other people for sales purposes.

By now, I saw a pattern which, unfortunately, Hannah had not seen. Still, not knowing all the facts, I thought it was dangerous for me to opine about Reggie's character structure. Rather, I pointed out to Hannah that she seemed to be accepting all of his explanations, which, taken together, seemed to suggest a pattern. Instead of feeling anything negative about Reggie, she accepted his criticism that she was jealous, which, in fact, she was. She was jealous that he paid attention to other women. She would then dismiss her own conclusions, not be critical, and believe his explanations.

My attempt to explain her taking in ("introjection of") his apparent gaslighting (trying to convince her she was crazy) was successful. She could see this, but when she thought about breaking up with him, she became terrified. This led us to study of the origins of her anxiety.

Much of her anxiety was generated by guilt over the physical damage she imagined inflicting on Reggie. When she finally got to her anger, it was graphic, brutal, and not surprisingly, involved thoughts of damaging his genitalia. She also wished to torture him in some vague way, but these thoughts made her feel weird and guilt ridden. Due to these conflicts, she had blamed herself and had accepted his accusations that she was hyperjealous.

Hannah finally broke up with Reggie. To check her view of reality, she used his password to a dating website. She found out he was bisexual, a swinger, and for years had been advertising himself as unattached.

I invited Hannah to think with me about how her guilt had developed. Hannah recalled that her mother, whom she had not mentioned much, was never able to attune herself to Hannah. Her mother had been hospitalized several times for severe mental illness, and when at home, was off by herself, staring into space. Her mother could rarely respond appropriately when Hannah was growing up.

Hannah, instead, had become attached to a woman teacher in her Episcopal Sunday school, who became a surrogate mother during Hannah's adolescence. When Hannah was 8 years old, her father had died from cancer.

Her childhood had left her with a terror of being alone, a terror that had been reinforced when she found her husband cheating on her several years earlier. He had been unapologetic about it, and she therefore had to divorce him and finish raising her daughter on her own until the daughter went to college.

Hannah's morbid fear of being alone had allowed her to be seduced by her husband when she was a freshman in college. He was one of her graduate student teachers. She later found he had sexual dalliances with other girls while he had been dating her.

These experiences contributed to her conflicts about breaking up with her boyfriend, especially her worries that she would be alone forever, that she could not trust any man, and that he was as good as she could get (generalization).[20]

As Hannah was less inhibited about being critical of men she dated, she was able to briefly date and stop dating men who sounded at least moderately psychopathic, although they were successful. At the time that she finished her therapy with me, Hannah was not dating anybody, but she felt confident that she would be able to make good choices in the future, and she was no longer experiencing panic attacks.

---

20 Loeb (1982).

Problem 97
People Who Are Dating Someone Who Sounds Severely Mentally Ill

If people you are treating are dating someone who sounds mentally ill, they can break off the relationship with few consequences (except emotionally). If, however, they are married to that person, breaking up is difficult, practically challenging, and upsetting. It is easier to recognize someone's mental illness before deciding whether to get married.

How are you to discern if people are describing someone who is severely mentally ill? People may distort their reports, project parts of themselves onto the other person, blame the other person for their own problems, or not remember things clearly. Some people involved in a custody dispute fabricate bad things about the (ex-)spouse.

SHORT ANSWER

Most of the time, it is an error to diagnose someone else through the eyes of people you are treating. It is safer, if you think people are describing a mentally ill partner, to bring together the various complaints they have made about their partner (clarification) and suggest they think about how they are describing this other person.

EXAMPLE 1

I told Vladimir, "You have said your girlfriend, Sally, is a severe alcoholic, she has taken off her clothes in public, she vowed to never stop drinking, and she insists on freedom to date other men. You, on the other hand, have said you want a committed relationship with a woman who is not an alcoholic. I'm interested in how you think about all of this."

Vladimir then admitted that he also drank too much, and that sex with Sally was a "blast." Vlad, himself, took golf trips with male friends for weeks at a time, leaving Sally at home. Although he and Sally agreed that they were exclusive, he had dabbled in one-night stands with other women when traveling.

In other words, the case turned out to be quite complicated. The features of Vlad's problems that I was able to help him understand, eventually, included

- his own alcohol abuse as a way of relieving pain;
- his infidelity regarding Sally as a way of establishing distance—because he was afraid of emotional closeness in relationships; and
- fear of closeness due to (transference) expectations from his mother, sister, and a number of prior women with whom he had been involved.

When people are married or living together, projective blaming is a common cause of disturbance between them. It is usually a mistake to presume that the so-called mentally ill spouse is quite as disturbed as they are being described. Caution is indicated.

With some chagrin, I have sat through case presentations by therapists where they sided with people in treatment, and little weight was given to the feelings of the (nonpresent) spouse who was supposedly such a terrible person.

LONG ANSWER

Keeping the above caveats in mind, at times, when you hear of egregiously dangerous behavior by a spouse or partner of people you are treating, it may be imprudent not to comment. Still, I try to approach the denial used by people I am treating, rather than judging or issuing an uninformed diagnosis of the person described.

EXAMPLE 2

Mickey, a 34-year-old single man, had taken over his family retail business and was successful. He complained about Pam, a woman he was dating, "She's driving me crazy! I can't get her out of my mind."

He met Pam 6 months previously when she came into his store. She was single and unattached. He found her attractive, and they had pleasurable conversations that were unusual, in his experience. They shared a lot and enjoyed each other's company. When they began having sex, they enjoyed it immensely.

Everything was fine for about a month. Then, suddenly, Pam opined that they needed to "stop being serious." An old boyfriend had contacted her and she wanted to date him. Mickey was dumbfounded. He asked her how she could be in an intense relationship with him and then suddenly go back to a boyfriend she had not seen in a year.

Pam then confessed that she had been talking to her old boyfriend, and he had been pressuring her to come back to him. She felt she "owed him" another try. She asked Mickey to be patient.

Mickey was furious. Pam accused him of not understanding: dating her old boyfriend was nothing against Mickey. They parted in an unfriendly way, and Mickey had written her off when, 2 months later, she reappeared on his doorstep. She was apologetic, wanted to talk to him, and wound up having sexual intercourse with him that night.

Thinking that the old boyfriend was out of the picture, Mickey began to talk with her about him. She flew into a rage, accused him of being "possessive," and insisted on "space" and "time to think." Over the next few months, the same scenario repeated itself. Between contacts, she texted him salacious messages but would not respond to his texts for several days.

It took me weeks of once-a-week therapy to conclude that Mickey had not introduced distance into their relationship. He had not pushed her away; he had not been jealous or possessive. He had begun openly musing with her about getting engaged down the line and married. He told me, "I'm at that time of life where if I meet the right girl, I'd like to settle down and have a family."

He had made his intentions clear to Pam after they had sex. She had expressed apprehension about ever having children, but said she would consider it if he wanted it. Mickey blamed himself and wondered what he had done wrong. She would only tell him he wasn't patient enough: She needed "space."

Her episodic closeness and distance seemed to me to be characteristic of certain personality disorders.[21] Seeing as Pam was 29 years old, her oscillations could not be entirely chalked up to the immaturity of identity formation that is characteristic of teenagers.

I pointed out to Mickey that he kept making excuses for Pam's behavior, blaming himself, and not admitting to himself that she could have psychological problems. He clung to the idea that he had put her off somehow.

After some sessions with me, he called Pam to ask if there was anything he had done that caused her to back off from him. She told him there was nothing about him that made her run away. She just couldn't decide and still felt like she needed to see her old boyfriend for a while. She would not make Mickey any promises or give him any timetable.

Mickey asked me if I thought his bringing up marriage and children had put her off. I repeated what he had told me, namely that she was uncomfortable with the idea of children but that I could not be sure whether this was affecting her. He concluded that it must be, but in any case, he was "fed up."

I also focused on his minimization of her ambivalence toward him. Mickey then recalled not seeing his high school girlfriend as "weird" until she

---

21 "Comets"—Blackman (2003a, 2010).

was hospitalized for a schizophrenic break. When he was 6, his mother had a stillbirth; he had not thought about that until he was in treatment.

Mickey's guilt over those events caused him not to be judgmental (which he considered "aggressive") toward females. He also identified with his father, "the sweetest guy you'd ever want to meet," who never criticized anyone. Therefore, Mickey was slow to criticize and make judgments about Pam.

Mickey let Pam go, grieved, and developed better judgment about women he dated. About 7 months later, Pam called him, "wanting to talk." He mentioned to me that the same process that took months for him to understand the first time now took 2 minutes: first, he was excited to hear from her and they had intense, funny interchanges. When he asked her about her boyfriend, she said she needed space but now gave an apology about hurting Mickey. Within minutes, he recognized the old pattern repeating, and told her to stop calling him.

Within months, he had met an interesting woman who seemed much more stable and was not squeamish about marriage and children.

Problem 98
People Who Write Down
Long Dreams

Ernest Hartmann, a psychoanalyst and sleep researcher in New York City, for years requested that people he evaluated keep a "dream log." In this sort of diary, people wrote down their dreams and brought them in for study. He integrated people's reports of dreams with electroencephalographic findings. The results are fascinating.[22]

People recording their dreams can help you understand, through deciphering the symbolism, elements of their problems that had not been clear before. On the other hand, sometimes people can take up two-thirds of their sessions rereading their dreams, and the dreams are so lengthy that it's difficult to pay attention or to draw any conclusions that can be used therapeutically.

People who write down dreams are trying to comply with the therapeutic process, but it can sometimes be difficult. What should you do about this?

SHORT ANSWER

In most cases, unless the written dreams are causing difficulty by eating up large segments of time during therapy, I listen carefully for threads of meaning in the dreams. Alexander (1925), in an astute paper, pointed out that sequences of dreams often juxtapose material where defense, wish, and conflict are represented and tell a story. The first or last dream reported provides material to help formulate and understand problems.

I do not usually interfere with people's reports from their written records of dreams. I can usually follow the sequence, and that sequence is useful. When people start telling long dreams, though, I add something: Every minute or two, I interrupt to paraphrase and clarify what was going on in that part of the dream. When I do this, I have an easier time remembering what the dream was about, and it also helps the person reporting the dream (and me) keep track of the segments of the dream.

After their lengthy report, I then go over the six or seven segments that I found most significant.[23]

---

22 E. Hartmann (1973, 1982).
23 If somebody is in analysis, and I am sitting behind the couch, I may jot down notes about the material in the sequence in the dream, so I don't have to interrupt people. I do not generally take notes during face-to-face psychotherapy.

EXAMPLE 1

Darlene, a 51-year-old married woman whose two daughters were grown and married, had a sexual inhibition. She was conscious of feelings of ambivalence about sex, which bothered her and interfered with her enjoyment of sexual intercourse with her husband of 26 years. At a time when they should have been freer to enjoy sex, she persisted in having difficulties.

During one session, she brought in a written report of dreams:

1. I am at some sort of recital. I'm in the audience. There's this woman I know who used to teach me in high school. She was very bossy. She is bossing me around and I don't like it. I walk out of the room.

2. Now, I am on a runway, like in a fashion show. I'm wearing this beautiful, sequined dress. It's really spectacular! It's the kind of thing I never wear. It has a slit up the back, but it's still tasteful. I really look gorgeous in it, and I'm walking up and down the runway feeling great. I know that people are looking at me, and I'm feeling great about that too.

3. Somehow, I'm in the attic of a wooden building. The building looks a little bit like the house I grew up in, and there is a dead woman, all dressed in black, lying in one of the bedrooms. I don't go in it. Instead, I go to this other room. For some reason, I jump out of the window, which is several stories high, but I land in a sort of lagoon. It's cold, though, and I notice that it's dark and black. There is some man there, but I'm afraid of alligators. I became terrified and I woke up."

The dreams took almost 20 minutes for her to recount. What we could see was that in the first dream, Darlene was feeling frustrated about being "in the audience." This reflected how she felt as a girl when her mother favored her brother. She remembered being "diminished" by her mother's attitude.

The second dream seemed to reflect feminine wishes to be beautiful, admired, and not be ashamed. I linked the first dream (mother criticizing) as a representation of guilt over sexual desires, creating her sexual inhibition.

The complex third dream suggested she felt danger in feeling competitive with her mother (dead woman). She wanted to be free of her mother (jumping out the window). But freedom brought with it the danger of sexuality with a man (alligators and man in lagoon). She also connected the water to the birth of her two children, with whom her "water had broken"[24] toward the end of labor.

---

[24] Premature rupture of the amniotic sac.

These thoughts correlated with her wish to have another child; but her husband had objected. Intellectually she thought two children were fine, but she had wanted to have a son. She had two daughters. The wishes to have a son were complex and took months to understand; they were "dark and murky."

Finally, dream 3 represented suicidal ideation Darlene had after the birth of her daughters. Each time, she felt guilty about having surpassed her mother. Each time, she felt vindicated by giving birth to daughters, whom she could raise in a much better fashion than her mother had done with her. She vowed not to treat her daughters as second-class citizens. She also yearned for a male child to please her mother, though, who openly favored her brother over her.

LONG ANSWER

S. Freud (1900) realized that writing down dreams could be a resistance to understanding them. People tend to be inaccurate when they write dreams down.

Some people lose what they had written down. They read the dreams, but are opaque to any study of them and want the therapist to "just tell me what it means."

Usually the therapist does not know what the dream means. You need the thoughts of the dreamer, in relation to different aspects of the dream, to be accurate in understanding symbolism—especially about specific conflicts. Therefore, if people write down long dreams but don't tell you their thoughts about them, the dreams (a) act as a way of avoiding getting closer to the therapist, (b) are distorted and "filtered" through the writing process, and (c) can lead the therapist into tangential and sometimes "wild" analysis.[25] Wild analysis occurs when therapists project their own conflicts onto the dreams or make a wild guess without information from the dreamer.

Women who write down dreams often harbor conflicts over masturbation—usually they feel inhibited about revealing masturbatory activity and fantasies. Writing and reading lengthy dreams is sort of "mental masturbation," where the woman (a) symbolically avoids discussion of masturbation fantasies; (b) lives out the fantasy in disguised form, by "playing with herself"; and (c) does not let the therapist in.

Not letting the therapist in has several common meanings. One is relief of anxiety about emotional closeness. This anxiety, originating before age 3 and recurring in adolescence, is a common culprit when grown women are inhibited about sex.

---

25 S. Freud (1910).

During the first genital phase[26] and adolescence, "letting a man in" can take on sexual symbolism. The report of a lengthy, written dream therefore can also indicate a wish to let the therapist in (a male or female therapist may represent a male—intruding in private areas), but reading the dream keeps the therapist out.

Written dreams may show symbolism about the writing process, as described in the following e-mail from Chang Wan, a therapist I was teaching in China in an online training program (CAPA).

EXAMPLE 2

During a videoconferenced class, Chang Wan reported a reluctance she felt to present case material in a different class. The material concerned Mu Ling, an agoraphobic woman who felt humiliated about secretly looking at men's crotches.

During class, I mentioned a countertransference called *concordant identification* (Racker, 1953), where the therapist unconsciously identifies with the person in treatment. I told Chang Wan that I suspected she had identified with Mu Ling. In other words, like Mu Ling in public, Chang Wan feared humiliation in the other class.

Following this discussion, Chang Wan sent me the following:[27]

Dear Jerry,

Many thanks for your interpret and encourage me send you this case. That made me refreshed suddenly. In the class, I have no time to tell you the most interesting thing about my case and myself. Let me expose it first:

In this session, I felt more relax and close to Mu Ling. At the night, before sleep, I think about Mu Ling again. She's afraid of expose herself what? I also have same feeling before several years ago, till now I still have it sometimes. Taking this question, I fall in sleep, then got a dream in Saturday morning. Seems there is an answer in it:

"I lie on the bed, catch sight of my penis. It's fresh and strong, smooth and long, straight up like a pen, as thin as finger. I don't feel surprise. I know I have it, too! I want to hide it, feel shy, and I won't want others see it.

"I look at him, a middle-age man, lie on opposite side of the bed, his penis is thick and relaxed. He is still sleeping. Seems there is a middle age woman sleeping beside him. I can't see her clearly."

---

26 Ages 2 to 7. See Blackman (2010), Chapter 10.
27 The therapist (different real name) gave me written permission to use this letter. Mu Ling is also a made-up name. I have described this case previously (Blackman, 2011).

I think this dream is telling my Oedipus complex. I yearn for father's penis, identify with father, hope myself was a boy, have more power, energy and success. I deny my female identity, so I can't see mother clearly, hope she was invisible.

Penis like a pen, that means I want to have more achievement on writing...Presenting a case like this in English is my first time. It's very hard but very useful. Striving for my people...also make me feel stronger. I'm eager for showing myself, but also afraid of that, want to hide it, my ambition and competitive power, like before.

Today (after Jerry's class) I remembered a film, Princess Diary. I have seen it thousand times. That's a Cinderella story, an invisible, inferior teenager finally become a bright, responsible, brave princess. That's also my dream.

Problem 99
Consulting With and Treating Family Members of People You Are Already Treating

It is common for therapists to evaluate and treat members of the same family who live with each other.[28] Some therapists treat siblings and their mother in individual therapy at the same time. This approach has arisen, I think, because of the work in family therapy started by Virginia Satir, John Bell, Murray Bowen, and Salvador Minuchin.

Although family work can be helpful when family conflicts involve children in grade school or early high school, my impression is that the more individuated the children have become in middle or late adolescence, the less family therapy is successful.

So, should you treat a husband and wife individually? Should you treat a parent and a child individually? Simultaneously or sequentially?

SHORT ANSWER

Most of the time, in my opinion, it is not a good idea to try to treat "nuclear" family members at all. An exception is child-centered counseling, where you attempt to help parents with advice about a preschooler, a school-age child, or an early adolescent.

Trying to point out internal conflicts to parents may produce resistance to counseling when they have not identified themselves as subjects for treatment. They may recoil from the notion that they need treatment. In favorable circumstances, where parents realize they have problems, I refer them to a colleague for individual and/or marital work. I think this works out much better.

I do not treat siblings for the following reasons:

- Most adolescents are mildly suspicious—afraid to tell you confidential things. If you also treat their sibling, they will be more defensive (repression).

- Sibling rivalry will inevitably be stimulated about you. You can inflame the rivalry if you allow siblings see you (even if they want to).

---

28 I know of one case where the therapist tried to treat an elderly couple with their married sons in a family session. The result was a disaster.

Often, you need to make an exception to confidentiality when people you treat are psychotic. If psychotic people are married, you may need to meet with the spouse to get input about how the psychotic partner is faring. Psychotic people often have to be hospitalized and rehospitalized and need their medications changed. Individual meetings with close family members are often required. It is best to obtain a written release from the psychotic person to meet with the family members. If not, you can try meeting with that person, the caretaker, the spouse, or others, together.

EXAMPLE 1

Dan was a 25-year-old, somewhat functional, so-called ambulatory schizophrenic man, whose father lived alone in a different state. Dan's father had obtained my name from a colleague, made the initial referral phone call, and paid my fees. That (supportive psychotherapy) treatment lasted about 2 years, during which Dan became more stable.

> **TIP**
> Avoid the trap of meeting individually with spouses of people you are treating. They may tell you a damaging "secret" that will create untenable conflicts.

Eventually, Dan was able to sustain himself, found a teaching position in another state where his mother (whom he had not seen in several years) lived, and planned to move near her. Throughout his treatment, with Dan's written permission, I spoke to his father a number of times on the phone to give the father an update on Dan's condition. Dan was agreeable to this, and it was important for me to learn quite a bit from his father, as well.

LONG ANSWER

For quite a while, if the spouse of a person I was treating in psychotherapy wanted to consult me individually, I would allow this (with the written permission of the person in treatment). It gave me certain information about the spouse, was usually interesting, and sometimes facilitated my empathy toward the person I was treating.

However, I have stopped doing this. For one thing, people who are having marital problems sometimes get divorced. When they do, if you have had a consultation with each spouse, they may very well each subpoena you as a witness in their divorce. It's tough enough to maintain confidentiality if only one of the people has consulted you, but it is doubly difficult if they have both done so.

Another serious problem is that one or both of the spouses may have cheated on the other. If one of them confesses this to you, even if you have written releases from both of them, this information puts you in an untenable position. For example, you are treating a woman who wants you to meet with her husband. On meeting with her husband privately, he confesses he's been having an affair, but asks you not to tell his wife. Even if you are released from confidentiality in writing, you now know that he is doing something destructive to the marriage. You will no doubt feel a responsibility to help the woman that you are treating, although her husband wants you to keep this secret. This situation can also occur the other way, if you are treating a man and his wife confesses to you, confidentially, that she is having an affair.

You can try to "handle" all this, but you are bound to falter, and, at the very least, you will get a headache. My advice is, don't do it, unless you are doing marital therapy and have made it clear, at the outset, that you will not keep confidences from either party.

There is only one occasion in my career when I have had a successful experience treating a parent and then sequentially treating one of her children.

EXAMPLE 2

Eleanor initially had been working too hard, neglecting her children, and experiencing quite a bit of pain from her own preoccupations and worries about everything. We were able to understand her obsessions over a period of about 3 years, and she successfully finished her treatment with me.

About a year later, she called me about her daughter, Jennifer, a senior in high school who had developed mild anorexia nervosa. She requested that I evaluate Jennifer and consider treating her. Jennifer knew that I had treated her mother, but this was all right with both mother and daughter. Jennifer actually had confidence that I could help her since I had helped her mother.

This was a short-term treatment, during the last 6 months of Jennifer's high school career. The anorexia had been relatively acute, was not severe, and did not require hospitalization. Jennifer was about 20 pounds underweight and had been purposely restricting food. The symbolism of this was quite readily definable:

1. Jennifer was terrified about leaving home and leaving her mother.
2. She had regressed to oral mechanisms (conflicts about food), which distracted her from a difficult decision about whether to have sexual

intercourse with her boyfriend, who, like her, would be leaving for college soon.

3. She had never been able to face any anger at her mother. Her mother had always been preoccupied (obsessed) with her safety, and she resented this. The resentment came into conflict with love and some guilt, so she was simultaneously

   a. punishing herself by not eating and
   b. expressing her wish, symbolically, to depend on her mother, who she knew would attend to the eating and do something.

Interestingly, during the mother's treatment, the mother had desisted from much of her overprotective behavior, and her daughter knew this. This improvement made it easier for me to treat the daughter.

Jennifer was not finished with therapy when she graduated from high school, although she had gained 10 pounds. She was going to Europe for 2 months to study. She was then going to attend an Ivy League school in the fall. She was receptive when I referred her to a colleague in that city, and I heard from her 4 years later, when she graduated, that she had successfully finished treatment with my colleague in her junior year.

Problem 100
When People "Don't Get It": Are They Using Denial or Are They Psychotic?

Not infrequently, people who are seriously disturbed tell their therapist something that sounds unrealistic. They may plan something that defies judgment, not seem to "get" what's going on around them, use bizarre verbiage, or blame others.

How do you distinguish denial (defense) from a break in reality testing (defect)?

SHORT ANSWER

Denial means that people are capable of seeing reality, but because something is upsetting, they tell themselves it is not true. They may do this by saying to themselves that it does not exist, by using certain magic words, by engaging in certain acts, or by developing certain fantasies.[29] If people have a pretty good grip on reality, but they are using denial to shield themselves from feeling something painful, they will usually respond to the therapist saying so.

In other words, you can try saying to people, "I believe that you are not paying attention to the reality of this situation because it is too painful." If people have intact reality testing, integrative functioning, and abstraction ability, they will respond to your explanation with emotion and a realization of how they have been ignoring something painful or dangerous.

If people argue with you about a simple reality instead of seeing the denial, you are likely dealing with a breakdown in reality testing—causing delusions. Treatment of them will include management of their environment, supportive techniques, and medicine.

LONG ANSWER

People can deny things by engaging in certain acts.

---
29 A. Freud (1936).

EXAMPLE 1

Rick, a local psychiatrist, consulted me for supervision on an inpatient case. He had evaluated Rita in an emergency room. She was an operating room technician in a different hospital. Two years prior, she had had a child by Wendell, a male Episcopal minister who was married to someone else. Just prior to the ER visit, Wendell had gone to Rita's house and gotten embroiled in an argument with her that became physical, although they had mutual restraining orders on each other granted by the court. Their child was in foster care.

Soon thereafter, Rita overdosed on Celexa and wound up in the emergency room; relatives had brought her. When she saw Rick, she was terrified that she would never see her child again. She feared that Wendell would kidnap the child and disappear from the United States. Rick learned from her relatives that Wendell maintained his position as a minister, his wife had apparently forgiven him for his infidelity, and they were in marital therapy with someone else.

Rick had opined to Rita that there was no danger to the child, and that her worries about the father were unrealistic. Rick said to her that she had not paid attention to the reality and that her overdose had not been based on a realistic appraisal of her situation. Rita accused Rick of knowing nothing: The child would be kidnapped. She had no reason to live. She would walk out of the hospital and kill herself. After orderlies detained her, she threatened to sue everyone.

> **TIP**
> Attempting to explain denial of a blatant truth may be very helpful: if the person understands, then insight-directed therapy may be effective; if they cannot understand, then you'll know the diagnosis is more serious and medication may be required.

At that point, a staff member filed a motion for a temporary detention order so that Rita could be held in the hospital. She quieted down but yelled while being transferred to the mental hospital, "I'll go, but it's under protest!"

I pointed out to Rick that his confrontation of Rita's "denial" of reality had failed. That failure was a useful diagnostic and prognostic tool in clarifying her delusional thinking.[30] Now Rick knew that therapy to help Rita understand symbolic meanings of her misperceptions would not help. She needed neuroleptic (antipsychotic) medication.

---

30 See Blackman (2003a), Chapter 8.

EXAMPLE 2

Jimmy, a 37-year-old engineer, had been hospitalized for suicidal ideation with no attempts. When I saw him as an outpatient (after he was discharged from the hospital), he was already taking an antidepressant. He and his wife, Leila, were separated but not yet divorced. Leila had custody of their two children.

Jimmy had been hospitalized after Leila had hung up the phone on him.

She had asked Jimmy to babysit for the children over the weekend while she traveled to a different state to visit a boyfriend—a "Platonic relationship." Leila was there Friday through Sunday. When she returned, she asked Jimmy to leave the house. Jimmy went back to his apartment, then called Leila to persuade her that they should get back together. Although she denied it, he felt strongly that her inviting him to babysit meant she wanted to reunite with him.

When she resisted, he had lectured her on her bad morals. He threatened to kill himself if she would not reunite with him. Leila had hung up on him and called the police, who picked him up and brought him to a mental hospital.

After hearing this story and getting more history of the marriage, it seemed to me that Leila was probably having an affair with the other man and may have been seeing him while married to Jimmy. I pointed out to Jimmy that, "You continuing to call and argue with your wife is a way of trying to convince yourself that you're not losing her."

Jimmy then argued with me. He said, "Well, then why would she have me come stay in the house and babysit for the kids?" I responded, "Most likely, it is because you come at the right price—free. The children need to see you, anyway, so she can have you babysit for free and get the child visitation done. Her actions do not mean she wants to get back with you. You're misinterpreting this because you wish it were not true. You're kidding yourself if you think she'll reconcile with you. She isn't, and by the way, she has another boyfriend."

At this point, Jimmy cried and screamed for 10 minutes. He yelled, "She doesn't know what she's doing! She's ruining the marriage! It's hurting the children!" I agreed with him that divorce was painful to children and that she was ruining the marriage. However, he couldn't do anything about her decisions. He then cried some more.

Finally, I explained that his suicidal thoughts indicated he turned much of his rage toward his wife on himself because he felt helpless. He agreed with me.

I saw Jimmy for two more sessions. He did not attempt suicide. I referred him to a therapist who would accept assignment from his insurance company.

Ten years later, I received a release form from a psychiatrist who was treating him. I called her. She said Jimmy was still upset about the divorce but had accepted it. His wife had remarried. Jimmy had not attempted suicide or been hospitalized since I had seen him.

The point is that, in this situation, my confrontation of Jimmy's denial was effective in helping Jimmy go from having severe suicidal urges to being able to face the painful reality in his life. With help, he was able to "get it"; once he stopped denying the truth, he could adjust his behaviors and expectations accordingly.

Problem 101
How to Improve Diagnosis and Choice of Techniques

In Part A, I go over some specifics of technique that were mentioned in Problem 1. More on this can be found in other references.[31]

In Part B, I review more details about diagnostic distinctions. For those of you who get into this, the way I do,[32] I have listed different phenomena you can see during evaluation and treatment that can further guide you about what you might say or do to help people during sessions.

---

31 Volkan (2011), Brenner (2006), Blackman (2003a, 2010).
32 Blackman (2010).

A. More on Supportive and Interpretive Techniques

SUPPORTIVE TECHNIQUES

Instructions

Ask people to tell you more about the reasons they consulted you. Ask questions about specifics of what they say and do at work, in relationships, and what solutions they have already tried.

Interventions

- Advise about language or behavior.
- Model by describing what you would do.
- Compliment a positive function or attribute of theirs.
- Agree with people's opinions, when appropriate.
- Debate alternative viewpoints with them.
- Persuade them that you are correct.
- Give (or refer for) medication to relieve painful affects.
- Teach (give information) regarding marriage, relationships, and child rearing.
- Reassure them about their choices (if they seem appropriate).
- Encourage healthy approaches and hobbies.
- Abreact (help to "vent" emotions) where grieving is blocked.
- Exhort behaviors ("You need to speak to your boss about that.").
- Hospitalize (if people pose a severe danger to themselves or others).

INTERPRETIVE TECHNIQUES

Instructions

Some people are self-starters and need no instructions. They immediately talk about themselves. Other people need some help getting started. They need you to explain what they should tell you, namely, all their thoughts and feelings about

- their chief complaint;
- their important relationships, past and present;
- their dreams and daydreams;

- their reactions to what you say;
- other thoughts about the treatment, both good and bad; and
- any stray thoughts they may have while they are talking to you.

Exploration

During the first evaluation, ask about a dozen questions, including:

1. What is troubling you?
2. When and where does it occur, and how long has it been going on? (Looking for precipitating factors.)
3. With whom are you living? (To get an idea of the general structure of their lives.)
4. How do you support yourself?
5. Do you trust anyone? Or have any friends? (Gives an idea about "object relations" problems—ability to form close, trusting relationships.)
6. What issues are there in your current serious relationship (if you have one)? (Data about current conflicts.)
7. Have you had any medical, obstetrical, or surgical problems? What medicines are you taking? (Reactions and expectations.)
8. Do you drink excessively or use drugs? (Impulse control.)
9. Are you involved in any legal action? (Their conscience, motives, values, and potential risk to you.)
10. Have you considered or tried killing yourself or others? If so, when and how? (Suicide risk, affect tolerance.)
11. Do you hear someone or something talking to you, but when you look you see no one? (Break in reality testing.)
12. Do you think people are watching you and/or talking about and/or plotting against you? (Breaks in reality testing.)

When an evaluee has friends and answers "no" to the last five questions, I generally ask very few questions during treatment but instead formulate and discuss his or her defenses (the defenses make you want to ask questions),[33] which is usually effective.

---

[33] For a discussion on how to find unconscious defenses, see Blackman (2003a), Chapter 6. Also, there are several exceptions to "The Rule Against Questions." See Blackman (2010), Chapter 4.

When you ask too many questions, people may be cooperative but stop treatment after just a few sessions. When therapists ask questions instead of mentioning defenses (see below), people feel invaded and angry (Problem 77) but guilty because the therapist has been nice. So, to avoid all that conflict,[34] they become defensive and don't come back. This seems strange: People were so cooperative in answering the therapist's questions—but *compliance* is a defense against angry defiance—the latter of which people "act out" by not showing up later.

Confrontation

You bring an unconscious defense or character trait to a person's awareness.

Example

You say, "You are joking, but I can tell this is painful."

Generally, don't confront affects. I usually won't say, "I think you are angry" (confrontation of affect). I might say, "I think you are somehow unaware of (or hiding or running away from) being angry" (confrontation of defense).

Clarification

You sum up a pattern that has been clear to you but not clear to the person you are treating. For instance, you say,

"From what you've told me, you shied away from sex with your first wife, you've found excuses to avoid your current wife, and you seem to be feeling inhibited about discussing your problems with me."

Current-day Interpretation[35]

You explain your perspective on people's current-day conflicts among *wishes*, *guilt*, *realities*, *affects*, and *defenses*.

Example

You say, "Jim, I think the panic that kept you from getting in your wife's car actually started an hour earlier when she criticized you for cursing. First, you felt put down, but you were too embarrassed to let yourself think

---

34 See Dorpat (2000).
35 For a definition of compromise formation and dynamic interpretation, see Brenner (2006) and Blackman (2003a, 2003b).

about it. Her criticism also made you angry at her, but as usual you felt guilty about getting angry. To relieve the guilt and embarrassment, you got passive and apologized to your wife. But I think that, without realizing it, you were angry at yourself for being passive and critical of her for being prudish. When you didn't get in her car, it was a 'perfect storm': You expressed your wish to run away from her, as well as your anger at her, but apologized, relieving your guilt." If Jim asks you to repeat all that, by all means do so.

Transference and Resistance Interpretation

You find how people are not cooperating with treatment (not following *instructions*). What they do or say in fighting the treatment instructions is based on an expectation that you will be like others from their past (relatives, friends, teachers).

Dream, Daydream, and Masturbatory Fantasy Interpretation

The dreamer reports thoughts about different aspects of the dream, and then, with the dreamer's help, you figure out the symbolism of the hidden wishes, affects, and defenses that explain parts of the dreamer's chief complaint or other parts of the pathology. You can do the same with daydreams[36] and masturbation fantasies.[37]

Reconstruction of the Past or Present

You take a stab at what might have happened in the recent or remote past— that someone can't recall—and present your educated guess to that person. If you are close to correct, the person in treatment will confirm or negate your theory with new memories and thoughts. This sometimes helps provide explanations for some of their current apparently irrational problems.[38] If the person does not remember anything new, or doesn't see any connections to your speculation, you are most likely wrong; in which case, don't push it.

---

36 Raphling (1996).
37 Marcus and Francis (1975).
38 Blum (2005).

B. More Information on Diagnosis

BASIC MENTAL FUNCTIONS (EGO FUNCTIONS), SUPEREGO, EGO STRENGTHS, OBJECT RELATIONS

AIRS / SE / ES / OR[39]

1. **AIRS** Abstraction/Integration/Reality-testing/Self-preservation (4 Basic Mental [Ego] Functions)

   There can be damage, in adults, to any of the four basic mental functions of

   - abstraction
   - integration
   - reality testing
   - self-preservation

   The damage can be caused by

   - heredity
   - physical illnesses
   - brain deterioration
   - severe, overwhelming affects

   You can use the algorithm in Table 1, more or less like this:

   People with deficits are *not* candidates for explanatory ("interpretive") treatment; they do not have the strength to tolerate such techniques.[40] When people have deficits, you can relieve their painful affects to help them adapt.

   Table 1
   Diagnosis Algorithm

DAMAGE	TREATMENT
Damaged **Abstraction, Integration, Reality Functions**	*Neuroleptic medication*
Add Suicide attempt (damaged **self-preservation**)	*Add antidepressant medication*
Add damage to **affect tolerance**, resulting in agitation, sleeplessness, clanging, flight of ideas (manicky symptoms)	*Add antimanic medicines and/or mood stabilizers*
Add damaged sleep–wake cycle	*Add hypnotics*

---

39 In this section, I use acronyms that help my students memorize these most important principles of mental status assessment.

40 For opposing opinions, see Rosen (1953), Boyer (1986), and Searles (1976).

You may want to withhold medications briefly in situations of trauma, such as with rape and concentration camp survivors. Traumatized people (meaning emotions broke down their abilities to organize and think) need support: verbalization (abreaction) and empathic understanding. People with illnesses that affect the brain (intoxication, pheochromocytoma, cerebral astrocytoma) need treatment for those diseases.

People who show disturbances in judgment and adaptation (two other important functions) are a mixed bag as far as treatability goes. Although some need the supportive techniques (Problems 1 and 101 [A]), most suffer with conflicts and personality problems that caused their mistakes. Find their transferences and defensive operations (counterphobic attitudes, passivity) and conflicts, and explain them.

2. **SE** Super Ego (F.I.R.E.-L.I.G.H.T.S.)

Deficits can occur in the normal adult attitudes listed in Table 2.

The more people lack **F**airness, **I**ntegrity, **R**eliability, **E**thics (FIRE)- **L**awfulness, **I**deals, **G**uilt, **H**onesty, **T**rustworthiness, and **S**hame (LIGHTS), the more a psychopathic (or antisocial) trait is added to their other problems.

Adults with multiple severe deficits are usually *entirely untreatable by any means*. The delusional, violent murderer and the sadistic rapist of children have, metaphorically speaking, the metastatic malignant melanoma of mental illness. They may have sad life stories and some may have been victims of abuse by others, but usually the only help that can benefit someone with such a severely damaged conscience is the type provided through our correctional system or other institutionalization.

Some people seem to have deficits ("lacunae") in their conscience, but actually don't. They may be

Table 2
Firelights

Normal Superego Function	Deficit
FAIRNESS	Doesn't consider facts before decisions
INTEGRITY	Inconsistent with ideas about self
RELIABILITY	No follow-through on what is promised
ETHICS	Does not follow known moral code
LAWFULNESS	Breaks society's laws
IDEALS	Has no goals for self
GUILT	Not self-critical for errors
HONESTY	Does not usually tell the truth
TRUSTWORTHINESS	Cannot be trusted with secrets
SHAME	No concern for others' opinions

- obsessive-compulsive people who *defensively* break the hold their conscience has on them by acting unethically, illegally, and so forth. (Their "acting out" involves the defenses of "undoing" and "provocation of punishment"; both relieve guilt.)
- immature (superego elements not yet fully developed)—the reason for more lenient laws regarding many adolescent crimes.[41]

These people, unlike narcissistic psychopaths, may be treatable.

3. **ES** Ego Strengths

- *Impulse control* damage is found in obesity, bulimia, sex addition, drug and alcohol addiction, infidelity, and violent temper outbursts. When deficits are found, treatment usually requires group support, supportive advice, and/or cognitive-behavioral techniques (such as testing reality for the person in treatment).
    - In exceptional cases, the impulsivity is *defensive*. To tell the difference between faulty impulse control versus impulsivity as a defense, try discussing how the impulse is being used to relieve pain. For example, you can say to the person you are treating, "You are overeating (or overdrinking) to relieve your painful grief" (defense against depressive affect). If the impulsivity is defensive, the person will experience a painful affect-discharge (crying or being sad) and think more about the pain. If the impulsivity is not defensive, the person is likely to respond with something like, "I just like to drink. That's all."
- *Affect tolerance* damage causes people to have trouble working and concentrating. With such damage, those functions get melted down by even mildly intense emotions that others can normally withstand.
    - The cause of this weakness in tolerating feelings is often disruption to secure-organized *attachments in early childhood* or failures of *individuation* during adolescence.
    - When adults have weaknesses in affect tolerance, they can suffer with meltdown of the concentration function, easily confused with Attention Deficit Disorder (a developmental delay of concentration ability).

---

41 A surprisingly sophisticated exposition on the problems of diagnosis and treatment selection for juvenile delinquents is found in the song, "Officer Krupke" in *West Side Story.*

- Treatment of adults with this weakness can require anxiolytic and/or antidepressant medication, *containing* (supportively listening and absorbing someone's feelings),[42] and other supportive techniques—as long as AIRS (autonomous ego functions, above) are more or less intact.

- *Containing primary process,* when damaged, allows symbolic, dream-like images into consciousness—causing "bizarre" thoughts. People who express bizarre thoughts look sicker to therapists and laypeople alike. The more primary process breaks into consciousness, the more people will require neuroleptic medication. Frequently, in such cases, AIRS are damaged, as well.

4. **OR** **O**bject **R**elations (*Warm-E.T.H.I.C.S.*)

If AIRS are damaged, the person's difficulties with *Warmth, Empathy, Trust, Holding environment, Identity, Closeness, and Stability* in relationships can be handled with neuroleptic medication and relational techniques.

If AIRS are intact but the "object relations" elements italicized above are damaged, you can use interpretive, supportive,[43] and relational techniques.

Relational techniques involve some self-disclosure by the therapist in an attempt to correct people's weaknesses in trust and emotional closeness. In treating adults, self-disclosure becomes complicated by sexuality (feelings by the person in treatment that your self-disclosure is at best a tease, or at worst that you are coming on to them); sufficient abstraction ability is required to understand the complex interactions.

Explanatory techniques are useful if AIRS and Ego Strengths are not too damaged, and object relations functioning is no more than slightly impaired (in other words, when people's capacities for trust, empathy, and closeness are only mildly or moderately problematic). When this is the case, you can confront

- unconscious distancing,
- fears of loss of identity that occasion that defense, and
- different patterns of establishing closeness alternating with distancing defenses against "selfobject fusion anxiety."[44]

---

42 Bion (1963).
43 Volkan (2009).
44 Akhtar (1994).

SUMMARY OF DIAGNOSIS, TREATMENT SELECTION, AND TECHNIQUE

Explanation of conflicts is effective when AIRS/SE/ES/OR are all intact. People without deficits will

- trust you fairly quickly;
- not be terribly put off by the upsurges of feelings they experience (some people have told me, "I'm not here to feel good! I need to get this fixed!"); and
- be able to reintegrate their newfound knowledge for more adaptive functioning and relief of symptoms.

As deficits in AIRS/SE/ES/OR increase, people are less responsive to explanations. Add supportive interventions or medication, the more deficits are present.

When AIRS/SE/ES/OR are all working pretty well, go ahead and

- *confront* defenses,
- *clarify* patterns and conflicts,
- *explain* (*dynamically interpret*) current conflicts among wish, guilt, affect and defense; and
- figure out the meanings of (*interpret*)
  - dreams,
  - *links* to the past,
  - resistances, and
  - *transferences* to you based on experiences with different people from different stages of the person's life.

References

Abend, S. (1975). An analogue of negation. *Psychoanalytic Quarterly* 44:631–637.
Abraham, K. (1923). Contributions to the theory of the anal character. *International Journal of Psychoanalysis* 4:400–418.
Adatto, C. (1970). Snout-hand behavior in an adult patient. *Journal of the American Psychoanalytic Association* 18:823–830.
Adkins, D. (Director). (2001). *Novocaine* [Motion picture]. United States: Artisan Entertainment. Retrieved from http://www.imdb.com/title/tt0234354/
Aisenstein, M. (2007). On therapeutic action. *Psychoanalytic Quarterly* 76S:1443–1461.
Akhtar, S. (1994). Object constancy and adult psychopathology. *International Journal of Psychoanalysis* 75:441–455.
Akhtar, S. (1996). "Someday.." and "if only.." fantasies: Pathological optimism and inordinate nostalgia as related forms of idealization. *Journal of the American Psychoanalytic Association* 44:723–753.
Akhtar, S. (Ed.). (2011). *The electrified mind: Developmental, pathological and therapeutic problems in the era of email and the Internet*. Lanham, MD: Jason Aronson.
Alexander, F. (1925). Dreams in pairs and series. *International Journal of Psychoanalysis* 6:446–452.
Almansi, R. (1960). The face-breast equation. *Journal of the American Psychoanalytic Association* 8:43–70.
Alpert, A. (1959). Reversibility of pathological fixations associated with maternal deprivation in infancy. *Psychoanalytic Study of the Child* 14:169–185.
American Psychiatric Association. (2000). *Diagnostic and statistical manual of mental disorders* (4th ed., Text rev.). Washington, DC: Author.
American Psychiatric Association Practice Guidelines. (2012). Assessing and treating suicidal behaviors: A quick reference guide. *Psychiatry Online*. http://psychiatryonline.org/content.aspx?bookid=28&sectionid=1663420#111943.
Arlow, J. (1979). The genesis of interpretation. *Journal of the American Psychoanalytic Association* 27S:193–206.
Arlow, J. (1995). Stilted listening: Psychoanalysis as discourse. *Psychoanalytic Quarterly* 64:215–233.
Bach, S. (2006). *Presentation at to the annual meeting of the Virginia Psychoanalytic Society*. Charlottesville, VA, April 26.
Beck, A. (1967). *Depression: Causes and treatment*. Philadelphia: University of Pennsylvania Press.
Beck, A. (1983). Cognitive therapy of depression: New perspectives. In P. J. Clayton & J. E. Barrett (Eds.), *Treatment of depression: Old controversies and new approaches* (pp. 265–290). New York: Raven.

Beebe, B. (2004). Faces in relation. *Psychoanalytic Dialogues* 14:1–51.

Beebe, B., & Lachmann, F. (1988). The contribution of mother–infant mutual influence to the origins of self- and object -representations. *Psychoanalytic Psychology* 5:305–337.

Bion, W. (1963). *Elements of psycho-analysis.* London: Heinemann.

Bion, W. (1970). *Attention and interpretation.* London: Tavistock.

Bird, B. (1955). *Talking with patients.* Philadelphia, PA: Lippincott.

Blackman, J. (1994). Psychodynamic technique during urgent consultation interviews. *Journal of Psychotherapy Practice and Research* 3:194–203.

Blackman, J. (1997). Teaching psychodynamic technique during an observed analytic psychotherapy interview. *Academic Psychiatry* 35:148–154.

Blackman, J. (2002). On childless stepparents. In S. Cath & M. Shopper (Eds.), *Stepparenting: Creating and recreating families in America today.* New York: Routledge pp. 168–182.

Blackman, J. (2003a). *101 defenses: How the mind shields itself.* New York: Routledge.

Blackman, J. (2003b). Dynamic supervision concerning a patient's request for medication. *Psychoanalytic Quarterly* 72:469–475.

Blackman, J. (2010). *Get the diagnosis right: Assessment and treatment selection for mental disorders.* New York: Routledge.

Blackman (2011). Defenses in the 21st century. *Synergy: Psychiatric writing worth reading* 16(2):1–7. Retrieved from http://www.fcmhs.ca/SynergySummer2011.pdf

Blatt, S. (1992). The differential effect of psychotherapy and psychoanalysis with anaclitic and introjective patients: The Menninger Psychotherapy Research Project revisited. *Journal of the American Psychoanalytic Association* 40:691–724.

Blatt, S. (1998). Contributions of psychoanalysis to the understanding and treatment of depression. *Journal of the American Psychoanalytic Association* 46:723–752.

Blechner, M. (2007). Approaches to panic attacks. *Neuro-Psychoanalysis* 9:91–100.

Bleuler, E. (1950). *Dementia præcox—Or the group of schizophrenias.* New York: International Universities Press. (Original work published 1911)

Blos, P. (1960). *On adolescence.* New York: International Universities Press.

Blos, P. (1967). The second individuation process of adolescence. *Psychoanalytic Study of the Child* 22:162–186.

Blum, H. (2005). Psychoanalytic reconstruction and reintergration. *Psychoanalytic Study of the Child* 60:295–311.

Blum, H., & Galenson, E. (1978). The psychology of women. *Journal of the American Psychoanalytic Association* 26:163–177.

Bollas, C. (1999). On the loss of confidence in psychoanalysis. *International Psychoanalytical Association (IPA) Newsletter* 8(2). Retrieved from http://www.academyprojects.org/leboll1.htm

Bonovitz, C. (2011). Evolving personifications: The contribution of interpersonal theory to an understanding of development. *Contemporary Psychoanalysis* 47:578–587.

Bowlby, J. (1944). Forty-four juvenile thieves: Their characters and home-life. *International Journal of Psychoanalysis* 25:19–53.

Boyer, B. (1986). Technical aspects of treating the regressed patient. *Contemporary Psychoanalysis* 22:25–44.

Brazelton, T., Christophersen, E., Frauman, A., Gorski, P., Poole, J., Stadtler, A., & Wright, C. (1999). Instruction, timeliness, and medical influences affecting toilet training. *Pediatrics* 103(Supplement):1353–1358. Retrieved from http://pediatrics.aappublications.org/cgi/content/full/103/6/S1/1353#B8

Brenner, C. (1959). The masochistic character: Genesis and treatment. *Journal of the American Psychoanalytic Association* 7:197–226.

Brenner, C. (1982). *The mind in conflict.* Madison, CT: International Universities Press.

Brenner, C. (2006). *Psychoanalysis: Or mind and meaning.* New York: Psychoanalytic Quarterly.

Bretherton, I. (1992). The origins of attachment theory: John Bowlby and Mary Ainsworth. *Developmental Psychology* 28:759–775. Retrieved from http://www.psychology.sunysb.edu/attachment/online/inge_origins.pdf

Brooks, R. (Director). (1977). *Looking for Mr. Goodbar* [Motion picture]. United States: Paramount Pictures. Retrieved from http://www.imdb.com/title/tt0076327/

Brown, S. (2003). *The crush.* New York: Grand Central Publishing/Hachette Book Group.

Buie, D. (1981). Empathy: Its nature and limitations. *Journal of the American Psychoanalytic Association* 29:281–307.

Calef, V., & Weinshel, E. (1981). Some clinical consequences of introjection: Gaslighting. *Psychoanalytic Quarterly* 50:44–66.

Celenza, A. (2006). Sexual boundary violations in the office. *Psychoanalytic Dialogues* 16:113–128.

Centers for Disease Control and Prevention. (2011, October 19). *More than 1 in 10 in U.S. take antidepressants.* Retrieved from http://thechart.blogs.cnn.com/2011/10/19/more-than-1-in-10-in-u-s-take-antidepressants/

Charcot, J. (1877). *Lectures on the diseases of the nervous system: Delivered at La Salpêtrière.* Translated by Sigerson, G. London: New Sydenham Society (published 1881).

Clarke, S. (2008). *Promiscuous.* New York: Aphrodisia Press.

Cohen, K. (2008). *Loose girl: A memoir of promiscuity.* New York: Hyperion.

Cohen, M. (1993). The negative therapeutic reaction, maternal transference, and obsessions. *American Journal of Psychoanalysis* 53:123–136.

Dewald, P. (1982). Serious illness in the analyst: Transference, countertransference, and reality responses. *Journal of the American Psychoanalytic Association* 30:347–363.

Dorpat, T. (2000). *Gaslighting, the double-whammy, interrogation, and other methods of covert control in psychotherapy and analysis.* Northvale, NJ: Aronson.

Easser, B. R. (1974). Empathic inhibition and psychoanalytic technique. *Psychoanalytic Quarterly* 43:557–580.

Erikson, E. (1950). *Childhood and society.* New York: Basic Books.

Erikson, E. (1968). *Identity, youth, and crisis.* New York: W.W. Norton.

Fine, B., Brenner, C., & Waldhorn, H. (1975). *Alterations in defenses during psychoanalysis.* New York: International Universities Press.

Firestein, S. (2001). *Termination in psychoanalysis and psychotherapy.* Madison, CT: International Universities Press.

Fishkin, R., & Fishkin, L. (2011). The electronic couch: Some observations about Skype treatment. In S. Akhtar (Ed.), *The electrified mind: Developmental, pathological and therapeutic problems in the era of email and the Internet.* Northvale, NJ: Aronson, pp. 99–112.

Fonagy, P., Gyorgy, G., Jurist, E., & Target, M. (2005). *Affect regulation, mentalization, and the development of self.* New York: Other Press.

Fournier, J., DeRubeis, R., Hollon, S., Dimidjian, S., Amsterdam, J., Shelton, R., & Fawcett, J. (2010). Antidepressant drug effects and depression severity. *Journal of the American Medical Association* 303(1):47–53.

Freud, A. (1936). *The ego and the mechanisms of defense.* New York: International Universities Press.

Freud, S. (1900). The interpretation of dreams. *Standard Edition* 4:5.
Freud, S. (1901). The psychopathology of everyday life. *Standard Edition* 6:vii–296.
Freud, S. (1905). Fragment of an analysis of a case of hysteria. *Standard Edition* 7:1–122.
Freud, S. (1910). "Wild" psycho-analysis. *Standard Edition* 11:219–228.
Freud, S. (1913). On beginning the treatment (further recommendations on the technique of psycho-analysis I). *Standard Edition* 12:121–144.
Freud, S. (1916). Some character-types met with in psycho-analytic work. *Standard Edition* 14:309–333.
Freud, S. (1917). Mourning and melancholia. *Standard Edition* 14:237–258.
Freud, S. (1919). "A child is being beaten": A contribution to the study of the origin of sexual perversions. *Standard Edition* 17:175–204.
Freud, S. (1923). The Ego and the Id. *Standard Edition* 19:1–66.
Freud, S. (1926). Inhibitions, symptoms and anxiety. *Standard Edition* 20:75–176.
Gabbard, G. (1994a). On love and lust in erotic transference. *Journal of the American Psychoanalytic Association* 42:385–403.
Gabbard, G. (1994b). Sexual excitement and countertransference love in the analyst. *Journal of the American Psychoanalytic Association* 42:1083–1106.
Gabbard, G. (1996). The analyst's contribution to the erotic transference. *Contemporary Psychoanalysis* 32:249–272.
Gaiman, N. (2002). *Coraline*. New York: HarperCollins.
Galenson, E., & Roiphe, H. (1980). The preoedipal development of the boy. *Journal of the American Psychoanalytic Association* 28:805–827.
Gill, B. (1998). *Cilantro*. Retrieved from http://www.fatfree.com/archive/1998/nov/msg00105.html
Glover, E. (1931). The therapeutic effect of inexact interpretation: A contribution to the theory of suggestion. *International Journal of Psychoanalysis* 12:397–411.
Glover, E. (1968). *The technique of psycho-analysis.* New York: International Universities Press.
Goldberg, A. (2002). Self psychology since Kohut. *Progress in Self Psychology* 18:1–13.
Goldberger, M. (1988). The two-man phenomenon. *Psychoanalytic Quarterly* 57:229–233.
Good, M. (Ed.). (2005). *The seduction theory in its second century: Trauma, fantasy, and reality today* (2nd ed.). Madison, CT: International Universities Press.
Goodman, A. (1998). *Sexual addiction: An integrated approach*. Madison, CT: International Universities Press.
Gray, J. (1993). *Men are from Mars, women are from Venus*. New York: HarperCollins.
Gray, P. (1994). *The ego and the analysis of defense*. Madison, CT: International Universities Press.
Greenson, R. (1972). Beyond transference and interpretation. *International Journal of Psychoanalysis* 53:213–217.
Greenson, R. (2008). The working alliance and the transference neurosis. *Psychoanalytic Quarterly* 77:77–102.
Gutheil, T., & Gabbard, G. (1993). *The concept of boundaries in clinical practice: Theoretical and risk-management dimensions*. American Psychiatric Association. Retrieved from http://kspope.com/ethics/boundaries.php
Hanson, C. (Director). (2005). *In her shoes* [Motion picture]. United States: Twentieth Century Fox. Retrieved from http://www.imdb.com/title/tt0388125
Harar, R., Kumar, S., Saeed, M., & Gatland, D. (2004). Management of globus pharyngeus: Review of 699 cases. *Journal of Laryngology and Otology* 118:522–527.
Hartmann, E. (1973). *The functions of sleep*. New Haven, CT: Yale University Press.

Hartmann, E. (1982). From the biology of dreaming to the biology of the mind. *Psychoanalytic Study of the Child* 37:303–335.

Hartmann, H. (1939). *Ego psychology and the problem of adaptation.* New York: International Universities Press.

Hartmann, H. (1965). *Essays on Ego psychology.* New York: International Universities Press.

Herzog, J. (1980). Sleep disturbance and father hunger in 18- to 28-month-old boys—The Erlkönig syndrome. *Psychoanalytic Study of the Child* 35:219–233.

Herzog, J. (2001). *Father hunger: Explorations with children and adults.* Hillsdale, NJ: Analytic Press.

Hoch, P., & Polatin, P. (1949). Pseudoneurotic forms of schizophrenia. *Psychiatric Quarterly* 23:248–276.

Jaffee v. Redmond. (1996). *The federal psychotherapist-patient privilege [Jaffee v. Redmond, 518 U.S. 1]: History, documents, and opinions.* Retrieved from http://www.jaffee-redmond.org

Joffe, W., & Sandler, J. (1979). Adaptation and individuation: An illustrative case. *Bulletin of the Anna Freud Centre* 2:127–161.

Johnson, A., & Szurek, S. (1952). The genesis of antisocial acting out in children and adults. *Psychoanalytic Quarterly* 21:323–343.

Kanzer, M. (1952). The transference neurosis of the Rat Man. *Psychoanalytic Quarterly* 21:181–189.

Karme, L. (1981). A clinical report of penis envy: Its multiple meanings and defensive function. *Journal of the American Psychoanalytic Association* 29:427–446.

Kernberg, O. (1975). *Borderline conditions and pathological narcissism.* New York: Aronson.

Kernberg, O. (1998). Aggression, hatred, and social violence. *Canadian Journal of Psychoanalysis*, 6:191–206.

Killingmo, B. (1989). Conflict and deficit: Implications for technique. *International Journal of Psychoanalysis* 70:65–79.

Kirsch, I., Moore, T., Scoboria, A., & Nicholls, S. (2002). The Emperor's new drugs: An analysis of antidepressant medication data submitted to the U.S. Food and Drug Administration. *Preventive Treatment* 5, Article 23.

Kleeman, J. A. (1966). Genital self-discovery during a boy's second year—A follow-up. *Psychoanalytic Study of the Child* 21:358–392.

Kliman, G., & Rosenfeld, A. (1983). *Responsible Parenthood: The child's psyche through the six-year pregnancy.* New York: Henry Holt.

Knight, R. (2005). The process of attachment and autonomy in latency. *Psychoanalytic Study of the Child* 60:178–210.

Kohut, H. (1959). Introspection, empathy, and psychoanalysis—An examination of the relationship between mode of observation and theory. *Journal of the American Psychoanalytic Association* 7:459–483.

Kohut, H. (1971). *The analysis of the self.* New York: International Universities Press.

Kramer, S. (1983). Object-coercive doubting: A pathological defensive response to maternal incest. *Journal of the American Psychoanalytic Association* 31S: 325–351.

Kramer, S., & Akhtar, S. (1988). The developmental context of internalized preoedipal object relations—Clinical applications of Mahler's theory of symbiosis and separation-individuation. *Psychoanalytic Quarterly* 57:547–576.

Kramer, S., & Prall, R. (1978). The role of the father in the preoedipal years. *Journal of the American Psychoanalytic Association* 26:143–161.

Kramer-Richards, A. (1992). The influence of sphincter control and genital sensation on body image and gender identity in women. *Psychoanalytic Quarterly* 61:331–351.

Kris, A. (1981). On giving advice to parents in analysis. *Psychoanalytic Study of the Child* 36:151–162.

Langs, R. (1973). *The technique of psychoanalytic psychotherapy.* New York: Jason Aronson.

Lauper, C. (1983). Girls just want to have fun. On *She's So Unusual* [Record]. Retrieved from http://www.songfacts.com/detail.php?id = 667

Lehr, E. D. (1975). *King Lehr and the gilded age.* New York: Arno Press. (Original work published 1935)

Levin, S. (1969a). A common type of marital incompatibility. *Journal of the American Psychoanalytic Association* 17:421–436.

Levin, S. (1969b). Further comments on a common type of marital incompatibility. *Journal of the American Psychoanalytic Association* 17:1097–1113.

Levy, K., Wasserman, R., Scott, L., Zach, S., White, C., Cain, N., Clarkin, J., Kernberg, O. (2006). The development of a measure to assess putative mechanisms of change in the treatment of borderline personality disorder. *Journal of the American Psychoanalytic Association* 54:1325–1330.

Lewin, B. (1948). The nature of reality, the meaning of nothing, with an addendum on concentration. *Psychoanalytic Quarterly* 17:524–526.

Lewin, B. (1955). Dream psychology and the analytic situation. *Psychoanalytic Quarterly* 24:169–199.

Loeb, F. (1982). Generalization as a defense. *Psychoanalytic Study of the Child* 37:405–419.

Lorand, S. (1937). Dynamics and therapy of depressive states. *Psychoanalytic Review* 24D:337–349.

Lorand, S., & Console, W. (1958). Therapeutic results in psycho-analytic treatment without fee—(Observation on therapeutic results). *International Journal of Psychoanalysis* 39:59–64.

Mahler, M. (1968). *On human symbiosis and the vicissitudes of individuation.* New York: International Universities Press.

Mahler, M., Pine, F., & Bergman, A. (1975). *The psychological birth of the human infant.* New York: Basic Books.

Makari, G. (2008). *Revolution in mind: The creation of psychoanalysis.* New York: HarperCollins.

Malawista, K., Adelman, A., & Anderson, C. (2011). *Wearing my tutu to analysis and other stories: Learning psychodynamic concepts from life.* New York: Columbia University Press.

Marcus, I. (1971). The marriage-separation pendulum: A character disorder associated with early object loss. In I. Marcus (Ed.), *Currents in psychoanalysis.* New York: International Universities Press, pp. 361–83.

Marcus, I. M. (1980). Countertransference and the psychoanalytic process in children and adolescents. *Psychoanalytic Study of the Child* 35:285–298.

Marcus, I. (2004). *Why men have affairs.* Jefferson, LA: Garrety Printing.

Marcus, I., & Francis, J. (1975). *Masturbation from infancy to senescence.* New York: International Universities Press.

Masterson, J., & Rinsley, D. (1975). The borderline syndrome: The role of the mother in the genesis and psychic structure of the borderline personality. *International Journal of Psychoanalysis* 56:163–177.

Mayo Clinic. (2012). *Stress management.* Retrieved from http://www.mayoclinic.com/health/assertive/SR00042

McCrae, C., Wilson, N., Lichstein, K., Durrence, H., Taylor, D., Bush, A., & Riedel, B. (2003). "Young old" and "old old" poor sleepers with and without insomnia complaints. *Journal of Psychosomatic Research* 54:11–19.

McDevitt, J. (1983). The emergence of hostile aggression and its defensive and adaptive modifications during the separation-individuation process. *Journal of the American Psychoanalytic Association* 31:273–300.

McDevitt, J. (1997). The continuity of conflict and compromise formation from infancy to adulthood: A twenty-five-year follow-up study. *Journal of the American Psychoanalytic Association* 45:105–126.

Menninger, K. (1933). Psychoanalytic aspects of suicide. *International Journal of Psychoanalysis* 14:376–390.

Mitchell, S. (1990). Discussion: A relational view. *Psychoanalytic Inquiry* 10:523–540.

Mitchell, S. (2000). You've got to suffer if you want to sing the blues. *Psychoanalytic Dialogues* 10:713–733.

Moffat. (2002). *Coupling,* Season 3, Episode 4, "Remember This."

Moloy, P., & Charter, R. (1982). The globus symptom: Incidence, therapeutic response, and age and sex relationships. *Archives of Otolaryngology* 108:740–744.

Nichols, M. (Director). (2004). *Closer* [Motion picture]. United States: Columbia Pictures. Retrieved from http://www.imdb.com/title/tt0376541/

Novick, J., & Novick, K. (1996). *A fearful symmetry: The development and treatment of sadomasochism.* Northvale, NJ: Aronson.

Paniagua, C. (1997). Negative acting in. *Journal of the American Psychoanalytic Association* 45:1209–1223.

Paniagua, C. (1998). Acting in revisited. *International Journal of Psychoanalysis* 79:499–512.

Parens, H. (1991). A view of the development of hostility in early life. *Journal of the American Psychoanalytic Association* 39S:75–108.

Parker, K. (2008). *Save the males: Why men matter, why women should care.* New York: Random House.

Parker, R. B. (2009). *Night and day.* New York: PG Putnam's Sons/Penguin.

Person, E. (1986). Male sexuality and power. *Psychoanalytic Inquiry* 6:3–25.

Pine, F. (1985). *Developmental theory and clinical process.* New Haven, CT: Yale University Press.

Pizzi, C., Rutjes, A., Costa, G., Fontana, F., Mezzetti, A., & Manzoli, L. (2011). Meta-analysis of selective serotonin reuptake inhibitors in patients with depression and coronary heart disease. *American Journal of Cardiology* 107(7):972–979.

Porter, C. (1934). *Anything goes* [Record]. Retrieved from http://www.youtube.com/watch?v = 3aeQ3DmKU7A

Racker, H. (1953). A contribution to the problem of countertransference. *International Journal of Psychoanalysis* 34:313–324.

Raphling, D. (1989). Fetishism in a woman. *Journal of the American Psychoanalytic Association* 37:465–491.

Raphling, D. (1996). The interpretation of daydreams. *Journal of the American Psychoanalytic Association* 44:533–547.

Renik, O. (1996). Knowledge and authority in the psychoanalytic relationship. *Psychoanalytic Quarterly* 55:1–265.

Renik, O. (1998). Getting real in analysis. *Psychoanalytic Quarterly* 67:566–593.

Renik, O. (1999). Playing one's cards face up in analysis. *Psychoanalytic Quarterly* 68:521–539.

Roose, S., & Johannet, C. (1998). Medication and psychoanalysis: Treatments in conflict. *Psychoanalytic Inquiry* 18:606–620.

Roose, S., & Stern, R. (1995). Medication use in training cases: A survey. *Journal of the American Psychoanalytic Association* 43:163–170.

Rosen, J. (1953). *Direct analysis: Selected papers*. New York: Grune and Stratton.

Rothfuss, P. (2009). *The name of the wind*. New York: Daw Books.

Rothfuss, P. (2011). *The wise man's fear*. New York: Daw Books.

Rothstein, A. (1998). *Psychoanalytic technique and the creation of analytic patients*. Madison, CT: International Universities Press.

Sadock, B., Sadock, V., and Ruiz, P. (2009). *Kaplan and Sadock's Comprehensive Textbook of Psychiatry*. Phila.: Lippincott, Williams, & Wilkins, pp. 1432–3, 1486–7, & 1523.

Sander, F. (2004). Psychoanalytic couple therapy. *Psychoanalytic Inquiry* 24:373–386.

Sandler, J. (1960). The background of safety. *International Journal of Psychoanalysis* 41:352–356.

Sandler, J. (1981). Character traits and object relationships. *Psychoanalytic Quarterly* 50:694–708.

Sarnoff, C. (1976). *Latency*. New York: Aronson.

Schilder, P. (1939). The psychology of schizophrenia. *Psychoanalytic Review* 26:380–398.

Schlesinger, H. J. (1995). The process of interpretation and the moment of change. *Journal of the American Psychoanalytic Association* 43:663–688.

Schur, M. (1966). *The id and the regulatory principles of mental functioning*. New York: International Universities Press.

Schwaber, E. A. (1998). From whose point of view? The neglected question in analytic listening. *Psychoanalytic Quarterly* 67:645–661.

Searles, H. (1965). *Collected papers on schizophrenia and related subjects*. New York: International Universities Press.

Searles, H. (1976). Psychoanalytic therapy with schizophrenic patients in a private practice context. *Contemporary Psychoanalysis* 12:387–406.

Seinfeld, J. (Creator.). (1990–1998). *Seinfeld* [Television program]. Retrieved from http://www.imdb.com/title/tt0098904/mediaindex

Semuels, A. (2009, February 24). Television viewing at all-time high. *Los Angeles Times*. Retrieved from http://articles.latimes.com/2009/feb/24/business/fi-tvwatching24

Shakespeare, W. (1602). *Hamlet*. Retrieved from http://shakespeare.mit.edu/hamlet/full.html

Sheets-Johnstone, M. (2002). Taking Freud's "bodily ego" seriously. *Neuro-Psychoanalysis* 4:41–44.

Shengold, L. (1967). The effects of overstimulation: Rat people. *International Journal of Psychoanalysis* 48:403–415.

Sifneos, P. (1987). *Short-term dynamic psychotherapy: Evaluation and technique*. New York: Springer.

Spitz, R., & Wolf, K. (1946). Anaclitic depression—An inquiry into the genesis of psychiatric conditions in early childhood, II. *Psychoanalytic Study of the Child* 2:313–342.

Stein, M. (1988). Writing about psychoanalysis: II. Analysts who write, patients who read. *Journal of the American Psychoanalytic Association* 36:393–408.

Stevenson, D. (2000). *Not so innocent*. Lincoln, NE: iuniverse.com. Retrieved from http://www.amazon.com/Not-So-Innocent-Donald-Stevenson/dp/0595003842/ref = sr_1_1?ie = UTF8&qid = 1327595411&sr = 8–1

Stoller, R., Buxbaum, E., & Galenson, E. (1976). Psychology of women—(1) Infancy and early childhood; (2) Latency and early adolescence. *Journal of the American Psychoanalytic Association* 24:141–160.

Stolorow, R., & Atwood, G. (1989). The unconscious and unconscious fantasy: An intersubjective-developmental perspective. *Psychoanalytic Inquiry* 9:364–374.

Tarachow, S. (1963). *An introduction to psychotherapy.* New York: International Universities Press.

Ticho, E. (1972). The development of superego autonomy. *Psychoanalytic Review* 59:217–233.

Volkan, V. (1982). *Linking objects and linking phenomena.* New York: International Universities Press

Volkan, V. (1988). *Six steps in the treatment of borderline personality organization.* Northvale, NJ: Aronson.

Volkan, V. (2009). *Searching for the perfect woman: The story of a complete psychoanalysis.* Lanham, MD: Jason Aronson.

Volkan, V. (2011). *Psychoanalytic technique expanded: A textbook on psychoanalytic treatment.* Istanbul, Turkey: OA Publishing.

Waelder, R. (2007). The principle of multiple function: Observations on overdetermination. *Psychoanalytic Quarterly* 76:75–92. (Original work published 1936)

Warner, S. L. (1991). Psychoanalytic understanding and treatment of the very rich. *Journal of the American Academy of Psychoanalysis and Dynamic Psychiatry* 19:578–594.

Wilson, C., Hogan, C., & Mintz, L. (1992). *Psychodynamic technique in the treatment of the eating disorders.* Northvale, NJ: Aronson.

Winnicott, D. (1953). Transitional objects and transitional phenomena—A study of the first not-me possession. *International Journal of Psychoanalysis* 34:89–97.

Wolfe, B. (1985). The costs of compliance. *Progress in Self Psychology* 1:147–163.

Wolfe, T. (1987). *The bonfire of the vanities.* New York: Picador.

Wyler, W. (Director). (1946). *The best years of our lives* [Motion picture]. Retrieved from http://www.imdb.com/title/tt0036868/

Yoest, C. (2007). *Reasoned audacity.* Retrieved from http://www.charmaineyoest.com/2007/02/a_woman_needs_a_man_like_a_fis.php

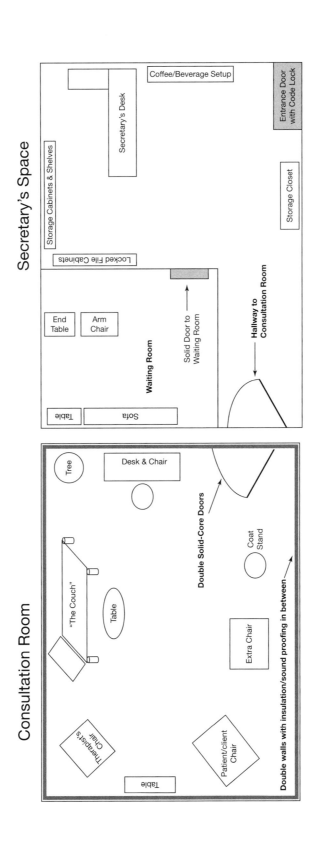

Index

AA *see* Alcoholics Anonymous
abortions 166
Abraham, K. 94
abuse *see* alcohol abuse; child abuse
accusations 159–61
acting in 109; *see also* boundary crossings
acting out: definition of 109; impulsive people relating to 122–5; *see also* boundary crossings
addiction 68–70
adolescents: alcohol abuse by 73; dressing provocatively 329; garrulousness in 162; sitting in your chair 188–9
advertising 208
advice: conflict from 262–3; giving 262–7
affairs: by impulsive people 123–5; by self-centered people 89–90; unfaithful people 242–4, 271
affect tolerance 368–9
affluence *see* financially successful people
age 102
aggression: hostile-aggressive transference 120; hostile-aggressivized transference 120–1; verbal attacks 119–21
AIRS (abstraction, integration, reality testing, self-preservation): conflict relating to 6; diagnosis relating to 6, 366–7; medicine relating to 23
Akhtar, Salman 43, 254
"Akhtar's sign" 92

alcohol abuse: by adolescents 73; causes of 68–9, 70; delirium tremens 69; for emotional pain 74; for guilt 72–3; as hereditary disease 68–9; by impulsive people 123–5; for masculinity 70; masturbation relating to 70; for social reasons 73; by women 73
alcoholics: addiction of 68–70; detoxification of 69; differential diagnosis of 68; with impaired conscience 71; narcissistic 72; schizophrenic 71–2; suicidal 219; types of 71–4; withdrawal symptoms of 69
Alcoholics Anonymous (AA) 68–70, 71, 311
anaclitic depression: definition of 25; in infants 310–11
analytic listening 48
anger turned in on self 217–18
anorexia 173
antidepressants 23–7, 271; *see also* medicine
antipsychotic medicine 23
anxiety 147–8, 246–7
appointment setting: cancellations 67; chronically late people relating to 65–7; missing appointments and 204–7; by patient's assistant 293–6
articles, professional 272–3
ARTS (affect tolerance, regulation of impulses, trust, superego) 6
asking how you are feeling: as boundary crossing 184–7; case studies on 184, 185–7; handling 185; as social norm 184

asking therapist questions: handling 235; about physical condition 236–7; about quitting employment 237–8; about themselves 236; about training 236
assertiveness training 84
attentive listening 48
auditory hallucinations 17–18
authority: names, titles and 298–9; procrastinators relating to 81
avoidance: of chief complaint 14; of pain 40–1; passive people relating to 86; sexual 49–50; understanding themselves before you do as 127

babysitters 66
Bach, Sheldon 238
Beck 227
befriending therapist 297–300
The Best Years of Our Lives (Wyler) 97
billing *see* payment
binary stars 158
Bion, W. 47
bizarre chief complaints 17
blaming, projective 345
blindness 98–9
books 272–3
borderline personality disorder: couch relating to 160; not wanting to leave relating to 157–8; obsessional people with 51, 52
borrowing magazine: case study on 199; handling 198–9; reasons for 199
boundaries 111
boundary crossings: accusation, "you're not paying attention" 159–61; asking how you are feeling 184–7; asking therapist questions 235–8; borrowing magazine 198–9; boundary violation 111; bringing child or baby to session 165–9; bringing parent to session 151–4; bringing spouse to session 146–50; bringing their own drinks 190–4; checking time 177–80; dating secretary 140–1; demanding medicine 208–10; by enactors 142–5; erotic 116–18; garrulousness 162–4; gifts 112–15; hugging 129–32; by impulsive people 122–5; missed appointments 204–7; moving furniture 211–14; not hanging up coats 195–7; not paying bill 200–3; not wanting to leave 155–8; parting shots 181–3; by self-centered people 89–92; silent people 170–3; sitting in therapist's chair, adolescents 188–9; sleeping in waiting room 215–16; standing up and walking around 174–6; by suicidal people 217–26; talking to secretary 137–9; by those with bad experience with prior therapist 231–4; touching 133–6; understanding of themselves before you do 126–8; undressing in front of you 133–6; verbal attacks 119–21; women dressing provocatively 329–32
Brenner, C. 94
bringing child or infant to session: as boundary crossing 165–9; case study on 166–9; handling 165; reasons for 165–6; symbolism of 166
bringing own drink to session: case studies on 190, 192–4; obsessive compulsive people and 190–1; reasons for 191
bringing parent to session: handling 151; problems from 152–4
bringing spouse to session: as boundary crossing 146–50; confidentiality relating to 146; diagnosis relating to 147, 148–9; example of 147–50; handling 146–7; marital therapy relating to 146
Brown, Sandra 85
bullies: depression relating to 77–8; differential diagnosis of 75; masochism relating to 75; oral demanding 79; psychopathic 77; psychotic 76–7; reasons for 75; sadism relating to 75, 79; treatment of 75–9
bumping into people outside of office 285–7

calming interactions 3
cancellations 67
carrot and stick position 202

Caruso, George 191
castration depressive affect 70, 87
casual sex 105
CBT *see* cognitive-behavioral technique
character traits: of binary stars 158; malignant 257; of obsessional people 51
Charcot, J. 56, 325–6
checking time: as boundary crossing 177–80; control relating to 177; by obsessional people 177; reasons for 178
chief complaints: avoidance of 14; bizarre 17; diagnosis from 17–20; FOOI relating to 14–15; unclear 13–16; vague responses relating to 14–15; working alliance relating to 13–14; *see also* understanding problems
child abuse 256–7, 309
childbearing: depression relating to 27; marriage relating to 27; menstruation and 327–8; pregnancy 166, 328; sex after 28–9, 294–6
child-centered counseling 310–14
children: adolescents 73, 162, 188–9, 329; bringing, to session 165–9; crying infants 311; developmental phase 314; infants with anaclitic depression 310–11; masculinity relating to 313; masturbation by 311–12; sex after newborn 28–9, 294–6; sitting in therapist's chair 188–9; sleeping arrangements of 28–9, 311–12; toilet training 311
chronically late people: exceptions regarding 66; excuses from 67; to sessions 65–7
civil cases 304, 305
clarification 5, 277
client evaluations 303–4
closeness 171
clothing: not hanging up coat 195–7; provocative dress 329–32; undressing in front of you 133–6
cognitive-behavioral technique (CBT): background on 227–8; case studies on 229–30; considerations when using 228; depression relating to 228; description of 3; ideals relating to 228; self-image relating to 228; uses for 4, 7; when not working 227–30
colloquialism 333; *see also* wiseguys
complementary identification 50
compliant talkers: case studies on 246–7; handling 245
compulsions 93–5; *see also* obsessional people
concordant identification 49, 50, 351
condescending attitude 334–5; *see also* wiseguys
confessing confusion 277
confidentiality 146
conflicts: from advice 262–3; AIRS relating to 6; ARTS relating to 6; visible disabilities relating to 96–7; Waelder's formulation of 28
confrontation 5, 364
confusion, confessing 277
conscience 71
consultations, from third-party 308–9
containing: Bion on 47; definition of 47; dreams relating to 50; empathy relating to 48; example on 49–50; listening relating to 47–8; *Men Are from Mars, Women Are from Venus* relating to 47; passive 48–9; primary process 369
contracting for safety 219–20
control: checking time relating to 177; financially successful people relating to 59; impulse 368; resistance relating to 39
conversations 11–12
conversion symptoms 55–7
co-sleeping 316–17
couch 160
counterphobic people 100–1
countertransference: complementary identification as 50; concordant identification as 50, 351; definition of 241; empathy compared to 240, 241; to marital arguments 250–3; roots of 250; to unfaithful people 242–4
criminal cases 309
The Crush (Brown) 85

crying: infants 311; interruption during 49; not wanting to leave relating to 155
cunnilingus 192
current-day interpretation 364–5

damaged functions 21
Daniel, Emad 34–6
Darwin, Charles 69
dating: of secretary, as boundary crossing 140–1; of someone mentally ill 344–7
death: mourning 22, 24; seniors relating to 103
dedifferentiation 221
defenses: of financially successful people 58; of highly intelligent people 61, 64; of obsessional people 94
defensiveness 368
delirium tremens 69
demanding medicine: as boundary crossing 208–10; case study on 210; controversy relating to 208; handling 209–10
denial 357–60
dependency 37–8, 39
depression: anaclitic 25, 310–11; antipsychotic medicine relating to 23; bullies relating to 77–8; CBT relating to 228; childbearing relating to 27; diagnosis of 18; excess guilt causing 24; ideals relating to 27, 252; in infants 310–11; introjective 25; loss causing 25; marriage relating to 26–7, 252–3; medicine for 23–7; from mistakes 24; from mourning 24; secondary 25–6, 224–6, 334–5; suicidal people relating to 224–6; tip regarding 18
detoxification 69
developmental phase 314
diagnosis: AIRS relating to 6, 366–7; algorithm 366; bringing spouse to session relating to 147, 148–9; from chief complaints 17–20; of depression 18; differential 17, 68, 75; ego strength relating to 368–9; F.I.R.E.L.I.G.H.T.S. relating to 367–8; of highly intelligent people 62–4; improvement of 361; information on 366–9; object relations relating to 369; of obsessional people 51–4; of procrastinators 80–1; summary of 370; super ego relating to 367–8
Diagnostic and Statistical Manual of Mental Disorders (DSM) 75
differential diagnosis: of alcoholics 68; of bullies 75; definition of 17
disabilities, not visible 98–9
disabilities, visible: conflicts relating to 96–7; Hartmann, H., on 98; Kohut on 98; later-acquired 97; Schilder on 96; self-image relating to 96
discharging from treatment 202
divorce 304
domination fantasies 241
dreams: containing relating to 50; interpretive technique on 365; masturbation relating to 350–1; writing of 348–52; see also fantasies
dressing provocatively 329–32
drug use 91; see also alcohol abuse
DSM see Diagnostic and Statistical Manual of Mental Disorders

eating disorders 173
ego: strength 368–9; super 367–8
18 types of thought content 35
elevator phobics 301–2
e-mailing 290–2
Emde, Robert 311
emotional distancing 59
emotional overload 40–1
emotional pain 41, 74
emotion verbalization 144
empathy: containing relating to 48; countertransference compared to 240, 241; problems with 161; of therapist 240, 251
employment 237–8
enactors: description of 142; handling 142; symbolic behavior relating to 143–5; symptomatic behavior relating to 142
endings 155–6
entitlement: self-centered people relating to 89, 90–1; seniors acting with 102–4

erotic boundary crossings: exploitation relating to 116; handling 116–18; hugging as 129; reasons for 116–17; seduction 135–6, 232–3; undressing in front of you 133–6
erotic transference 117
erotized transference 118
excess guilt 24
explanatory technique *see* interpretive technique
exploitation 116

family 353–6
Family of Origin Issues (FOOI) 14–15
fantasies: about domination 241; hermaphroditic 82
fee discussions 288–9; *see also* payment
"figuring you out" 248–9
financially successful people: control relating to 59; defenses of 58; emotional distancing by 59; psychotherapy of 58–60; shame relating to 59–60
F.I.R.E.-L.I.G.H.T.S. 367–8
first name use: authority relating to 298–9; handling 297–8; titles relating to 298–9
FOOI *see* Family of Origin Issues
forgetting 233
fragging 282
frame of treatment 11–12, 111, 283–4
Freud, Sigmund 98, 111, 239, 258
friends 338–40
furniture: couch 160; moving of 211–14; sitting in therapist's chair 188–9

garrulousness: in adolescents 162; as boundary crossing 162–4; handling 162–3; as resistance 162
gaslighting: case study on 341–3; definition of 341; handling 341
genital phase 144, 242, 351
germs 51, 52
gifts: acceptance of 113; as boundary crossing 112–15; case study on 113–14
giving advice: case studies on 264–7; handling 262–3; problems with 262; resistance relating to 263
globus hystericus 325–8

Gray, J. 47, 105
guilt: alcohol abuse because of 72–3; depression relating to 24; excess 24; passive people relating to 86; procrastinators relating to 80–1; women and 166

hallucinations: auditory 17–18; negative 195
Hartmann, Ernest 346
Hartmann, H. 98, 334
hereditary disease 68–9
hermaphroditic fantasy 82
highly intelligent people: defenses of 61, 64; diagnosis of 62–4; intellectualization relating to 61, 62–3; psychotherapy of 61–4; shame relating to 61, 64
holding environment 47
homosexuality 243
hostile-aggressive transference 120
hostile-aggressivized transference 120–1
hostile-destructive impulsivity 123–5
hugging: as boundary crossing 129–32; as erotic boundary crossing 129; example on why not to 131–2; exception to 130; handling 129–31; tip regarding 129
hyperneat people 51
hyperpunctual people 51

ideals: CBT relating to 228; depression relating to 27, 252
identification: complementary 50; concordant 49, 50, 351
identity constancy 160
impaired conscience 71
impulse control 368
impulsive people: acting out relating to 122–5; affairs by 123–5; alcohol abuse by 123–5; boundary crossing by 122–5; oral impulsivity 123; sexual and hostile-destructive impulsivity 123–5; symptomatic behavior of 120; tip for 122
income dependency 37–8, 39
infants: anaclitic depression in 310–11; bringing, to session 165–9; crying

311; sex after newborn children 28–9, 294–6; *see also* children
initial evaluation 37
instruction: for interpretive technique 4, 362–3; for supportive technique 3–4
insurance carriers 13, 320
intellectualization 61, 62–3, 269
intelligent people *see* highly intelligent people
interpretation: description of 4; trial 53
interpretive technique: clarification in 5, 364; confrontation in 5, 364; current-day interpretation 364–5; description of 3, 4; on dreams 365; exploration in 363–4; instruction for 4, 362–3; on masturbation 365; pointing out in 4; questions to ask with 363; reconstruction relating to 365; resistance interpretation 365; supportive technique, alternating between 33–6; transference interpretation 365; uses for 6
interruption 49
intervention: as invasion 274–5; for supportive technique 362
introjective depression 25
invasion 274–5
isolation of affect 93

Jaffee v. Redmond 304

Kanzer, Mark 175
Karme 161
Kissinger, Henry 299–300
Kliman, Gilbert 311
Knight, Edward H. 294
Kohut, H. 98, 223, 228
Koy, Albert P. 181
Kris, Anton 310

latency 144, 160
lateness: chronically late people 65–7; procrastinators 80–3
later-acquired disabilities 97
lawyer client evaluations 303–4
Lingyun, Cao 316
The Lion King 86

listening: analytic 48; attentive 48; containing relating to 47–8; not, accusation of 159–61
litigation 303–4
loss 25

males: passive 85; promiscuous 107–8; wiseguys 333–7; "yes dear" 87–8
malignant traits 257
Marcus, Irwin 241
marijuana use 91
marital therapy 146, 251
marriage: bringing spouse to session 146–50; childbearing relating to 27; condescending attitude in 334–5; countertransference regarding marital arguments 250–3; depression relating to 26–7, 252–3; divorce 304; "male yes dear" relating to 87–8; masturbation in 146; sexual avoidance in 49–50; unfaithful people 242–4, 271
masculinity: alcohol abuse for 70; children relating to 313
masochism 75
masturbation: alcohol relating to 70; by children 311–12; dreams relating to 350–1; interpretive technique relating to 365; in marriage 146
Medicare 319–20
medicine: advertising of 208; AIRS relating to 23; antidepressants 23–7, 271; antipsychotic 23; controversy around 208; damaged functions relating to 21; demanding 208–10; for depression 23–7; methodology relating to 209; during mourning 24; neuroleptic 21, 24; Premarin 334; prescription 208–10; short-time use of 21; suicidal people relating to 217; after trauma 367; when to use 6, 21–2, 209
Men Are from Mars, Women Are from Venus (Gray) 47, 105
menstruation 327–8
missing appointments: as boundary crossing 204–7; case studies on

205–7; handling 204–5; not showing up 67
mistakes 24
mothers: babysitters relating to 66; child or infant brought to session by 165–9; *see also* women
motivation 85
mourning 22, 24
moving of furniture: as boundary crossing 211–14; case studies on 211–14; handling 211

names: authority, titles and 298–9; first name use 297–300
narcissistic people 72, 298; *see also* self-centered people
negative cognitive triad 227
negative hallucination 195
negative therapeutic reaction 255, 259
neuroleptic medicine 21, 24
neurotic behavior: obsessional people with 51, 94; of promiscuous people 107; of seniors, entitled 103; women with 161
neurotic symbolism 156–7
neutrality 239
newborn children 28–9, 294–6; *see also* children; infants
Night and Day (Parker) 235
Nixon, Richard 299–300
note taking 43
"not getting it" 357–60
not hanging up coat: handling 195–6; reasons for 195, 196–7; resistance relating to 195; symbolism of 196
not letting you speak *see* garrulousness
not paying attention 159–61
not paying bill: as boundary crossing 200–3; exceptions for 203; handling 200–2; reasons for 201–2
not showing up 67; *see also* missing appointments
Not So Innocent (Stevenson) 338
not wanting to leave: borderline personality disorder relating to 157–8; crying relating to 155; endings relating to 155–6; handling 155–6; neurotic symbolism relating to 156–7;
as pattern 155; separation relating to 155–6

object constancy 160
object relation: diagnosis relating to 369; not listening relating to 160–1; suicidal people relating to 219, 220
obsessional people: Abraham on 94; with borderline personality disorder 51, 52; Brenner on 94; bringing own drink to session and 190–1; character traits of 51; checking time by 177; defenses of 94; diagnosis of 51–4; germs relating to 51, 52; isolation of affect relating to 93; neurotic 51, 94; rumination relating to 52, 93; schizophrenic 51; sex relating to 94–5; studies on 51; symptoms of 51; treatment of 51–2; trial interpretation for 53
obsessions 93
obsessive compulsive people 93–5
old old 102
oral demanding bullies 79
oral impulsivity 123
out of network providers 319–20

pain: avoidance of 40–1; emotional 41, 74; pleasure-unpleasure principle 40; resistance relating to 40–1
panic attacks 148–50; *see also* anxiety
parents: brought to session 151–4; child-centered counseling 310–14; mothers 66, 165–9
Parker, Robert B. 235
parting shots: case studies on 181–3; description of 181; handling 181, 182; Koy relating to 181
passive containing 48–9
passive people: assertiveness training for 84; avoidance relating to 86; complexity of 85; example of 85–6; female 85; guilt relating to 86; male 85; male "yes dear" 87–8; motivation for 85; punishment relating to 84; self-centered people on 89; sex relating to 85–6
patients: appointment setting by assistant of 293–6; asking about

themselves 236; befriending therapist by 297–300; dating someone mentally ill 344–7; elevator use by 301–2; "figuring you out" 248–9; first name use by 297–300; friends with other patients 338–40; reading professional articles and books by therapist 272–3; in social settings 285–7; understanding themselves before you do 126–8; untreatable 309; who don't like you 255–7; writing of dreams by 348–52; you don't like 254–5
payment: billed unfairly 231, 233; fee discussions 288–9; lowering fees 288–9; not paying bill 200–3
perfectionistic behavior 51
phobic people: counterphobic people 100–1; elevator phobics 301–2
physical illness or condition: conversion symptoms 55–7; psychotherapy relating to 55–7; questions about 236–7; regression relating to 55; seniors relating to, entitled 103; symbolic 56
planes of psychotherapy 28–32
pleasure-unpleasure principle 40
pointing out 4
preconscious automatisms 334
pregnancy 325; abortions 166; *see also* childbearing
Premarin 334
preparation 42–4
prescription medicine 208–10; *see also* medicine
primary process 369
prior therapists: bad experiences with 231–4; billing unfairly by 231, 233; boundary crossings by 231–4; case studies on 231; forgetting by 233; seduction relating to 232–3
problems *see* chief complaints; understanding problems
procrastinators: authority relating to 81; description of 80; diagnosis of 80–1; examples of 81–3; guilt relating to 80–1; reasons for 80–2
professional articles and books 272–3

projective blaming 345
promiscuous people: casual sex and 105; description of 105; examples of 106–8; female 105–7; male 107–8; neurotic behavior of 107; suicidal 106; treatment for 105–6
prostitutes 192
provocative dress 329–32
psychopathic bullies 77
psychotherapy: conversations compared to 11–12; of financially successful people 58–60; frame of 11–12, 111, 283–4; of highly intelligent people 61–4; income dependency from 37–8, 39; physical illness relating to 55–7; planes of 28–32; preparation for 42–4; quitting, premature 37–8; resistance to 42–3; therapeutic barrier of 111
psychotic bullies 76–7
psychotic people: bizarre chief complaints relating to 17; splitting relating to 218
punishment 84

questions: asking therapist, as boundary crossing 235–8; with interpretive technique, 363; about physical condition 236–7; about quitting employment 237–8; to schizophrenic people 278; about theoretical orientation 268–71; too many, by therapist 251, 276–8; about training 236
quitting: of employment, questions about 237–8; psychotherapy, premature 37–8

"Rat Man" 174
reaction, negative therapeutic 255, 259
reading therapist's professional articles and books 272–3
reconstruction 365
regression 55
relational techniques 369
resistance: control relating to 39; emotional overload relating to 40–1; garrulousness as 162; giving advice

relating to 263; initial evaluation relating to 37; interpretation 365; not hanging up coat relating to 195; not wanting to leave 155–8; pain relating to 40–1; to psychotherapy 42–3; silent people relating to 170
Rothfuss 263
rumination 52, 93

sadism 75, 79
sadistic personality disorder *see* bullies
sadomasochistic behavior 244
safety, contracting for 219–20
SAS *see* sociotropy-autonomy scale
Schilder, Paul 95
schizophrenic people: alcoholic 71–2; obsessional 51; questions to 278; suicidal 219
secondary depression: description of 25–6; suicidal people relating to 224–6; wiseguys relating to 334–5
second opinions 305–7
secretary: dating of, as boundary crossing 140–1; responsibilities of 137; talking to, as boundary crossing 137–9
seduction: prior therapists relating to 232–3; undressing in front of you as 135–6
self-centered people: affairs by 89–90; "Akhtar's sign" in 92; boundary crossing by 89–92; entitlement relating to 89, 90–1; examples of 89–92; on passive people 89
self-esteem 96, 223–4
self-image: CBT relating to 228; visible disabilities relating to 96
seniors, entitled: causes of 103; death relating to 103; description of 102; neurotic behavior of 103; physical illness relating to 103; treatment for 102–4
separation 155–6
sessions: bringing own drink to 190–4; bumping into people outside of 285–7; cancellations of 67; children or infants brought to 165–9; not wanting to leave 155–8; parent brought to 151–4; people chronically late to 65–7; spouses brought to 146–50; traveling long distances to 315–18
sex: casual 105; cunnilingus 192; erotic boundary crossings 116–18, 129, 133–6; fantasies 241; after newborn children 28–9, 294–6; obsessional people relating to 94–5; passive people relating to 85–6; promiscuous people 105–8; with prostitutes 192; seduction 135–6, 232–3; with therapist 240; *see also* masturbation
sexual avoidance 49–50
sexual impulsivity 123–5
sexualization 331
shame: financially successful people relating to 59–60; highly intelligent people relating to 61, 64
siblings 353
sight 98–9
silent people: as boundary crossing 170–3; case studies on 171–3; closeness relating to 171; handling 170; resistance relating to 170
sitting in therapist's chair 188–9
Skype 291–2, 315–16
sleeping arrangements: of children 28–9, 311–12; co-sleeping 316–17
sleeping in waiting room: as boundary crossing 215–16; case studies on 215–16; reasons for 215
social norm 184
social settings 73, 285–7
sociotropy-autonomy scale (SAS) 227
splitting 218
spouse 146–50; *see also* marriage
standing up and walking around: as boundary crossing 174–6; case study on 175–6; handling 174; Kanzer on 175; reasons for 174–5
Stevenson, Donald V. 338
stirring comments 3
subpoena 304
suicidal ideation 152, 350
suicidal people: alcoholic 219; anger turned in on self 217–18; boundary crossing by 217–26; case studies

on 218; contracting for safety 219–20; depression relating to 224–6; handling 217–18, 219–20; medicine relating to 217; object relation relating to 219, 220; promiscuous 106; schizophrenic 219; secondary depression relating to 224–6; self-esteem relating to 223–4
suicide threats 281
super ego 367–8
supportive technique: Daniel relating to 34–6; description of 3, 33; instructions for 3–4; interpretive technique, alternating between 33–6; interventions for 362; uses for 6
symbolic behavior 56, 141–2, 143–5
symbolism: of bringing child or infant to session 166; neurotic 156–7; of not hanging up coat 196
symptomatic behavior: of enactors 142; of impulsive people 120
symptoms: conversion 55–7; of obsessional people 51; withdrawal 69

talking: compliant talkers 245–7; garrulousness 162–4; to secretary 137–9; verbal attacks 119–21; verbalizing emotions 144; "you know" said repetitively 323–4
technology: e-mailing 290–2; Skype 291–2, 315–16
telephone triage 306
testifying 303–4
theoretical orientation 268–71
therapeutic barrier 111
therapist: asking questions of, as boundary crossing 235–8; bad experiences with, prior 231–4; befriending, by patient 297–300; empathy of 240, 251; "figuring you out," by patient 248–9; marital 251; not paying attention 159–61; patients not liked by 254–5; patients who don't like 255–7; professional articles and books by, patients reading 272–3; questions by, too many 251, 276–8; sex with 240; threats to 279–82
therapist-patient privilege 304

third-party payers 13
third-party pressure 308–9
thought content 35
threats: handling 279–81; suicide 281; to therapist 279–82
throat clearing 325–8
time: checking of, by patient 177–80; policy on 177–8; traveling long distances to sessions 315–18
titles 298–9
toilet training 311
tolerance, affect 368–9
touching: boundary crossing and 133–6; hugging 129–32
trainees 286
training: assertiveness 84; questions about 236; toilet 311
transference: boundaries relating to 111; erotic 117; erotized 118; hostile-aggressive 120; hostile-aggressivized 120–1; interpretation 365
trauma 160, 367
traveling long distances to sessions 315–18
treatment: of bullies 75–9; for counterphobic people 100; discharging from 202; of family members 353–6; of obsessional people 51–2; other, second opinions while in 305–7; over Skype 291–2, 315–16; for promiscuous people 105–6; for seniors acting with entitlement 102–4
trial interpretation 53
trust problems 161

unclear chief complaints: case studies on 15–16; vague responses relating to 14–15; working alliance relating to 13–14
understanding problems: denial relating to 357–60; "not getting it" 357–60; tip for 20
understanding themselves before you do: as avoidance 127; as boundary crossing 126–8
undressing in front of you: as boundary crossing 133–6; handling 133, 134–5; as seduction 135–6

unfair billing 231, 233
unfaithful people: case studies on 243, 271; countertransference to 242–4; women 243–4; *see also* affairs
unresponsiveness 258–61
untreatable patients 309
unusual situations: colloquialism 333; dreams, writing of 348–52; family, treatment of different members of 353–6; friends, patients who are 338–40; gaslighting 341–3; globus hystericus 325–8; not understanding 357–60; patients who are dating someone mentally ill 344–7; throat clearing 325–8; wiseguys 333–7; women dressing provocatively 329–32; "you know" said repetitively 323–4

vague responses 14–15
verbal attacks: handling 119; hostile-aggressive transference 120; hostile-aggressivized transference 120–1; reasons for 119
verbal brutality 333
verbalization of emotions 144
Vidal, Gore 59–60

visible disabilities *see* disabilities, visible
Volkan, V. 198

Waelder, R. 28
walking around 174–6
Warm-E.T.H.I.C.S. 369
Winnicott, D. 47
wiseguys 333–7
withdrawal symptoms 69
women: alcohol abuse by 73; childbearing 27–9, 294–6, 327–8; dressing provocatively 329–32; guilt and 166; menstruation 327–8; mothers 66; with neurotic behavior 161; passive 85; pregnancy 166, 328; promiscuous 105–7; unfaithful 243–4
working alliance: chief complaints relating to 13–14; description of 11–12, 13; factors of 9
Wyler, W. 97

"yes dear" 87–8
"you know" said repetitively 323–4
young old 102
"you're not paying attention" 159–61